SYMBOLIC COMPUTATION

Artificial Intelligence

N.J. Nilsson: Principles of Artificial Intelligence. XV, 476 pages, 139 figs., 1982

J.H. Siekmann, G. Wrightson (Eds.): Automation of Reasoning 1. Classical Papers on Computational Logic 1957–1966. XXII, 525 pages, 1983.

J.H. Siekmann, G. Wrightson (Eds.): Automation of Reasoning 2. Classical Papers on Computational Logic 1967–1970. XXII, 638 pages, 1983.

L. Bolc (Ed.): The Design of Interpreters, Compilers, and Editors for Augmented Transition Networks. XI, 214 pages, 72 figs., 1983.

R.S. Michalski, J.G. Carbonell, T.M. Mitchell (Eds.): Machine Learning. An Artificial Intelligence Approach 572 pages, 1984.

L. Bolc (Ed.): Natural Language Communication with Pictorial Information Systems. VII, 327 pages, 67 figs., 1984.

J.W. Lloyd: Foundations of Logic Programming. X, 124 pages, 1984.

A. Bundy (Ed.): Catalogue of Artificial Intelligence Tools. XXV, 150 pages, 1984. Second, revised edition, IV, 168 pages, 1986.

M.M. Botvinnik: Computers in Chess. Solving Inexact Problems. With contributions by A.I. Reznitsky, B.M. Stilman, M.A. Tsfasman, A.D. Yudin. Translated from the Russian by A.A. Brown. XIV, 158 pages, 48 figs., 1984.

C. Blume, W. Jakob: Programming Languages for Industrial Robots. XIII, 376 pages, 145 figs., 1986.

N. Cercone, G. McCalla (Eds.): The Knowledge Frontier. Essays in the Representation of Knowledge. 552 pages, 93 figs., 1987.

Nick Cercone   Gordon McCalla
Editors

The Knowledge Frontier
Essays in the Representation of Knowledge

With 93 illustrations

Springer-Verlag
New York Berlin Heidelberg
London Paris Tokyo

Nick Cercone
Computing Science Department
Simon Fraser University
Burnaby, British Columbia
Canada V5A 1S6

Gordon McCalla
Department of Computational Science
University of Saskatchewan
Saskatoon, Saskatchewan
Canada S7N 0W0

Library of Congress Cataloging in Publication Data
The Knowledge Frontier.
    (Symbolic computation—artificial intelligence)
    Bibliography: p.
    Includes index.
    1. Artificial intelligence.   2. Knowledge, Theory of.
3. Linguistics—Data processing.   I. Cercone, Nick.
II. McCalla, Gordon.   III. Series: Symbolic computation.
Artificial intelligence.
Q335.K57   1987   006.3′3   87-13019

Text prepared by the editors in camera-ready form.

Printed and bound by R.R. Donnelley & Sons, Harrisonburg, Virginia.
Printed in the United States of America.

9 8 7 6 5 4 3 2 1

ISBN 0-387-96557-2 Springer-Verlag New York Berlin Heidelberg
ISBN 3-540-96557-2 Springer-Verlag Berlin Heidelberg New York

Table of Contents

List of Tables

List of Figures

Preface

Knowledge representation is perhaps the most central problem confronting artificial intelligence. Expert systems need knowledge of their domain of expertise in order to function properly. Computer vision systems need to know characteristics of what they are "seeing" in order to be able to fully interpret scenes. Natural language systems are invaluably aided by knowledge of the subject of the natural language discourse and knowledge of the participants in the discourse. Knowledge can guide learning systems towards better understanding and can aid problem solving systems in creating plans to solve various problems. Applications such as intelligent tutoring, computer-aided VLSI design, game playing, automatic programming, medical reasoning, diagnosis in various domains, and speech recognition, to name a few, are all currently experimenting with knowledge-based approaches.

The problem of knowledge representation breaks down into several subsidiary problems including what knowledge to represent in a particular application, how to extract or create that knowledge, how to represent the knowledge efficiently and effectively, how to implement the knowledge representation scheme chosen, how to modify the knowledge in the face of a changing world, how to reason with the knowledge, and how to use the knowledge appropriately in the creation of the application solution. This volume contains an elaboration of many of these basic issues from a variety of perspectives.

The Knowledge Frontier: Essays in the Representation of Knowledge is an outgrowth of the **IEEE Computer** Special Issue on Knowledge Representation (Cercone and McCalla, 1983) which briefly overviewed the field as it was in 1983. Since some time has passed since then, and since many of the papers appearing in the special issue had to be very brief, the editors of that collection felt it was appropriate to update and enhance the special issue, and to this end have put together the current volume. There are 17 papers in this collection, 6 of them brand new, 7 of them enhanced versions of papers appearing in the special issue (in most cases considerably enhanced), and 4 of them essentially unchanged. In addition, there were 4 papers appearing in the special issue which, unfortunately, were not available for this volume.

As in any edited collection, it is important for the editors to try to enhance the integration, uniformity, and accessibility of the papers as much as possible. Naturally, when 17 different papers and 26 different authors are involved, this endeavour can never be fully successful, but we have at least made a start. The authors were asked to write abstracts for their papers to summarize the main contributions. They were also asked to review each others' submissions so as to try to indicate the points of contact connecting their paper with perspectives expressed in other papers. We as editors read all the papers, inserted the odd pointer back and forth to related research in other papers, created an index of relevant terms, performed the typesetting (except for the figures) to achieve uniformity of presentation style, compiled a unified reference list, and, of course, wrote this preface. We believe that the collection maintains the approachability to non-AIers of the IEEE Computer special issue while still having enough grist for even the most ardent AIer's mill. The remainder of this preface overviews the main contributions of each paper, tries to tie together the main issues raised in the various papers, and explains the organization of the book.

The papers in this book are organized into six sections: I. Overview, II Logic, III. Foundations, IV. Organization, V Reasoning, and VI. Applications. Each of the papers is slotted into one of the sections, although there is much overlap in content among the various papers and several of them could have readily fit into more than one section. The sections have been arranged so that they can be read in order (more or less), although the degree of interconnectedness is high enough that certain aspects of each chapter can only be fully appreciated after the insights of many other chapters have been accomodated.

I. Overview

In the Overview section are two chapters, What is Knowledge Representation, by Nick Cercone and Gord McCalla, and Knowledge Representation: What s Important About It, by Bill Woods. These chapters provide a context for the rest of the book. The Cercone and McCalla chapter overviews the different approaches taken to knowledge representation, explaining at least briefly the strengths and weaknesses of each. Seven different (but interrelated) styles of knowledge representation are outlined: logical representations, semantic networks, procedural representations, logic programming, frame-based representations, production system architectures, and knowledge representation languages. All of these approaches find further elaboration in subsequent chapters, with special attention being paid to logical approaches (see section II), semantic networks (see section IV), logic programming (see Elcock's paper, Chapter 7, Dahl's paper, Chapter 12, and the Poole, Goebel, and Aleliunas paper, Chapter 13), and frames (see section VI, especially the Havens and Mackworth paper).

Woods' contribution to the Overview section looks at basic requirements for any knowledge representation scheme, and considers a number of important issues which arise in dealing with these requirements. After discussing the nature of models and reasoning in knowledge representation (including inherent limitations), Woods outlines three classes of knowledge that a knowledge representation system should support: knowledge acquisition, perception, and planning. The role of generalization is then discussed and the KL-One representation scheme is presented to allow concrete illustration of much of the discussion. KL-One is a representation formalism combining aspects of both frame-based and semantic network schemes. The important notions of expressive adequacy (what a representation scheme is capable of representing) and notational efficacy (the scheme's actual shape and structure) are contrasted. These notions re-appear in several places in the remainder of the book, sometimes labelled differently. Two aspects of notational efficacy are discussed in more detail: computational efficiency (speed of inference) and conceptual efficiency (ease of representation), important attributes of any representation scheme as can be seen in many other chapters. Woods concludes his paper with a discussion of the role of predicate calculus in knowledge representation and suggests limitations on predicate calculus as a representation formalism.

II. Logic

Section II, Logic, further considers the influence of logic

on knowledge representation, an influence which, while strong from the beginning of artificial intelligence, has been growing in the last decade. The section consists of three chapters dealing with various aspects of logic. David Israel's paper Some Remarks on the Place of Logic in Knowledge Representation clarifies the role which logic plays (or should play, at least) in knowledge representation. Israel suggests that the many debates about logic can be divided into two main categories: arguments about logic as a representation formalism, and arguments about logical reasoning. It is entirely possible to support using logic, with its precise syntax and semantics, as a representation formalism while arguing that traditional deductive theorem proving methodologies are not workable for logical reasoning. In fact, the recent non-monotonic reasoning systems do just this (see the Webber, Marek, and Poole, Goebel, and Aleliunas chapters - Chapters 4, 6, and 13 respectively - for discussions of aspects of non-monotonic logic, especially default logic). Supporting Woods' arguments about expressive adequacy and notational efficiency, Israel concludes that the real problems are what knowledge to represent and reasoning with this knowledge effectively.

The next chapter in this section, Bonnie Webber's paper Logic and Natural Language, looks at how several different kinds of logic can be helpful in modelling aspects of natural language. In particular the use of default logic to reason about presuppositions, the use of modal logic to help in planning utterances, and the use of temporal logic for reasoning about time-dependent linguistic phenomena are discussed. Default logic receives further attention in Marek's paper (Chapter 6) and especially in the Poole, Goebel, and Aleliunas paper (Chapter 13). Temporal reasoning of various sorts gets much further play in several other chapters, especially the three chapters in section IV, and Firby and McDermott's paper (Chapter 14). Webber's paper, while concentrating on a specific aspect of natural language understanding (namely logic), illustrates one of the major applications of artificial intelligence with a strong need for knowledge representation. As such, it should be considered as an augmentation to the applications considered in section VI.

The final chapter in the Logic section is Commonsense

and Fuzzy Logic by Lotfi Zadeh. In a long and detailed presentation, Zadeh presents a particular brand of logic, fuzzy logic, for modelling approximate or fuzzy reasoning. Normal logics, such as predicate calculus, don't handle uncertainty, although it seems to be a major phenomenon in the real world. To handle this notion of fuzziness, Zadeh proposes that commonsense knowledge consists largely of dispositions, which are propositions with implicit fuzzy quantifiers such as "most", "usually", etc. Zadeh concentrates on precisely defining a notion of test-score semantics for representing the meaning of such dispositions. The basic idea behind test-score semantics is that the meaning of a disposition can be interpreted by a process which assigns it meaning based on the meanings of constituent relations in an explanatory database. The explanatory database is comprised of relations whose meaning is known to the creator of the database. This notion of semantics has interesting points of contact with other approaches, especially with Doyle's ideas of translating informal semantics directly into formal semantics (see Chapter 8). Zadeh concludes his discussion with a brief outline of an inferential system for fuzzy logic, although such reasoning is not a central theme of his paper.

III. Foundations

Section III, Foundations, follows up many of the concerns of section II by considering a number of issues at the foundations of knowledge representation. In his paper Basic ·Properties of Knowledge-Based Systems I, Wictor Marek presents a number of formal properties of a rule-oriented knowledge representation scheme based on representing knowledge in a formalism similar to that for relational databases. This formalism has obvious points of contact with both rule-oriented representation formalisms and formalisms based on logic (see the Elcock and Dahl papers - Chapters 7 and 12 - especially). Of particular concern to Marek are issues of completeness and consistency of a knowledge base, and the notion of default reasoning (discussed for natural language by Webber). General consistency and completeness checking algorithms are given, and a number of properties of these algorithms are formally proven. Another interesting facet of

Marek's treatment is his ability to give a definition of the adequacy of a set of rules, a limited formal version of Woods' expressive adequacy.

Ted Elcock's paper entitled First Order Logic and Knowledge Manipulation: Some Properties of Incomplete Systems is an ideal follow-up to Marek's exposition, especially on the issue of completeness. In this chapter Elcock is concerned with issues raised by the implicit sequencing which any logic-based programming language imposes on the order of the derivation of the proof of some consequence, and the fact that an effective procedure to derive such a consequence must necessarily be incomplete in the sense that pragmatic time and space constraints could mean that a valid consequence is missed. To focus his discussion, Elcock introduces Absys, a logic-based representation language which predates both the Planner and Prolog logic programming languages and which anticipates much of their approach. Absys is an ideal vehicle for exploring the issue of incompleteness since it allows dynamic re-ordering of the order of elaboration of a proof under the influence of the changing binding environment as the proof proceeds, and hence has the capability of finding consequences more flexibly (and possibly more often) than a non-dynamic language. Elcock also proposes that aggregation (similar to that discussed in the papers in section IV and by Havens and Mackworth in Chapter 16) will be another useful tool in constraining proofs since composite relations can be manipulated directly rather than always having to appeal to the simple relations which comprise them. Elcock's discussion of Prolog and its strengths and weaknesses (especially in comparison to Absys) makes an interesting contrast to Dahl's elaborations (Chapter 12), and the THEORIST system of Poole, Goebel, and Aleliunas (Chapter 13).

The final entry in Section III is Jon Doyle's paper Admissible State Semantics for Representational Systems which considers the very important issue of specifying the formal semantics of a knowledge representation scheme. Doyle proposes a particular kind of semantics called admissible state semantics which avoids some of the complexities of purely logic-based approaches to semantics. The naturalness of this approach to semantics is achieved by distinguishing between objects external to the reasoning system, whose semantics are specified using standard model theory, and objects internal to the system, whose semantics are specified directly in admissible state semantics.   Any language can be used to specify the interpretation of the internal states without having to pretend that this language is itself the representation.   In particular, logic can be used to precisely specify the interpretation of a representation without the representation itself necessarily being logical.   Doyle briefly considers a number of knowledge representation formalisms and indicates how admissible state semantics can be useful in precisely specifying their semantics. In particular, inheritance in semantic networks (such as those discussed in Section IV) and in the schema (frame) based representation language SRL are considered, as are aspects of Minsky's K-lines theory of memory.   Semantics forms an important aspect of other papers as well, particularly Zadeh's paper and that of Shapiro and Rapaport (Chapter 11).

IV. Organization

One of the prime concerns of knowledge representation is how to organize knowledge for efficient retrieval and effective reasoning. This is the subject of section IV, Organization. The section starts with an examination by Len Schubert, Mary Angela Papalaskaris and Jay Taugher of several special inference methods.   Entitled Accelerating Deductive Inference: Special Methods for Taxonomies, Colours and Times, the paper shows how to perform efficient inference in various hierarchies and how to elegantly handle the representation of colour and time.   In particular the ubiquitous IS-A and PART-OF relationships are considered, and a number of inference mechanisms specifically tailored to these relationships are discussed.   Although efficient, these methods have the drawback of being incomplete (in the Elcock sense above).   The representation of colour is another interesting problem, especially being able to infer relationships among colours (e.g. "lime is compatible with green, but black isn't"), and Schubert, Papalaskaris, and Taugher devise an interesting geometric technique for easily being able to perform such inferences. Representing and reasoning about time is also a common problem in knowledge representation (and one tackled by a number of authors in this book see for example Tsotsos and Shibahara - Chapter 10 - and Firby and McDermott - Chapter 14). After discussing a number of different approaches, the authors come up with a scheme consisting of pseudo-times, time chains, and time graphs for which very efficient algorithms to check for relative orderings, overlap, inclusion, duration, elapsed time, etc., can be written. The paper concludes with a discussion of how to combine the various special purpose algorithms with more general purpose inference methods (such as those used by Prolog). In contrast to Marek's general purpose, but exponential-time, algorithms, the hybrid proposed here provides "a basis for constant-time or near constant-time simplification and generalized resolution, factoring, subsumption testing, and tautology elimination in the taxonomic, colour, and temporal domains". Echoing Woods and Elcock, Schubert, Papalaskaris, and Taugher conclude that the methods of symbolic logic need to be augmented with special methods to achieve efficiency.

Next in Section IV is John Tsotsos' and Taro Shibahara's paper entitled Knowledge Organization and Its Role in Temporal and Causal Signal Understanding: The ALVEN and CAA Projects. The paper starts by outlining a representation scheme which organizes frames into PART-OF and IS-A hierarchies, and which has varied facilities for handling time. There are many points of similarity between this representation and that outlined in Schubert, Papalaskaris, and Taugher, as well as with the KL-One scheme outlined by Woods, the SnePs semantic network formalism of Shapiro and Rapaport (Chapter 11), and the Maya representation scheme underlying the vision system described by Havens and Mackworth (Chapter 16). Reasoning is achieved using a mixture of goal-directed, model-directed, failure-directed, data-directed, and temporal searches, which make use of the various links in the representation scheme to help guide the searches. Much more about reasoning can be found in other chapters, especially those in Section V and the Havens and Mackworth chapter (Chapter 16).

Two medical expert systems which use the Tsotsos and Shibahara representation scheme are described: ALVEN analyzes left ventricular motion from x-ray images; and CAA detects and analyzes heart rhythm anomalies from electrocardiograms.

CAA makes use of a number of additional knowledge representation features to those mentioned above, most notably causal links of various kinds, projection links connecting concepts in different "stratified" knowledge bases, and statistical reasoning (based on probability theory, not fuzzy logic) for handling situations without sufficient information or for determining "goodness-of-fit". These applications are described in some detail and augment the applications discussions of section VI.

Section IV then concludes with SNePs Considered as a Fully Intensional Propositional Semantic Network by Stu Shapiro and Bill Rapaport. This paper is a lengthy summary of a long-term semantic network research project, and is an excellent illustration of the many different organizational (and other) aspects with which semantic network designers must be concerned. SNePs has many sub-components, including a user language, various editors, a logic-based representation language based on higher-order rather than the first-order logic underlying most logic-based languages (e.g. Prolog), an English-like interface, and an inference package. Also described is CASSIE, a cognitive agent modelled in SNePs. In contrast to many network schemes, SNePs gives the user much power to create his/her own arc labels. The arcs represent structural links between nodes; and the nodes represent propositions, entities, properties and relations. All nodes in SNePs are intensional (although some may also have external reference). This fact, when combined with the fact that all information, including propositions, can be represented in nodes, leads Shapiro and Rapaport to consider SNePs to be a fully intensional propositional network formalism rather than an inheritance network formalism such as KL-One or the schemes outlined in the previous two chapters. Despite this ostensible difference with other schemes, many representation techniques used in other formalisms can be handled in SNePs, including subset, class membership, time, booleans, beliefs, and aspects of quantification; and many kinds of inference can be undertaken, including property inheritance in generalization hierarchies.

Shapiro and Rapaport provide precise rules for both the syntax and semantics of SNePs. Semantics is particularly interesting in SNePs, being based on the philosophical theory of objects promoted by Meinong early in this century. This approach to semantics allows precision to be given to the intensional objects at the heart of SNePs. Moreover, there seems to be an intriguing parallel between the SNePs focus on Meinongian semantics for intensional objects, and Doyle's concern with providing admissible state semantics for internal objects (distinct from the semantics for external objects). SNePs has also proven useful in a number of applications including database management, recognizing addresses in the sorting of mail, diagnosing diseases of the nervous system, reasoning about digital circuits, revising beliefs, and understanding natural language. These, too, should be added to the repetoire of applications outlined in Section VI.

V. Reasoning

In addition to organizing knowledge, a representation scheme must also reason about that knowledge and this is the concern of section V, Reasoning. In her paper Representing Virtual Knowledge Through Logic Programming, Veronica Dahl starts the section by discussing how logic programming, in particular Prolog, can be used to represent virtual (implicit) knowledge as well as explicit knowledge. The paper is a readable overview of Prolog and explains its power as a logical reasoning system. Although it is basically laudatory, the paper does consider some of the current limitations of Prolog and points out research aimed at overcoming some of these limitations and extending Prolog's applicability. Of particular interest is Dahl's own research into how to detect false presuppositions in natural language queries using a Prolog-based approach (another application besides those discussed in Webber's paper of using knowledge-based techniques in natural language understanding). Explaining as it does the basics of Prolog, the chapter forms a nice companion paper to other discussions of logic programming, particularly Elcock's paper, and the Poole, Goebel, and Aleliunas paper which follows next.

David Poole, Randy Goebel and Romas Aleliunas describe Theorist: A Logical Reasoning System for Defaults and Diagnosis which overcomes some of the shortcomings of Prolog as a knowledge representation system, particularly for reasoning. The Theorist approach is based on the idea that reasoning can be looked at as constructing theories which explain observations, and then using these theories in further reasoning, in much the same way as scientific theories explain observations about the world and suggest further research directions. A Theorist knowledge base consists of hypotheses, facts, and observations. A theory is defined to be a consistent subset of the hypotheses and facts which implies (and thus explains) the observations. Theorist contains a uniform deduction mechanism which seeks to construct such theories. This framework is a powerful one; the authors show how it can be used in default reasoning, diagnosis, learning, and user modelling. The implementation of a prototype Theorist interpreter is discussed, and a Prolog version of such an interpreter is given. It constitutes a full first order clausal theorem prover. Theorist suggests an elegant new way of unifying a lot of heretofore disparate representation issues, and as such is quite provocative. It certainly augments many of the logical discussions outlined in Section II (especially the Israel and Webber papers) and the theoretical analyses of section III, as well as forming an appropriate follow-up to Dahl's discussion of Prolog.

Next in Section V Jim Firby and Drew McDermott consider the problems of temporal planning in their paper entitled Representing and Solving Temporal Planning Problems. This lengthy exposition focusses almost exclusively on the problems of reasoning with knowledge rather than how to precisely formalize the knowledge or how to appropriately organize the knowledge. The particular reasoning topic chosen is temporal planning, i.e. automatically creating plans that solve problems whose solution have a number of time-dependent steps (such as occur in robotics tasks, for example). Two implemented systems, the Time Map Manager and the Heuristic Task Scheduler, are used to illustrate a variety of temporal representation and reasoning issues. The Time Map Manager is a system for building and reasoning about time maps, where a time map is a partially ordered network of tasks, ordering constraints, and task effects. Among the issues dealt with by the Time Map Manager are representing the time map as a temporally scoped predicate calculus database (another kind of logic to complement those of Section III), implementing the system in DUCK (a knowledge representation language with similarities to some of the logic programming formalisms), "fuzzifying" temporal distances in the time map (another approach to uncertainty besides Zadeh's and Tsotsos' and Shibahara's), using something called "clipping" to indicate constraints on the persistence of certain assertions in the time map (useful for solving aspects of the frame problem), and allowing various search strategies including temporal forward chaining and causal forward chaining (more inference strategies to go along with those already discussed by Schubert, Papalaskaris, and Taugher, and by Tsotsos and Shibahara, and the hybrid top-down/bottom-up recogniton scheme discussed by Havens and Mackworth in Chapter 16).

The Heuristic Task Scheduler finds a total temporal order for a set of tasks which may have many subtle order-dependent interactions among them. Not only can the Heuristic Task Scheduler deal with some situations where the Time Map Manager fails, it also can handle both incremental changes and some kinds of continuous change. The Heuristic Task Scheduler works with plans described in the Bumpers planning language, a language which represents plans as a collection of tasks to achieve a goal, a set of constraints on the goal, and a set of resources to be used in carrying out the plan. Bumpers has been used in robot planning tasks.

Since the Time Map Manager and the Heuristic Task Scheduler complement one another, Firby and McDermott speculate that the two might be combined into one powerful temporal planning system. Even now, the two systems illustrate many of the subtle problems which occur when solving problems in temporal domains. Finally, it should be noted that the notions of time discussed here form an interesting augmentation of the Schubert, Papalaskaris, and Taugher ideas on time, as well as of the Tsotsos and Shibahara approaches to time.

The final paper in this section, Analogical Modes of Reasoning and Process Modelling by Brian Funt, presents WHISPER, an interesting approach to reasoning using direct representations called analogs. WHISPER is a simulation which is able to look at an unstable configuration of blocks and, through use of a parallel processing retina and procedures to manipulate this retina, is able to predict how the blocks will fall. In contrast to all the other representations discussed in this volume, the WHISPER approach is non-propositional, but is, instead an analog of a physical process. Rather than merely describing WHISPER's capabilities, the paper focusses on the issues raised by such analogical reasoning. It provides much food for thought about the considerable diversity of approaches to representation, about how much of human reasoning is, in fact, based on analogs, and what exactly the role of analogs might be in knowledge representation.

VI. Applications

Although both papers in Section VI, Applications, take an issue-oriented approach, they both look at knowledge representation from the perspective of particular applications. Bill Havens and Alan Mackworth in their paper Representing Knowledge of the Visual World overview the need for knowledge representation in computational vision applications and the properties that are desireable in any such knowledge representation scheme. Many of the same issues raised by Woods are discussed by Havens and Mackworth and are given focus through a particular working vision system, called Mapsee2. Two different approaches to vision are outlined, high-level vision, driven by the goals of the vision system, and early vision, driven by the data contained in the input image. Havens and Mackworth persuasively argue that these are just two ends of a spectrum, and that an approach that integrates both data-driven and goal-driven methodologies is needed. The Mapsee2 system has been developed which tries to find such a middle-ground. Mapsee2 is based on the idea of schemata (frames) arranged in specialization (IS-A) and composition (PART-OF) hierarchies, well known organizations of knowledge (see the papers in Section III especially). These hierarchies are used to support a powerful and interesting scheme for recognizing an input scene from an image. Low-level schemata in the composition hierarchy are cued (instantiated) directly from the image, high-level schemata are cued by presupposed knowledge of the scene being looked at, and a search is carried out to connect the high-level and low-level schemata into a comprehensive description of the scene. This search works both top-down, as high-level schemata hypothesize lower-level schemata which seem likely according to the system's knowledge of the world, and low-level schemata are amalgamated into higher-level schemata along the composition hierarchy. Using this hybrid search scheme, Mapsee2 can achieve procedural adequacy (similar to Woods' computational efficency), and, through the structure of the schemata and their organization, Mapsee2 also exhibits descriptive adequacy (similar to Woods' expressive adequacy). Mapsee2 faces similar problems to those faced by the Tsotsos and Shibahara vision systems (especially ALVEN), and uses many of the same techniques (especially organizational). Its hybrid recognition scheme seems useful far beyond vision applications.

Hassan Reghbati and Nick Cercone conclude both Section VI and the book with their paper On Representational Aspects of VLSI-CADT Systems which overviews the burgeoning interest among circuit designers in the use of knowledge representation techniques of various sorts to aid in the design of very large scale integrated circuits. Any representation of knowledge for VLSI-CADT systems must take into account the multiple perspectives with which it is possible to view a circuit, including the design perspective, where the structure or behaviour of a circuit is viewed at a conceptual level, and the structural perspective, which views the circuit in terms of its components. It must also deal with the fact that most circuit designers start without having a precise idea of what they want. Finally, it must handle the different motivations of circuit designers; some are concerned with the synthesis of circuits, others with the analysis of already synthesized circuits. To handle this variety of perspectives and goals, a number of different kinds of knowledge are needed, including knowledge of implementation methods, control knowledge, and causal knowledge. A selection of specific knowledge representation techniques are presented such as block diagrams, behavioural representations, physical representations, electrical representations, sticks, etc. The paper discusses qualitative reasoning and its use in circuit analysis, logic programming to solve basic VLSI design problems, and knowledge-based diagnosis of faulty circuits. Several applications are used to illustrate the arguments, with particular emphasis on natural language interfaces (with the CLEOPATRA interface for computer assisted design being used to focus much of this discussion). Overall the paper shows that knowledge representation techniques are moving out of the laboratory into actual use in difficult real world problems, a fitting conclusion to the book.

We hope that the reader will find this book readable and informative. We certainly believe that the many ideas presented here form a comprehensive snapshot of the "state of the art" in knowledge representation, and a provocative introduction to the many intriguing and subtle issues underlying this most central area of artificial intelligence.

We have enjoyed the challenge of trying to integrate a variety of research into a reasonably uniform collection. We owe a great deal of thanks to each contributor for both his/her writing and rewriting efforts and also his/her reviewing efforts. We thanks our reviewers for helping us to integrate this collection. We would also like to acknowledge the help we have received preparing this manuscript for publication. Lynn Montz of Springer-Verlag was a constant stream of encouragement. For helping to input some of the material into the typesetting system, we thank Mila Yee-Hafer. We acknowledge the editing support we received from Carol Murchison. To Ed Bryant we owe a debt of graditude for modifying the Scribe system in places where our special requirements made it necessary to do so and also for providing invaluable technical support and advice. Finally, we would like to thank the Laboratory for Computer and Communications Research at Simon Fraser University for the use of their facilities.

Nick Cercone, Editor

Gord McCalla, Editor

October 1986

1. What Is Knowledge Representation?

Nick Cercone

Laboratory for Computer and Communications Research
School of Computing Science
Simon Fraser University
Burnaby, British Columbia, CANADA V5A 1S6

Gordon McCalla

Department of Computational Science
University of Saskatchewan
Saskatoon, Saskatchewan, CANADA S7N 0W0

Abstract

In this chapter, we overview eight major approaches to knowledge representation: logical representations, semantic networks, procedural representations, logic programming formalisms, frame-based representations, production system architectures, and knowledge representation languages. The fundamentals of each approach are described, and then elaborated upon through illustrative examples chosen from actual systems which employ the approach. Where appropriate, comparisons among the various schemes are drawn. The chapter concludes with a set of general principles which have grown out of the different approaches.

Based on the paper, Approaches to Knowledge
Representation, G. McCalla and N. Cercone, appearing in COMPUTER,
Volume 16, Number 10, October, 1983.

1.1. Introduction

When computer vision systems interpret a scene, they benefit greatly when they have knowledge about the kinds of objects they "see". Medical diagnostic systems need to know the characteristics of the diseases being diagnosed. Without knowledge of the application environment, or *domain knowledge*, and knowledge of the intended audience, natural language understanding systems could not properly comprehend the phrases and sentences they process. What we need, then, is a suitable way to represent such knowledge. For this reason, artificial intelligence (AI) researchers are preoccupied with what is known as *knowledge representation*. According to Brachman and Levesque, (Brachman and Levesque, 1985), "[Knowledge representation]...simply has to do with writing down, in some language or communicative medium, descriptions or pictures that correspond in some salient way to the world or some state of the world." Knowledge representation is basically the *glue* that binds much of AI together, but it has its own set of problems.

In contrast to conventional database systems, AI systems require a knowledge base with diverse kinds of knowledge. These include, but are not limited to, knowledge about objects, knowledge about processes, and hard-to-represent *commonsense* knowledge about goals, motivation, causality, time, actions, etc. Attempts to represent this breadth of knowledge raise many questions:

- How do we structure the explicit knowledge in a knowledge base?

- How do we encode rules for manipulating a knowledge base's explicit knowledge to infer knowledge contained implicitly within the knowledge base?

- When do we undertake and how do we control such inferences?

- How do we formally specify the semantics of a

knowledge base?

- How do we deal with incomplete knowledge?

- How do we extract the knowledge of an expert to initially "stock" the knowledge base?

- How do we automatically acquire new knowledge as time goes on so that the knowledge base can be kept current?

An excellent overview for the specialist in knowledge representation is provided in (Brachman and Smith, 1980), while summaries for the nonspecialist are given in (Barr and Feigenbaum, 1981) and (Brachman and Levesque, 1985). This paper is intended to provide some background to knowledge representation research by mapping out the basic approaches to knowledge representation that have developed over the years. It should also serve as an introduction to this collection by providing context for the other articles.

In most early AI systems, knowledge representation was not explicitly recognized as an important issue in its own right, although most systems incorporated knowledge indirectly through rules and data structures. Some early researchers did address representation issues more directly. For example, the SIR reasoning system used LISP property lists to represent and make inferences about information acquired from users, (Raphael, 1968); the Deacon system used ring structures to encode many kinds of knowledge, including time-variant information, (Craig, 1966); and the question-answering system of (Black, 1968) stressed the need to make (and control) inferences about stored knowledge.

During the late 1960's knowledge representation slowly emerged as a separate area of study. Several different approaches to knowledge representation began to manifest themselves and have resulted in the various formalisms in use today. The most important current approaches are logical representations (especially first-order logic), semantic networks, procedural representations, logic programming, frame-based representations, production system architectures, and knowledge representation languages. These are not mutually exclusive, and methodologies developed from these various perspectives often influence each other, but they do form a convenient division for the purposes of explication.

We now present an overview of these major approaches to representing knowledge.

1.2. Logic representations

The usefulness of *first-order logic* in a knowledge representation context became evident during the 1960's, primarily as a result of research into mechanical theorem-proving and early attempts at building question-answering systems. A good overview of this research area is given in (Nilsson, 1971). Much research was directed at investigating the use of the resolution principle as an inferencing technique in various applications (for example, question-answering). Other research attempted to recast logical formalisms in a more computationally oriented framework. Examples include the Planner formalism, (Hewitt, 1972); the Strips planning paradigm, (Fikes and Nilsson, 1971); and more recently the widely used Prolog programming language (see Section 5). This body of work has led to intense discussion regarding the pros and cons of logic-based approaches to representation. Concern has been expressed about the lack of an explicit scheme to index into relevant knowledge, the awkwardness of handling changing or incomplete knowledge, and the perceived limitations of deductive inference. However, logic advocates muster counterarguments to many of these concerns, and there is no doubt that the formal precision and interpretability of logic are useful and supply certain kinds of expressiveness that other knowledge representation schemes lack.

To illustrate how logic is used in an AI system, let us examine how it might be used in a natural language understanding system. In linguistics, there is a notion of *logical form* (LF); however, the artificial intelligence version of LF is quite different from LF as discussed by linguists. The AI versions of logical form attempt to capture semantic and pragmatic notions in addition to the syntactic aspects dealt with by the linguists' LF. In addition the logical form is not only the target language into which surface language is translated, but it often also is used to represent knowledge about the domain of discourse, as might be expected. Such knowledge, contained in a *knowledge base*, is useful for disambiguating the exact meaning of a natural language surface form. It is from this notion of LF that computational linguists specify the inferential machinery which provides natural language "front-ends" to database systems, natural language question-answering systems, etc., with the power to carry out their respective tasks.

Most often the LF into which natural language is translated is logic itself, see (Rosenschein and Shieber, 1982). Usually, the logic chosen is some variant of the predicate calculus, where both the natural language input and the knowledge relating to the input are represented in the form of (possibly quantified) propositions in the predicate calculus. Conjunctive normal form is often used, where each proposition is a conjunction of disjunctions of literals (atomic formulae composed of predicates and terms, where predicates are functions of variables over a domain of discourse). This form has several advantages, the most important of which is the ability to mechanize the process of making logical inferences from the statements in the knowledge base using an automated resolution theorem proving procedure for deducing facts from other facts in a knowledge base consisting of statements in conjunctive normal form, (Robinson, 1965).

In predicate calculus representation schemes, the precise syntax and semantics of the form and the existence of an automated inference procedure provide the complete description required; in other words, an internal form is incomplete without a specification of what it means and how it is to be

used.[1]   This is one of the major advantages of predicate
calculus as a representation scheme.   Another major advantage
of   the   predicate   calculus   approach   is   having   a   uniform
representation for all knowledge.   This uniformity tends to
make it easy to integrate the information contained in the
input with the knowledge already in the knowledge base.   The
uniformity of logic as a representation also makes the control
structure for programs manipulating knowledge quite simple.
Using only the first order predicate calculus, the expressive
power is sufficient to represent almost anything that we can
formulate precisely (for example, most of mathematics). It is
the case, however, that some problems seem to be more
conveniently and compactly represented by higher than first-
order logic and by modal logic, which has led to a debate
about whether first-order logic is sufficient.

    There is very little debate about one issue: constraints on
time and space make pure predicate calculus fairly unworkable
in any practical setting.   The number of predicates needed to
describe any real world situation would be immense, and the
attempt   to   make   them   fully   consistent   would   be   nearly

---

[1]The need to specify the semantics of a formalism has been well established
for some time in logic and mathematics, but was realized surprisingly recently
in computer science and artificial intelligence.   However, it is now a common
assumption shared by much of computer science that no data structure makes
sense unless what it means is precisely specified.   In computer science, this
usually means that the processes which use a data structure and modify it
must be specified along with the form of the data structure.   In artificial
intelligence, there are two schools of thought.   One school, the formal school,
chooses a formal approach (for example, denotational semantics) to specify what
the objects and relations in the internal form mean.   The other school, the
procedural school, specifies the meaning of an internal form via the procedures
which interpret it.   In either case, both the procedural and the formal schools
must concern themselves with how the form is used.   In particular, the
internal form into which surface natural language is interpreted must be used
by procedures which carry out the action(s) required by the surface language.
Each different type of logical form has a set of procedures usually used in
conjunction with it (for example, network forms have arc traversal algorithms;
predicate calculus representations employ logical inference procedures; etc.).
Among the most interesting internal forms from this point of view are
procedural representations, which are directly processed by a programming
language interpreter.

impossible. Moreover, the dynamic nature of the real world would rapidly make any collection of predicates obsolete. The problem of maintaining a knowledge base is thus extremely critical. Unfortunately, predicate calculus is particularly inappropriate for representing changing information. A standard difficulty which arises is the "frame problem" - how to distinguish those things which do not change as time goes by from those that do. See (McCarthy and Hayes, 1969) for a good discussion of this and other issues.

1.2.1. Default logic

There has thus been a fair amount of investigation into ways of extending the power of predicate calculus (while maintaining its formal semantics) to handle situations where knowledge is incompletely specified or changing. This work is known under the general label of *nonmonotonic logic*, that is, logic where the truth values of predicates can change over time. The special issue of the Artificial Intelligence Journal (Bobrow, 1980) is a good overview of the various approaches which launched the investigations into nonmonotonic logic. For some other more recent work see (Levesque, 1981), (Reiter and Crisculo, 1983), (McCarthy, 1984), (Delgrande, 1984), and (Etherington, Mercer, and Reiter, 1985).

To give the flavour of the nonmonotonic approach, we cite an example from Reiter and Crisculo on default logic (one brand of nonmonotonic logic). The notion of a default rule can be formalized as

$$\frac{\alpha(x) \cdot M\beta_1(x),....,M\beta_n(x)}{w(x)}$$

where $\alpha(x)$, $\beta_1(x),....,\beta_n(x)$, $w(x)$ are all first order formulae whose free variables are among those of $x = x_1,...., x_m$. This rule should be interpreted as meaning that for all individuals $x_1,...., x_m$, if $\alpha(x)$ is believed and if each of $\beta_1(x),....,\beta_n(x)$ is consistent with our beliefs, then $w(x)$ may be believed. Thus "typically dogs bark" can be represented as $DOG(x)$: M $BARK(x)/BARK(x)$. The use of such default rules allows notions like "normally", or "in the absence of information to the contrary", or "typically", etc., to be captured in the knowledge base, and relieves the designer of the knowledge base from the necessity of having to explicitly state each and every exception to each and every rule. The other approaches to nonmonotonic logic have a similar flavour.

1.2.2. Fuzzy logic

Before leaving logical representations altogether, one other logical approach should be briefly mentioned. An issue not really dealt with well by predicate calculus is uncertainty, that is, representing statements which aren't always strictly true or false. *Fuzzy logic* (Zadeh, 1979a) handles apparent imprecision by attaching various numeric measures of credibility to propositions, a priori. There is some debate within the knowledge representation community about the usefulness of fuzzy logic and whether surface imprecision in fact only hides deeper regularities which can be ferreted out by studying the circumstances under which a proposition is true or false, rather than the proportion of the time it is true or false. Zadeh in some sense responds to this criticism by showing, particularly, how fuzzy logic can be used in natural language understanding, (Zadeh, 1983a). For a discussion of the implications of fuzzy logic for knowledge representation, see Zadeh's article in this book (Chapter 5).

1.3. Semantic networks

Another approach to representing knowledge is through use of graph structures called *semantic networks*. There are many varieties of semantic network, each emphasizing different kinds of relationships among the information represented in the network. However, all network schemes are based on the idea of knowledge represented in graph structures, with nodes representing concepts connected by links representing *semantic* relationships between the concepts. Similar in representational power to predicate calculus, semantic networks are distinguished from such propositional representation schemes because of their concern with how *close* concepts are to one another in the network, and by interpretation by procedures which traverse the various links from concept to concept in order to make inferences.

The following examples of semantic networks illustrate their perspicuity and kinship to logical representations. The first example represents the propositional content of the sentence *John gives the book to Mary*, see Figure 1-1(a). The unlabelled node represents the *giving* event; the other link/node pairs represent the various *cases* associated with the event. This is similar in content to an equivalent set of well-formed formulae in the predicate calculus, except that it is a graphical representation, and it explicitly shows that each binary relationship pertains to the same event.

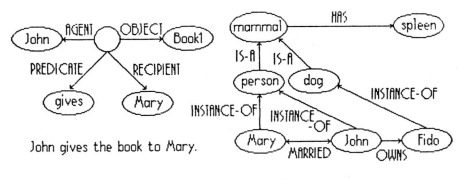

Figure 1-1: Semantic Networks

Figure 1-1(b) depicts a small IS-A hierarchy, one of the most intensively investigated kinds of semantic network organisation. Properties at higher levels in the IS-A hierarchy can be inherited by instances at lower levels, for example, Fido has a spleen, as do John and Mary. Such inheritance is a limited version of logical deduction and forms a central inference technique employed in most semantic network formalisms. Formulating the precise semantics of inheritance has been the subject of much research, (Brachman, 1983); (Mylopoulos, Shibahara, and Tsotsos, 1983). The IS-A relationship allows a large scale saving of space over an equivalent predicate calculus formulation by storing a fact at the most general possible level to be shared by many facts beneath it. There is also reason to believe that humans employ something very much like IS-A. Collins and Quillian suggest that, frequently, questions which people could easily answer on the basis of explicitly stored propositions are nevertheless answered through inference facilitated by a hierarchical organisation, (Collins and Quillian, 1972), such as that illustrated in Figure 1-1(b).

Figure 1-2 demonstrates the expressive power of semantic networks to represent non-trivial quantified expressions. The network is in a precise notation which, while being as formal as the equivalent logical representation, is more perspicuous. Moreover, the interconnections among the concepts are made overt and suggest link traversal inference schemes quite different from logical deduction. For more details of the notation used in Figure 1-2 and its usefulness as a representation scheme see (Schubert, Goebel, and Cercone, 1979).

Semantic networks are really an attempt to model the associative capabilities which humans seem to employ so successfully when reasoning by analogy, speaking metaphorically, or resolving anaphoric references. From a semantic network point of view, associative connections can be made between concepts directly linked or at least close to one another in the network. Several approaches to semantic networks propose explicit associative searches, the most well known being Quillian's *intersection search* techniques, (Quillian, 1968); (Quillian, 1969). For example, to comprehend a sentence like "The rain drums on the shelter" to mean "The rain falls on the shelter and produces a hollow sound like someone beating on a drum" would require a *correct* intersection between the concepts *rain* and *drum*. Various hierarchies have been defined to facilitate these associative searches. In addition to the IS-A hierarchy described above, other hierarchical organisations such as the PART-OF hierarchy,

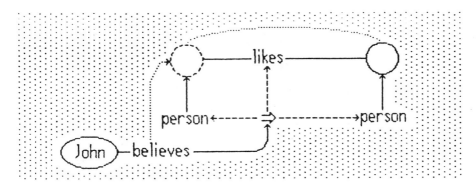

"John believes that everyone likes someone."
[John believes (∀x) (∃y) [[x person] ⇒
     [[y person] & [x likes y]]]

Figure 1-2:   The Expressive Power of Semantic Networks

(Mylopoulos, Shibahara, and Tsotsos, 1983), or the visibility lattice, (Hendrix, 1975), are also useful for suggesting directions to search for relevant information or for constraining the kind of search undertaken.   Such searches constitute the processes which manipulate and interpret a semantic network.   However, the semantics of such associative searches are not nearly as well understood nor as agreed upon as resolution is for predicate calculus representations.

Semantic networks have stimulated intense interest in their use as a propositional knowledge representation in reasoning and understanding systems since their introduction by Quillian and subsequent generalisations, (Shapiro, 1971a), (Schubert, 1975), (Cercone and Schubert, 1975), (Woods, 1975), (Levesque and Mylopoulos, 1979).   They have been successfully exploited for concept learning, (Winston, 1970); natural language understanding, (Schank, 1972), (Schubert, Goebel, and Cercone, 1979); and deductive reasoning, (McSkimmin and Minker, 1977). Semantic networks have affected psychological theories of cognition, (Collins and Quillian, 1972), (Norman and Rumelhart, 1975), (Wilson, 1980); the development of knowledge representation languages. (Brachman, 1979), (Mylopoulos, Shibahara, and Tsotsos, 1983); and machine architecture, (Fahlman, 1980).

1.3.1. Partitioned networks

We consider several examples in greater detail. *Partitioned networks* is the term Gary Hendrix coined for his version of semantic networks, (Hendrix, 1979). In addition to discussing various network notations and notions for encoding a number of different kinds of knowledge, he discusses the concept of partitioning networks for organisational reasons.[2] According to Hendrix,

> "The central idea of partitioning is to allow groups of nodes and arcs to be bundled together into units called *spaces*, which are fundamental entities in partitioned networks, on the same level as nodes and arcs." (Hendrix, 1979)

This idea is similar to the notion of *planes* espoused by (Scragg, 1975). Spaces can overlap; every node and arc in the network belongs to one or more space. For convenience, related bundles of spaces are further grouped into *vistas*, and most network operations purport to operate on the collections of nodes and arcs that comprise vistas. Although vistas can be created freely and arbitrarily, this freedom is seldom exercised, and most superimposing organisational schemes tend to be hierarchical.

After delineating structures for logical deduction (logical connectives, quantification, and a deduction algorithm), Hendrix turns his attention to various uses attributed to partitioned networks, including: inheriting information, judgmental

---

[2]Hendrix discusses the inclusion of taxonomic information, general statements involving quantification, information about processes and procedures, delineation of local contexts, beliefs, and wishes, and the relationship between various syntactic units and their interpretations.

reasoning, reasoning about processes, and natural language understanding. We consider two examples from Hendrix.

Hendrix decries the many network schemes which have been devised that handle *information inheritance* either incorrectly or through a complicated system of ad-hoc rules and structures. He correctly points out that one typical failure of most systems is the failure to distinguish properties of sets (such as cardinality) from properties of individual members of a set. *Quantification* (universally quantified statements generally restrict set membership), *case roles* (case arcs designate only instances of functions), and *delineation* play central roles for structuring inheritance rules in Hendrix's approach. Delineation names and restricts the participants of situations in a situation set. For example, the delineation of the set *ownings* corresponds to the formula

$$\forall x\{\text{member}(x, \ ownings)$$
$$\rightarrow \ \exists y, z, t1, t2[\text{member}(y,\text{Legal.persons}) \ \& \ \text{agent}(x,y)$$
$$\& \ \text{member}(z, \text{Physobjs}) \ \& \ \text{obj}(x,z)$$
$$\& \ \text{member}(t1, \text{Times}) \ \& \ \text{start-time}(x,t1)$$
$$\& \ \text{member}(t2, \text{Times}) \ \& \ \text{end-time}(x,t2)]\}.$$

To reason effectively about processes, Hendrix offers convenient structures for encoding both operators and *state of the world* models. This *state-space* approximation has long been utilised in artificial intelligence models for planning, and Hendrix's refinements allow the important aspects of processes to be considered uniformly and handled efficiently, for example, decomposition of processes into sequences of subprocesses.

Hendrix has implemented partitioned networks in INTERLISP, with existing networks composed of over 5000 network structures in place as of the paper's writing. One rule-based inference system, PROSPECTOR (Duda, 1978), used Hendrix's partitioned network formalism, as did the discourse model of P. Cohen (Cohen, 1978).

1.3.2. Marker propagation schemes

To further illuminate the usefulness of the semantic network approach, and the subtleties, let us examine Fahlman's various "marker propagation" schemes for overcoming the *symbol-mapping problem*, (Fahlman, 1975), (Fahlman, 1979), (Fahlman, 1982). The symbol mapping problem was originally posed by Scott Fahlman as follows, "Suppose I tell you that a certain animal - let's call him Clyde - is an elephant. You accept this simple assertion and file it away with no apparent display of mental effort. And yet as a result of this simple transaction, you suddenly appear to know a great deal about Clyde. If I say that Clyde climbs trees or plays the piano or lives in a teacup, you will immediately begin to doubt my credibility. Somehow, "elephant" is serving as more than a mere label here; it is, in some sense, a whole package of relationships and properties and that package can be delivered by means of a single IS-A statement". The means by which the symbol *elephant* is mapped onto the various implications of *elephanthood* is called the symbol mapping problem.

Fahlman conceived of a of parallel processing *machine* in which each conceptual entity (Clyde, elephant, gray) is represented by a hardware device called a *node* and each node has a distinct serial number, a few bits of type information, and storage for about a dozen *marker bits*. The machine has a centralised control to these nodes over a shared party-line bus. Other simple hardware devices, *links*, are used to represent relationships between nodes; links have a few bits of type code and a number of wires that can be connected to nodes in interesting ways. Links can respond to commands in parallel. Marker bits can propagate throughout the network to effect relationships and change structures. By moving markers from node to node in parallel, the machine can perform certain deductions and searches (for example, property inheritance) very quickly.

The actual hardware implementation of the machine, presently underway at Carnegie-Mellon University, poses some difficulties, though with current hardware technology it is easy to put thousands of nodes and links on a chip. The problem is to form connections between nodes and links as new knowledge is added. These connections must be private lines between nodes and links, otherwise all of the parallelism will be lost. Fahlman has recently proposed a solution to this using a hashnet scheme and has sketched a design for a million element machine, (Fahlman, 1980).

In addition to developing the parallel network notion, Fahlman developed a knowledge representation language called NETL, (Fahlman, 1979). A NETL simulator was implemented in MACLISP. NETL provides the following facilities:

- The creation of a new individual of a given type (for example, Clyde)

- The creation of a new prototype description (for example, elephant)

- The division of an existing class into non-overlapping subclasses (*living thing* into *animal* and *vegetable*), and the detection of any attempt to violate the split.

- The creation of inheritance *roles* within a description. Roles may be given a default value, etc.

- The creation of type-roles that are to be filled with a set of objects within the description of a particular individual.

- The creation and processing of exceptions to general statements.

- The creation of new relation-types and the compound links to represent them.

- The creation of a hierarchy of context areas, their parts and subparts, and scoping of statements within these areas.

- The representation of individual actions and events

in a hierarchy of event-types and the use of time contexts to represent the effect of an action upon the universe.

- The creation of hypothetical universes that differ from the real universe in certain specified ways.

- The separation of the defining properties of a set from its incidental properties.

- The use of simple network re-organisation strategies to perform abstraction and learning.

1.3.3. Topic hierarchies

It is clear that any system designed for reasoning about its world can efficiently exploit property inheritance within generalisation (IS-A) hierarchies or relationship inheritance in aggregation (PART-OF) hierarchies.   What complicates this problem is that conceptual entities typically consist of many components, for example, parts of an object, the participants of an action, or the departments of an organisation.

Moreover, mere access to elephant knowledge via inheritance does not guarantee swift question-answering or consistency checking. Imagine hundreds of facts impinging on *Clyde, elephant, mammal,* etc. and attempt to do a Quillian-like *activation search* to particular attributes, such as colour or appearance. This would, in all likelihood lead to a combinatorial explosion when trying to construct inference chains to answer relatively simple queries like *What colour is Clyde?* or *Does Clyde live in a teacup?*.

To overcome problems such as this, we note two features which these examples illustrate. One is the need to classify propositions *topically* as colour propositions, location propositions, size propositions, etc. This classification scheme should help us to avoid the exhaustive search for combinations of propositions which yield a desired conclusion. The other is the need for access to just those propositions about a concept which belong to one of the above topics. A topic is defined as a *predicate over proposition-concept pairs*. For example, *colouring* is a predicate which is considered to be true for the proposition *a zebra has black and white stripes* in relation to the concept *zebra*. Another topic predicate which is true for that proposition in relation to *zebra* is *appearance*; in fact, appearance holds for any proposition-concept pair for which *colouring* holds. That is, appearance is a *supertopic* of colouring, and, conversely, colouring is a *subtopic* of appearance.

Topic predicates can be stored in a semantic network, linked by subtopic and supertopic relationships. Together, these form a *topic hierarchy* (or several topic hierarchies), (Schubert, Goebel, and Cercone, 1979). Topic hierarchies provide a basis for organising the propositions attached to a node. A possible topic hierarchy for physical objects is shown in Figure 1-3, which provides an attempt to comprehensively classify knowledge about physical objects with minimal overlap between categories. The *subconcept* topic is intended to be a slot not only for genuine subconcept relationships (that is, necessary subsumption) but also for contingent subsumption relationships and for *instances* of a concept. Similar notions apply for superconcept relationships.

Once a topic hierarchy has been defined for a particular kind of node, the propositions attached to any node of that kind can be organised in accordance with the hierarchy. This is accomplished by superimposing an access structure called a *topic access skeleton* upon the attached propositions. A topic access skeleton *mimics* a part of the topic hierarchy, namely that part which is needed to supply access paths to all the available propositions about the node, when these are attached to the appropriate terminal topics.

For example, if the only facts known about Clyde are that he is an elephant and likes to eat peanuts, these would be attached to the access skeleton

```
           |object type
Clyde ——+
           |behaviour —— self—maintenance —— feeding
```

If elephants, in turn, are known to be very large, grey, rough-skinned mammals, and Clyde is known to be an instance of an elephant, these facts would be attached to the access skeleton.

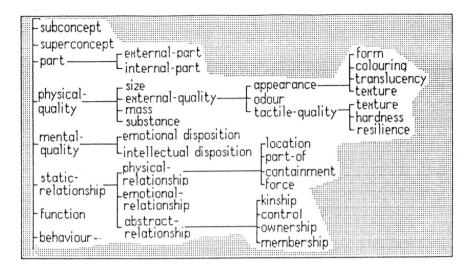

Figure 1-3:   A Topic Hierarchy for Physical Objects

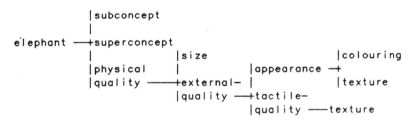

Note that *texture* appears twice, making the *rough-skinned* predication available both as an aspect of appearance and as a tactile quality. In implementations a topic hierarchy and corresponding access skeletons need not be strictly tree-structured since a single *texture* node can be used, with pointers to it from both the *appearance* and *tactile-quality* nodes, (Schubert, Goebel, and Cercone, 1979).

Topically organised networks facilitate different kinds of inferences about objects, and their kinds. A mechanism has been implemented for performing automatic topical classification of propositions. The proper topical classification of propositions in general depends on their *logical form* and on the nature of the predicative concepts involved. *Time* and *storage* tradeoffs have been studied and a clever *path contraction* algorithm implemented which guarantees descent time in the tree-like topic hierarchies, and subsequent access to propositions they encode, to be proportional to $\log n_{max}$, the maximum number of propositions attached to any concept.

1.3.4. Propositional networks

To conclude the overview of various semantic network formalisms, let us examine Shapiro's SNePS system, (Shapiro, 1979a) (also see Chapter 11, this volume). SNePS is the culmination of over a decade of work on semantic networks. Discussion of the SNePS user language, SNePSUL, can serve as a focus on what can be done in SNePS. Embedded in LISP, SNePSUL provides facilities for defining arc labels, adding information, examining network structures, deleting nodes, finding nodes and performing deductive inference on nodes. SNePS is not a particular semantic network, and thus different semantic network notations can be easily implemented in SNePS since it provides the basic mechanisms for constructing such disparate networks.

Deduction in SNePS may be triggered automatically by utilising the function DEDUCE instead of FIND, or the function ADD, a generalisation of BUILD. Thus, SNePS provides explicit deduction rules, and these rules exist in the network as *rule nodes*. Rule nodes represent a formula of molecular nodes using connectives such as AND-entailment, OR-entailment, etc., and existential, universal, and numerical quantifiers.

SNePS is also capable of performing backward inference in its deduction rules and also a restricted form of forward inference. SNePSUL functions may be activated as actions on the arcs of an augmented transition network grammar, so that natural language sentences can be parsed directly into SNePS networks.

Despite their extensive usefulness there has been much debate as to whether semantic networks are *mere notational*

variants of predicate calculus or, in fact, whether they really
do offer something beyond a first-order scheme. (Woods, 1975);
(Hayes, 1977).   The proponents of the logical point of view
maintain that logic is the only representation scheme really
needed.   Are they correct?

1.3.5. Semantic networks and logic

Although on the surface the various representation
schemes can look quite different, many of the differences
vanish when examined closely.   One means of doing this is to
use first-order logic as the measuring stick with which they
can all be appraised.   That is, by making some assumptions
about the precise interpretation to be given each different type
of form (since, apart from first-order logic itself, these forms
do not have well defined semantics), concepts represented in
these formalisms can usually be mapped onto more or less
equivalent representations in first-order logic.   Such a mapping
can illustrate much about the representational power of each
type of form, but unfortunately ignores many methodological
differences distinguishing the forms; that is, it obscures the fact
that each of the different surface representations suggests
different issues to be studied, different knowledge structures,
and different inference techniques.

In particular, it is misleading to consider that semantic
networks may represent only a clever indexing scheme for
first-order formulae, or that knowledge representation languages
(see below) bias the commitment of the system designer to a
small set of "knowledge" primitives. The respective power of
these (largely) notational differences lies in the uses to which
each is put. It is doubtful that the associative matching
procedures of (Winston, 1970) or the intersection search
techniques of (Quillian, 1968) would have been discovered if a
linear logical notation had been favoured instead of a network
scheme, even though in both cases the expressive power of each
formalism reduces to predicate calculus restricted to binary
predicates.   Another example: the problem of integrating the
information content of a natural language sentence into a
semantic network raises issues of where in the network to add

the information, issues not raised in a predicate calculus scheme where it is sufficient simply to add a predicate representing the meaning of the input to a list of well-formed formulae. The conclusion is that, regardless of theoretic import, methodological differences are important, especially given the artificial intelligence concern with performance issues.

1.4. Procedural representations

Knowledge can also be stored in the form of *procedures* rather than in the form of propositions. The knowledge embedded in procedures can be accessed either directly or using the technique of pattern directed procedure invocation, (Hewitt, 1972). Advocates of knowledge representation through procedural embedding stress that the kinship between the way people use the knowledge they possess and the variety of activities people perform and their intellectual behaviour is due in large part to the "procedures" they possess for carrying out their activities.

1.4.1. Winograd's work

The most persuasive champion of the procedural point of view has been Terry Winograd, whose Ph.D. thesis, (Winograd, 1972), described a system of procedures that interpreted and generated a wide variety of natural language sentences pertaining to stacking and unstacking blocks (the system "existed" in a microworld that came to be known as *the blocks world*). Winograd chose the programming language MICRO-PLANNER (based on Hewitt's PLANNER formalism) as the ultimate internal form for his interpretation procedures. That is, a command such as

Pick up the big red block and put it in the blue box

would be translated into a MICRO-PLANNER program which, when executed, would achieve the required action. This program could also be examined or manipulated as data by other procedures if it was necessary for them to access or alter the interpretation at any time.

We indicate some of the power and influence of the procedural approach on AI modes of thinking by showing how Winograd's thesis work delineated various issues which subsequently became important. Of course, as in most AI approaches, the procedures used to interpret and generate language have a paramount importance. But, Winograd has gone further and has suggested, (Winograd, 1976), that the semantics of the meaning representation itself should be procedural as well, following up on a notion of Woods, (Woods, 1967). This initial elaboration of *procedural semantics* generated vigorous debate about the novelty and importance of the supposed shift of perspective that proceduralism constituted, (Dresher and Hornstein, 1976a), (Dresher and Hornstein, 1977), (Dresher and Hornstein, 1976b), (Johnson-Laird, 1977), (Winograd, 1977), (Schank and Wilensky, 1977), and (Fodor, 1978).

A related issue initiated by Winograd's work was the so-called *procedural/declarative* controversy in artificial intelligence: the initial shots were fired by (Winograd, 1975). Debate swirled over issues raised by the nature of the internal form used to represent the meaning of natural language.[3] On one side of the debate were those supporting procedures as a representation language. On the other side were those that claimed that procedures, although interesting as a representational form, were difficult for other procedures to reason with and should be supplemented or even supplanted by more "declarative" (data-like) constructs. The debate eventually died away when both sides conceded that any scheme, declarative or procedural, has to have processes of various kinds interpret it, and that for a given application, a representation scheme is better the more easily it can be interpreted.

In his SHRDLU system, (Winograd, 1972), Winograd was

---

[3]This procedural-declarative controversy is the artificial intelligence incarnation of the old philosophical distinction between *knowing how* and *knowing that*; proceduralists assert that our knowledge is primarily knowing how, while declarativists believe that a set of quite general *procedures* exist for manipulating specific facts describing particular knowledge domains.

able to control the complexity of studying a wide variety of phenomena by limiting his domain to a microworld. This has since become a standard technique in artificial intelligence research, and at least a short term way of allowing broad issues to be studied with some subtlety. Eventually, of course, lessons learned in microworlds must be generalised to richer, real world domains. The attempt to extend pure procedural models tends to run into a "complexity barrier", (Winograd, 1974), and this is one of the major criticisms of the procedural approach when contrasted to more declarative schemes. However, the linguistic intuitions gained in a microworld can be applied more generally, even if the system itself cannot be directly extended. A good example of such growth towards reality can be found in the sequence of work on story understanding by Schank's students, where lessons learned in the MARGIE system, (Schank, Goldman, Reiger, and Reisbeck, 1973), were applied to SAM, (Cullingford, 1978), which provided a foundation for PAM, (Wilensky, 1978), which in turn was instrumental in the design of POLITICS, (Carbonell, 1981). Another good example is the work at University of Pennsylvania, in general supervised by Bonnie Webber, where insights into general linguistic issues are an outgrowth of the creation of a number of systems, (Kaplan, 1982), (Mays, 1980), (McCoy, 1982), (McKeown, 1982), built in the "microworld" of providing natural language access to databases.

Another important aspect of Winograd's work was his system's ability to achieve an interaction of syntax, semantics, and pragmatics, allowing information from whatever "level" to be used when appropriate. For example, once his parser identified a syntactically valid constituent, the semantic routines would be called before the rest of the input was parsed to determine if the constituent "made sense" in the blocks world. This aspect of his work foreshadowed a general concern with control, and reinforced the necessity for AI models (particularly procedural models) to pay heed to these issues. Wherever possible, his system used knowledge to reduce search. His approach, though, was application dependent, specifically tailored to the kinds of language used in the blocks world. Since then, more general models of control have been posited in AI, including work on *scripts*, for example, (Schank and Abelson, 1977), which package together ready made inferences, *plans*, for example, (Schank and Abelson, 1977), which can be concocted using AI problem solving techniques, and *special purpose inference schemes*, for example, inheritance of information in generalisation hierarchies, (Schubert, Goebel, and Cercone, 1979).

1.4.2. Procedural semantic networks

Recognizing the importance of procedural representations, researchers at the University of Toronto developed a system called PSN (procedural semantic network), which is still used today. We describe their approach to procedural semantic network representations which formalises traditional semantic network concepts within a procedural framework. (Levesque, 1977) and (Levesque and Mylopoulos, 1979) describe the underlying considerations which went into the development of PSN.

The Toronto group cite two problems with the classical approach to defining semantic networks in which, at best, the networks are interpreted in terms of the semantics of classical *logic*. The first of these problems include the specification of concepts whose properties change over time. The formalism developed by (Schubert, 1976) can handle such specifications, admittedly in a perhaps cumbersome manner. The other, more serious problem concerns itself with the control issues involved in *using* a representation; for example, no distinction is normally made between an inference rule that *can* be used from one that *should* be used. To progress beyond these problems, the Toronto researchers based their semantic network representation on programs.

The components of the procedural semantic network representation include *classes*, *relations*, and *programs* that are all (but not the only) objects. A *class* is a collection of objects sharing common properties; these objects are said to be *instances* of the class and may themselves be classes. A *relation* is a mapping from one class to another class (from the *domain* to the *range*). Relations can be considered as classes with *assertions* as instances. Finally a *program* is a class whose instances are called *processes* and correspond to program activations. Four basic operations, defined by attaching four programs to each class or relation, include: *add*ing an instance to a class, *remove*ing an instance from a class, *fetch*ing an instance of a class, and *test*ing membership of an instance in a class.

The organisation of the semantic network is considered to be basically an *abstraction mechanism* in terms of which details from a lower level of representation are suppressed. Two abstraction mechanisms which are considered correspond to *generalisation/specialization* - the so called IS-A hierarchy - and *aggregation/decomposition* for composing groups of interrelated objects into single functional units. A further distinction is made between *structural properties*, for example, PUPIL, a relation that always holds between a grade and a single student, and *assertional properties*, for example, MARK which is a relation mapping grades into numeric values and can be changed without altering what the grade is intended to represent. Furthermore, some relations, like GRADE, are represented as having both structural and assertional properties, since it depends upon two parts, neither of which is important enough to be defined independently as the relation.

The approach to quantification is somewhat simplistic by design - the IS-A hierarchy expresses a simple universal quantification and the PART-OF hierarchy implicitly expresses existential quantification. Rather than introduce specialised machinery to treat the full range of quantification problems (scope, nesting, etc.), quantification is treated procedurally (constructively) as in PLANNER, (Hewitt, 1972). IS-A and PART-OF provide a convenient declarative supplement to the usual procedural definitions. This is typical of semantic network formalisms: the full power of the approach is trimmed in the interest of efficiency, perspicuity, or simplicity.

Subsequent generalisation of classes to include *metaclasses* permits objects to be organised along an *instance hierarchy* as well as an IS-A and a PART-OF hierarchy. In addition, the use of metaclasses clarify the operation of inheritance, for example, the metaclass RELATION inherits the attributes of CLASS, that is, the four program slots, but specifies new defaults: the four standard programs for relations.

Programs (*procedures* and *functions*) are required for the specification of the behaviour of classes and relations. They are characterised by: (i) *prerequisite*, a logical statement that must be true before the body can be executed; (ii) *body*, an action for procedures or an expression for functions; (iii) *effect*, an action performed after a successful completion of the body; and (iv) *complaint*, an action or expression to be used after an unsuccessful completion of the body. Since programs are classes, they can be organised along the IS-A hierarchy and benefit from inheritance rules.

Levesque and Mylopoulos discuss advantages of their formalisation of semantic networks, in particular the usefulness of incorporating procedures directly into the network, (Levesque and Mylopoulos, 1979). These advantages include:

● A semantic foundation for semantic networks is provided using programs.

● The IS-A and instance hierarchies are useful and provide explicit rules for inheritance.

● Structural and assertional properties are differentiated and their characteristics are explored.

● The metaclass is introduced as a method of representing certain aspects of the representation within the representation itself.

● Programs are integrated directly into the representation as classes having all of the usual characteristics (for example, inheritance).

1.5. Logic programming

Combining logic and procedures is the idea behind *logic programming*, manifested in programming languages like Prolog, (Colmerauer, 1973a). In this approach, procedural and logical representation schemes are combined into one form: *logic programs*. Initially growing out of research into automated reasoning, more recently logic programming has been explicitly explored in a natural language context, (Dahl, 1981); (Hadley, 1985).

The power of logic programming derives from the fact that declarative sentences in predicate calculus are also programs, a particularly useful merging of declarative and procedural styles in that inferencing capabilities can be achieved without undue loss of perspicuity. There is also a uniformity in representation between the processes which interpret the natural language and the notation into which the language is translated, and it is very easy to incorporate the information content of the natural language input into the knowledge base. Prolog as a particular logic programming language has the further advantage of being able to share some of the precision of predicate calculus as a formal notation.

To informally introduce the logic programming paradigm, we examine Prolog in more detail. Knowledge is expressed in Prolog as either facts or rules. Thus *loves(John, Mary)* represents the fact that "John loves Mary". Rules take the general form

$$P_1 \text{ if } (P_2 \text{ and } P_3 \text{ and } ... \text{ and } P_n)$$

where the P_i's are predications. The general rule that "Mary loves everyone who loves her" can be stated

$$\text{loves(Mary, x) if loves(x, Mary)}$$

Once facts and rules are defined, Prolog's inference mechanism proves goals by finding clauses which unify with the goal, and in turn proving the goals in the body of those clauses. A backtracking mechanism is used to cycle through alternate clauses that unify with a goal. For example, if we want to know "who loves Mary?" [loves(x, Mary)] given the facts and rules

```
1. loves(John, Mary)
2. loves(sibling(x), x)
3. loves(Mary, x) if loves(x, Mary)
4. loves(Mary, Bill)
```

Prolog would find x=John and x=sibling(Mary). On the other hand, in the query "who does Mary love?" [loves(Mary,z)],

Prolog would find z=Bill, z=sibling(Mary), and z=John.

In many ways, this type of representation for natural language is not new. The use of MICRO-PLANNER (Winograd, 1972) was quite similar, although MICRO-PLANNER, as implemented, does not share Prolog's formal underpinnings, since it is based on the less well-understood Planner formalism developed by Hewitt, (Hewitt, 1972).   MICRO-PLANNER quickly fell into disfavour, since users could not control its "blind backtracking" search. Prolog programmers use the *cut* operator to prevent blind backtracking - *cut* effectively fixes certain bindings to variables and does not allow them to change thenceforth.   If too many cuts are needed to make a Prolog program execute in reasonable time, the program becomes quite opaque, and many of the advantages of Prolog as a comprehensible, declarative, formally tractable language disappear.   Whether *cuts* will eventually bring Prolog to the same fate as MICRO-PLANNER remains to be seen. The plethora of current research into logic programming suggests that every effort will be made to overcome problems such as this.

1.6. Frame-based representations

Propositional representation schemes, such as semantic networks, predicate calculus, or logic programming representations, have been criticised as imposing only a local organisation on the world, (Bobrow, 1975).   Organizational theories of knowledge can be characterized as clustering related knowledge into "chunks".   The idea is that storing knowledge in chunks will reduce the computation required to access knowledge, since once a particular chunk has been accessed, all knowledge relevant to that chunk is immediately available in the chunk itself.   Chunking had been investigated in psychological research for some time, for example, (Bartlett, 1932); (de Groot, 1967).

The first computational theory to embody the idea of chunks was Minsky's *frames proposal*, (Minsky, 1975).   In an incredibly short time, the notion of frames became the basis of another major school of thought on knowledge representation.

The salient feature of frames is simply the idea of grouping pieces of knowledge which may be useful for understanding a particular concept or situation. Dividing a knowledge base into frames has become common in a variety of applications such as computational vision, using schemata (Havens, 1977), and natural language understanding, using scripts (Schank and Abelson, 1977), (McCalla, 1978). Frames are particularly useful when used to represent knowledge of certain stereotypical concepts or events.

Figure 1-4 illustrates a frame for a stereotypical restaurant. The *pointers* represent *slots* which must be assigned to specific instances of restaurant type, restaurant alternatives, restaurant location(s), and restaurant food style frames when a particular restaurant is *recognized*. Most frame formalisms provide a variety of mechanisms to help in filling in slots, which range from pre-specified *defaults* to major capabilities for inference. Once a frame has been instantiated, many inferences can be made about the state of the world (for example, in a dining room frame, once a dining room is recognized, inferences about the existence of a dining room table, chairs, windows, a chandelier, etc., can be made). Some of these inferences are contained directly in the frame itself (for example, the existence of the table and chairs); other inferences can be made from the fact that a frame is usually statically related to other frames, most importantly by the IS-A relationship (for example, the existence of windows may be a fact inherited from the fact that dining room is a room, and all rooms have windows). Many approaches to frames deal at length with how and when to make such inferences. Often a distinction is made between scripts (Schank and Abelson, 1977) with little capacity for inference and more procedurally oriented frames. This distinction has helped to fuel the procedural/declarative controversy, mentioned above.

It appears to us that the fundamental differences between networks and frames can be traced to the fact that the concept of a frame is largely *functional* rather than *structural*; that is, a memory structure is regarded as a frame because of the kinds of knowledge and capabilities attributed to it, rather than because of any specific structural properties. Thus, frame theorizing can take either of two forms: design of specific

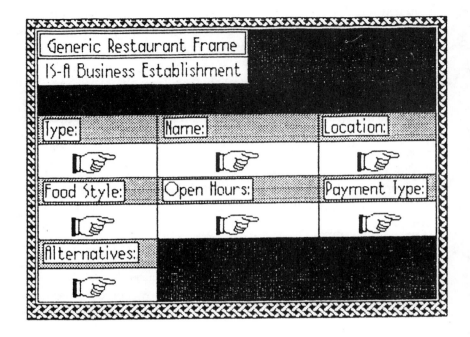

Figure 1-4:   A Frame for a Stereotypical Dining Room

frame structures, (Bobrow and Winograd, 1977), (Roberts and Goldstein, 1977), (McCalla, 1978), (Havens, 1977), or demonstration of specific frame-like capabilities in existing structures such as scripts, (Schank and Abelson, 1975), or nets, (Scragg, 1975).

Frames, scripts, and schemata organise the knowledge which they represent according to the function of that knowledge.   The following example illustrates the functional organisation for frames, specifically the associative access of *frame slots*.   Knowledge associatively accessed via frame slots can be procedurally embedded; execution of these procedures provides computational comprehension for concept and context. In the sentences:

```
John unlocked his car.
He used his key.

John graded the exam.
He used his key.
```

the meaning of *key* is different in the second sentence than in the last sentence; comprehension of its different meanings depends upon the *unlockingcars* frame and the *gradingexams* frame. The frames might contain slots for carkeys and examinationkeys, or slots for other frames to explain car and examination keys. The frames might also contain information about the kind and use of keys in general. The description of *his key* guides clever access mechanisms to select the appropriate slot.

Scragg's proposed network version of this idea characterizes *car* and *exam* as *key nodes* with *weak links* to the parts of a car and exam respectively, and to other information about these concepts. Weak links and their inverses are distinct from propositional links within a net, and serve the exclusive purpose of gathering together into a *plane* useful information about a particular concept. Similar to the way in which frames trigger subframes and other frames, mention of "car" and "exam" would activate the corresponding key nodes.

The crucial part of Scragg's theory concerns the operation of the access mechanism which seeks the referent of "the key". First, the possible meanings (nodes) of this term are accessed and then all inverse weak links from these nodes are followed. This mechanism starts its search *outside* the active plane and works (*gropes*) its way back. This is probably more efficient than groping *forward* from an active key node in search of a "key" of some kind. However, consider *one couple was dancing* and *the man kept stepping on the woman's toes*. One shudders at the thought of the access mechanism tracing inverse weak links from *man* and *woman* back to all planes in which a man or a woman is a participant.

One suggestion, (Schubert, Goebel, and Cercone, 1979), is to associate a *concept access skeleton* with every concept which is distinct from the topic access skeleton and has as its leaves the participants in the knowledge about the root concept. Thus, for example, in *John was gardening* and *the spade became muddy* the "gardening spade" might well be accessible via the concept access skeleton of gardening, whereas no playing card is likely to reside in that context.

No *rote* solution is likely to work in all cases of associative referent determination. Reasoning is surely required to select the most plausible sense of "spade" in the example *John opened the trunk of the car* and *he took out a spade.*

The semantics of functionally organised representations are frequently treated as a computational rather than a representational issue. To be effective, *procedural semantics* must distinguish between implementing a well-specified notion and specifying a notion by implementing it. For example, the selection of replacement frames is treated differently in all frame-based systems as a computational problem to be solved by clever implementation rather than through well specified semantics which delineate various selection classes.

Knowledge representation languages, such as KL-One (Brachman, 1979), KRL (Bobrow and Winograd, 1977), FRL (Roberts and Goldstein, 1977), etc., have sprung up based on the idea of frames. These languages provide primitives which allow the user to define new frames, to specify links to and from the frames (which effectively embed the frames in a semantic network), to indicate "slots" to be filled in, to put conditions on the kinds of variables which fill the slots, to specify inferences which can be made once slots are filled, and much else beside.

Frames combine many of the advantages of semantic network and procedural representations. Each frame is a node in a semantic network; procedures are incorporated explicitly where they are needed to make inferences to fill in slots or after the slots are filled. Frame systems which are developed as knowledge representation languages also have an interpreter which, in a sense, provides a semantics for the frame system (and certainly makes precise both the internal form and the processes which manipulate it). However, as with semantic networks, most approaches to frames blur many distinctions and are unclear on others. For example, are links in a frame making an assertion or are they part of the essential meaning of the frame? More recent approaches to frames have started to deal with the problem of making such subtleties clear; see, for example, the Krypton system (Brachman, Fikes, and Levesque, 1983).

1.7. Production system architectures

Production system architectures are another way of representing knowledge. Proposed by Newell, production systems were originally presented as models of human reasoning, (Newell, 1973). A set of production rules (each essentially a *pattern → action* pair) (see Figure 1-5) operates on a short term memory buffer of relevant concepts, although recent versions tend to have an unlimited memory of concepts. A basic control loop tries each rule in turn, executing the *action half* of the rule only if the *pattern half* matches. Representing knowledge as *pattern → action* pairs has proven to be a very natural way of extracting and encoding rule-based knowledge in many applications, and now production systems are widely used to construct special-purpose knowledge-based systems, so-called expert systems. Various abstract production systems, such as EMYCIN were devised to make this task easier, (van Melle, 1980).

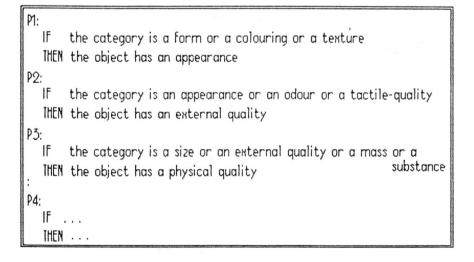

```
P1:
    IF   the category is a form or a colouring or a texture
    THEN the object has an appearance
P2:
    IF   the category is an appearance or an odour or a tactile-quality
    THEN the object has an external quality
P3:
    IF   the category is a size or an external quality or a mass or a
    THEN the object has a physical quality            substance
    :
P4:
    IF   . . .
    THEN . . .
```

Figure 1-5:   Productions from a Typical Expert System

The production system data base typically stores state information about a domain, while the production rules specify how state changes in the data base can be effected. Production systems differ from most frames, scripts, schemata, and semantic networks in that they include methods for changing the information stored. This essential nature of production systems precludes a direct correspondence with any single part of the network organizations, frame-based schemes, or even a typical database management system paradigm. The data base component of production systems gives them the appearance of a (naive) database management scheme which, with a suitable interface, would provide a comprehensive information management tool.

However, production system data bases lack a unique data model. The structure of each data base and its production rules is determined by the application. Production systems manage data bases in a more structured manner than do most AI systems, and provide a framework in which to explore issues of representation.

Currently, the terms *production system* and *expert system* are used nearly interchangeably. However, this was not always so. Rule based (expert) systems originated during the early 1960s at Stanford and M.I.T. before the production system architecture was even invented. DENDRAL (Buchanan, 1969) was a heuristic program which performed organic chemical analysis. The MACSYMA system (Mathlab, 1977) of symbolic integration and formula simplification was developed at M.I.T. Both systems were designed to manipulate and reason about symbolically expressed problems which were known to be difficult for humans to solve, partly due to the large number of possible solutions. The early rule-based systems incorporated efficient algorithms to search through a potentially (combinatorially) explosive domain of possible solutions.

When, in 1973, Newell elaborated the idea of production systems to represent rule-based reasoning, it became possible to use this idea to build "expert systems" (Newell, 1973). A wide range of problems requiring expertise were addressed. MYCIN provides consultative advice on diagnosis and therapy for infectious diseases (Shortliffe, 1976). INTERNIST consults in the domain of internal medicine (Pople, 1977). PROSPECTOR is a geological "hard rock" mineral exploration system (Duda, 1978). BUGGY identifies a student's misconceptions about basic arithmetic computations (Brown and Burton, 1978). SOPHIE is an intelligent CAI (Computer Aided Instruction) system which teaches students problem solving skills by student trial and error (Brown, Burton, and Bell, 1974). Automatic programming systems like PSI (Green, 1977) and legal expert systems (McCarty and Sridharan, 1981) are further examples of the range of problems which are being addressed by expert systems derived from the production system architecture formalism.

The latest development in rule-based systems is recognition of the important role played by the knowledge engineer, who is responsible for incorporating the knowledge and methodology of many experts into the expert system. Hayes-Roth et al. (Hayes-Roth, Waterman and Lenat, 1983) and Weiss and Kulikowski (Weiss and Kulikowski, 1984) describe the development of expert systems as a cumulative trial and error process during which databases grow and production rules are adapted as the expert system grows more similar to human expertise. Expert system development languages are available to assist in the implementation of expert systems. EMYCIN, was used to develop expert systems for pulmonary disfunction, structural analysis, psychiatric analysis, and education. AGE is used to build knowledge based programs (Nii and Aiello, 1979), and OPS is a domain independent production system language (Forgy and McDermott, 1977).

Paradoxically, production system architectures have seldom been used for constructing natural language understanding systems. Since the main advantages of production systems as a knowledge representation seem to lie first in the ease with which they allow knowledge to be extracted from an expert and encoded, second their ability to be directly executed, and third their ability to be readily modified once their action has been observed, we observe that these aspects do not directly pertain to the problem of providing a nice *logical form* for natural language analysis. However, there is some reason to believe that knowledge encoded in production systems may be useful in other roles than directly simulating expertise. Clancey,

(Clancey, 1982), for example, has used productions initially extracted for the MYCIN expert system, as the basis of an intelligent tutoring system which teaches the rules underlying MYCIN to students. Such "passive" use of production systems for reasoning and inference may foreshadow their more widespread use in applications like natural language processing.

1.8. Knowledge representation languages

During the late-1970's *knowledge representation languages* (KRLs) slowly emerged as a separate vechicle for representing knowledge. Several different languages were quickly developed, such as KL-One (Brachman, 1979), KRL (Bobrow and Winograd, 1977), FRL (Roberts and Goldstein, 1977), etc. More recently, the KRYPTON (Brachman, Fikes, and Levesque, 1983) system attempted to separate representational issues from control issues in a knowledge representation language. We discuss two of the more recent of these KRLs: KL-One and KRYPTON.

1.8.1. KL-One

KL-One is a language for representing knowledge to support reasoning in artificial intelligence programs. Originally developed at Bolt Beranek and Newman Inc. [BBN] in the late 1970's, it has attracted a sizable following consisting of those who use the formalism to structure domain models on paper and those who use the original INTERLISP implementation developed at BBN. Today, several other versions and implementations exist, and an annual workshop is held by KL-One users.

KL-One is based on the *structured inheritance networks* developed by Brachman, (Brachman, 1979). Essentially KL-One has two sublanguages - a *description* language and an *assertional* language. The description language allows the user to define an extensible set of conceptual terms that are used to make assertions. The assertional language is used to make statements about the world. Thus, the descriptive language is used to form a description for the compound "a man from

Mars" from simpler KL-One descriptions for "a man" and "Mars", but this carries no assertional force.

KL-One is based on the *structural conceptual object* (or concept) as its building block. This kind of "object" replaces the "proposition" of the traditional semantic network as a basic structuring unit, and thus the representational level appropriate for discussing KL-One as a knowledge representation language is *epistemological* rather than *propositional*. Thus, KL-One comprises a set of *epistemological primitives* for structure types and structure forming relations.

The principle elements of KL-One descriptions are *concepts*, generic and individual. Generic concepts, "general terms" in Quine's sense, (Quine, 1960), and individual concepts can be illustrated by the contrast between *a man from Mars* (generic) and *the man from Mars* (individual). Generic concepts are arranged in a definitional taxonomy which represents their subsumption relations and this is referred to as a definitional taxonomy (very similar to the IS-A hierarchy discussed at length earlier). Concepts inherit at least part of their definition from their superConcepts.[4]

Figure 1-6 illustrates a KL-One representation of the concept for a simple "arch" which has three bricks as its parts. R1 is a *Role* that expresses the fact that this arch has one "lintel", which must be a "wedge-brick". The *RoleD* link relates the concept "arch" and one of its role descriptions; the *V/R* (value/restriction) points to the type predicate that must be satisfied (true) of the eventual role filler, and the *number* link restricts the number of fillers of the role. *Modality* links indicate the importance of the attribute to the concept. Other roles and links are defined in a similar manner.

The definitional components of a KL-One concept include:

1. The definitions of its subsuming concept (its superConcept)

2. Its local internal structure expressed in

---

[4]KL-One places a strong emphasis upon precise definitions for concepts.

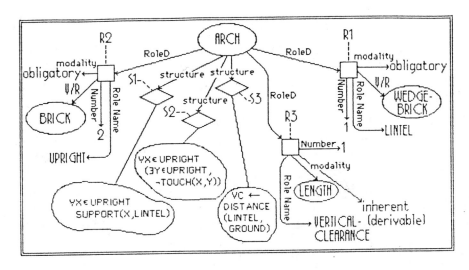

Figure 1-6:   A KL-One Concept for a Simple Arch

a. *Roles,* which describe potential relationships
    between instances of the Concept and other
    closely associated Concepts (that is, those of
    its properties, parts, etc.), and

b. *Roleset Relations,* which express the
    interrelationships among the functional Roles.

A superConcept serves as proximate genus, while the
internal structure expresses essential differences. Roles come in
two flavours in KL-One: *RoleSets,* which capture the notion
that a given functional role of a Concept can be filled in the
same instance by several different entities, and *IRoles,* or
instance Roles. Since the functional Roles defined by RoleSets
can be played by more than one individual at a time, RoleSets
have number restrictions to express cardinality information.

Definitional generic knowledge in KL-One is expressed in
a taxonomic inheritance structure. This network is formed by
inter-Concept inheritance Cables (such as the superConcept link)

which pass the structure of definitions. The inheritance Cable is the primary description-formation operator of KL-One. This definitional relationship which is established by the Cable is akin to lambda-abstraction, such as that between A and B in $B(x)=lambda(x)[A(x)$ & ...]. Thus, subConcepts are defined in terms of the superConcepts.

Not all terms used in KL-One can be completely defined via the term-forming operators. KL-One provides a mechanism for introducing *primitive* terms from which other terms may be defined, and these definitions, vis-a-vis KL-One, are incomplete. They are referred to in KL-One as *Concepts.

Inter-Role relations are expressed by modifier links; there are four such relationships: *restriction, differentiation, particularisation,* and *satisfaction.* These relationships bear the brunt of the structured inheritance carried by Cables.

KL-One Roles are assigned local "names" and inherit them from superRoles. Role-fillers provide for the explicit representation of roles and provide the representation with a set of inter-Role relations, known as RoleSet relations [RSR], such as RoleValueMap [RVM]. A RVM expresses a simple relationship between two sets of Role-fillers - either identity or inclusion. Another RSR is the Structured Description [SD], which expresses how the Roles of the Concept interrelate and how they relate to the Concept as a whole via the use of *ParaIndividual Concepts,* or parameterised versions of other Concepts. In general, RSRs express quantified relationships among RoleSets as set mappings.

KL-One also provides mechanisms for *Contexts* and *Nexuses,* structureless entities which serve as loci for co-reference statements, and *Meta-Descriptions* which are references to internal entities, and which allow for attached procedures and the incorporation of arbitrary data to KL-One Concepts.

Further discussion of KL-One's usefulness in illuminating knowledge representation subtleties and resolving issues can be found in Woods' chapter in this volume (Chapter 2).

1.8.2. KRYPTON

KRYPTON is an experimental knowledge representation system which focusses on a *functional* specification of the knowledge base. Derived in part from previous experiences with KL-One and PSN, the authors of the system provided *operations* needed for interacting with a knowledge base without assuming anything about the internal structure of the knowledge base. These operations are divided into *TBox*, a terminological kind of operation, and *ABox*, an assertional kind. Essentially, the TBox deals with the formal equivalent of noun phrases, such as *a person with at least three children*, and the ABox operates with the formal equivalent of sentences, such as *every person with at least three children owns a car*. The TBox supports two kinds of expressions: *concept expressions*, similar to frames or KL-One Concepts, and *role expressions*, which are slots or KL-One Roles. In Krypton, TBox expressions are very strictly controlled, and only a small number of specific operators exist for concept and role expressions (about a dozen).

Just as TBox expressions are constructed compositionally from simpler TBox expressions, the ABox language allows ABox sentences to be constructed compositionally from simpler ABox sentences. The major difference between the ABox language and a standard first order logical language lies in the primitive sentences. The *predicate symbols* are taken to be *independent, primitive, domain-dependent* terms, and since the TBox language allows specification of such terms, the nonlogical symbols in the ABox language correspond to the terms of the TBox language. The TBox has structured terms organized taxonomically, while the ABox contains first-order sentences whose predicates come from the TBox, and a separate symbol table maintains the names of the TBox terms.

There are two ways of interfacing with a KRYPTON knowledge base: *Tell*, which augments the knowledge base, and *Ask*, which extracts information from the knowledge base. Tell takes an Abox sentence and asserts that it is true, and this changes the knowledge base. Ask takes a sentence and asks if it is true, and the result is determined on the basis of the current theory held by the knowledge base and the vocabulary used in the sentence, as defined in the TBox.

KRYPTON's service as a knowledge representation system is completely specified by these operations. Thus, in this functional view, KRYPTON's knowledge base is treated like an *abstract data type* characterised by a set of operations. The KRYPTON system attempts to deal with problems which arise when frames are used as a representation language, for example, confusing structural and assertional facilities.

1.8.3. Other languages

There are other knowledge representation languages currently in practical use; for example, LOOPS is an extension of the INTERLISP-D programming environment which combines procedures, object-orientation, and the rule-based paradigm in one language. Undoubtedly other knowledge representation languages will be developed in the future. Until knowledge representation experts agree on the basic ingredients of epistemological primitives for such languages, we are afraid that they will be useful only to a handful of specific applications for which they are best suited, or will prove to be too complex to provide a sound basis on which to build the complex knowledge-based systems of the future.

1.9. Concluding remarks

In a very real sense, knowledge representation is at the core of most artificial intelligence research. Much of AI's ongoing effort is devoted to research into knowledge representation, both into the formal and computational properties of the various knowledge representation schemes which we have described, and also into the use of knowledge representation in artificial intelligence applications and elsewhere.

This chapter has illustrated many possible artificial intelligence representation paradigms, including logical representations (particularly first order predicate calculus and esoteric logics), semantic networks, frames, procedures, logic programming, production systems, knowledge representation languages, and variations on these. We conclude this chapter by

outlining some general knowledge representation principles
which can be drawn from this diversity of research:

- information of many different kinds must be
  capable of being represented, including knowledge of
  the world, knowledge about goals and (sometimes)
  intentions, knowledge of context, and so on;

- knowledge representation is relativistic - the best
  kind of knowledge representation scheme is often
  dependent on the particular requirements of a given
  application;

- knowledge should be representable to all depths -
  there is no absolute level of primitives which
  cannot be "opened-up";

- the processes which manipulate a knowledge
  representation scheme are important; moreover they
  should run in *reasonable* space and time;

- it is important that a knowledge representation
  scheme be precisely formulated - ad-hocness is no
  longer satisfactory;

- artificial intelligence approaches to knowledge
  representation do not have exclusive access to all
  the answers - other areas of inquiry into intelligent
  behaviour are extremely useful and have been
  influential on AI knowledge representation research;
  hopefully, too, the AI approach will be influential
  on other areas of inquiry.

We hope that future knowledge representation research
will begin to coalesce into a more uniform endeavour, united
by adherence to principles such as these.

Acknowledgements

We would like to thank our friends and colleagues for many useful insights provided over the years. In addition, we thank our reviewers who have helped to make this a much more accurate and readable article. We also wish to express our gratitude to Canada's Natural Science and Engineering Research Council for its financial support of our various research endeavours. Finally, we would like to acknowledge the fact that much of this article is based on the IEEE Computer special issue paper "Approaches to Knowledge Representation", and the fact that we have also occasionally adapted aspects of various other papers we have written over the past couple of years (Cercone and McCalla, 1984), (McCalla and Cercone, 1985), (Schubert, Goebel, and Cercone, 1979), (Cercone, McCalla, and McFetridge, 1986).

2. Knowledge Representation: What's Important About It?

William A. Woods

Applied Expert Systems, Inc.
Harvard University
Cambridge, Massachusetts

Abstract

In this chapter the basic requirements for a knowledge representation scheme are examined. The nature of models and reasoning is discussed, and characteristics of various aspects of representation are outlined (including knowledge acquisition, perception, planning, and generalization). The knowledge representation language KL-One is introduced in order to clarify these notions with actual examples. Then, the expressive adequacy of a knowledge representation scheme (what it is capable of representing) is contrasted to the notational efficacy of a scheme (its actual shape and structure). Two aspects of notational efficacy receive special attention: computational efficiency (speed of inference) and conceptual efficiency (ease of representation). The chapter concludes with arguments about the role of predicate calculus in the representation of knowledge.

Based on the paper, What's Important About
Knowledge Representation, William A. Woods, appearing in COMPUTER,
Volume 16, Number 10, October, 1983.

2.1. Introduction

In computer science, a good solution often depends on a good representation. For most applications in artificial intelligence, the choice of representation is especially important, since the possible choices are more diverse and the forcing criteria are less clear. A suitable representational system is crucial for encoding the knowledge and the states of reasoning of intelligent agents that can understand natural language, characterize perceptual data, or learn about their world. This is because the representational primitives, together with the system for their combination, effectively limit what such systems can perceive, know, or understand (see Figure 2-1).

Figure 2-1:   A Priori Choices Limit What a Computer Can
Perceive or Know

This chapter will discuss a number of issues that serve as goals for knowledge representation research. The objective is to discover general principles, frameworks, representational systems, and a good set of representational primitives for dealing with an open-ended range of knowledge. By "representational primitives" I mean to include not only

primitive concepts but (especially) the primitive elements and
operators out of which an open-ended range of learned concepts
can be constructed. The focus of the chapter will be on the
problems that arise when designing representational systems to
support any kind of **knowledge-based system** -- that is a
computer system that uses knowledge to perform some task. I
will first discuss some philosophical issues concerning the
nature of knowledge and its relationship to the world and then
consider a variety of issues that a comprehensive knowledge
representation system must address.

The general case of a knowledge-based system can be
thought of as a reasoning agent applying knowledge to achieve
goals. Although the representational problems that need to be
solved for many less ambitious knowledge-based systems may
be simpler than those for a universal reasoning agent, the
general principles are nevertheless the same.

2.2. Knowledge for reasoning agents

The role of reasoning for an intelligent agent is depicted
in Figure 2-2. Such an agent is perpetually engaged in an
infinite loop of perceiving things, reasoning about them, and
taking actions. The actions are determined by a set of internal
beliefs, goals, and objectives in interaction with what is
perceived. A major task for such an agent is to acquire a
model of the world in which it is embedded and to keep its
model sufficiently consistent with the real world that it can
achieve its goals. Knowledge of the world consists of two
kinds of things -- **facts** about what is or has been true (the
known world state), and **rules** for predicting changes over
time, consequences of actions, and unobserved things that can
be deduced from other observations (the generalized physics/
logic/ psychophysics/ sociology of the world).

An unavoidable characteristic of the internal model of the
world is that it is at best an incomplete model of the real
external world. In addition, it may be partly in error due to
false assumptions and invalid reasoning. Differences between
the internal model and the real world arise from a variety of
sources, including (but not limited to):

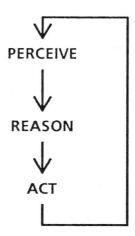

Figure 2-2:　The Reasoning Loop for an Intelligent System

- changes that have happened in the world since the agent recorded some fact about it (the world won't hold still);

- the inability of the agent to learn in a reasonable amount of time everything it could know in principle (there's too much to know);

- and limitations of the knowledge representation system that preclude it from even conceptualizing certain things about the world (the world is richer than we can imagine).

(These are fundamental limitations that can't be avoided by more careful reasoning or avoiding unwarranted assumptions.)

Although it may not be apparent at first glance, this characterization is as accurate for many computer application systems as it is for a biological or artificial creature. It is a fair characterization of the function that a data base system is intended to support, as well as a good model of the situation of an intelligent expert system. This perspective can be taken as a general characterization of the kinds of systems that require knowledge representation, and it can serve as a focus for the general problems that a knowledge representation system should solve. Specifically, it suggests that a knowledge representation system should support perception, reasoning, planning and controlling actions.

2.3. Modeling the external world

One theory of intelligence (Dennett, 1978) conjectures that the essence of intelligence comes from a kind of internalized natural selection in which the intelligent agent has an internal model of the world against which it can try out hypothesized courses of action. This allows it to evaluate expected results without exposing it prematurely to the dangers of real actions in the real world. Whether this is the essence of intelligence or not, it is clearly a useful ability and an important role for knowledge representation -- both in intelligent creatures and in computer artifacts.

Viewing the knowledge base of an intelligent agent as a **model** of the external world focuses attention on a number of problems that are not normally addressed in data base systems or knowledge-based expert systems. For example, the questions of how the individuals and relationships in the model relate to the external world are not usually part of the competence of a data base system. This role is filled at the time of input by a data entry specialist, after which the data base behaves as if its contents **were** the world. If a person querying the data base wonders what the terms in the data base are supposed to mean (e.g. how is "annual coal production in Ohio" actually determined), there is nothing in the competence of the system to support this need. What's missing is a characterization of the relationship between the internal model and the world "out there".

Typical data base systems support the storage and retrieval of "facts" about the world and certain aggregation and filtering operations on them, but do not perform operations of perception to map situations in the world into data base contents. Nor do they perform planning operations leading to action in the world (unless you count report generators and graphics displays as actions in the world). The utility of a traditional data base system rests in its support of an overall human activity in which the perception and action aspects are performed by the human users and maintainers of the data base. However, the objectives of the overall combination of data base and its human "partners" are similar to those of our canonical intelligent agent. Thus an ideal data base (or knowledge base) would be evaluated in terms of its support for the same kinds of reasoning, perception, and planning activities as performed by our intelligent agent (although in some cases, parts of these activities are performed by human agents interacting with the system).

2.4. Perception and reasoning by machine

Increasingly, computer systems are being called upon to perform tasks of perception and reasoning as well as storage and retrieval of data. The problem of automatically perceiving larger patterns in data is a perceptual task that begins to be important for many expert systems applications. Recognition of visual scenes, natural language parsing and interpretation, plan recognition in discourse understanding, and continuous speech understanding are generic classes of perceptual problems which reasoning agents may be called upon to perform. Domain specific instances are tasks such as medical diagnosis, mass spectrographic analysis, or seismic signal interpretation. The roles of a knowledge representation system in perception are important to all of these tasks.

Similarly, deductive reasoning applied to the information provided by perception is essential to the analysis of situations and the planning of actions in knowledge-based systems. Such reasoning is required to draw conclusions from facts, to connect known facts to enabling conditions for actions and expectations, to determine applicability of actions to situations, to evaluate alternative hypothetical actions, to determine when expectations and hypotheses are violated, to structure plans to achieve goals, and to detect inconsistencies among goals and to resolve them. Many of these activities involve the application of deductively valid rules of inference as in a formal predicate calculus.

Other reasoning processes that can be applied to such information include: (a) drawing "nonmonotonic" conclusions from limited amounts of information, (b) determining degrees of likelihood or confidence of a supposition through probabilistic reasoning such as Bayesian analysis, (c) conceptualizing and naming new entities through constructive actions such as planning and designing, and (d) maximization or "satisficing" processes that seek the best choice among alternatives (for example, the best fit to some specification, the best account of some data elements).[5] These reasoning processes do not consist of drawing deductively valid conclusions, and their operations differ in many respects from those of deductive inference.

All of the above processes make use of knowledge or information and draw conclusions. Some system of knowledge representation is implicit in all of these processes for recording and representing both the input information and the conclusions that are drawn. Whatever representational system is chosen will play an important role in organizing the information and in supporting the internal substeps of the reasoning and/or perceptual processes.

It is important to realize that the reasoning involved here is dealing with a model of the world, not the real one. The model imposes an abstraction on the real world, segments the world into entities, and postulates relationships among them. Reasoning systems can draw conclusions about entities and propagate the consequences of assumptions, but do not deal directly with the world. Perceptual processes interact with the

---

[5]"Nonmonotonic" conclusions are conclusions that are drawn in the face of explicit lack of knowledge and would not be made if certain information were known. Although the term is of relatively recent coinage, an early example is Alan Collins' "lack of knowledge principle" (Collins, 1975), a principle for concluding that some property is not true of an object if it is not known to be true and enough is known about the object to be confident that the property in question would have become known if it were true. "Satisficing" is a term coined by Herbert Simon (Simon, 1956) for processes that are similar to optimization processes except that there is a criterion for what constitutes a sufficiently good solution to stop searching for something better -- that is, a process that seeks a "good enough" solution.

world to populate the internal model.   Actions performed by
the agent can affect both the external world and the internal
model.   These distinctions are fundamental for keeping track of
what's going on in the knowledge base of a reasoning agent.
Figure 2-3 illustrates some elaborations of the basic reasoning
loop to begin to take account of this distinction.   Notice that
at the point of action, there is an element of expectation
introduced into the model to record the effect that the action
is expected to have.   Expectations have two roles: (1) the
intended effect is modeled directly in the internal model of the
world, and may be compared with the system's perceptions to
determine if the action has succeeded, and (2) expectations
condition perception by preparing the reasoning system to
perceive what is expected (with consequent risks of only
perceiving what is expected).

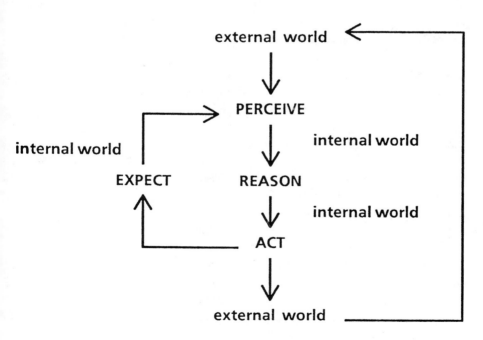

Figure 2-3:   Modeling the External World

2.5. The Nature of the world and its models

There are at least two ways to view the world and our perception of it. One way views the world as an ideal entity, perceived through sensors that are limited and prone to error, so that it is necessary to infer the hidden real world from the measurements of our sensors. A classic example of such a situation is that of a hidden Markov process, whose state transitions are only visible through their effects on a probabilistic output function that does not uniquely determine the underlying state. In this view, the nature of the "real world" can be inferred through reasoning or calculation (given enough data).

Another way to view the same situation is that the world is as it is, and is too complex and detailed to ever be captured or even fully conceived by any reasoning agent. In this view, the world as it presents itself to our senses is the ultimate reality, and the ideal models that we construct are just that -- models -- whose fidelity is traded off against the simplicity and efficiency of their use. From this latter perspective, it is not necessary to postulate objective reality to the idealized models, but only to consider them from the perspective of their utility in predicting the behavior of the world. All that is necessary is predictability within sufficient tolerances of precision and accuracy that the reasoning agent can achieve its goals well enough for the species to survive. One model can be more "true" than another in that it predicts more than the other, and there can even be incomparable models that predict different things, each of which is equally "true" (faithful).

The second of the above perspectives seems to account best for the situation of a knowledge-based computer system (and probably our human situation as well) -- the state of the world is far more detailed and its behavior more diverse than we could possibly replicate in a model with fewer states. In most mathematical models used by physicists and engineers, an intentional approximation is used to eliminate inessential attributes of the problem and focus on the essence. Hence the introduction of idealized concepts such as point masses and frictionless surfaces. From the perspective of our understanding of the world, we realize the nature of such approximations and can characterize the kinds of things that these idealized models leave out.   When we look closely at our most complete perspective, however, we find it likely that our best and most thorough understanding of the world is still, like the mathematical abstractions, only an approximate idealization, and there is no larger perspective available to us from which we can understand its limitations.   Thus, it appears that any reasoning we could do, and any understanding of the world we could have, must necessarily be an approximation.

An example of this limitation is weather simulation.   The instabilities in the atmosphere that can be introduced by even a small temperature difference (below the levels of precision that we could expect to measure and use on the scale required to simulate the weather) can lead after a sufficient period of time to quite dramatic differences in the ensuing weather patterns. Hence it would be impossible to capture a fully accurate and precise initial state for a weather simulation, even if the model of the equations that govern the behavior of the weather were to be totally correct.   Moreover, even if one could capture all the relevant information, it would be difficult to simulate the weather faster than it actually happens using any computational engine with fewer resources than the atmosphere itself.   One can view the actual weather system as a highly parallel engine that determines its behavior more quickly and accurately than any existing computational artifact does.   This line of reasoning leads to the possible conclusion that the most accurate, timely simulation of the weather may be the weather itself.

What's true of the weather is a part of what's true of the world.   Hence, for purposes of an intelligent agent, models of limited fidelity appear to be a practical, if not logical, necessity if they are to be of any predictive use at all.

2.6. The functions of a knowledge representation system

In the most general case, a knowledge representation system must support a number of different activities.

Different techniques may be appropriate for representing different kinds of things and for supporting different kinds of activities, but there is a substantial overlap in the use of knowledge for different purposes. This forces us in some cases to either find a representational system that supports multiple uses of knowledge or else represent the same knowledge several times in different representational systems. All other things being equal, it would be desirable to have a representational system in which knowledge that has multiple uses will have a single representation that supports those uses. One reason for this is the cost of acquiring and maintaining independent representations. On the other hand, when issues of efficiency for different uses impose conflicting demands on a representation, and the benefits are sufficient to overcome the costs of acquiring, storing, and maintaining multiple representations, then one would prefer separate representations tailored to their use. In the next three sections, we will discuss three broad classes of use of knowledge that a knowledge representation system should support and some of the demands that they impose on a knowledge representation system.

2.7. The knowledge acquisition problem

From the above perspective, it seems that the best any intelligent agent can hope for is to gradually evolve a more and more faithful and useful model of the world as its experience with the world and its experience with its own needs for prediction accumulate. This is true also for any computer knowledge base that is to perform some task or assist some human to do so. Thus, a primary role of a knowledge representation system must be to support this evolutionary acquisition of more and more faithful models that can be effectively applied to achieving goals or tasks (at least up to the point where the additional complexity and cost of using a more faithful model outweighs the additional benefits to be gained).

Some of the issues that need to be addressed are:

- how to structure a representational system that will be able to, in principle, make all of the important distinctions;

- how to remain noncommittal about details that cannot be resolved;

- how to capture generalizations so that facts that can be generalized don't have to be learned and stored individually;

- how to recognize efficiently when new knowledge contradicts or modifies existing hypotheses and previous knowledge, and how to know/discover/decide what to do about it;

- how to represent values of time dependent attributes; and

- how to acquire knowledge dynamically over the system's lifetime -- especially to assimilate pieces of knowledge in the order in which they may accidentally be encountered rather than in a predetermined order of presentation.

2.8. The perception problem

In addition to the problems of acquiring a knowledge base, an intelligent agent must use knowledge to advance its goals. This requires being able to perceive what's happening in the world in order to act appropriately. It is necessary for the agent to perceive that it is in a situation in which knowledge is applicable, and to find the knowledge that is relevant to the situation. It is necessary to use knowledge to support the perception of what is the same and what has changed from a previously known state of the world. Among other things, knowledge will be used to perceive new individual entities that are present but formerly unknown and to identify new perceptions with preexisting concepts of known individuals where appropriate.

Some of the issues that need to be addressed here are:

- how to generate and search a space of possible hypotheses without combinatorial explosion;

- how to find the relationships between elements that have been identified and roles they could play in larger percepts;

- how to recognize when one perceptual hypothesis is a duplicate of another;

- how to find the best characterization of the situation; and

- how to deal with errors in input or partially ill-formed perceptions.

2.9. Planning to act

Like perception, planning to act can introduce new elements into the internal world that were not there before -- namely, the planned actions and their expected results. Planning is one of the kinds of action that the system can execute. It is one of a class of **internal actions** which differ from **overt actions** in that their effects happen in the internal, rather than the external, world. (We will ignore here the philosophical implications of the fact that the agent's internal world is a part of the real external world.) Internal actions require a knowledge representation system to be able to represent such things as plans, goals, hypotheses, and expectations.

Some of the issues that need to be addressed here are:

- how to share large amounts of common knowledge between alternative hypotheses and different points in time;

- how to structure a plan to support monitoring for its successful execution;

- how to represent and trigger contingency plans and dynamically replan when something goes wrong;

- how to simulate and evaluate a plan;

- how to record the expectations and objectives that motivate a plan and recognize when a plan is no longer relevant; and

- how to plan for multiple and possibly competing objectives.

2.10. Role of a conceptual taxonomy for an intelligent agent

A fundamental problem for an intelligent computer agent that cuts across many of the above activities is analyzing a situation to determine what to do. For example, many expert systems are organized around a set of "production rules," a set of pattern-action rules characterizing the desired behavior of the system (Davis, Buchanan, and Shortliffe, 1977). Such a system operates by determining at every step what rules are satisfied by the current state of the system, then acting upon that state by executing one of those rules. Conceptually, this operation entails testing each of the system's rules against the current state. However, as the number of rules increases, techniques are sought to avoid testing all of them.

One approach to the problem of determining which rules apply has been to assume that the pattern parts of all such rules are organized into a **structured taxonomy** of all the situations and objects about which the system knows anything. By a taxonomy, I mean a collection of concepts linked together by a relation of **generalization** so that the concepts more general than a given concept are accessible from it. By a structured taxonomy I mean that the concept descriptions have an internal structure so that, for example, the placement of concepts within the taxonomy can be computationally determined. A characteristic of such a taxonomy is that information can be stored at its most general level of applicability and indirectly accessed by more specific concepts said to "inherit" that information.

If such a taxonomic structure is available, the action parts of the system's rules can be attached to the concept nodes in the structure as pieces of "advice" that apply in the situations described by those concepts. The task of determining the rules applicable to a given situation then consists of classifying the situation within the taxonomy and inheriting the advice. Thus, a principal role that a conceptual taxonomy can play is to serve as a conceptual "coat rack" upon which to hang various procedures or methods for the system to execute (see Figure 2-4). A conceptual taxonomy can organize the pattern parts of a system's rules into an efficient structure that facilitates recognition as well as a number of other activities that a knowledge representation system must support.

2.11. The structure of concepts

In building up internal descriptions of situations, one needs to use concepts of objects, substances, times, places, events, conditions, predicates, functions, individuals, etc. Each concept can be characterized as a configuration of attributes or parts, satisfying certain restrictions and standing in specified relationships to each other. A knowledge representation system that focuses on this type of characterization is the system KL-One.[6]

Space does not permit a complete exposition of KL-One in

---

[6]KL-One is the collaborative design of a number of researchers over an extensive period. Principal developers (besides myself) have been Ron Brachman, Rusty Bobrow, Jim Schmolze and David Israel. Hector Levesque, Bill Mark, Tom Lipkis, and numerous other people have made contributions. Within this large group are different points of view regarding what KL-One is or is attempting to be. Over time those views have evolved substantially. What I say here represents primarily my own view, and may not be totally congruent with the views of my KL-One colleagues.

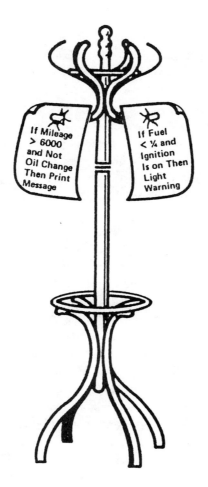

Figure 2-4:   A Conceptual Coat Rack for Organizing Advice

this article.   However, I want to use KL-One notations to illustrate the kinds of taxonomic organizations I am advocating. In this section, I will present a brief overview of the taxonomic structures in KL-One as a context for subsequent discussion.   For a more complete exposition of KL-One, see (Brachman and Schmolze, 1985).

A **concept** node in KL-One has an associated set of **roles** -- a generalization of the notions of attribute, part, constituent, feature, etc.   In addition, it has a set of **structural conditions** expressing relationships among the roles.   Concepts are linked

to more general concepts by a relation called SUPERC. The
more general concept in such a relationship is called the
superconcept and is said to **subsume** the more specific
subconcept. Some of a concept's roles and structural
conditions are attached to it directly, while others are
inherited indirectly from more general concepts.

The concepts and roles of KL-One are similar in structure
to the general data-structure notions of record and field or to
the "frame" (also called "schema" or "unit") and "slot" of AI
terminology. However, there are several differences between a
KL-One concept and these data structure notions. These
differences include the way that subsumption is defined and
used, the presence of structural conditions attached to a
concept, the explicit relationships between roles at different
levels of generality, and the general intent of KL-One
structures to model the semantics and conceptual structure of
an abstract space of concepts (as opposed to being merely a
data structure in a computer implementation).

This last point may require some elaboration. The goal
of KL-One is not per se to produce a particular computer
system, but rather to force the discovery and articulation of
general principles of knowledge organization and structure.
Expressive adequacy is an important driving force in KL-One
research, emphasizing the semantics of the representation and its
adequacy to make the kinds of subtle distinctions that people
make when conceptualizing complex ideas. (The importance of
the semantics of a semantic network is discussed elsewhere
(Woods, 1975).) The KL-One effort has been more of an
exercise in applied philosophical investigation of abstract
conceptual structure than a design of computer data structures.

2.12. An example of a conceptual taxonomy

The kind of taxonomic structure that I want to advocate
is illustrated by the example in Figure 2-5. Here, using KL-
One notation, concepts are represented by ellipses and roles by
circled squares. At the top of the figure is a high-level
concept of Activity having roles for Time, Place, and
Participants, which are inherited by all concepts below it.

Below Activity, to the right, is the concept for a Purposive Activity, which differentiates (DIFFS) the general role for Participants into an Agent (the participant that has the purpose) and Other Participants. Purposive Activity introduces a new role called Goal to represent the purpose of the activity.

Below Purposive Activity is the fairly specific, but still generic, concept of Driving to Work. This concept modifies the Goal of Purposive Activity by adding Getting to Work as a value restriction (V/R), indicating that whatever fills the Goal must be an instance of Getting to Work. It also introduces a new role called Destination, with Place of Work as its value restriction. A structural condition (not shown) attached to the concept would specify how the Place of Work related to the Getting to Work goal -- that is, that it is the Destination of the Getting to Work goal. Driving to Work in Massachusetts is, in turn, a specialization of Driving to Work, with its Destination restricted (MODS) to a Place in Massachusetts. Driving to work in Massachusetts is also a specialization of a Dangerous Activity with a Risk of Physical Harm.

This figure illustrates the kind of taxonomy one would expect to have in an intelligent computer agent, including both high-level abstractions and quite specific concepts. As such a taxonomy is used and evolves, there is always room for inserting new levels of abstraction between existing ones. In fact, a well-defined classification procedure implemented in the KL-One system can automatically place a new description into a taxonomy, linking it by SUPERC connections to the concepts that most specifically subsume it and those that it in turn subsumes.

2.13. The need for taxonomic organization

In most expert-system applications, a task description often satisfies several rules simultaneously, no one of which accounts for all of the task or supplants the relevance of the others. For example, adding an object to a display simultaneously changes the display and displays an object. Advice (the action parts of the rules) associated with both activities must be considered. Moreover, one description of a

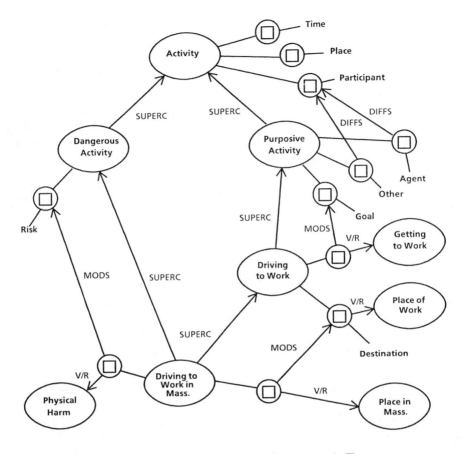

Figure 2-5:   An Example of a Conceptual Taxonomy

situation may subsume another more specific description, and their advice may supplement or contradict each other. Thus, conventions are required to determine which advice takes precedence when conflicts arise.

For independent rules in a classical production-rule system, such conflicts may be discovered only when a conflicting situation occurs as input. In a taxonomic classification structure, however, the subsumption of the conditions of one rule by another can be discovered when the rule is assimilated into the taxonomy -- at which time the person entering the rule can address the question of how the two rules should interact. The advice associated with the more specific rule then can explicitly include the information to override or supplement the more general rule.

Assimilating rules into a taxonomic knowledge structure not only facilitates the discovery of interactions at input time, but also promotes a compactness in the specification of the rules. By relying on the fact that concepts inherit information from more general concepts, one can usually create the concept for the pattern part of a new rule merely by adding a minor restriction to an existing concept.

In KL-One, when one wants to create a description of a situation that is more specific than a given one, it is only necessary to mention those attributes being modified or added; one does not have to copy all of the attributes of the general situation. Besides facilitating compact memory storage, this feature also facilitates updating and maintaining the consistency of the knowledge base by avoiding the creation of duplicate copies of information (which can then be independently modified and could accidentally be modified inconsistently).

The ability to assimilate new descriptions into an existing taxonomy at any level permits an evolutionary system design that can achieve the same standards of rigor as a top-down design without requiring concepts to be defined in a predetermined order. For most applications, even if one could get the initial design carefully laid out in a rigorous top-down mode, subsequent changes (for example, required changes in accounting policies induced by new tax laws) will require the ability to modify the system in more flexible ways. A system's taxonomy of recognizable situations and situational elements should be viewed as an evolving knowledge structure that, like a person's world view, continues to be refined and developed throughout the lifetime of the system.

2.14. Recognizing/analyzing/parsing situations

A taxonomic structure can have considerable advantages for the process of recognizing that some of the elements currently perceived constitute instances of a known situation. Roughly, this process consists of discovering that those elements can be interpreted as filling roles in descriptions known to the system. Merely characterizing a situation as an instance of a single existing conceptual description is not usually sufficient. In general, a description of a situation must be a composite object, parts of which will be instances of other concepts assembled together in formally permitted ways.

Recognizing a situation is similar to parsing a sentence, although it is considerably more complex. Whereas the grammatical relationships between parts of a sentence are fixed, the relationships among the "constituents" of a situation may be arbitrary. These relationships include events preceding one another in time; people, places, and physical objects in various spatial relationships with each other; people in physical or legal possession of objects; people in relationships of authority to other people; and people having certain goals or objectives.

One technique for efficiently recognizing situations is to use a "factored" knowledge structure (Woods, 1980) in which the common parts of different rules are merged so that their testing is done only once. Examples of factored knowledge structures include classical decision trees and typical ATN grammars. With such structures, one can effectively test a large set of rules without considering the rules individually. The taxonomic structures embodied in KL-One can provide a factored representation for parsing situations. Determining the most specific concepts that subsume the input situation can be done by using the chains of links from the elements of the situation to the roles of higher level concepts in which they can participate, using generalizations and extensions of the algorithms used to parse sentences.

The suitability of a representation for supporting algorithms of this sort is an important aspect of a knowledge representation system. A version of this technique using KL-One has been successfully applied in the PSI-Klone system, where an ATN parser is coupled with a KL-One taxonomy that organizes the semantic interpretation rules for a natural-language understanding system (Bobrow and Webber, 1980).

2.15. Two aspects of knowledge representation

Two aspects of the problem of knowledge representation need to be considered. The first, **expressive adequacy**, has to do with the expressive power of the representation -- that is, what it can say. Two components of expressive adequacy are the distinctions a representation can make and the distinctions it can leave unspecified to express partial knowledge. A second aspect, **notational efficacy**, concerns the actual shape and structure of the representation as well as the impact this structure has on the operations of a system. Notational efficacy, in turn, breaks down into such components as computational efficiency, conceptual clarity, conciseness of representation, and ease of modification.

It is important to distinguish expressive adequacy from notational efficacy, since the failure to clarify which issues are being addressed has exacerbated numerous arguments in this field. For example, an argument that first-order predicate calculus should be used because it has a well-understood semantics partially addresses expressive adequacy, but does not explicitly mention the issue of notational efficacy. The argument could be understood as advocating the use of the notations traditionally used by logicians, and in some cases this may even be what is meant. However, it is possible to invent many different notational systems, each having a first-order logic semantics, but having different attributes of notational efficacy.

To provide reasonable foundations for the practical use of knowledge in reasoning, perception, and learning, knowledge representation research should seek notational conventions that simultaneously address expressive adequacy and notational efficacy. A representational system is required that will be adequate for a comprehensive range of different kinds of inference and will provide computational advantages to inferences that must be performed often and rapidly. One class of inference that must be performed rapidly and efficiently is the characterization of one's current situation with respect to a taxonomically organized knowledge network.

2.16. Expressive adequacy

However efficient a representation may be for some purposes, it is all for naught if it can't express necessary distinctions. In seeking a representation, one must avoid choosing a set of primitives that either washes out such distinctions as those among "walk," "run," "amble," "drive," and "fly", or overlooks the commonality between these specific concepts and the general concept "move." A structured inheritance network such as KL-One permits both benefits. As they become important, new distinctions can be introduced by refining or modifying existing concepts. Moreover, it is always possible to introduce more general concepts that abstract details from more specific ones. The explicit taxonomic structure allows one to move freely among different levels of generality, rather than being required to fix a single level of detail at which to characterize knowledge. Figures 2-6, 2-7, 2-8, and 2-9 illustrate this kind of ability.

Figure 2-6 illustrates how a number of Roger Schank's abstract transfer concepts (MTRANS, ATRANS, PTRANS, and PROPEL) (Schank and Rieger, 1974) relate to each other and to some more general concepts. Figure 2-7 illustrates how ATRANS relates to several more specific concepts (the balloons below the small diamonds signify structural conditions that characterize how the details of the more specific actions relate to the more general one). Figure 2-8 illustrates how the specializations of one class of entity (Legal Entity in this case) can induce a corresponding space of specializations of an action that applies to such entities, presenting more specialized concepts for a variety of interesting classes of entity that can serve as the recipient of an ATRANS. Figure 2-9 illustrates both kinds of subclassification of the abstract verb Like. This kind of taxonomic organization allows one to capture generalizations at the level of Transfer, Directed Action, or Action on an Object while still being able to store facts at the level of specific actions such as Loan or Give. The more

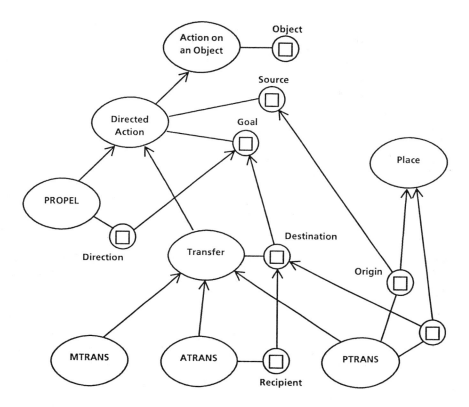

Figure 2-6:   Transfers and Directed Actions

specific concepts will automatically inherit information stored at the more general levels.

Common problems in axiomatizing a domain in the traditional predicate calculus are choosing the set of predicates and deciding what arguments they will take. Inevitably, these decisions leave out distinctions that might be important for another purpose, such as time variables, situation variables, intermediate steps, and provisions for manner adverbial modification. Incorporating revisions of such decisions in a complex system could amount to redoing the axiomatization. One of the goals of KL-One, toward which some progress has been made, is to provide a terminological component for such axiomatizations (that is, KL-One concepts provide the predicate

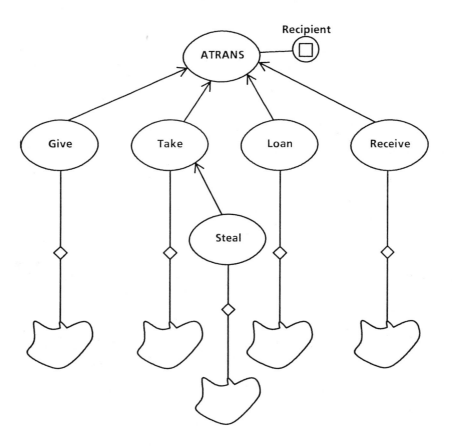

Figure 2-7:   Some Kinds of ATRANS

inventory for the axiomatization) so that, for example, the time
role of activities (see Figure 2-5) can be virtually ignored in
expressing an axiom in which time does not figure prominently,
and yet remain present implicitly (or be added later) when a
situation is encountered in which it is important.

Another need is an ability to refer to what we know,
believe, suspect, or conjecture and to represent our varying
states of knowledge over time. Often we need to record the
sources of pieces of knowledge and evidence for that
knowledge. The ability to refer to concepts as entities as well
as to use them to refer to their instances, and the ability to
represent propositions as entities (about which assertions can be
made) as well as to believe them, are both critical to this

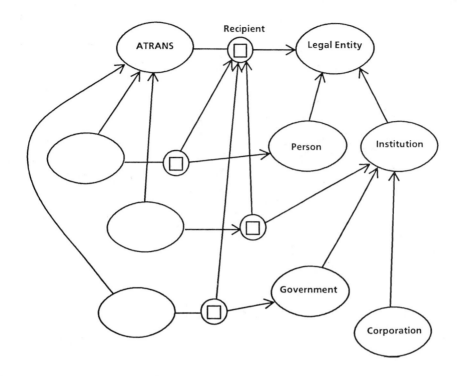

Figure 2-8:   More Kinds of ATRANS

ability.

2.17. Notational efficacy

Expressive adequacy is a minimal requirement for a knowledge representation system. Eventually, one wants a framework in which the assimilation of arbitrary new information is not only possible but also is in some sense natural. For example, one would like small changes in knowledge to require small changes in the knowledge base, so that learning processes or even incremental debugging can be expected to eventually converge. Moreover, there must be operators for making fine adjustments as one gets close to the

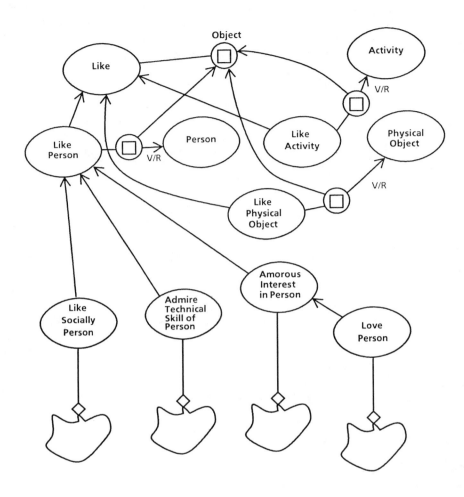

Figure 2-9:   Kinds of Like

correct state.   Thus, an aspect of a knowledge representation
system that is important for knowledge acquisition and learning
is an analog of the mathematical property of compactness --
that is, there should be points in the space of possible

knowledge states that are arbitrarily close to the state of knowledge one wants to reach (in some suitable sense of "close"). It is necessary for the representation to be able to express not only the desired target knowledge, but also all of the intermediate states of knowledge that must be passed through along the way. If the knowledge representation system cannot represent some of the intermediate states or if the topology of the space of representations is such that you can't get from one learning state to another without major detours or major reorganization, then learning will be difficult at best. This kind of support for knowledge acquisition is one element of notational efficacy.

Notional efficacy issues can be subdivided into issues of **computational efficiency** and **conceptual efficiency**. The aspects just discussed that support knowledge acquisition are primarily elements of conceptual efficiency. Elements ∶ of computational efficiency have to do with the utility of notations for supporting a variety of algorithms. Examples include some of the factoring transformations (which can reduce combinatoric search) and the use of links to access concepts related to other concepts (which can reduce searching and matching). Some aspects of a knowledge representation may support both computational and conceptual efficiency. For example, assimilating the pattern parts of rules into a taxonomic knowledge structure (to facilitate the discovery of interactions at input time) and the inheritance of common parts of those patterns (to provide a compactness in the rule specifications) are features that support both efficiency of operation and the conceptual efficiency of the knowledge acquisition and organization processes. The fact that sharing common parts of different rules can conserve memory storage and facilitate updating as well as minimizing duplicate testing of conditions is another such element.

In summary, a knowledge representation is called upon not only to express an adequate model of a domain of knowledge, but also to support a variety of computational and conceptual activities involved in acquiring and using that model.

2.18. The relationship to formal logic

Many hold the opinion and have argued strongly that **formal logic**, by which they usually mean the **first order predicate calculus** with its customary syntactic notations, provides all that one needs for knowledge representation. By this account, all that is necessary to represent knowledge is to axiomatize the appropriate information. Someone else, or perhaps the same person, will then produce an efficient general purpose theorem prover or reasoning engine for using that axiomatization to perform tasks. Others, who perceive that something more than this is required for reasonable efficiency, nevertheless still view notations such as semantic networks as alternative encodings of things that can be expressed in predicate calculus, and they characterize the meaning of these notations in terms of equivalent predicate calculus terms and predicates.

While it is true that the first order predicate calculus is able to axiomatize the behavior of any computational system, this does not mean that the properties of those systems follow from the predicate calculus. On the contrary, one can axiomatize any rule-governed behavior that one can rigorously specify, whether it's nature is deductively valid or not, logic-like or not. The difficult issues mostly stem from determining what the behavior should be and how to efficiently bring it about. This work remains whether the medium is a predicate calculus notation or some other representational formalism.

Thus, the predicate calculus alone is not the solution. Moreover, the notations and style of activity associated with predicate calculus axiomatization can in some cases be misleading or distracting (or unnecessarily constraining) rather than helpful. For example, the semantic approach to belief modelling based on sets of possible worlds a la Hintikka and Kripke leads to models of belief with the undesirable consequences that the modeled agent must be assumed to believe all the logical consequences of his other beliefs (including all the truths of arithmetic -- whether known to any mathematician or not). Likewise, although one can use the basic predicate calculus machinery to prove the existence of an individual satisfying certain properties, the predicate calculus machinery gives us no operator to name that individual and refer to it by name in subsequent reasoning. (Skolem functions and individual constants provide names for individuals conceived by the system designer in setting up the formal system, but there is no notion of process in the predicate calculus within which a name could be coined in the course of reasoning and then used later.) The classical Tarskian model of first-order logic provides a good way to characterize the necessary truths and the consequences of hypotheses in any situation (determined by the individuals in it and the predicates that are true of them), but it provides no machinery for characterizing the relationship between two situations. For example it gives no leverage for characterizing what happens to a situation as a result of introducing a new individual.

The issues raised previously about sharing information across alternative hypotheses or points in time, the creation of new structures in response to perception or planning, and many other tasks are not directly supported by the basic inferential and semantic machinery of the predicate calculus. Thus, there are a number of problems that need to be solved that are not inconsistent with a predicate calculus approach, but are nevertheless not solved merely by adopting the predicate calculus as a representation. These issues remain to be solved and addressed whether predicate calculus or some other representational system is used.

Finally, even if the predicate calculus is taken as the basis for part or all of a knowledge representation system, there remain issues of representation dealing with how best to structure the axioms and how to organize them to support efficient reasoning. Even within the family of predicate calculus approaches, there are such different representational techniques as Skolem-functions versus explicit existential quantification, Skolem-normal form, conjunctive normal form, clausal representations, etc. -- all different notations sharing a basic semantic framework, but adopting different representations in order to support particular reasoning disciplines.

What I have said here is not meant to argue against the value of interpreting a representational system in terms of a predicate calculus perspective in order to understand those aspects that are equivalent to predicate calculus notions. I do, however, argue that the ordinary notations and semantics of the predicate calculus are insufficient by themselves -- they need to be supplemented with additional machinery in order to solve many of the problems. This would include adding machinery for the modalities (necessity, possibility, contingent truth), machinery for the creation of referential names and attaching them to a characterization of their meanings, and machinery for nonmonotonic reasoning, as well as coming to grips with some nonfirst-order problems such as reasoning about properties. In addition, there are other mechanisms required for dealing with perception and creative actions such as planning that are not customary in traditional formal logic. The next section will consider one such issue.

2.19. Concepts are more than predicates

The search for a clean semantics for semantic networks has led some researchers to adopt an assumption that the nodes or arcs in a semantic network are simply alternative notations for the equivalent of predicate calculus predicates. In this section, I will present some counter arguments to that position. To illustrate the points, I will use the classical blocks-world arch example, illustrated in Figure 2-10. In this figure, an arch is an assembly of three blocks, two of which are called uprights and the third is called a lintel. The balloon at the bottom signifies a structural condition about how the blocks have to be related to each other in order for them to constitute an arch -- that is, the lintel has to be supported by the uprights and there must be space between the uprights. The concept of such an arch specifies both that the arch is composed of three things which are individually blocks as well as the relationships that have to hold among them to be an arch.

We might consider identifying this concept of an arch with a predicate in the predicate calculus. However, there are a number of candidates, each of which might have equal claim to being the predicate represented by the arch concept. One of these is a predicate on three blocks that characterizes the

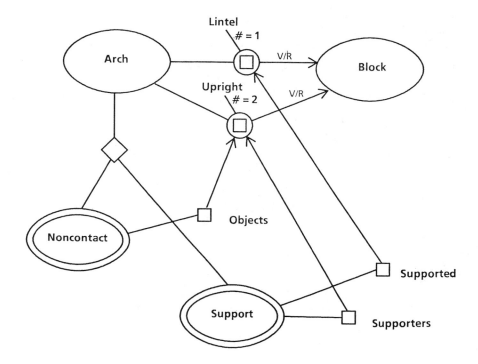

Figure 2-10:   A Blocks-World Arch

relationship that the blocks must have in order to be an arch (i.e., the predicate of the structural condition). Let us call it ARCH(X, Y, Z). Another is a predicate of one argument that is true of an individual arch. Let us call it ARCH'(X). Still another is a predicate that is true of a situation S if there is an arch present in the situation. Suppose we call it ARCH''(S). Either of the first two, if not the third, appear to have a good claim to be the predicate that we would mean by the concept Arch (if that was all we meant by the concept). I would suggest, however, that the concept of an arch is something slightly different from any of these predicates, and yet has all three of these predicates (and more) associated with it. The concept is an abstraction that ties together a number

of related predicates that characterize what an arch is. The
concept also serves some other functions as well, such as
serving as a place to keep records about one's experience with
arches.

One of the elements of the arch concept that is missing
from an identification of the concept with one of the simple
arch predicates is the notion of what it would take to build
one. The predicate ARCH(X,Y,Z), for example, is true of three
blocks if they stand in a certain relationship. When viewed as
an abstract set of ordered triples (as in a standard predicate
calculus semantics) it does not provide a very useful object to
serve as a plan for building an arch. If there do not happen
to exist three blocks in an arch configuration, then the
predicate ARCH(X,Y,Z) has the empty extension and there is
not much structure there to use as a plan. Yet one of the
things that we know about an arch is what its parts are and
how they are arranged. The arch concept is at least a
constellation of such predications (as uninstantiated, second-
order, metalevel objects capable of being instantiated or as
conceptual objects capable of being manipulated by reasoning
and planning activities as entities in their own right -- e.g., as
subgoals to be achieved).

Another inadequacy of the concept-is-predicate view is the
lack of anything that characterizes when two instances of a
concept are to be considered the same or different. For
example, two views of the same arch, one identifying a
particular support with the X argument and the other
identifying it with the Y argument should not count as two
different arches. This is another piece of information that we
know about arches and is part of the arch concept. I have
suggested elsewhere (Woods, 1986) that a kind of object can be
characterized by its recognition conditions and a "sameness"
predicate that defines what counts as two instances versus one.
One can conceive of two different kinds of object that share
the same recognition conditions but have different sameness
predicates. For example, one can distinguish an "ordinary
triangle" (which merely has three sides and three corners) from
an "oriented triangle" (which in addition has a top and a
bottom). Depending on one's perspective, a given instance of
the former will be interpretable in different ways as

instantiating the latter.   When thinking in these terms, it becomes apparent that "same" is a relation not of two arguments but of three -- we must consider whether two things X and Y are the same Z, where Z is a concept and X and Y are instances of it.   We may have two distinct oriented triangles that are nevertheless the same triangle.   Thus, one of the things that may be associated with a concept is a sameness predicate, and this predicate stands in a qualitatively different relation to the concept from the predicates making up the conditions' that any instance must satisfy.

Finally, there is nothing in either ARCH or ARCH' (as abstract sets of ordered tuples) that characterizes the relationship between the arch as an individual and the individual blocks that make it up.   There is nothing there to provide guidance to an inference engine that should conceptualize :an individual arch when it perceives a constellation of three blocks in the appropriate relationship or to a planner that needs to know what subgoals to attempt in order to construct an arch.

The above discussion should convince the reader that there is something more to a concept than simply a predicate. A concept has an associated set of predicates as well as being a mental object that can support learning and planning.   Note that I am not talking here about specific internal implementational structures.   Rather, my notion of a concept should be interpreted as the abstraction that such implementational structures would stand for.   The important issue is that a representational object representing a concept stands for more than a single predicate, and in the abstract world of concepts, there is structure that can be exploited for learning and planning.

2.20. Conclusions

This chapter has discussed a number of issues of knowledge representation that go beyond merely being able to express a correct semantics.   The discussion began with a consideration of the relationship between knowledge and the world and the use of knowledge by reasoning agents (both biological and mechanical). Specifically, a knowledge representation system is called upon to support activities of perception, learning, and planning to act. A number of issues are presented that a knowledge representation system must address to support these activities, and an argument is put forth that the mechanisms of traditional formal logic, such as the predicate calculus, while important to our understanding, are not by themselves sufficient to solve all of the problems. In particular, notational aspects of a knowledge representation system are important both for computational and conceptual reasons.

Two aspects of a knowledge representation system are important -- expressive adequacy (the ability to make important distinctions and the ability to avoid undesired distinctions) and notational efficacy (the aspects of the notation that support both computational efficiency and conceptual activities such as knowledge acquisition and learning).

I have argued that taxonomic classification structures can advance both expressive adequacy and notational efficacy for intelligent systems. Such techniques, I believe, eventually will be applicable throughout computer science. Emphasizing the expressive adequacy and conceptual efficiency of a representation -- rather than solely the computational efficiency of data structures -- prepares the way for a general methodology of representation that will transcend different applications and different implementation techniques. Ultimately, this trend should lead to a way of specifying computational behavior in terms of high-level conceptual operators that match the conceptual structures of the human programmer, factoring out the issues of implementational efficiency for separate consideration or even automatic compilation.

The increased emphasis on abstract data types and "object-oriented" programming (Robson, 1981) mark the beginning of this trend. The next logical step is generalizing the notion of abstract data types to the level of abstraction, inheritance, and expressive adequacy present in a sophisticated knowledge representation system. This step could produce a new style of programming which (Goodwin, 1979) has termed "taxonomic programming." This style of programming can have enormous advantages in flexibility, extensibility, and maintainability, as well as for documentation, user education, error reduction, and software productivity. Moreover, such representations can make it possible to combine independently developed systems to produce integrated systems more powerful than the mere union of their parts.

3. Some Remarks on the Place of Logic in Knowledge Representation

David J. Israel

Center for the Study of Language and Information
and SRI International
333 Ravenswood Avenue
Menlo Park, California

Note: A later and more extensive version of this material has appeared under the title *A Short Companion to the Naive Physics Manifesto*, as the last chapter of **Formal Theories of the Commonsense World**, edited by Hobbs and Moore, Ablex Publishing Corporation, Norwood, N.J., 1985.

Abstract

What is the place of logic in knowledge representation? It is argued that the answer to this question depends on what one means by *logic*. Various alternative conceptions are briefly scouted, with an eye to separating out what are, in fact, separate issues.

Based on the paper, The Role of Logic in Knowledge Representation,
D. Isreal, Appearing in COMPUTER, Volume 16, Number 10, October, 1983.

3.1. Introduction

If we think of artificial intelligence as being founded during the Dartmouth Conference of 1956, then it's fair to say that since this field of study began, AI researchers have debated the appropriateness of adopting as a representational formalism a language of the kind devised, used, and studied by logicians. And, if we are to believe *Science* magazine, the debate continues:

> Theoreticians...have reached no consensus on how to solve the AI problem--on how to make true thinking machines. Instead, there are two opposing philosophical viewpoints, and a flurry of research activity along these two directions. The different viewpoints were represented at a recent meeting of the American Association for Artificial Intelligence by Marvin Minsky and John McCarthy...
>
> McCarthy believes that the way to solve the AI problem is to design computer programs to reason according to the well-worked-out languages of mathematical logic, whether or not that is actually the way people think. Minsky believes that a fruitful approach is to try to get computers to imitate the way the human mind works, which he thinks, is almost certainly not with mathematical logic.

The debate, clearly enough, is about the role that "logic" can play in solving "the AI problem". But not much beyond that is clear. I will attempt in this chapter to sort out *some* of the issues involved in this debate. In particular, I'm going to suggest that the failure to sort them out is one reason for the long life and inconclusive nature of the disagreement. First, however, something must be said by way of introduction.[7]

All parties to the debate agree that a central goal of

---

[7]This essay is best seen as a minor addendum to works by (Hayes, 1977) and (Moore, 1982), to both of which I am sorely indebted.

research is that computers must somehow come to "know" a good deal of what every human being knows about the world and about the organisms, natural or artificial, that inhabit it. This body of knowledge (indefinite, no doubt, in its boundaries) goes by the name "common sense." The problem we face is how to impart such knowledge to a robot. That is, how do we design a robot with a reasoning capacity sufficiently powerful and fruitful that when provided with some sub-body of this knowledge, the robot will be able to generate enough of the rest to intelligently adapt to and exploit its environment? We can assume that most, if not all, common-sense knowledge is general, as in the knowledge that objects fall unless they are supported, that physical objects do not suddenly disappear, and that one can get wet in the rain (Nilsson, 1982). We can further assume that a robot's knowledge of particular facts regarding its current situation is input from its sensors.

I am assuming here that the "AI problem," or "knowledge representation problem," is the problem posed above. But what do parties to the debate have in mind when they speak of "logic"?

3.2. What is logic?

What is logic? Defining logic is no easy task, even if we are considering only formal systems developed by mathematical logicians. These systems were originally created and studied with an eye toward precisely characterizing a symbolic language within which all mathematical propositions could be expressed. More particularly, logicians wanted a language within which they could express a set of basic mathematical truths or axioms, from which all the rest could be generated by applying a finite set of precisely characterized (combinatorial) rules of proof that could be shown to be truth-preserving.

In short, the languages of mathematical logic were not meant for general use. Their developers did not claim they were universal symbolisms for unrestricted application - that is, that everything thinkable could be adequately expressed in them. Indeed, it was not even held that everything sayable in a natural language could be expressed in a formalized logical language-- surely much commonsense knowledge can be expressed in English; recall the three examples of commonsense knowledge represented earlier. Of course, that these formalisms were not devised with the goal of expressing commonsense knowledge, that is, of solving the AI problem, does not mean that they cannot be used in this manner. Before we can dismiss their usefulness, we must demonstrate particular failures of representational adequacy, perhaps with explanations in terms of the differences between mathematical knowledge and commonsense knowledge.

Some attempts have been made in this direction. Doubts have been raised about the adequacy or appropriateness, for example, of the "basic" language of logic - the language of the first-order predicate calculus. Of course, it is not obvious that these translate into doubts about the adequacy of logical languages in general. There is nothing in the spirit of the McCarthy camp (see *Science* excerpt presented earlier) to rule out the use of many different logical languages in addressing the representation problem. Moreover, many of these doubts have been based on criticisms of some *particular* way of formally representing some body of knowledge.

These considerations are best translated into objections to the way that objects, properties, and relations of the domain have been conceived or represented, *not* as objections to the language of logic itself. Adopting a logical language does not mean adopting one particular way of "cutting the world at its joints," a way that was arguably inappropriate to many domains and for many purposes. As a representational formalism, a logical language is just a tool. The effectiveness of this tool in carrying out a certain task depends on how it is used. A commitment to standard logical formalisms does not carry along with it a commitment to a particular metaphysics or ontology, let alone to a particularly inappropriate one.

For the most part, those in the Minsky camp seem to assume that the presumed enormity of the differences between mathematics and common sense, together with the fact that the formalisms of mathematical logic were meant for and are fine for the former, somehow *guarantees* the inadequacy of such languages for the latter. Moreover, this guarantee somehow relieves "the enemies of logic" of the obligation to actually demonstrate this inadequacy in any detail.

Before briefly surveying some of the alleged "inherited" maladaptive traits of logical formalisms, we need to distinguish three aspects of such formalisms.

A formal language is determined by specifying a vocabulary, broken into syntactic types, and then developing a set of formation rules for generating complex expressions, in particular, complex well-formed terms and/or formulas of the language. All these specifications must be mechanical or algorithmic.

Having determined the syntax of a language, we can then go on to specify a semantics for the language in a way that mirrors the recursive specification of its syntax. We can thus assign semantic values to the primitive non-logical expressions of the language, with different types of semantic value being associated with the different syntactic types. Such assignments are also called models or interpretations. We can then give a set of interpretation rules that determines semantic values of complex expressions as a function of the semantic values of their constituents and the syntactic formation rules used to generate them. For instance, the meaning of the logical constants - for example, the truth-functional connectives and quantifiers - can be given by interpretation rules that assign values to complex expressions containing them.

Finally, we can specify a deductive apparatus for the language. This apparatus can take many forms, but all involve specifying a set of transformation rules whose applicability to a set of sentences can be effectively determined and whose output, typically a sentence, can likewise be determined. Moreover, these rules must "jibe" with the semantics we have specified for our language. For example, if the premises of a rule are valid--true in every interpretation, according to our semantics - then so too is the conclusion of the rule. Such rules are said to be sound with respect to validity. We might also require that the rules be truth-preserving.

3.3. On being logical

Now that we've gone to the trouble of characterizing a logical system, what more can be said about the issues dividing McCarthy and Minsky? A crucial point (already alluded to above) is that certain objections to how well logic applies to the AI problem have not really been aimed at the expressive capabilities of logical languages. Rather they have been directed at the claim - to which the "friends of logic" are supposedly committed - that *commonsense reasoning* or *inference* could be adequately captured by running a sound theorem-prover over such a language. It is on these points that I intend to concentrate. Indeed much of the *Science* article by G. Kolata is devoted to a particular instance of this mode of objection - the problem of default reasoning or of "nonmonotonic logic."

Remember the claim, "...the way the human mind works, which is almost certainly not with mathematical logic." Kolata presents conflicting viewpoints on the relation between mathematical and commonsense reasoning. Thus, McCarthy answers Minsky:

> Minsky never liked logic, says McCarthy, "when difficulties with mathematical reasoning came up, he felt they killed off logic. Those of us who did like logic thought we should find a way of fixing the difficulties." Whether logical reasoning is really the way the brain works is beside the point, McCarthy says. "This is A(RTIFICIAL) I(ntelligence) and so we don't care if it's psychologically real.

The same tendency is evident in Minsky's recent article in *AI Magazine* (Minsky, 1982), "Why People Think Computers Can't."

> Many AI workers have continued to pursue the use of logic to solve problems. This hasn't worked very well, in my opinion; logical reasoning is more appropriate for displaying or confirming the (*results*) of thinking than for thinking itself. That is, I

suspect we use it less for solving problems than we use it for explaining the solutions to other people and--much more important--to ourselves.

It seems that *both sides* assume the commitment to use a logical language as a representation language carries with it the ineluctable commitment to some sound algorithmic deductive apparatus as the central or sole nonperceptual generator of new knowledge or new beliefs. But the first commitment is quite independent of the second: the second, much more contentious than the first. Having specified a formal, logical language and its semantics, we can freely specify any transformation rules. They need not be sound; they need only be mechanically applicable. That is, the conditions of their "legal" applicability must be determined solely by evaluating the syntactic structures of sentences. For instance, we might be able to come up with rules that embody useful principles of plausible or probabilistic reasoning, or even of analogical reasoning. An important point here is that the applicability of these rules can depend on the occurrences of *nonlogical*, descriptive expressions in sentences as well as on the occurrences of the logical constants. That is, the rules can be specified for a particular domain, and they need not be sound. Thus, they need not constitute a *deductive* apparatus.

Holding that the rules need not be sound does not mean we ignore the semantics of the language in specifying the inferential procedures that operate on its sentences. It simply frees us to experiment. What we want is a set of rules that collectively embodies - in a form that can be syntactically codified - fruitful and generally reliable modes of reasoning. The rules need not be our own, and they certainly need not be discovered by introspection. They must, however, on reflection seem reasonable to us. But how exactly do we go about devising mechanizable rules that embody rational principles of belief fixation and revision if we don't completely grasp the meanings of the sentences on which those rules act? This question raises one very strong argument for using a formal logical language: namely, we can obtain precise accounts of what sentences in such a language mean.

3.4. Reasoning and logic

To bring out the freedom we have in our choice of rules, we must clearly distinguish between reasoning and proof. Minsky seems to be claiming that the application of deductively sound rules of proof does not play an important part in commonsense reasoning. McCarthy is prepared to be neutral on this point. Surely these viewpoints suggest an agreement between parties that reasoning is distinct from logic - and they are right. Exemplary reasoning can often lead us from true beliefs to false ones. Reasoning often involves going out on a limb a little, going beyond what we are absolutely sure of or take for granted. Indeed, reasoning can often lead us to give up some of the beliefs from which we began - even when we have not set out purposefully to put those beliefs to the test (in contrast to proofs by refutation or to reductio ad absurdum proofs in logic).

To take a simple case, suppose you accept - among other things, of course - some sentence of the form "if P, then Q" and accept the antecedent. Should you, must you, accept the consequence? The answer is "not necessarily," because you may have tremendously good *overall* reasons for believing not-Q, and these might lead you to give up belief in either the conditional or its antecedent. Further, rules of proof are local; they apply to a given set of sentences according to their individual syntactic forms. Reasoning, on the other hand, can often be global; one must try not only to take into account all the relevant evidence on hand but also to get more evidence if the immediate evidence is judged insufficient. That judgment and judgments about the relevance and weights of evidence are typically the products of reasoning.

It may appear that logical proof is being opposed to reasoning. The correct view seems to be that logical proof is a tool used in reasoning. Hence, talk about "logical reasoning" is inappropriate especially if it connotes that reasoning is "illogical" or nonlogical reasoning.

Two further points should be made. If we look at the history of science, we can see part of the force of Minsky's claim that "logical reasoning [sic] is more appropriate for displaying or confirming the *results* of thinking than for thinking itself." Logicians who produce axiomatic formalizations of a body of knowledge - when such formalizations come at all - are doing so after the scientists have done their work. However, we cannot assume that proof, deductive inference, has played no part or only an insignificant part in the scientific work. Moreover, with respect to commonsense knowledge, the "science" has long since done most of its job; we already know a whole lot about the way the world works. It is not so much a task of making new discoveries (although surely there must be some new knowledge to acquire) as it is the problem of codifying and systemizing existing knowledge precisely. There *may* be reasons for doubting the adequacy of logical formalisms for *this* task; but these doubts are apart from the claims about the adequacy of deductively sound rules of proof.

The claim that deductively valid rules of proof are *all* that is required is extraordinarily strong, however. It says that everything a robot needs to know, even in a constrained, but real environment, is a deductive consequence of the things we "tell" it - together with the particular facts delivered by its sensors. The only way a robot can learn new things, then, except those it learns by perceiving, is to deduce them from what it already knows. Quite independent of determining how people do this is the difficulty of arranging things so that successful artificially intelligent beings can do it this way. Of course, we should not give up trying to formulate as much as we can as systematically as we can.

3.5. Nonmonotonic logic

Much of Kolata's article is devoted to a discussion of one species of commonsense reasoning that is supposedly beyond the purview of logic. The problem is seen as one of dealing with exceptions. Minsky sees this problem as a defect of "logic" that can be traced to its origins - and an especially glaring defect, it is:

> Logical systems work very well in mathematics, but that is a well-defined world. The only time when you can say something like, "if *a* and *b* are integers,

then *a* plus *b* always equals *b* plus *a*," is in mathematics...Consider a fact like "Birds can fly." If you think that commonsense reasoning is like logical reasoning, then you believe there are general principles that state, "If Joe is a bird and birds can fly, then Joe can fly." Suppose Joe is an ostrich or a penguin? Well, we can axiomatize and say if Joe is a bird and Joe is not an ostrich or a penguin, then Joe can fly. But suppose Joe is dead? Or suppose Joe has his feet set in concrete? The problem with logic is once you deduce something you can't get rid of it. What I'm getting at is that there is a problem with exceptions. It is very hard to find things that are always true.

This problem with logic is allegedly due to monotonicity - if a sentence *S* is a logical consequence of a set of sentences *A*, then *S* is (still) a logical consequence of any set of sentences that includes *A*. So, if we think of *A* as embodying the set of beliefs we started with, the addition of new beliefs cannot lead to the "logical" repudiation of old consequences. (Once you deduce something, you can't get rid of it.) Thus, as McCarthy says:

A proper axiomatization is one in which a proof exists for all conclusions that are ordinarily drawn from these facts. But what we know about common sense is that that's asking for too much. You need another kind of reasoning-- nonmonotonic reasoning...If you know I have a car, you may conclude that you can ask me for a ride. If I tell you the car is in the shop, you may conclude you can't ask me for a ride. If I tell you it will be out of the shop in 2 hours, you may conclude you can ask me. [As more premises are added, the conclusion keeps changing.]

In my opinion, the alleged defect of logic is no defect at all; indeed, it has nothing directly to do with logic. Logic does not tell you what to hold on to nor what to get rid of. That is the job of reasoning, which is surely a nonmonotonic process. Finding out or coming to believe new things often gives us good reason for repudiating old favorites (see example given in the first paragraph on this page). Throwing away our initial beliefs is in no way illogical - especially if we throw them away because what they logically entail conflicts with what we have overwhelming reasons to believe. This is one reason for not talking about "premises" in reasoning. Another has to do with the global nature of reasoning - in principle, it is nothing less than a whole theory that operates as what is given and, in practice, it is often sizeable chunks of theory. Surely it's odd to think of an entire theory as a premise.

Just as logic doesn't tell us what beliefs to keep, it doesn't tell us what beliefs to throw away. In particular, it doesn't tell us what to do when we discover, with its help, that we hold inconsistent beliefs. It tells us only that, in this case, not all our beliefs can be true. The fact that, in many standard logics, anything and everything follows from a contradiction is quite irrelevant - if, that is, we distinguish clearly between logic and reasoning, and see the former as a tool used in the latter. (There are logics defined over perfectly standard languages in which not everything follows from a contradiction.)

The problem that Minsky and McCarthy are addressing is deep, and McCarthy,[8] among others, has made a significant technical contribution. (McCarthy, 1980) The crucial point, though, is that nothing in the debate about nonmonotonic logic argues against the use of a standard logical language, with some standard semantic account, as a representation language for artificial intelligence. The only requirement is that "logic" be kept in its proper place. As Minsky himself says, (Minsky, 1982)

> But "logic" simply isn't a theory of reasoning at all. It doesn't even try to describe how a reasoning process might work. It is only a partial theory of how to *constrain* such a process...

---

[8] but not alone: see (Bobrow, 1980)

If it doesn't even try, it can scarcely be said to "botch the job," can it?

3.6. Conclusion

Efforts to solve the knowledge-representation problem, according to McCarthy, share two major obstacles: deciding what knowledge to represent and getting answers out of a computer in a reasonable time. The key thing we have not formulated is the facts of the commonsense world, and even if we do manage to represent them, we sill have the second problem.

Though we have probed only a few facets of the disagreement between McCarthy and Minsky, I am sure Minsky would second McCarthy's characterization of the representational problem. Before we spend too much time worrying about the adequacy of a particular representational formalism, we should have some better idea about what we want to represent. The more self-consciously and systematically we set out to make explicit those beliefs about the world we usually take for granted - the ones too obvious even to mention - the more likely we are to see that the real problem facing us is to figure out how to find and apply those parts of our common sense that are especially relevant to the task at hand.

Acknowledgements

This research was supported in part by the Defense Advanced Research Projects Agency, monitored by the Office of Naval Research under contract N00014-77-C-0378, and in part by ONR under contract N00014-77-C-0371.

4. Logic and Natural Language

Bonnie Lynn Webber

Department of Computer and Information Science
University of Pennsylvania
Philadelphia, Pennsylvania 19104

Abstract

To understand and generate natural language requires some means of representing knowledge. A particularly appropriate tool in this endeavour is logic. In this chapter, three kinds of logic (default, model, and temporal) are introduced and their use in resolving certain natural language representational issues is outlined.

4.1. Introduction

Logic is that branch of knowledge concerned with truth and inference - that is, with determining the conditions under which a proposition is true or one proposition may be inferred from others. Such knowledge is essential for communication since most of our beliefs about the world come, not from direct contact with it, but from what others tell us and from what we in turn tell others.

Therefore, it is not surprising that logic underlies a wide range of current research on natural language interactions with machines, including parsing (Pereira and Warren, 1980), semantic interpretation (Woods, Kaplan, and Nash-Webber, 1972), and reasoning about an agent's goals in order to understand his utterances, (Allen, 1982). However, not just first-order logic but also more powerful - or at least very different - forms of logic are being used in understanding and generating natural language.

This article discusses three of these forms: *default* logic, used in computing presuppositions; *modal* logic, for planning utterances to enlist help; and *temporal* logic, for offering competent database monitors and correcting certain user misconceptions.

What I hope the reader gains from this discussion is a sense of logic's preeminence in providing "natural" natural-language interactions with machines. Understanding and generating language are exercises in reasoning. For reasoning, logic is our best tool.

4.2. Default logic for computing presuppositions

The notion of "presupposition" comes from linguistics. In pragmatic terms, the presuppositions of an assertion, a question, or a command are those propositions a speaker must be assuming as background for his utterance.

For example, when a speaker asks "Is it 'undelete' that I type to recover a file?" he or she must be assuming something can be typed to recover a file. The presupposition is revealed in the it-cleft construction "It BE X that Y," where what is presupposed is the open sentence Y with its variable bound by an existential quantifier. As another example, if a speaker simply asserts "Mary has stopped smoking," he or she must be assuming as background that there was a time in the past when Mary was smoking, a presupposition reflected in the word "stopped."

In any interaction, it is important for participants to recognize whether their background assumptions are compatible. Otherwise, one participant will utter things that do not make sense to the other, who will respond in completely unexpected ways. For example, if a user asks a system to stop printing out a file, the request shows that the user assumes the system *is* printing out that file. If the system hasn't started to print out the file, or has completed the task, it cannot cooperatively respond as the user intends: it cannot stop. Likewise, the user who asks a system "Which math majors failed CSE251?" has assumed there *are* math majors. If there aren't, the system cannot respond as the user intends. Its response of "none" might be misunderstood as meaning that all math majors passed, (Kaplan, 1982). The only way to respond cooperatively to an utterance revealing incompatible assumptions is to try to reconcile that incompatibility.

From a logical viewpoint, the odd thing about presuppositions is that they can be "blocked." That is, the speaker can clarify that he or she *doesn't* assume the propositions his or her utterance might otherwise presuppose. In the following two examples, the speakers block presuppositions by using initial "if" clauses:

- "If you're printing out FOO.MEM, then stop."

- "If there are any math majors, which of them failed CSE251?"

If a system is going to correctly recognize a user's background assumptions in order to remember or try to correct them, it cannot treat asserted propositions and presupposed propositions in the same way.

One recent approach (Mercer and Reiter, 1982) to determining whether a presupposed proposition actually reflects a person's assumption is based on what Reiter calls "default logic," (Reiter, 1980). In this type of logic, the usual set of axioms used in deduction is augmented by a set of "default rules" used to infer conclusions that cannot otherwise be deduced. Such conclusions, although consistent with the world as currently known, have not been verified as true. Were more to be learned about the world, they might have to be retracted. However, one often needs to make them to proceed in a world about which we have only partial knowledge.

Mercer and Reiter's insight is that presuppositions are like defaults: when trying to identify a speaker's background assumptions, one includes the proposition carried by a presupposition - unless one has information that the speaker doesn't make that assumption. They represent the potential presuppositions of lexical items and syntactic constructs as default rules, checking their contextual consistency by using the logic's proof theory. Essentially this theory treats presuppositions as inferences made in the absence of knowledge - that is, as defaults. If the context provides contrary information, the inferences aren't made. One example is given below, while other examples are found in (Mercer and Reiter, 1982).

Consider the verb "regret" in two sentences whose objects are "that" clauses (that is, embedded propositions):

A. John regrets that Mary came to the party.

B. John doesn't regret that Mary came to the party.

As with all "factive" verbs, given no information to the contrary, one understands the speaker to have assumed the embedded proposition - in this case, that Mary came to the party. This presupposition of factive verbs can be represented by the two default rule schemas

$$\frac{\text{FACTIVE}(P) \ \& \ P(A,X) \ : \ M \ X}{X}$$

$$\frac{\text{FACTIVE}(P) \ \& \ \sim P(A,X) \ : \ M \ X}{X}$$

where *A* stands for the agent of the factive verb, and *X* stands for the embedded proposition. A default rule (and hence, the schemas for such rules) consists of three parts:

- a *prerequisite* that must be satisfied for the default to apply,

- a set of *assumptions* that must be consistent for the consequent to be inferred, and

- the *consequent* itself.

These two schemas specify (1) the prerequisite that if *P* is factive and if agent *A* predicates either *P* or *NOT P* of *X* and (2) the consistency assumption *(M)* that it is consistent to believe the speaker assumes *X*, the consequent is that one should believe the speaker makes that assumption.

As shown above, sentence B asserts ~REGRET(j,COME(m,party)). It is consistent to believe that, given no context, the speaker assumes COME(m,party). By the second default schema, one draws that conclusion. On the other hand, in the sentence

    C. John doesn't regret that Mary came to the party,
       because she didn't come to the party.

the speaker asserts through the "because" clause that ~COME(m,party). Hence, it is not consistent to believe the speaker assumes COME(m,party) and the presupposition is not generated.

The above presentation departs from Mercer and Reiter's presentation, (Mercer and Reiter, 1982), where the positive form of a factive (for example, sentence A) is treated as entailing the truth of its complement and the relationship is represented by a standard axiom schema

    FACTIVE(P) + P(a,X) $\rightarrow$ X

I have treated both forms as leading to the same potential presupposition to deal with the case of "if" constructs, where the potential presupposition in either case can be blocked by making it part of the antecedent, as in "If Mary came to the party, then John regrets it."

4.3. Modal logic for planning utterances

Logic and deduction also play significant roles in generating natural language. For example, suppose there is something you cannot do but someone else can or would do for you, were he or she to know of it. What you can do is formulate a request that informs that other person of what you want done and do so in such a way that he or she recognizes how to do it, if he or she doesn't already know. The success of an utterance such as "Could you hand me that ratchet wrench in the toolbox next to the hammer?" comes from (1) directing the person's attention to the thing in the toolbox next to the hammer, (2) informing the person that it is a ratchet wrench (if he or she doesn't already know it), and (3) requesting the person to hand it to you.

Producing a successful utterance may require reasoning about what that agent does or doesn't know and what you must do to get him or her to know it. However, reasoning about knowledge, action, and the effect of action on knowledge is not within the scope of first-order logic, assuming its standard semantics, partly because "knowledge" predicates are opaque. Unlike standard predicates, "knowledge" predicates do not permit the substitution of equivalent terms, such as if RUN(John,2kms) is true, then so is RUN(John,1.24miles). Even if KNOW(John, 2kms = 2kms) is true, the statement KNOW(John, 2kms = 1.24miles) may not be, since John may know nothing about metric conversion. The problem is that action changes the world and what is known about it, falsifying things that were previously true and vice versa. First-order logic, with its standard semantics, stands for eternal verities.

Modal logic, on the other hand, can be applied to reasoning about knowledge and action as a consequence of its concern with "necessity" and "possibility." Those concerns led philosophers to introduce the notion of a "consistent state of affairs" or "possible world." Necessity corresponds to truth in all possible worlds, while possibility corresponds to truth in some possible world. One can then look at knowledge and action as relating possible worlds. That is, worlds *w1* and *w2* may be related by *w2*'s consistency with what some agent knows in *w1* or with the result of some action performed in *w1*.

A major problem, though, is making such logic computationally tractable. One particularly elegant solution (Moore, 1980) involves translating (that is, axiomatizing) into first-order logic the "possible worlds" interpretation. These "possible worlds" then become things one can reason about (that is, part of one's ontology), in addition to people, wrenches, etc.

Research described by Appelt shows the application of this logic to language generation, (Appelt, 1982). Axioms are given that relate, for example, the ACT of informing someone of a proposition with (1) the precondition that the informer KNOW the proposition to be true and (2) the consequence that the hearer then KNOWS that the informing ACT has taken place. Since the proposition must be true for it to be the object of the act of informing, the hearer knows the proposition. Using such reasoning, the system (Appelt, 1982) can generate such potentially more effective utterances as "Remove the pump with the wrench in the toolbox" when it believes that the listener knows what the pump is attached to (and thus does not need to be told what to remove it from) but does *not* know either the right tool or its location. Such utterances as "Remove the pump" or "Remove the pump from the platform" would not be as effective.

4.4. Temporal logic for reasoning about futures

Reasoning about change - what can be, what could be, what could have been - plays a large role in conversational behavior. When a person doesn't know the answer to someone else's question, one reasons about whether one might know it later. If the answer might leave the other person unsatisfied, one reasons about whether one might have a better answer later on. If so, one can offer to provide it at that time. For example:

```
A:  Did Eric register for physics?

B1: I don't know.  Shall I let you know
    when I find out?

B2: No. Shall I let you know if he
    registers next term?
```

Of course, it is important not to make a misleading offer:

```
A:  Is Los Angeles less than 300 miles
    from San Francisco?

B:  No, but shall I let you know if it ever is?
```

One also reasons about change in recognizing and correcting people's misconceptions about events and states and their relationships over time. Rather than merely answering a question that reflects such a misconception - and possibly misleading rather than helping the person - one tries to figure out which event, state, or relationship he or she has misunderstood and tries to correct it. For example:

```
A:  Is John registered for CSE110?

B:  No, he can't be.  He already advance-
    placed it.
```

To have asked the question, A must believe it is possible for John to be registered. To have replied as he or she did, B must have reasoned from the advance-placement event of the past that he knows that this possibility is wrong and that there is no future time when John could be registered for the course.

Neither first-order logic with its standard semantics nor modal logic is adequate for reasoning about change. Modal logic *per se* does not provide a good handle on sequences of events. A system is needed that can reason from past events (or states of the database) to what can be true afterwards, including possibly the present. The latter is very much like update constraints for maintaining database consistency. However, in general, update constraints are not expressed in a form that admits reasoning about possible change. A system that does admit such reasoning is an extension of the propositional branching-time temporal logic (Ari, Manna, and Pneuli, 1981) documented by Mays, (Mays, 1982). This form of logic is appropriate for reasoning about what may be, what will be, or what can never be. Systems that can reason about possible future states of the database have been termed "dynamic database systems."

Only a brief description of this logical system and its uses is possible here. This system treats the past as a linear sequence of time points up to and including a reference point that, for simplicity, can be called *now*. The future is treated as a branching structure of time points that go out from and include the reference point. A set of complex operators is available to quantify propositions regarding the points they are asserted to hold over. For example:

```
AGq: proposition q holds at every
         time of every future;

EXq: proposition q holds at the
         next point in some future; and

Pq:  proposition q holds at some
         time in the past.
```

Two classes of axioms describe the relationship between events and states in the past, present, and future. The first class contains *logical axiom schemas* that apply to temporal assertions in general - for example, if prior to *now*, Pq was true (that is, LPq), then Pq is still true *now* (that is, LPq --> Pq). "Specialization" axioms relate general and more specific operators. For example, if for all times in every future q will be true (that is, AGq), then, more specifically, q will be true at the next time in every future (that is, AGq --> AXq).

The second class of axioms contains *nonlogical axioms* describing relationships that hold in the particular domain. For example, let q stand for "student passes course" and r for "student is registered for course":

```
(1) HAG(r  →  EXq)

(2) HAG(Pq  →  ~r)
```

(Most nonlogical axioms are taken to have held and to continue to hold forever - hence, the complex operator HAG around the implication.) The first axiom states the continuing rule that a student who is *now* registered for the course *may next* pass it. The second axiom states that a student who has already passed a course is not *now* registered for it.   Consider these two questions

        Q1: Did John pass CSE110?

        Q2: Is John registered for CSE110?

in the following situations:

        S1: r — John is registered for CSE110.

        S2: Pq — John already passed CSE110.

In the first situation - where the answer to Q2 is a simple "Yes" - axiom (1) allows the system to respond to Q1 with the offer

        A1: No, but he's currently registered for it.
            Shall I let you know if he passes?

If he's registered, there is at least some next state in which he passes.

In the second situation - where the answer to Q1 is a simple "Yes" - axiom (2) allows the system to respond to Q2 with the correction

        A2: No, he can't be. He already passed.

If he has passed, there never will be any *now* when he is registered.

Like the work discussed throughout this article, developing and applying modal temporal logic to improve the versatility of question-answering systems is still in the early stages. Nevertheless, the approach presages success.

4.5. Conclusion

As I have tried to show, logic is the tool of choice in a wide range of efforts aimed at extending the scope and quality of natural-language interactions with machines. Why this is true seems clear: logic is our best tool for reasoning, and reasoning is needed in both analyzing and generating purposeful utterances.

5. Commonsense and Fuzzy Logic

L. A. Zadeh

Department of Electrical Engineering
and Computer Sciences
University of California, Berkeley
Berkeley, California 94720

Abstract

Implicit in the fuzzy-logic-based approach to commonsense knowledge representation is the thesis that conventional logical systems do not provide an appropriate framework for representing and inferring from commonsense knowledge.

The principal ideas underlying the fuzzy-logic-based approach are (a) that commonsense knowledge consists for the most part of *dispositions*, that is, propositions which are preponderantly but necessarily always true; and (b) that a disposition may be interpreted as a proposition with implicit fuzzy quantifiers such as *most, mostly, usually, frequently*, etc. For example, the disposition *birds can fly* may be interpreted as the proposition *(most) birds can fly*, where *most* is an implicit fuzzy quantifier which represents the fuzzy proportion of birds which can fly among birds. Similarly, the disposition *a cup of coffee costs about fifty cents* may be interpreted as *(usually) a cup of coffee costs about fifty cents*, in which *usually* is an implicit fuzzy quantifier and *about fifty cents* plays the role of a usual value of the variable *Cost(Cup(Coffee))*.

Viewed in this perspective, standard logical systems do not provide an appropriate framework for representing and inferring from commonsense knowledge because such systems make no provision for fuzzy quantifiers and thus are incapable of accomodating the concept of dispositionality - a concept which plays an essential role in commonsense knowledge and commonsense reasoning.

This paper describes an approach to dispositionality based on fuzzy logic and outlines its application to commonsense reasoning and knowledge representation.

Based on the paper, Commonsense Knowledge
Representation Based on Fuzzy Logic, Lofti Zadeh, appearing in **COMPUTER**,
Volume 16, Number 10, October, 1983.

5.1. Introduction

It is widely agreed at this juncture that one of the important - and least well-understood - problem areas in artificial intelligence relates to the representation of commonsense knowledge (Hobbs and Moore, 1984). In general, such knowledge may be regarded as a collection of propositions exemplified by: *snow is white, icy roads are slippery, most Frenchmen are not very tall, Alice is very intelligent, if a car which is offered for sale is cheap and old then it is probably not in good shape, heavy smoking causes lung cancer,* etc. Representation of propositions of this type plays a particularly important role in the design of expert systems.

The conventional knowledge representation techniques based on the use of predicate calculus and related methods are not well-suited for the representation of commonsense knowledge because the predicates in the propositions which represent commonsense knowledge do not, in general, have crisp denotations. For example, the proposition *most Frenchmen are not very tall* cannot be represented as a well-formed formula in predicate calculus because the sets which constitute the denotations of the predicate *tall* and the quantifier *most* in their respective universes of discourse are fuzzy rather than crisp. **Furthermore, there is no mechanism in predicate calculus for computing the cardinality of a fuzzy denotation.**

More generally, the inapplicability of predicate calculus and related logical systems to the representation of commonsense knowledge reflects the fact that such systems make no provision for dealing with uncertainty. Thus, in predicate logic, for example, a proposition is either true or false and no gradations of truth or membership are allowed. By contrast, in the case of commonsense knowledge, a typical proposition contains a multiplicity of sources of uncertainty. For example, in the case of the proposition *if a car which is offered for sale is cheap and much more than ten years old then it is probably not in good shape,* there are five sources of uncertainty:(i) the temporal uncertainty associated with the fuzzy predicate *much more than ten years old;* (ii) the uncertainty associated with the fuzzy predicate *cheap;* (iii) the uncertainty associated with the fuzzy predicate *not in very good shape*; (iv) the probabilistic uncertainty associated with the event *the car is not in good shape*; and (v) the uncertainty associated with the fuzzy characterization of the probability of the event in question as *probable*.

The approach to the representation of commonsense knowledge which is described in this paper is based on the idea that the propositions which characterize commonsense knowledge are, for the most part, *dispositions* (Zadeh, 1983b), that is, propositions with implicit fuzzy quantifiers. In this sense, the proposition *tall men are not very agile* is a disposition which upon explication is converted into the propositions *most tall men are not very agile*. In this proposition, *most* is an explicit fuzzy quantifier which provides an approximate characterization of the proportion of *men who are not very agile* among *men who are tall*.

To deal with dispositions in a systematic fashion, we shall employ *fuzzy logic* – which is the logic underlying *approximate* or *fuzzy reasoning* (Bellman and Zadeh, 1977), (Zadeh, 1975). Basically, fuzzy logic has two principle components. The first component is, in effect, a translation system for representing the meaning of propositions and other types of semantic entities. We shall employ the suggestive term *test-score semantics* to refer to this translation system because it involves an aggregation of the test scores of elastic constraints which are induced by the semantic entity whose meaning is represented (Zadeh, 1979b).

The second component is an inferential system for arriving at an answer to a question which relates the information which is resident in a knowledge base. In the present paper, the focus of our attention will be the problem of meaning representation in the context of commonsense knowledge, and our discussion of the inferential component will be limited to a **brief discussion of fuzzy syllogistic reasoning** (Zadeh, 1985).[9]

---

[9]A more detailed discussion of the inferential component of fuzzy logic may be found in (Zadeh, 1977a); (Zadeh, 1979b). Recent literature, (Mamdani and Gaines, 1981), contains a number of papers dealing with fuzzy logic and its applications. A description of an implemented fuzzy-logic based inferential system is given in (Balwin and Zhou, 1982) and (Noguchi, Umano, Mizumoto, and Tanaka, 1976).

5.2. Meaning representation in test-score semantics

Test score semantics is concerned with the representation of the meaning of various types of semantic entities, for example, propositions, predicates, commands, questions, modifiers, etc. Knowledge, however, whether commonsense or not, may be viewed as a collection of propositions. For this reason, we shall restrict our discussion of test-score semantics to the representation of meaning of propositions.

In test-score semantics, as in PRUF (Zadeh, 1978), a proposition is regarded as a collection of elastic, or, equivalently, fuzzy constraints. For example, the proposition *Pat is tall* represents an elastic constraint on the height of Pat. Similarly, the proposition *Charlotte is blonde* represents an elastic constraint on the color of Charlotte's hair. And, the proposition *most tall men are not very agile* represents an elastic constraint on the proportion of men who are not very agile among tall men.

In more concrete terms, representing the meaning of a proposition, *p*, through the use of test-score semantics involves the following steps.

1. Identification of the variables X_1, ..., X_n whose values are constrained by the proposition. Usually, these variables are implicit rather than explicit in *p*.

2. Identification of the constraints C_1, ..., C_m which are induced by *p*.

3. Characterization of each constraint C_i, by describing a testing procedure which associates with C_i a test score τ_i representing the degree to which C_i is satisfied. Usually τ_i is expressed as a number in the interval [0,1]. More generally, however, a test score may be a probability/possibility distribution over the unit interval.

4. Aggregation of the partial test scores τ_1, ..., τ_m into a smaller number of test scores τ^*_1, ..., τ^*_k, which

are represented as an *overall vector test score* $\tau = (\tau^*_1, ..., \tau^*_k)$. In most cases $k=1$, so that the overall test scores is a scalar. We shall assume that this is the case unless an explicit statement to the contrary is made.

It is important to note that, in test-score semantics, the meaning of p is represented not by the overall test score τ but by the procedure which leads to it. Viewed in this perspective, test-score semantics may be regarded as a generalization of the truth-conditional, possible world and model-theoretic semantics (Cresswell, 1973). However, by providing a computational framework for dealing with uncertainty – which the conventional semantic systems disregard – test score semantics achieves a much higher level of expressive power and thus provides a basis for representing the meaning of a much wider variety of propositions in a natural language.

In test-score semantics, the testing of the constraints induced by p is performed on a collection of fuzzy relations which constitute an *explanatory database*, or *ED* for short. A basic assumption which can be made about the explanatory database is that it is comprised of relations whose meaning is known to the addressee of the meaning-representation process. In an indirect way, then, the testing and aggregation procedures in test-score semantics may be viewed as a description of a process by which the meaning of p is composed from the meanings of the constituent relations in the explanatory database. It is this explanatory role of the relations in *ED* that motivates its description as an *explanatory database*.

As will be seen in the sequel, in describing the testing procedures we need not concern ourselves with the actual entries in the constituent relations. Thus, in general, the description of a test involves only the frames[10] of the constituent relations, that is, their names, their variables (or

---

[10]In the literature of database management systems, some authors employ the name *schema* to describe what we call a *frame*. More commonly, however, the term *schema* is used in a narrower sense (Date, 1977), to describe the frame of a relation together with the dependencies between the variables.

attributes) and the domain of each variable. When this is the case, the explanatory database will be referred to as the *explanatory database frame*, or *EDF* for short.

As a simple illustration, consider the proposition

$$p \;\equiv\; \textit{Debbie is a few years older than Dana.} \qquad (5.2.1)$$

in which $\equiv$ stands for *is defined to be*. In this case, a suitable explanatory database frame may be represented as[11]

$$EDF \;\equiv\; POPULATION[Name; \; Age] \;+\; FEW[Number; \; \mu],$$

which signifies that the explanatory database frame consists of two relations: (a) a nonfuzzy relation *POPULATION[Name; Age]*, which lists names of individuals and their age; and (b) a fuzzy relation *FEW[Number;μ]*, which associates with each value of Number the degree, μ, to which *Number* is compatible with the intended meaning of *few*. In general, the domain of each variable in the *EDF* is implicitly determined by p, and is not spelled-out explicitly unless it is necessary to do so to define the testing procedure.

As another example, consider the disposition[12]

$$d \;\equiv\; \textit{snow is white,}$$

which is frequently used in the literature to explain the basic ideas underlying truth-conditional semantics.

To construct an *EDF* for this disposition, we first note that what is generally meant by *snow is white* is *usually snow is white*, in which *usually* may be interpreted as a fuzzy

---

[11]We employ uppercase letters to represent relations and denotations of predicates. Some of the notation in this paper has been changed from that of the author due to typsetting limitations.

[12]As was stated earlier, a *disposition* is a proposition with implicit fuzzy quantifiers. (Note that this definition, too, is a disposition.) For example, the proposition *small cars are unsafe*, is a disposition, since it may be viewed as an abbreviation of the proposition *most small cars are unsafe*, in which *most* is a fuzzy quantifier. In general, a disposition may be interpreted in more than one way depending on the manner in which the implicit fuzzy quantifiers are restored.

quantifier. Consequently, on the assumption that the proposition

$p \equiv$ *usually snow is white*   (5.2.2)

is a restoration of d, a natural choice for the *EDF* would be

$EDF \equiv WHITE[Sample;\mu]+USUALLY[Proportion;\mu].$ (5.2.3)

In this *EDF*, the relation *WHITE* is a listing of samples of snow together with the degree, μ, to which each sample is white, while the relation *USUALLY* defines the degree to which a numerical value of *Proportion* is compatible with the intended meaning of *usually* (Figure 5-1).

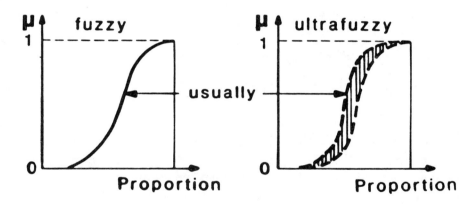

Figure 5-1:   Representation of the Fuzzy Temporal Quantifier *usually*.

In proposition (5.2.1), the constrained variable is the difference in the ages of Debbie and Dana. Thus,

$X \equiv$ *Age(Debbie) - Age(Dana).*   (5.2.4)

The elastic constraint which is induced by p is determined by the fuzzy relation *FEW*. More specifically, let Π_X denote the possibility distribution of X, that is, the fuzzy set of possible values of X. Then the constraint on X may be expressed as the *possibility assignment equation* (Zadeh, 1977b)

$$\Pi_X = FEW, \qquad\qquad (5.2.5)$$

which assigns the fuzzy relation FEW to the possibility distribution of X. This equation implies that

$$\pi_X(v) \equiv Poss\{X=v\} = \mu_{FEW}(v), \qquad\qquad (5.2.6)$$

where $Poss\{X=v\}$ is the possibility that X may take v as its value; $\mu_{FEW}(v)$ is the grade of membership of v in the fuzzy relation FEW; and the function π_X (from the domain of X to the unit interval) is the *possibility distribution function* associated with X.

For the example under consideration, what we have done so far may be summarized by stating that the proposition

$$p \equiv Debbie\ is\ a\ few\ years\ older\ than\ Dana$$

may be expressed in a canonical form, namely,

$$X\ is\ FEW, \qquad\qquad (5.2.7)$$

which places in evidence the implicit variable X which is constrained by p. The canonical proposition implies and is implied by the possibility assignment equation (5.2.5), which defines via (5.2.6) the possibility distribution of X and thus characterizes the elastic constraint on X which is induced by p.

The foregoing analysis may be viewed as an instantiation of the basic idea underlying PRUF, namely, that any proposition, p, in a natural language may be expressed in the canonical form (Zadeh, 1983b)

$$can(p) \equiv X\ is\ F, \qquad\qquad (5.2.8)$$

where $X = (X_1, ..., X_n)$ is an n-ary *focal variable* whose constituent variables $X_1, ..., X_n$ range over the universes $U_1, ..., U_n$, respectively; F is an n-ary fuzzy relation in the product space $U = U_1 \times ... \times U_n$ and $can(p)$ is an abbreviation for the *canonical form of* p. The canonical form, in turn, may be expressed more concretely as the possibility assignment equation

$$\Pi_X = F, \tag{5.2.9}$$

which signifies that the possibility distribution of X is given by F. Thus, we may say that p *translates* into the possibility assignment equation (5.2.9), that is,

$$p \rightarrow \Pi_X = F, \tag{5.2.10}$$

in the sense that (5.2.9) exhibits the implicit variable which is constrained by p and defines the elastic constraint which is induced by p.

When we employ test-score semantics, the meaning of a proposition, p, is represented as a test which associates with each ED (that is, an instantiation of EDF) an overall test score τ which may be viewed as the *compatibility* of p with ED. This compatibility may be interpreted in two equivalent ways: (a) as the truth of p given ED; and (b) as the possibility of ED given p. The latter interpretation shows that the representation of the meaning of p as a test is equivalent to representing the meaning of p by a possibility assignment equation.[13]

The connection between the two points of view will become clearer in Section 5.4, where we shall discuss several examples of propositions representing commonsense knowledge. As a preliminary, we shall present in the following section a brief exposition of some of the basic techniques which will be needed in Section 5.4 to test the constituent relations in the explanatory database and aggregate the partial test scores.

---

[13]As is pointed out in (Zadeh, 1979b), the translation of p into a possibility assignment equation is an instance of a *focussed* translation. By contrast, representation of the meaning of p by a test on EDF is an instance of an *unfocussed* translation. The two are equivalent in principle but differ in detail.

5.3. Testing and translation rules

A typical relation in *EDF* may be expressed as $R[X_1; ...; X_n; \mu]$, where R is the name of the relation; the X_i, $i = 1, ..., n$, are the names of the variables (or, equivalently, the attributes of R), with U_i and v_i representing, respectively, the domain of X_i and its generic value; and μ is the grade of membership of a generic n-tuple $v = (v_1, ..., v_n)$ in R.

In the case of nonfuzzy relations, a basic relation operation on R which is a generalization of the familiar operation of looking up the value of a function for a given value of its argument, is the so-called *mapping operation*. The counterpart of this operation for fuzzy relations is the operation of *transduction*.

Transduction may be viewed as a combination of two operations: (a) *particularization*[14] which constrains the values of a subset of variables of R; and (b) *projection*, which reads the induced constraints on another subset of variables of R. The subsets in question may be viewed as the *input* and *output* variables, respectively.

To define particularization, it is helpful to view a fuzzy relation as an elastic constraint on n-tuples in $U_1 \times ... \times U_n$, with the μ-value for each row in R representing the degree (or the test score) with which the constraint is satisfied.

For concreteness, assume that the input variables are X_1, X_2, and X_3, and that the constraints on these variables are expressed as canonical propositions. For example

$$X_1 \text{ is } F$$

and

$$(X_2, X_3) \text{ is } G,$$

where F and G are fuzzy subsets of U_1 and $U_2 \times U_3$, respectively. Equivalently, the constraints in question may be

---

[14]In the case of nonfuzzy relations, particularization is usually referred to as *selection* or *restriction*.

expressed as

$$\Pi_{X_1} = F$$

and

$$\Pi_{(X_2, X_3)} = G$$

where Π_{X_1} and $\Pi_{(X_2, X_3)}$ are the respective possibility distributions of X_1 and X_2, X_3. To place in evidence the input constraints, the particularized relation is written as

$$R^* \equiv R[X_1 \ is \ F; \ (X_2, X_3) \ is \ G] \tag{5.3.1}$$

or, equivalently, as

$$R^* \equiv R[\Pi_{X_1} \ is \ F; \ \Pi_{(X_2, X_3)} \ is \ G]. \tag{5.3.2}$$

As a concrete illustration, assume that R is a relation whose frame is expressed as

$$RICH[Name; \ Age; \ Height; \ Weight; \ Sex; \ \mu], \tag{5.3.3}$$

is which Age, Height, Weight, and Sex are attributes of Name, and μ is the degree to which Name is *rich*. In this case, the input constraints might be:

$$Age \ is \ YOUNG$$

$$(Height, \ Weight) \ is \ BIG$$

$$Sex \ is \ MALE$$

and, correspondingly, the particularized relation reads

$$R^* \equiv RICH[Age \ is \ Young; \ (Height, \ Weight) \ is \ BIG;$$
$$Sex \ is \ MALE \tag{5.3.4}$$

To concretize the meaning of a particularized relation it is necessary to perform a *row test* on each row of R. Specifically, with reference to (5.3.1), let $\tau_1 = (v_{1t}, \ ..., \ v_{nt}, \ \mu_t)$ be the tth row of R, where $v_{1t}, \ ..., \ v_{nt}, \ \mu_t$ are the values of $X_1, \ ..., \ X_n$, μ, respectively. Furthermore, let μ_F and μ_G be the respective membership functions of F and G. Then for τ_t, the test scores for the constraints on X_1 and (X_2, X_3) may be expressed as

$$\tau_{1t} = \mu_F(v_{1t})$$

$$\tau_{2t} = \mu_G(v_{2t}, v_{3t})$$

To aggregate the test scores with μ_t, we employ the min operator $\downarrow$,[15] which leads to the overall test score for τ_t:

$$\tau_t = \tau_{1t} \downarrow \tau_{2t} \downarrow \mu_t. \qquad (5.3.5)$$

Then, the particularized relation (5.3.1) is obtained by replacing each μ_t in τ_t, t = 1, 2, ..., by τ_t. An example illustrating these steps in the computation of a particularized relation may be found in (Zadeh, 1979b).

As was stated earlier, when a fuzzy relation R is particularized by constraining a set of input variables, we may focus our attention on a subset of variables of R which are designated as *output* variables and ask the question: what are the induced constraints on the output variables? As in the case of nonfuzzy relations, the answer is yielded by projecting the particularized relation on the cartesian product of the domains of output variables. Thus, for example, if the input variables are X_2, X_3 and X_5, and the output variables are X_1 and X_4, then the induced constraints on X_1 and X_4 are determined by the projection, G, on the particularized relation $R^*[(X_2,X_3,X_5)$ is $F]$ on $U_1 \times U_2$. The relation which represents the projection in question is expressed as[16]

$$G \equiv X_1 \times X_2 \ R[(X_2,X_3,X_5) \ is \ F], \qquad (5.3.6)$$

with the understanding that $X_1 \times X_2$ in (5.3.6) should be interpreted as $U_1 \times U_2$. In more transparent terms, (5.3.6) may be restated as the *transduction*:

---

[15]Here and elsewhere in the paper the aggregation operation min ($\downarrow$) is used as a default choice when no alternative (for example, arithmetic mean, geometric mean, etc.) is specified.

[16]If R is a fuzzy relation, its projection on $U_1 \times U_2$ is obtained by deleting from R all columns other than X_1 and X_2, and forming the union of the resulting tuples.

If (X_2,X_3,X_5) *is* F, *then* (X_1,X_2) *is* G (5.3.7)

where G is given by (5.3.6). Equivalently, (5.3.7) may be interpreted as the instruction:

Read (X_1,X_2) *given that* (X_2,X_3,X_5) *is* F (5.3.8)

For example, the transduction represented by the expression

RICH[Age is YOUNG;(Height, Weight) is BIG;Sex is MALE]
   Name $\times$ μ

may be interpreted as the fuzzy set of names of rich men who are young and big. It may also be interpreted in an imperative sense as the instruction: read the name and grade of membership in the fuzzy set of rich men and all those who are young and big.

Remark. When the constraint set which is associated with an input variable, say X_1, is a singleton, say {a}, we write simply

$$X = a$$

instead of X *is* a. For example,

RICH[Age = 25; Weight = 136; Sex = Male] Name $\times$ μ

represents the fuzzy set of rich men whose age and weight are equal to 25 and 136, respectively.

5.3.1. Composition of elastic constraints

In testing the constituent relations in *EDF*, it is helpful to have a collection of standardized translation rules for computing the test score of a combination of elastic constraints $C_1, \ldots, C_k$ from the knowledge of the test scores of each constraint considered in isolation. For the most part, such rules are *default* rules in the sense that they are intended to be used in the absence of alternative rules supplied by the user.

For purposes of commonsense knowledge representation,

the principle rules of this type are the following.[17]

1. **Rules pertaining to modification** - If the test score for an elastic constraint C in a specified context is τ, then in the same context the test score for

   a. *not C is 1 - τ (negation)*   (5.3.9)

   b. *very C is τ^2 (concentration)*   (5.3.10)

   c. *more or less C is $\tau^{.5}$ (diffusion)*   (5.3.11)

   A graphical illustration of these rules is shown in Figure 5-2.

2. **Rules pertaining to composition** - If the test scores for elastic constraints C_1 and C_2 in a specified context are τ_1 and τ_2 respectively, then in the same context the test score for

   a. C_1 *and* C_2 *is* $\tau_1 \downarrow \tau_2$ *(conjunction), where* $\downarrow \equiv min$ (5.3.12)

   b. C_1 *and* C_2 *is* $\tau_1 \uparrow \tau_2$ *(disjunction), where* $\uparrow \equiv max$ (5.3.13)

   c. *If* C_1 *then* C_2 *is* $1 \downarrow (1 - \tau_1 + \tau_2)$ (implication)   (5.3.14)

3. **Rules pertaining to quantification** - The rules in question apply to propositions of the general form Q *A's are B's*, where Q is a fuzzy quantifier, for example, most, many, several, few, etc. and A and B are fuzzy sets, for example, tall men, intelligent

---

[17]A more detailed discussion of such rules in the context of PRUF may be found in (Zadeh, 1978).

men, etc. As was stated earlier, when the fuzzy quantifiers in a proposition are implied rather than explicit, their suppression may be placed in evidence by referring to the proposition as a *disposition*. In this sense, the proposition *overeating causes obesity* is a disposition which results from the suppression of fuzzy quantifiers in the proposition *most of those who overeat are obese.*

To make the concept of a fuzzy quantifier meaningful, it is necessary to define a way of counting the number of elements in a fuzzy set or, equivalently, to determine its cardinality.

There are several ways that this can be done (Zadeh, 1983c), (Wygralak, 1986). For our purposes, it will suffice to employ the concept of a *sigma-count*, which is defined as follows.

Let F be a fuzzy subset of $U = \{v_1, \ldots, v_n\}$ expressed symbolically as

$$F = \mu_1/v_1 + \ldots + \mu_n/v_n = \Sigma_{i=1}^{n} \mu_i/v_i \qquad (5.3.15)$$

or, more simply, as

$$F = \mu_1 v_1 + \ldots + \mu_\nu v_\nu \qquad (5.3.16)$$

in which the term μ_i/v_i, $i = 1, \ldots, n$, signifies that μ_i is the grade of membership of v_i in F, and the plus sign represents the union.[18]

The sigma-count of F is defined as the arithmetic sum of the μ_i, that is,

$$\Sigma \, Count(F) \equiv \Sigma_i \, \mu_i, \; i = 1, \ldots, n \qquad (5.3.17)$$

with the understanding that the sum may be rounded, if need be, to the nearest integer.

---

[18]In most cases, the context is sufficient to resolve the question of whether a plus sign should be interpreted as the union or the arithmetic form.

Furthermore, one may stipulate that the terms whose grade of membership falls below a specified threshold be excluded from the summation. The purpose of such an exclusion is to avoid a situation in which a large number of terms with low grades of membership become count-equivalent to a small number of terms with high membership.

The *relative sigma-count*, denoted by $\Sigma\, Count(F/G)$ may be interpreted as the proportion of elements of F which are in G. More explicitly,

$$\Sigma\, Count(F/G) = \frac{\Sigma\, Count(F \cap G)}{\Sigma\, Count(G)} \qquad (5.3.18)$$

where $F \cap G$, the intersection of F and G, is defined by

$$F \cap G = \Sigma_i (\mu_B(v_i)) \downarrow \mu_G(v_i)/v_i, \quad i=1,...,n. \qquad (5.3.19)$$

Thus, in terms of the membership functions of F and G, the relative sigma-count of F in G is given by

$$\Sigma\, Count(F/G) = \frac{\Sigma_i \mu_F(v_i) \downarrow \mu_G(v_i)}{\Sigma_i \mu_G(v_i)}, \qquad (5.3.20)$$

The concept of a relative sigma-count provides a basis for interpreting the meaning of propositions of the form $Q\ A$'s *are* B's, for example, *Most young men are healthy* (Figure 5-3). More specifically, if the base variable (that is, the constrained variable) in the proposition in question is taken to be the proportion of B's in A's, then the corresponding translation rule may be expressed as

$$Q\ A\text{'s are } B\text{'s} \rightarrow \Sigma\, Count(B/A) \text{ is } Q \qquad (5.3.21)$$

or, equivalently, as

$$Q\ A\text{'s are } B\text{'s} \rightarrow \Pi_X = Q \qquad (5.3.22)$$

where

$$X = \frac{\Sigma_i \mu_A(v_i) \downarrow \mu_B(v_i)}{\Sigma_i \mu_A(v_i)} \qquad (5.3.23)$$

As will be seen in the following section, the quantification rule (5.3.23) together with the other rules described in this section provide a basic conceptual framework for the representation of commonsense knowledge. We shall illustrate the representation process through the medium of several examples in which the meaning of a disposition is represented as a test on a collection of fuzzy relations in an expanatory database.

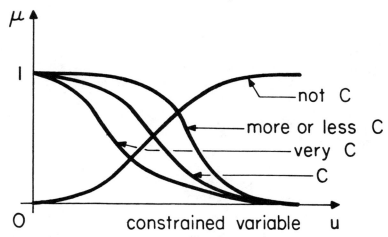

Figure 5-2:   Effect of Modifiers on an Elastic Constraint.

5.4. Representation of dispositions

To clarify the difference between the conventional approaches to meaning representation and that described in the present paper, we shall consider as our first example (**Example 1**) the disposition

$$d \equiv snow\ is\ white, \qquad (5.4.1)$$

which, as was stated earlier, is frequently employed as an

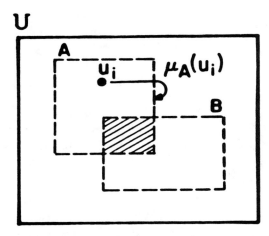

Figure 5-3: The Relative Sigma-count.

illustration in introductory expositions of truth-conditional semantics.

The first step in the representation process involves a restoration of the supressed quantifiers in d. We shall assume that the intended meaning of d is conveyed by the proposition

$p \equiv$ *usually snow is white*   (5.4.2)

As an *EDF* for (5.4.2), we shall use (5.2.3), that is,

$EDF \equiv WHITE[Sample;\mu]+USUALLY[Proportion;\mu].$ (5.4.3)

Let S_1, ..., S_m denote samples of snow and let τ_i, $i = 1$, ..., m, denote the degree to which the color of S_i matches white. Thus, τ_i may be interpreted as the test score for the constraint on the color S_i which is induced by *WHITE*.

Using this notation, the steps in the testing procedure may be described as follows:

1. Find the proportion of samples whose color is white:

$$\rho = \frac{\Sigma\ Count(WHITE)}{m} = \frac{\tau_1+...+\tau_m}{m}$$ (5.4.4)

2. Compute the degree to which ρ satisfies the constraint induced by *USUALLY*:

$$\tau = {}_{\mu}USUALLY[Proportion = \rho] \tag{5.4.5}$$

In (5.4.5), τ represents the overall test score and the right-hand member signifies that the relation $USUALLY$ is particularized by setting $Proportion$ equal to ρ and projecting the resulting relation on μ. The meaning of d, then, is represented by the test procedure which leads to the value of τ.

Equivalently, the meaning of any d may be represented as a possibility assignment equation. Specifically, let X denote the focal variable (that is, the constrained variable) in p. Then we can write

$$d \rightarrow \Pi_X = USUALLY, \tag{5.4.6}$$

where $X \equiv \dfrac{1}{m}\Sigma \, Count(WHITE)$

Example 2

To illustrate the use of translation rules relating to modification, we shall consider the disposition

$$d \equiv Frenchmen \text{ } are \text{ } not \text{ } very \text{ } tall \tag{5.4.7}$$

After restoration, the intended meaning of d is assumed to be represented by the proposition

$$p \equiv most \text{ } Frenchmen \text{ } are \text{ } not \text{ } very \text{ } tall \tag{5.4.8}$$

To represent the meaning of p, we shall employ an EDF whose constituent relations are:

$$
\begin{aligned}
EDF \equiv \; & POPULATION[Name; Height] + \\
& TALL[Height; \mu] + \\
& MOST[Proportion; \mu].
\end{aligned}
\tag{5.4.9}
$$

The relation $POPULATION$ is a tabulation of $Height$ as a function of $Name$ for a representative group of Frenchmen. In $TALL$, μ is the degree to which a value of $Height$ fits the description $tall$; and in $MOST$, μ is the degree to which a numerical value of $Proportion$ fits the intended meaning of $most$.

The test procedure which represents the meaning of p involves the following steps:

1. Let $Name_i$ be the name of the ith individual in POPULATION. For each $Name_i$, i = 1, ..., m, find the height of $Name_i$:

$$Height(Name_i) \equiv POPULATION[Name = Name_i]$$

2. For each $Name_i$ compute the test score for the constraint induced by TALL:

$$\tau_i = {}_\mu TALL[Height(Name_i)]$$

3. Using the translation rules (5.3.9) and (5.3.10), compute the test score for the constraint induced by NOT VERY TALL:

$$\tau'_i = 1 - \tau_i^2.$$

4. Find the relative sigma-count of Frenchmen who are not very tall:

$$p \equiv \Sigma\, Count(NOT.VERY.TALL/POPULATION)$$

$$= \frac{\Sigma_i \tau'_i}{m}$$

5. Compute the test score for the constraint induced by MOST:

$$\tau = {}_\mu MOST[Proportion - p] \qquad (5.4.10)$$

The test score given by (5.4.10) represents the overall test score for d, and the test procedure which yields τ represents the meaning of d.

Example 3

Consider the disposition

$$d \equiv overeating \ causes \ obesity \qquad (5.4.11)$$

which after restoration is assumed to read

$$p \equiv most \ of \ those \ who \ overeat \ are \ obese. \qquad (5.4.12)$$

To represent the meaning of p, we shall employ an *EDF* whose constituent relations are:

$$EDF = POPULATION[Name; \ Overeat; \ Obese] + \qquad (5.4.13)$$
$$MOST[Proportion; \ \mu].$$

The relation *POPULATION* is a list of names of individuals, with the variables *Overeat* and *Obese* representing, respectively, the degrees to which *Name* overeats and is obese. In *MOST*, μ is the degree to which a numerical value of *Proportion* fits the intended meaning of *MOST*.

The testing procedure which represents the meaning of d involves the following steps:

1. Let $Name_i$ be the name of the ith individual in *POPULATION*. For each $Name_i$, i=1, ..., m, find the degrees to which $Name_i$ overeats and is obese:

$$\alpha_i \equiv \mu_{OVEREAT}(Name) \equiv$$
$$_{Overeat}POPULATION[Name=Name_i] \qquad (5.4.14)$$

and

$$\beta_i \equiv \mu_{OBESE}(Name) \equiv \ _{Obese}POPULATION[Name=Name_i]$$
$$(5.4.15)$$

2. Compute the relative-sigma count of *OBESE* and *OVEREAT*:

$$\rho \equiv \Sigma \ Count(OBESE/OVEREAT) = \frac{\Sigma_i \alpha_i \downarrow \beta_i}{\Sigma_i \alpha_i} \qquad (5.4.16)$$

3. Compute the test score for the constraint induced by *MOST*:

$$\tau = {}_{\mu}MOST[Proportion = \rho] \qquad (5.4.17)$$

This test score represents the compatibility of d with the explanatory database.

Example 4

Consider the disposition

$$d \equiv heavy\ smoking\ causes\ lung\ cancer \qquad (5.4.18)$$

Although it has the same form as (5.4.11), we shall interpret it differently. Specifically, the restored proposition will be assumed to be expressed as

$$p \equiv \begin{array}{l} the\ incidence\ of\ cases\ of\ lung\ cancer\ among \\ heavy\ smokers\ is\ much\ higher\ than\ among \\ those\ who\ are\ not\ heavy\ smokers \end{array} \qquad (5.4.19)$$

The *EDF* for this proposition is assumed to have the following constituents:

$$EDF \equiv POPULATION[Name;\ Heavy;\ Smoker;\ Lung;\ Cancer] +$$
$$MUCH\_HIGHER[Proportion\ 1;\ Proportion\ 2;\ \mu]. \qquad (5.4.20)$$

In *POPULATION*, *Heavy.Smoker* represents the degree to which *Name* is a heavy smoker and the variable Lung.Cancer is 1 or 0 depending on whether or not *Name* has lung cancer. In *MUCH_HIGHER*, μ is the degree to which *Proportion 1* is much higher than *Proportion 2*.

The steps in the test procedure may be summarized as follows:

1. For each $Name_i$, i=1, ..., m, determine the degree to which $Name_i$ is a heavy smoker:

$$\alpha_i \equiv {}_{Heavy.Smoker}POPULATION[Name=Name_i] \qquad (5.4.21)$$

Then, the degree to which $Name_i$ is not a heavy smoker is

$$\beta_i = 1 - \alpha_i \qquad\qquad (5.4.22)$$

2. For each $Name_i$ determine if $Name_i$ has lung cancer:

$$\lambda_i \equiv {}_{Lung.Cancer}POPULATION[Name=Name_i] \qquad (5.4.23)$$

3. Compute the relative sigma-counts of those who have lung cancer among (a) heavy smokers; and (b) non heavy smokers:

$$\rho_1 = \Sigma\, Count(LUNG.CANCER/HEAVY.SMOKER)$$

$$= \frac{\Sigma_i \lambda_i \downarrow \alpha_i}{\Sigma_i \alpha_i}$$

$$\rho_2 = \Sigma\, Count(LUNG.CANCER/NOT.HEAVY.SMOKER)$$

$$= \frac{\Sigma_i \lambda_i \downarrow (1-\alpha_i)}{\Sigma_i \alpha_i}$$

4. Test the constraint induced by $MUCH.HIGHER$:

$$\tau = {}_\mu MUCH.HIGHER[Proportion1=\rho_1;$$
$$Proportion2=\rho_2] \qquad\qquad (5.4.24)$$

Example 5
Consider the disposition

$$d \equiv small\ families\ are\ friendly \qquad\qquad (5.4.25)$$

which we shall interpret as the proposition

$p \equiv$ *in most small families almost all of the members are*
friendly with one another   (5.4.26)

It should be noted that the quantifier *most* in p is a second
order fuzzy quantifier in the sense that it represents a fuzzy
count of fuzzy sets (that is, *small families*).
  The *EDF* for p is assumed to be expressed by

$$EDF \equiv POPULATION[Name; \ Family.Identifier] +$$
$$SMALL[Number; \ \mu] +$$
$$FRIENDLY[Name \ 1; \ Name \ 2; \ \mu] +$$
$$MOST[Proportion; \ \mu] +$$
$$ALMOST.ALL[Proportion; \ \mu] \qquad (5.4.27)$$

The relation *POPULATION* is assumed to be partitioned (by
rows) into a disjoint families $F_i, \ ..., \ F_k$. In *FRIENDLY*, μ is
the degree to which *Name 1* is friendly toward *Name 2*, with
Name 1 $\neq$ *Name 2*.
  The test procedure may be described as follows:

1. For each family, F_i, find the count of its members:

$$C_i \equiv Count(POPULATION[Family.Ident=F_i]) \qquad (5.4.28)$$

2. For each family, test the constraint C_i induced by
   SMALL:

$$\alpha_i \equiv SMALL[Number = C_i] \qquad (5.4.29)$$

3. For each family, compute the relative sigma-count
   of its members who are friendly with one another:

$$\beta_i = \frac{1}{(C_i^2 - C_i)} \ \Sigma_{j,k}(_\mu FRIENDLY[Name \ 1 = Name_j;$$
$$Name \ 2 = Name_k]) \qquad (5.4.30)$$

where $Name_j$ and $Name_k$ range over the members of

F_i and $Name_i \neq Name_j$. The normalizing factor C_i^2 - C_i represents the total number of links between pairs of distinct individuals in F_i.

4. For each family, test the constraint on β_i which is induced by $ALMOST.ALL$:

$$\gamma_i = {}_\mu ALMOST.ALL[Proportion = \beta_i] \qquad (5.4.31)$$

5. For each family, aggregate the test scores α_i and γ_i by using the min operator ($\downarrow$):

$$\delta_i \equiv \alpha_i \downarrow \gamma_i \qquad (5.4.32)$$

6. Compute the relative sigma-count of small families in which almost all members are friendly with one another:

$$\rho = \frac{1}{k}(\delta_1 + ... + \delta_k) \qquad (5.4.33)$$

7. Test the constraint of ρ induced by $MOST$:

$$\tau = {}_\mu MOST[Proportion = \rho] \qquad (5.4.34)$$

The value of τ given by (5.4.34) represents the compatibility of d with the explanatory database.

The foregoing examples are intended to illustrate the basic idea underlying our approach to the representation of commonsense knowledge, namely, the conversion of a disposition into a proposition, and the construction of a test procedure which acts on the constituent relations in an explanatory database and yields its compatibility with the restored proposition.

A basic issue which will be addressed only briefly in the present paper is the following. Assuming that we have represented a collection of dispositions in the manner described above, how can an answer to a query be **inferred** from the representations in question? The following simple example is intended to illustrate the use of fuzzy logic for this purpose,

(Zadeh, 1983b).

Example 6
   Infer from the propositions

$$p_1 \equiv \textit{most Frenchmen are not tall} \qquad (5.4.35)$$

$$p_2 \equiv \textit{most Frenchmen are not short} \qquad (5.4.36)$$

$$q \equiv \textit{what is the average height of a Frenchman?} \qquad (5.4.37)$$

Because of the simplicity of p_1 and p_2, the constraints induced by the premises may be found directly. Specifically, let $h_1, \ldots, h_n$ denote the heights of $\textit{Frenchman}_1, \ldots, \textit{Frenchman}_n$, respectively. Then, the test scores associated with the constraints in question may be expressed as

$$\tau_1 - \mu_{\text{ANT MOST}}(\tfrac{1}{n}\Sigma_i \mu_{\text{TALL}}(h_i)) \qquad (5.4.38)$$

and

$$\tau_2 - \mu_{\text{ANT MOST}}(\tfrac{1}{n}\Sigma_i \mu_{\text{SHORT}}(h_i)) \qquad (5.4.39)$$

where ANT is an abbreviation for *antonym*, that is,

$$\text{quad}\mu_{\text{ANT MOST}}(v) = \mu_{\text{MOST}}(1 - v), \ v \in [0,1], \qquad (5.4.40)$$

and μ_{TALL} and μ_{SHORT} are the membership functions of *TALL* and *SHORT*, respectively. Correspondingly, the overall test score may be expressed as

$$\tau = \tau_1 \downarrow \tau_2. \qquad (5.4.41)$$

Now, the average height of a Frenchman and hence the answer to the question is given by

$$ans(q) = \tfrac{1}{n}\Sigma_i h_i. \qquad (5.4.42$$

Consequently, the possibility distribution of *ans(q)* is given by the solution of the nonlinear program

$$\mu_{\text{ans(q)}}(h) = \max_{h_1, \ldots, h_n}(\tau) \qquad (5.4.43)$$

subject to the constraint

$$h = \frac{1}{n}\sum_i h_i. \tag{5.4.44}$$

Alternatively, a simpler but less informative answer may be formulated by forming the intersection of the possibility distributions of $ans(q)$ which are induced separately by p_1 and p_2. More specifically, let $\Pi_{ans(q)|p_1}$, $\Pi_{ans(q)|p_2}$, $\Pi_{ans(q)|p_1 \& p_2}$ be the possibility distributions of $ans(q)$ which are induced by p_1, p_2, and the conjunction of p_1 and p_2, respectively. Then, by using the minimax inequality, (Zadeh, 1971), it can readily be shown that

$$\Pi_{ans(q)|p_1} \cap \Pi_{ans(q)|p_1} \supset \Pi_{ans(q)|p_1 \& p_2} \tag{5.4.45}$$

and hence we can invoke the entailment principle, (Zadeh, 1979a), to validate the intersection in question as the possibility distribution of $ans(q)$. For the example under consideration, the desired possibility distribution is readily found to be given by

$$Poss\{ans(q)=h\}=\mu_{ANT\_MOST}(\mu_{TALL}(h))\&\mu_{ANT\_MOST}(\mu_{SHORT}(h)). \tag{5.4.46}$$

5.5. Reasoning with dispositions

Much of human reasoning involves reasoning with commonsense knowledge. Typically, such reasoning involves *chaining* of two or more dispositions, as in

icy roads are slippery (5.5.1)

slippery roads are dangerous

----

icy roads are dangerous

in which the horizontal line separates the premises from the conclusion.

The conclusion in (5.5.1) is in accord with our experience, which is equivalent to saying that it is consistent with our commonsense knowledge. However, as shown in Figure 5-4 it is not true in general that

most A's are B's   (5.5.2)

most B's are C's

----

most A's are C's

even though it is true that

All A's are B's   (5.5.3)

All B's are C's

----

all A's are C's

Furthermore, as shown in (Zadeh, 1983c) the transitivity - or, equivalently, the property inheritance - represented by (5.5.3) is *brittle* in the sense that the replacement of the quantifier *all* in the premises of (5.5.3) by *almost all*, results in the replacement of *all* in the conclusion by the quantifier *none to all*, that is, by the interval [0,1]. What this implies is that, no matter how high is the degree of containment, δ, of A in B and B in C, so long as δ is not exactly equal to unity, the degree of containment of A in C may be any number in the interval [0,1]. This is illustrated graphically in Figure 5-4, which shows that A may have a high degree of containment in B. B may have a high degree of containment in C, and yet the degree of containment of A in C may be low or zero. The same phenomenon accounts for the invalidity of reasoning chains (5.5.4) and (5.5.5) below.

most UC students are residents of California   (5.5.4)

most residents of California are over thirty

----

most UC students are over thirty

cheap apartments in Paris are rare   (5.5.5)

what is rare is expensive

----

cheap apartments in Paris are expensive

A mode of reasoning in fuzzy logic which provides a

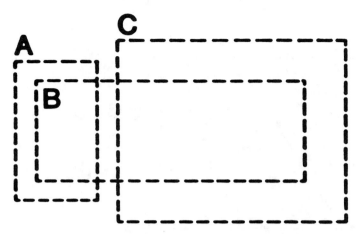

Figure 5-4:   The Brittleness of Property Inheritence.

basis for reasoning with dispositions is that of *fuzzy syllogistic reasoning.* (Zadeh, 1985). Such reasoning may be viewed as a generalization of syllogistic reasoning in Aristotelian logic, (Lukasiewicz, 1951).

As shown in (Zadeh, 1983b) and (Zadeh, 1985), a basic syllogism which plays an important role in chaining of dispositions is the *intersection/product syllogism.*

Q_1 *A's are B's* $\qquad\qquad\qquad\qquad\qquad\qquad$ (5.5.6)

Q_2 *(A ∩ B)'s are B's*

$(Q_1 \otimes Q_2$ *A's are (B ∩ C)'s*

where *A, B* and *C* are fuzzy sets; *A ∩ B* and *B ∩ C* are the intersections of *A* and *B* and *B* and *C*, respectively; Q_1 and Q_2 are arbitrary fuzzy quantifiers; and $(Q_1 \otimes Q_2)$ is the fuzzy product of the fuzzy numbers representing Q_1 and Q_2, (Kaufmann and Gupta, 1985), (Figure 5-5). For example,

most students are single $\qquad\qquad\qquad\qquad\qquad$ (5.5.7)

a little more than half of single students are male

(most $\otimes$ A little more than a half) of students are single and male.

A graphical illustration of this rule is shown in Figure 5-6.

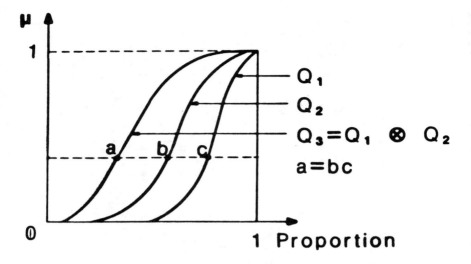

Figure 5-5:   The Intersection/Product Syllogism

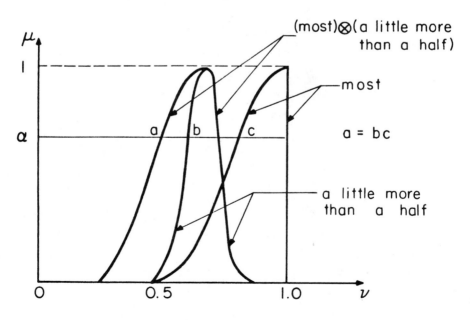

Figure 5-6:   A Graphical Illustration of the
Intersection/Product Syllogism

Through the use of *linguistic approximation* - which is

analogous to rounding to the nearest integer in ordinary arithmetic - the fuzzy number which represents the product of the fuzzy number *most* with the fuzzy number *a little more than a half* may be approximated by, say, *about a half*. In this way an approximate conclusion which follows from the premises in (5.5.7) may be expressed as shown below.

   about a half of students are single and male.

An important special case of the intersection/product syllogism results from making two restrictive assumptions about A, B, Q_1, and Q_2. Specifically, if B is assumed to be contained in A, the intersection of A and B becomes equal to B. In this case, since $B \cap C$ is contained in C, (5.5.6) may be rewritten as

Q_1 *A's are B's*   (5.5.8)

Q_2 *B's are C's*

$\geqslant (Q_1 \otimes Q_2)$ *A's are C's,*

where $\geqslant (Q_1 \otimes Q_2)$ should be read as *at least* $(Q_1 \otimes Q_2)$. Now, if the fuzzy quantifiers Q_1 and Q_2 are assumed to be *monotone non-decreasing* (Figure 5-7), that is,

$\geqslant Q_1 = Q_1$ (5.5.9)

$\geqslant Q_2 = Q_2$

which is true, for example, of the fuzzy quantifier *most*, then

$\geqslant (Q_1 \otimes Q_2) = Q_1 \otimes Q_2$ (5.5.10)

and the intersection/product syllogism becomes the *multiplicative chaining rule*

Q_1 *A's are B's*   (5.5.11)

Q_2 *B's are C's*

$(Q_1 \otimes Q_2)$ *A's are C's,*

which implies that the fuzzy relation of fuzzy-set-containment is *product transitive*.

As an illustration, we shall consider an example in which the containment relation $B \subset A$ holds approximately, as in the disposition

$$d_1 \equiv American\ cars\ are\ big, \qquad (5.5.12)$$

which upon restoration may be interpreted as the proposition

$$p_1 \equiv most\ American\ cars\ are\ big, \qquad (5.5.13)$$

Then, if the disposition

$$d_2 \equiv big\ cars\ are\ expensive \qquad (5.5.14)$$

is interpreted as the proposition

$$p_2 \equiv most\ big\ cars\ are\ expensive, \qquad (5.5.15)$$

we may conclude, by employing (5.5.11) that

$$d \equiv American\ cars\ are\ expensive \qquad (5.5.16)$$

with the understanding that the implicit fuzzy quantifier in d is, approximately, $most^2$, that is, the product of the fuzzy number $most$ with itself, Figure 5-8. As shown in (DuBois and Prade, 1985), analogous results may be obtained for chains in which the assumption of containment, $B \subset A$, is replaced by that of *reversibility*, namely, $Q\ A$'s are B's $\leftarrow \rightarrow$ $Q\ B$'s are A's, where $\leftarrow \rightarrow$ denotes semantic equivalence.

5.6. Concluding remark

The basic idea which underlies the approach described in this paper is that much of what is commonly referred to as *commonsense knowledge* may be regarded as a collection of dispositions. This idea serves as a point of departure for applying fuzzy logic to the representation of/and inference from commonsense knowledge. The fuzzy-logic-based computational framework for reasoning with dispositions is of relevance to the management of uncertainty in knowledge-based systems, especially in the context of inference under uncertainty in

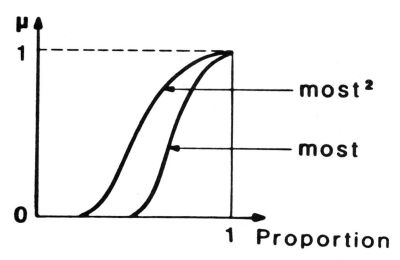

Figure 5-7:   Product Transitivity

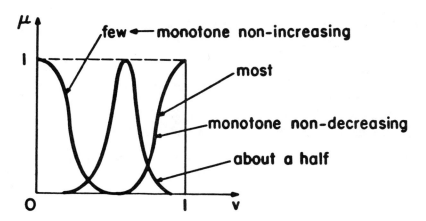

Figure 5-8:   Monotonicity of *most*

expert systems.

Acknowledgements

This research is supported in part by NSF Grant IST-8320416 and NASA Grant NCC-2-275. To Brian Gaines and Mildred Shaw.

6. Basic Properties of Knowledge Base Systems

W. Marek

Department of Computer Science
University of Kentucky
Lexington, Kentucky 40506-0027

Abstract

We consider rule-structured knowledge bases and investigate some of their basic properties. We propose an algorithm for the investigation of completeness and consistency of rule represented knowledge bases. We study some aspects of incomplete information in such systems.

6.1. Introduction

To the memory of
Witold Lipski Jr.
student, teacher and a friend

In this paper we propose a formalism for the description of knowledge bases. Present investigations in artificial intelligence tend to consider the knowledge base as a separate entity carrying the information relevant to the proper operation of the system. Usually, a system containing a knowledge base also possesses editing facilities allowing for instance inserting, deleting and modifying (cf. (Hayes-Roth, Waterman and Lenat, 1983), where a number of examples of knowledge bases are provided). This suggests a close connection with data bases. Indeed, some knowledge bases seem to resemble traditional databases, although carrying a special type of information.

This fact results in our attempt to reduce (at least some) knowledge bases to the familiar relational database formalism of Codd. This paper is a step in this direction. We notice that at the same time, we find some concepts and problems which do not seem to be addressed by Codd's paradigm.

Our approach is to describe knowledge as a set of rules. The reason for this is that rule based knowledge bases seem to appear in the majority of currently built expert systems, numerous examples can be found in the literature, for instance, see (Hayes-Roth, Waterman and Lenat, 1983). Even though various systems try to incorporate techniques coming from probabilistic methods (Bayesian techniques) or fuzzy logic, most of the currently built systems seem to avoid those tools (see chapter 5 for a discussion of fuzzy approaches). We believe that this paper will contribute to the foundations of knowledge engineering, providing a framework to describe various methods and problems related to knowledge bases.

As one application of the formalism introduced in our paper we investigate the problems of the completeness and consistency of the set of rules. This issue has been, informally, discussed in (Sowa, Scott, and Shortliffe, 1985) where an algorithm is proposed to treat these problems. This algorithm appears to be the most direct way of checking completeness; it amounts to producing a training table (see below) and checking if the rows match the rules. Our algorithm is much simpler and more feasible even if the domains of attributes are infinite (providing the collection of rules is linear (see below)).

6.2. Basic notions

A knowledge base system is a system $K=<r_1,...,r_n,A>$ where A is an attribute, r_1, ..., r_n are instances (typed relations) and A appears in each of the schemata R_1, ..., R_n (which are the schemata for r_1, ..., r_n respectively).

In the paper we will not distinguish between the attribute and its domain. In particular, when we say that a set B is a subset of an attribute A we mean that B is a subset of the <u>domain</u> of A.

Essentially the idea is that A represents the class (of descriptions) of expert advice (or expert actions). The relation $r_i \subseteq A_1 \times ... \times A_n \times A$ intuitively represents knowledge in the following form (each tuple $<a_1, ..., a_n, a>$ is a fact which is interpreted as follows):

```
If the value of the attribute A₁ is a₁
Andif the value of the attribute A₂ is a₂
    :
    :
Andif the value of the attribute Aₙ is aₙ
Then perform the action a.
```

Consequently, intuitively, the values of the attributes A_1, ..., A_n uniquely determine an action a of A. Even though this intuition seems very reasonable, it is not always the case; our knowledge may be (and often is) contradictory. There may be knowledge which for the same data (situation) prescribes different actions (medicine is a notable example). This is the case of inherently contradictory knowledge and, unfortunately, we need to accommodate this type of situation.

The instances r_1, ..., r_n are called *training tables* in the representation of the knowledge base system S.

A *rule* (with attributes A_1, ..., A_n and conclusion of type A) is a tuple $<B_1, ..., B_n, a>$ where $B_1 \subseteq A_1$, ..., $B_n \subseteq A_n$

and a ∈ A.

A rule **r** is *faithful* for the system **K** if and only if:

1. There is a unique relation r in **K** with a scheme $R(A_1, ..., A_n, A)$, and

2. Every tuple $<a_1, ..., a_n, a>$ where $a_1 \in B_1, ..., a_n \in B_n$ appears in r.

A set of rules **S** is faithful for the system **K** if every rule in **S** is faithful for **K**.

A set of rules is *adequate* for a system **K** if it is faithful for **S** and, in addition, for every relation r in **K** and every tuple $<a_1, ..., a_n, a>$ in r there is a rule r in **S**, r = $<B_1, ..., B_n, a>$ such that $<a_1, ..., a_n> \in B_1 \times ... \times B_n$.

The above definitions need some motivation. If we think about the training table as a collection of "recipes" (for a situation described by tuple $<s_1, ..., a_n>$ do a) then a rule **r** is faithful if a table consisting of tuples $<a_1, ..., a_n, a>$ (where $a_1 \in B_1, ..., a_n \in B_n$ and a is the conclusion of the rule **r**) is a subset of the table. Hence, a faithful rule describes a part of the information contained in the table **K**. On the other hand an adequate set of rules consists of faithful rules only, and, in addition, codes all the information included in **K**.

We have the following proposition:

PROPOSITION 2.1 There is a correspondence between the sets of rules and knowledge base systems. This correspondence is given by assigning to the set of rules **S** a system **K** for which **S** is adequate.

The converse of this proposition is, again, straightforward: each tuple may be treated as a (degenerate) rule. Yet, the question of how to generate a set of rules adequate for a knowledge base system turns out to be quite complicated. First of all, notice that there are many possible sets of rules adequate for a given knowledge base system. Hence, we should ask whether it is possible to assign effectively to a given system **K** a *minimal* (in some reasonable sense) set of rules **K**. One measure for minimality could be the least number of rules.

Notice that it would be very desirable to have a method of assigning to the system such a set of rules. This means that we would be able to assign, with a training table, the most compact description of the knowledge included in this table. Unfortunately, this is not feasible in practice as noted in the following result:

THEOREM 2.2. The problem of deciding if, for a given table **K** and a natural number M, there exists a set of rules **S** such that $|S| \leqslant M$ and **S** is adequate for **K** is NP-complete.

Proof: Checking if **S** is faithful for **K** is clearly polynomial (generate tuples from the rules in **S** and check if they belong to **K**; it there is a wrong tuple (that is, one that fails the second faithfulness test above) you will find it in at most $|K|$ steps.) Consequently, checking if **S** is adequate for **K** is again polynomial; we just mark the elements of **K** as we proceed through **S**, and in at most $|K|$ steps we will find not only if all of the tuples represented by **S** are in **K** but also if there is anything left in **K** unmarked. This shows that our problem is NP. To see that it is complete for that class notice that the problem of representing a formula in a clausal form is reducible to our problem.□

The size of the set of rules is not the only measure of complexity of the set of rules. Another one, which may be loosely interpreted as the length of a Prolog program representing the set of rules, follows.

Let us introduce the notion of the *weight* of a rule $\mathbf{r} = <B_1, ..., B_n, a>$ as $w(\mathbf{r}) = |B_1|+...+|B_n|$. Then set $w(\mathbf{S}) = \sum \{w(\mathbf{r}): \mathbf{r} \in \mathbf{S}\}$. We have an interesting result due to (Schlipf, 1986):

THEOREM 2.3. The problem of finding if the table **K** possesses an adequate set of rules of weight at most M is NP-complete.

Even though we have shown a representation of knowledge bases in the familiar framework of Codd's relational model of databases (cf. (Codd, 1970), (Maier, 1983), (Ullman, 1984)), the domain of knowledge base systems creates its own problems, not necessarily well enlightened in the general context of Codd's model. Of these, we will discuss the following issues: (1) completeness, (2) consistency, (3) dependency of actions on attributes, and (4) default reasoning.

Intuitively, a system **K** is complete if and only if it provides expert advice for every meaningful tuple of data. In order to formalize this property let us introduce the following definition:

DEFINITION

(1) A tuple $<a_1, ..., a_k>$ *matches* a rule $r = <B_1, ..., B_k, a>$ if $<a_1, ..., a_k> \in B_1 \times ... \times B_k$. If the tuple $<a_1, ..., a_k>$ matches r then we say that r provides the conclusion a for $<a_1, ..., a_k>$.

(2) A set of rules **S** is *complete* (for the attributes $A_1, ..., A_m$) if and only if for every scheme $R(A_1, ..., A_k, A)$ of the system **K** and every tuple $<a_1, ..., a_k> \in A_1 \times ... \times A_k$ there exists a rule r in **S** such that $<a_1, ..., a_k>$ matches r.

The notion of completeness of the set of rules possesses a counterpart in the relational model representation. We have

PROPOSITION 2.4 Let **S** be a set of rules adequate for the knowledge base system **K**. Then the set **S** is complete if and only if for every instance r of **K**, the projection $\pi_{A_1...A_k}(r) = A_1 \times ... \times A_k$ (where the scheme of r is $R(A_1, ..., A_k, A)$).

Why should we bother with the issue of completeness of **S** at all? We could introduce a new action, @, and define (Prolog-like) that the tuples not matching any of the present rules get the expert advice @ (with the intended meaning "I do not know" or "I am not able to deal with this situation"), thus making the system "artificially complete". Unfortunately, this procedure, especially at this stage of the organization of the system, leads to the following phenomenon: we do not know if the lack of knowledge (covered by the default rules) is intentional (due to the fact that the expert which creates the knowledge base is not able to cope with the situation) or accidental (due to the fact that the knowledge exists, but for some reason was not collected by the expert). In particular, when we set up (or modify) the knowledge base, we want to know that the answers which are provided are intentionally correct. We want to exclude the omissions by mistake and thus point out to the expert the incompleteness of his knowledge so that we (and he) may gain additional insight about the problems at hand.

The issue of consistency is, in a sense, easier to follow. We would like to be able to see that the expert's knowledge is consistent; in other words, it provides unambiguous advice in a given situation. As pointed out above, this seems to be the ideal situation which cannot really be attained in practice. The question of consistency is formalized in the following definition:

DEFINITION

A set of rules **S** is consistent if for every type $R(A_1, ..., A_k, A)$ and a situation $<a_1, ..., a_k> \in A_1 \times ... \times A_k$, if $<a_1, ..., a_k>$ matches two rules, r_1 and r_2 then r_1 and r_2 have the same conclusion.

The following result characterizes consistency in the terms of a relational model.

THEOREM 2.5. Let **S** be adequate for the system **K**. Then the set **S** is consistent if and only if every instance **r** in **K** (with the scheme $R(A_1, ..., A_k, A)$) satisfies the functional dependency $A_1, ..., A_k \rightarrow A$.

<u>Proof</u>: If **S** is consistent and $<a_1, ..., a_k, a>$, $<a_1, ..., a_k, b>$ belong to **r** then, since **S** is adequate for **K**, there must exist two rules, r_1 with the conclusion a and r_2 with the conclusion b such that $<a_1, ..., a_k>$ matches both r_1 and r_2. Hence a=b.

Conversely, if the functional dependencies as above are satisfied then assume that r_1, r_2 are two rules of the same type (say $A_1, ..., A_k$) and belong to **S**. Then if $<a_1, ..., a_k>$ matches both r_1 and r_2 then $<a_1, ..., a_k,$ *conclusion of* $r_1> \in r$ and similarly for the conclusion of r_2. Hence, these conclusions must be identical.□

The third issue, that of dependency of expert advice on the attributes, will be discussed in Section 6.5 and the defaults will be discussed in Section 6.6.

6.3. Completeness & consistency of rule-represented knowledge bases

Let us now consider rule represented knowledge bases. We may describe these as structures of the form:

$$<A_1, ..., A_n, A, S>$$

where S is a set of rules, each of the form:

$$r = <B_1, ..., B_r, a>$$

which may be more suggestively written as:

$$\frac{B_1, ..., B_n}{a}$$

where $B_j \subseteq A_j$ is the jth condition of the rule r and a is the conclusion of the rule r.

Let us assume for the purpose of this section that all rules are of the same type $<A_1, ..., A_n>$. This assumption is reasonable since every set of rules decomposes naturally into its subsets consisting of rules of the same type and the issues of completeness and consistency are related to each of these sets. [That is, S is complete if and only if for every type t, the set S_t consisting of rules in S of type t is complete]. In the present context the completeness and consistency of S take the following form:

Completeness:

$$\cup(B_1^i \times ... \times B_n^i) = A_1 \times ... \times A_n$$

Consistency:

$$(B_1^i \times ... \times B_n^i) \cap (B_1^j \times ... \times B_n^j) \neq \emptyset => a_i = a_j.$$

Let us again notice that the set of rules **S** is complete iff every legal situation is taken care of by some rule from **S**; that is, for every situation $<a_1, \ldots, a_n>$ there is a rule $r_i \in$ **S** such that $<a_1, \ldots, a_n>$ matches r_i. Consistency of the set **S** has a different meaning; it corresponds to the fact that the knowledge base provides unambiguous advice.

Before we address the problem of checking the completeness and consistency of a set **S**, let us look at the problem of missing conditions (which is closely connected to the null-values problem in data bases).

Assume that we are given a rule r: $<B_1, \ldots, B_m, a>$. This rule may be treated as the rule $<B_1, \ldots, B_m, B_{m+1}, a>$ with $B_{m+1} = A_{m+1}$. Indeed, we may think that the $m+1^{st}$ condition in the rule r is not specified since its value does not influence the conclusion. Yet it is possible that in our knowledge base there are both types $<A_1, \ldots, A_m>$ and $<A_1, \ldots, A_{m+1}>$. Hence the interpretation of the rule r is not clear in this case! As in the case of relational databases, the information on the $m+1^{st}$ attribute may be missing either because its value is *immaterial* or because the attribute itself is immaterial. Clearly, this issue is of practical importance and it was encountered by us in the implementation of the algorithms of Sections 6.3 and 6.4 (Hawrylak, 1985). Our solution is to determine which attributes are relevant to the rule (even though the values may be immaterial). Hence, from this point on, we shall assume that all relevant attributes are mentioned in the rule.

To check the completeness of the set of n rules (with m attributes) one needs (in principle) to generate all situations and see if they match a rule. If we assume that for all $1 \leqslant i \leqslant m$, A_i possesses s descriptors, then this most obvious algorithm needs $O(s^{m+1} \times m \times n)$ steps. One can safely assume that s is large. In that case, especially if $s >> 2^n$ the cost may be prohibitive. One cannot, in principle, exclude the case when s is infinite! Yet the algorithm given below allows us to lower sizably the complexity of the algorithm. If s is infinite then our algorithm works if the following condition is met: for every $1 \leqslant i \leqslant m$ there exists n_i such that all the sets B_j^i are finite with the possible exception of $j=n_i$. In case of linear rules (Section 6.4) the size of s is simply immaterial.

We proceed now to introduce the general case of completeness and consistency algorithms. Although these algorithms are quite complex in their general form, we will show, in Section 6.4, that some important special cases can have algorithms which are quite manageable.

In order to present the algorithm let us recall (c.f. (Kuratowski and Mostowski, 1982)) the notion of the constituent of the family of sets. Let Z be a set and assume that $\{C_1,....,C_k\}$ is a family of its subsets. For $T \subseteq Z$ define $0T = T$ and $1T = Z - T$. A *constituent* of the family $\{C_1,....,C_k\}$ is every set of the form:

$$K_{p_1 \cdots p_k} = p_1 C_1 \cap ... \cap p_k C_k$$

where $<p_1,....,p_k>$ is any sequence of zeros or ones.

Let us list below the basic properties of constituents:

1. If $<p_1,....,p_k> \neq <q_1,....,q_k>$ then $K_{p_1,....,p_k} \cap K_{q_1,....,q_k} = \emptyset$.

2. $\cup\, K_{p_1,....,p_k} = Z$

3. Union of the constituents corresponding to the sequences which on the ith coordinate take value 0 is the set C_i.

4. Union of the constituents corresponding to the sequences which on the ith coordinate take value 1 is the set $Z - C_i$.

The above properties of constituents play a crucial role in the correctness proof of the completeness-checking algorithm presented below (we do not give the correctness proof itself, but it could be reconstructed from properties 1 - 4). The constituents are nothing else but the atoms of the Boolean subalgebra $B(C_1, ..., C_k)$ of the algebra of all subsets of Z. The algebra $B(C_1, ..., C_k)$ is generated by the sets $C_1, ..., C_k$, (Halmos, 1963).

Finally let us introduce a notion of the *projection* of a rule. The projection of a rule $<B_1, ..., B_n, B_{n+1}, a>$ is the rule $<B_1, ..., B_n, a>$. Since the completeness checking does not involve the conclusions of the rules, we will not address this issue at this time.

Assume we are given a set of rules: $S = <r_1, ..., r_m>$ where each of the rules r_i has premises of the form: $<B_1^i, ..., B_n^i, B_{n+1}^i>$

We now present our *completeness-checking algorithm* which is a recursive on n - the number of attributes.

If $n = 0$, that is, all the premises look as follows: B_1^i then the completeness check of our rule system is equivalent to determining if:

$$\cup B_1^i = A_1$$

But this is equivalent to the fact that the constituent with the index constantly equal to 1 is empty. Symbolically:

$$\cup B_1^1 = A_1 <=> 1B_1^i \cap ... \cap 1B_1^m = \varnothing$$

Hence, in the case of $n = 0$ (that is, when we have just one attribute) we need to check whether or not the constituent $K_{1...1}$ is empty. If it is, the system is complete, otherwise it is not.

Assume now that we know how to check completeness of the rule system with at most n attributes. We now show how to check the completeness of a system with at most n+1 attributes.

To this end generate all the constituents of the family:

$$<B_{n+1}^1, ..., B_{n+1}^m>$$

(that is, take the last coordinate of each rule and generate the constituents). Observe that there are at most 2^m nonempty constituents and that it is possible that all may be nonempty.

For each constituent $K_{p_1...p_n}$ of the family:

$$<B_{n+1}^1, ..., B_{n+1}^m>$$

form an auxiliary family $S^1_{p_1...p_m}$ consisting of these rules r_j

that satisfy:

$$K_{p_1 \cdots p_m} \subseteq B^j_{n+1}$$

In particular, notice that p_j must be equal 0 if $\mathbf{r}_j$ belongs to the auxiliary family $\mathbf{S}^1_{p_1 \cdots p_m}$.

For each sequence $<p_1, \ldots, p_m>$ such that $K_{p_1 \cdots p_m} \neq \emptyset$ and for each rule $\mathbf{r}$ in $\mathbf{S}^1_{p_1 \cdots p_n}$ consider its projection to the set of attributes $A_1, \ldots, A_n$ - that is, omit the condition B_{n+1}. Call the projected set (that is, the set consisting of projections) $\mathbf{S}_{p_1 \cdots p_n}$. Recursively check its completeness.

If *all* the sets $\mathbf{S}_{p_1 \cdots p_n}$ are complete then the original set $\mathbf{S}$ is complete. Otherwise the set $\mathbf{S}$ is incomplete. Notice that in case of complete set $\mathbf{S}$ the equality:

$$\cup B^i_{n+1} = A_{n+1}$$

must hold. Otherwise, the constituent $1B^1_{n+1} \cap \ldots \cap 1B^m_{n+1} \neq \emptyset$ and by construction the set $\mathbf{S}^1_{1 \ldots 1}$ is empty, hence the set $\mathbf{S}_{1 \ldots 1}$ is empty, and, hence the rule set is incomplete.

We leave the following proposition without proof:

PROPOSITION 3.1. The above algorithm correctly checks the completeness of the set of rules $\mathbf{S}$.

The complexity of the above algorithm in the general case is exponential in n and k and, hence, it is not meant to be used in practice. In fact, this should not be that surprising, as we deal with properties somewhat approximating truth. Notice that in case of $n = 1$, the complexity of the algorithm is $O(s^2 \times m)$ [Check for each $a \in A_1$ if a matches any of the rules, $|A_1| = s$]. Next, observe that as n increases, there are at most 2^m sets of rules to be checked for completeness. This gives us a quite crude estimate:

$$O(s^2 \times m \times (2^m)^{n-1}) = O(s^2 \times m \times 2^{m(n-1)})$$

We will see that in the practically important, "linear" case the algorithm becomes polynomial (in m).

Before we move to the consistency problem of a set of rules let us make an observation which, though not changing the complexity of the algorithm, should be useful in the implementation.

PROPOSITION 3.2. It is enough, in the above algorithm, to consider only the inclusion-minimal sets $S_{p_1 \cdots p_k}$.

Next, we will discuss the consistency of the knowledge base, represented as a rule set **S**.

We assume that set $S = \langle r_1, \ldots, r_m \rangle$ of rules is given. Notice that rules with an identical conclusion do not lead to inconsistency; if a situation $\langle a_1, \ldots, a_n \rangle$ matches both rules r_i and r_j which have same conclusion, then there is no danger of erroneous advice. Consequently, we now check, for each pair $\langle i,j \rangle$ such that the conclusions of r_i and r_j are different, if there is a situation matching both the premises of r_i and r_j. If there is such a pair then the set **S** is inconsistent; otherwise, the pair $\langle r_i, r_j \rangle$ does not generate conflict. If no pair $\langle r_i, r_j \rangle$ generates inconsistency then the rule set **S** is consistent. Otherwise it is inconsistent.

PROPOSITION 3.3. The above algorithm correctly checks the consistency of a rule set **S**.

The argument for proposition 3.2. is straightforward and won't be repeated here.

As concerns the complexity of this algorithm notice that there are $O(m^2)$ pairs of rules. For each such pair, if the conclusions are different, we need to check if there exists a situation $\langle a_1, \ldots, a_n \rangle$ matching both rules. This in turn is equivalent to:

$$B^i_1 \cap B^j_1 \neq \emptyset, \ldots, B^i_n \cap B^j_n \neq \emptyset$$

Each of these n facts can be checked at the cost of $O(s^2)$ (where $s = \max (|A_i|)$). Consequently, the complexity of our algorithm is $O(m^2 \times s^2 \times n)$. We will see below that in the case of linear rules the complexity of our consistency algorithm decreases substantially and does not depend on s at all.

One notices that our algorithm for checking consistency is particularly suitable for parallel processing. Checking if the above intersections are nonempty can be done in parallel. Also notice that, in principle, the number of attributes in the rule is small. We observe that checking of the consistency of each rule (with the rest) can also be done in parallel.

If we know that the knowledge base is complete and we modify one of the rules $<B_1, ..., B_n, a>$ (substituting one or more rules in its place), then after this update we need to check only that the Cartesian product $<B_1 \times ... \times B_n>$ is covered by the new rules. This simple remark is very useful in the process of the maintenance of the completeness property and has been used explicitly in the system KBMS of (Hawrylak, 1985). Similarly, checking the consistency after updates can be greatly simplified.

The completeness of a rule-represented knowledge base can be always ensured by the use of the default rules (the very same way as it is done in Prolog). The checking of completeness is important because the use of default rules can hide various deficiencies of the knowledge base; for instance it may non-adequately reflect the expert's knowledge. Conceptually, default rules are "less important" than the original rules. This rationale was developed in (Sandewall, 1985), where rules coming from different experts are assigned different priorities. Needless to say default rules have the least priority. The rules are ordered, then, according to priorities and the conflicts are checked only between rules of same priority.

Finally let us notice that if we use default rules, then before we add them (to ensure completeness) we may use probabilistic methods (for instance generating randomly situations and checking if they match some rule) to make sure that our knowledge base is "complete with probability $\geq 1 - 1/n$".

6.4. The case of linear sets of rules

As introduced in Section 6.3, the set **S** of rules (and again for the purpose of this section we assume that all these rules are of the same type) consists of objects of the form:

$$\frac{B^i_1,...,B^i_n}{a_i}$$

Until now, we have not made any restrictions on the possible structure of the sets B^i_j, $1 \leqslant i \leqslant m$, $1 \leqslant j \leqslant n$. In this section, we see that under reasonable assumptions on this family of sets, the algorithms from Section 6.3 become more manageable; that is, their complexity is reduced sharply.

DEFINITION

(a) Let $<T, \leqslant >$ be a linearly ordered set. The subset $Z \subseteq T$ is a *segment* in $<T, \leqslant >$ if and only if for all x,y in Z, if $x \leqslant t \leqslant y$ then $t \in Z$.

(b) A family $<A_r>_{r \in R}$ of subsets of a set T is called *linear* if and only if there exists a linear ordering of the set T in which all A_r's are segments.

(c) A set of rules **S** is called *linear* if and only if for every $1 \leqslant i \leqslant n$ the family of sets $<B^S_i>_{1 \leqslant s \leqslant m}$ is linear.

The concept of linear family comes from the theory of file organization and has a rich history in the literature. The papers (Lipski, 1976), (Boland and Lekkerkerker, 1962), (Fulkerson and Gross, 1965), (Ghosh, 1972) and (Booth and Lueker, 1975) deal with the problem of linearity and related questions. In an outstanding paper, (Booth and Lueker, 1975), it is shown that there exists an $O(n)$ algorithm for deciding if a family of finite sets is linear. Notice that various expert system shells provide a facility for declaring linear systems of rules.

The reason for recalling this notion is that in practice the rule set is usually linear. We may also assume that the attributes are finite (although quite often we talk about values being real numbers we still can assume that there is only a finite set of possible values of an attribute). In that case all the segments become closed (that is, we may assume that they contain their extremities).

THEOREM 4.1. For every set of rules there exists an

equivalent, linear, set of rules. Moreover, we may assume that every constituent is a segment (in the corresponding ordering).

Proof: Order each of the attributes in such a way that every constituent becomes a segment (as we do not impose any restrictions other than this, it is clearly possible). We then begin splitting the rules as follows:

The rule:

$$\frac{B^i_1,...,B^i_n}{a}$$

is replaced by the *family* of rules:

$$\frac{D_1,...,D_n}{a}$$

where the D_j's are constituents.$\square$

It is clear that theorem 4.1. is of theoretical interest only, since the cost of replacing the set **S** by an equivalent linear set **S'** is prohibitive (in fact it is exponential).

Yet, if the set of rules **S** *is* linear we have a big gain. The reason for it is the following:

PROPOSITION 4.2. ((Lipski, 1976)) If **A** is a linear family of sets and the cardinality of A is k, then there are at most 2k nonempty constituents of **A**.

One notices that even if the family **A** is linear and consists of segments in the linear ordering $<T, \leqslant >$ not all of the constituents of **A** need to be segments. Yet there exists another ordering of the set T in which all the constituents are segments and, furthermore, if some constituents of **A** are not segments in the ordering $\leqslant$ still the number of "elementary" segments generated by **A** is bounded by 2k + 1. (Elementary segments are those generated by the consecutive endpoints of the sets of the family **A**.) This fact is proved by induction on the number k.

Just for the sake of completeness notice the following definition and proposition 4.3.

DEFINITION

(a) A family **A** of subsets of a set T is *nested* if and only if for every X,Y in **A**, $X \subseteq Y$ or $Y \subseteq X$.

(b) If $X \subseteq T$, $<T, \leqslant >$ is a linearly ordered set, then the *beginning* of X is its least element, and the *end* of X is its largest element.

(c) A family **A** of subsets of a set T is *weakly unnested* if and only if for all X and Y in **A**, if $X \subseteq Y$ then X and Y have a common beginning or common end.

PROPOSITION 4.3. (essentially (Lipski, 1976)) Let **A** be a family of segments of the set $<T, \leqslant >$ and assume that **A** is weakly unnested. Then every constituent of the family **A** is a segment.

The nested families are a basic tool of (Ghosh, 1972), where, in particular, it is shown that if **A** is a nested family then there exists an ordering of T (possibly different from the original one) in which **A** is nested but weakly unnested. As a consequence he proves that any extension of a nested family by one set is still linear.

Let us now modify the algorithm of Section 6.3 to accommodate the case of linear families of rules. To this end let us assume that each attribute A_i is linearly discretely ordered and finite. Under this assumption, and assuming that all B^j_i are segments, they must also be closed segments. Let us look at the inductive step of our algorithm. The family of at most m sets B^i_{n+1} determines at most 2m + 1 closed segments (some constituents may become sums of several segments, but there will be no more than 2m + 1 segments). Hence the number of segments in which the domain of the attribute A_{n+1} is split is *linear* in m (and not exponential, as in the general case). Consequently there are at most 2m + 1 families of rules (now in n attributes only) to be considered recursively. In addition, checking if the family $<B^i_1>_{1 \leqslant i \leqslant m}$ covers whole set A_1 becomes linear in m (the number of elements of A_1 does not play a role anymore!) You simply sort the segments according to their beginnings and ends and then check for gaps;

if the beginning of a segment is bigger than the end of the previous segment, then you need to see if the gap between them is nonempty. If so the collection does not cover the whole set A_1. Otherwise you continue. Taking it all together we get:

THEOREM 4.4. If the family of rules is linear then the (modified) algorithm of section 6.3 checks completeness in $O(m_n)$.

For the consistency checking algorithm we also notice a large improvement when dealing with a linear set of rules. The reason for this is that checking for overlapping of segments is simply constant! Indeed, just notice that segments [a,b] and [c,d] overlap exactly when either: $a \leqslant c \leqslant b$ or $c \leqslant a \leqslant d$. Hence at most four comparisons are necessary to establish the truth (or falsity) of this fact. Consequently, we have:

PROPOSITION 4.5. If the set of rules **S** is linear then the (modified) algorithm of Section 6.3 checks the consistency of **S** in $O(m^2 \times n)$.

Besides linearity there are other conditions which guarantee that the family of sets possesses "few" constituents. "Acyclicity", "admissibility" and other conditions appearing naturally in the investigations of "consecutive retrieval properties" imply similar results. For a general discussion of these concepts see (Ghosh, Kambayashi, and Lipski, 1983).

6.5. Dependency of rules on attributes

In many practical applications, we may find that some of the attributes A_i are superfluous. According to the "relational model" convention (see Section 6.2) this simply means that the relational representation of the knowledge base satisfies the dependency $U\text{-}A_i \rightarrow A_i$. Let us notice that although there is a fast algorithm checking the satisfaction of a dependency by an instance (see (Ullman, 1984) and references in that book) this does not help us if our knowledge base is represented as a collection of rules. Below we show how the consistency checking algorithm can be used for this purpose.

We generalize a notion of projection from Section 6.3 and introduce $proj_{A_{i_1} \dots A_{i_k}}(<B_1, \dots, B_n, a>)$ as $<B_{i_1}, \dots, B_{i_k}, a>$. The projection of a set of rules is the set of projections of its elements.

Similarly, we say that the relational representation of a knowledge base does not depend on the attributes $A_{k+1}, \dots, A_n$ if the instance r satisfies $A_1, \dots, A_k \rightarrow A$.

The following theorem connects the concept of projection and dependency of rules.

THEOREM 5.1. Let **S** be a consistent set of rules and r an instance be its relational representation. Then $r \models A_1, \dots, A_k \rightarrow A$ if and only if $proj_{A_1 \dots A_k}(\mathbf{S})$ is consistent.

Proof: Assume $r \models A_1, \dots, A_k \rightarrow A$. If $proj_{A_1 \dots A_k}(\mathbf{S})$ is inconsistent then there are two rules, r_i and r_j whose projections $A_1, \dots, A_k$ result in conflict, that is, there exists a situation $<a_1, \dots, a_k>$ matching both projections and in addition $a^i \neq a^j$. But then, by definition, there exist $<a^1_{k+1}, \dots, a^1_n>$ and $<a^2_{k+1}, \dots, a^2_n>$ such that $<a_1, \dots, a_k, a^1_{k+1}, \dots, a^1_n>$ matches r_i whereas $<a_1, \dots, a_k, a^2_{k+1}, \dots, a^2_n>$ matches r_j. But then both $<a_1, \dots, a_k, a^1_{k+1}, \dots, a^1_n, a^i>$ and $<a_1, \dots, a_k, a^2_{k+1}, \dots, a^2_n, a^j>$ belong to the instance r. However, this contradicts $r \models A_1, \dots, A_k \rightarrow A$. Assume now that $proj_{A_1 \dots A_k}(r)$ is consistent but that $r \models A_1, \dots, A_k \rightarrow B$ contains tuples $<a_1, \dots, a_k, a_{k+1}, \dots, a_n, a>$ and $<a_1, \dots, a_k, b_{k+1}, \dots, b_n, b>$ with $a \neq b$. But the above tuple must meet two rules r_1 and r_2 in **S**. If this is the case then $<a_1, \dots, a_k>$ matches both $proj_{A_1 \dots A_k}(r_1)$ and $proj_{A_1 \dots A_k}(r_2)$. The latter rules are clearly in conflict.☐

Since the functional dependencies possess the augmentation property we get the following corollary:

COROLLARY 5.2. Let $Z \subseteq \{A_1, \dots, A_n\}$ have the property that $proj_Z(\mathbf{S})$ is consistent but for every $A_j \in Z$ if $Z_j = Z - A_j$ then

$proj_T(\mathbf{S})$ is inconsistent. Then for every $T \supset Z$, $proj_Z(\mathbf{S})$ is inconsistent. Consequently A is a minimal set for which the projection is consistent.

We will call the sets considered in the corollary *minimal sets*. One should not confuse the notion of minimal set with that of the key. Inconsistent sets of rules do not possess a minimal set at all. If $\mathbf{S}$ is consistent then it possesses a minimal set and every such set is a key. Yet there may exist keys which are not minimal sets in the above sense (for instance when they contain A itself).

Corollary 5.2., together with the consistency checking algorithm of Section 6.3 lead to the algorithm of producing of the minimal set for the set of rules $\mathbf{S}$. We discharge an attribute as long as it possibly preserves consistency. After n runs (n is the number of attributes) we find the minimal set. Unfortunately this algorithm is dependent on the order of attributes. You may obtain every minimal set using the appropriate order of the set of attributes (just put your minimal set as the final segment of the list of attributes).

6.6. Partial information and defaults

In this section we discuss the problem of incomplete information for knowledge base systems (comprehensive treatment of the problem of incomplete information may be found in (Lipski, 1977)) and the problem of expert behaviour in that case. We show that some modes of expert methods for dealing with incomplete information can be mimicked by knowledge base systems. In particular we show that the choice of ordering of (complete) situations allows for the rational choice of treatment of incomplete situations.

To do this let us introduce the notion of a default over the knowledge base system.

A *partial situation* in the knowledge base system (for simplicity we treat the case of one instance only but it can be easily extended to the case of multiple instances as well) is a list:

$$s = <\; <A_{i_1}, a_{i_1}>\; ,...., <A_{i_k}, a_{i_k}>\; >$$

of tuples $<A_r, a_r>$, where A_r is an attribute and a_r its value. The collection of partial situations is endowed with a natural partial ordering $<<$. If we define $Dom(s) = \{A_{i_1}, ..., A_{i_k}\}$ to be the domain of s, the $s_1 << s_2$ means that $Dom(s_1) \subseteq Dom(s_2)$ and $s_2 | Dom(s_1) = s_1$.

Notice that every (total) situation is a partial situation and that, consequently, we have the following:

PROPOSITION 6.1. A system S is complete if and only if every partial situation can be extended in S to a complete one.

We have the following useful lemma:

LEMMA 6.2. Let t be a (complete) situation and Z_t the collection of all partial situations $<<$ - included in t. Then Z_t forms an ideal, that is, it is closed under $<<$.

Now let us look at what constitutes a default reasoning over partial situations. A *general default* is a mapping p from the collection of all partial situations to $A_1 \times ... \times A_n$ satisfying the condition

$$p(s) = t => s << t$$

One interprets such a function p as follows: an expert faces an incomplete situation s, but, in order to perform anything at all decides that the situation he faces is really $p(s)$ (and suggests the corresponding action). The composition of p and the expert advice $f: A_1 \times ... \times A_n \rightarrow A$ is the partial knowledge base system.

If no restriction on such general defaults are imposed then it is obvious that such functions exist (just use Proposition 6.1). Yet an expert does not seem to think in such a chaotic way. To see how a rational expert may deal with incomplete information, let us introduce the notion of *persistent default*.

DEFINITION

Let p be a default. We say that p is *persistent* if the following condition is met:

$$\text{If } p(s)=t \text{ and } s<<u<<t \text{ then } p(u)=t$$

The persistent default should be viewed as follows: a (dogmatic) expert faces a partial situation s and decides that in order to act he has to decide what situation he really faces. By default he decides that he really deals with the (complete) situation t. Subsequently, new information comes which, however, does not contradict his assumption (that he really faces t). At this point he still insists that he deals with t. Notice that in case of a general default he could change his course of action.

Subsequently we prove that persistent defaults exist. In fact, existence of yet stronger defaults will be proven. First some definitions.

DEFINITION
(1) Let $r=<B_1,....,B_k,a>$ be a rule. A partial situation $<<A_{i_1},a_{i_1}>,....,<A_{i_k},a_{i_k}>>$ matches r if and only if $a_{i_1} \in B_{i_1},....,a_{i_k} \in B_{i_k}$.
(2) Let S be a set of rules. Partial situations s_1, s_k are *indiscernible* with respect to S if s_1, s_2 have the same domain and if s_1, s_2 match exactly the same rules.

In case of complete situations, indiscernibility of t_1, t_2 means that for each j, the values on the jth coordinate belong to the same atom of the Boolean algebra B_j.

LEMMA 6.3. If s_1, s_2 are indiscernible partial situations and $s_1<<t_1$ where t_1 is a complete situation and S is a complete set of rules, then there exists t_2 indiscernible from t_1 such that $s_2<<t_2$.

Proof: Choose elements to extend s_2 from appropriate atoms (as indicated above).□
We now show the main result of this section:

THEOREM 6.4. If S is a collection of rules representing a complete knowledge base system S, then there exists a persistent and indiscernible (with respect to S) default on S.

Proof: Let $<t_1,....,t_l>$ be the enumeration of all complete situations. We may assume that for every situation t, all situations indiscernible from t form a segment in this enumeration. This is a reasonable assumption, since indiscernibility is an equivalence relation. We construct our default as follows: with every partial situation we associate the first complete extension appearing in the enumeration (alternatively we could say that we proceed in stages: first we consider t_1 and we assign t_1 to all partial situations which t_1 extends; then in stage n+1 we consider the set $Z=Z_{t_1} \cup ... \cup Z_{t_n}$. Define now, for $s \in Z_{t_{n+1}} -Z$, $p(s)=t_{n+1}$. One realizes that this defines the same concept, even if it does not look quite the same).

We need to prove that p is persistent and that p preserves indiscernibility. We prove persistency first. If $p(s_1)=t$ and $s_1 <<s_2 <<t$, then t is the first complete situation extending s_2. Indeed if t' extends s_2 then t' also extends s_1. Hence no element of our enumeration preceeding t can extend s_2 and since t extends s_2, $p(s_2)=t$.

Indiscernibility follows from Lemma 6.3. Let s_1, s_2 be indiscernible partial situations. By Lemma 6.3 they possess indiscernible complete extensions. The choice of the enumeration of complete situations $<t_1,....,t_l>$ was such that the indiscernible situations formed a segment. Hence, the first segment (consisting of indiscernible complete situations) where an extension of s_1 can be found and the similar segment for s_2 must coincide. Therefore the values of p assigned to s_1 and s_2 must be indiscernible.$\square$

The assignment $s\mapsto p(s)$ is, by necessity, non-monotonic; $s_1 <<s_2 \neq >p(s_1)=p(s_2)$ (to reach this conclusion we need in addition $s_2 <<p(s_1)$). This corresponds to the situation that on the basis of new information the expert may be forced to change his opinion.

In conclusion let us add that a stronger form of Theorem 6.4 can be proven; namely that the "segments" of functions satisfying the persistency condition can be extended to complete such functions.

The use of the word "default" is not accidental here. There is an alternative proof of Theorem 6.4 by means of appropriate coding within the default logic of (Reiter, 1980). The methods of (Sandewall, 1985) also apply here.

Finally one can ask *how* the default function p is obtained. As the function p is uniquely determined by the ordering of complete situations, we should say a word about the desired choice of such ordering. The ordering of the situations must be provided by the expert who establishes in this way the priority of certain situations. Once this priority is established, the default function p chooses the extending complete situation of highest priority.

6.7. Conclusion

In this chapter we considered rule-structured knowledge bases and have investigated some of their basic properties in formal terms. Algorithms for determining the completeness and consistency of rule-structured knowledge bases were proposed, and aspects of incomplete information were also investigated. The strength and limitations of the various algorithms were considered, in terms of their computational complexity and their usefulness to the knowledge representation endeavour.

Acknowledgements

It is my pleasant duty to express my gratitude to my colleagues from the Lexington "Logic and Computer Science Seminar": Tom Altman, Audrey Ferry, Forbes Lewis and Mirek Truszczynski. We acknowledge assistance of Iwona Hawrylak (c.f. (Hawrylak, 1985)) and discussions with John Schlipf and Michal Jaegermann. Needless to say that all the mistakes must be attributed only to the author. Research partially supported by NSF grant #DCR 8411600 and USDA grant # USDS/CSRS/84-CRSC-2-2524.

7. First Order Logic and Knowledge Representation: Some Problems of Incomplete Systems

E. W. Elcock

Department of Computer Science
The University of Western Ontario
London, Ontario, Canada N6A 5B7

Abstract

It is arguable that knowledge representation and use should be founded on a complete system. For example, if the knowledge representation language is to be first order logic, then we would like to express knowledge K under the assumption that we have available a sequenthood procedure *which is complete* in the sense that any true sequent K $\rightarrow$ G (G follows from K) is demonstrably true by the procedure. For example, our knowledge system might be based on finite clausal sequents for which there is indeed a procedure using resolution which has the completeness property.

Over the last decade an incomplete resolution system called Prolog has been elaborated and has become widely used. Prolog has intriguing analogies with Absys - an assertive programming system developed in 1968. Some issues of incompleteness important for knowledge manipulation are illustrated by comparing some aspects of the two systems.

Based on the paper, How Complete are Knowledge
Representation Systems, E. W. Elcock, appearing in COMPUTER,
Volume 16, Number 10, October, 1983.

7.1. Introduction

A critical problem of knowledge representation is that of expressing a body of knowledge and computing the consequence of the body of knowledge. We need a calculus that will make the expression of knowledge and this notion of consequence precise and straightforward. The standard logical formalisms have been designed with just these properties in mind: they are an obvious first choice for examination in a search for an ideal formalism. First order logic was essentially introduced as a calculus for capturing the expression of intuitively valid patterns of reasoning, patterns which are essentially abstracted from the content of what is being reasoned about (Robinson, 1979). Ideally, we would like to express our knowledge base in this calculus and have an algorithmic decision procedure which would decide whether any particular (well-formed) statement logically followed from the knowledge base.

Unfortunately, there is no effective procedure (algorithm) that will decide whether or not a particular arbitrary statement is indeed a logical consequence of an arbitrary knowledge base. First order logic is only what is called semi-decidable. That is, there are effective procedures which are complete in the sense that if and only if presented with a logical consequence will they establish that it is indeed such. We have to settle for these. More: we are really only interested in computationally *pragmatic* procedures (that is procedures which in most cases of interest need only feasible computational resources on available machines). A major step forward was the discovery that there are subsets of first order logic which lend themselves to such pragmatic procedures and yet which in principle are powerful enough to express any logical consequence expressible in the full system.

Robinson's resolution principle for the subset of first order logic using clausal form is the basis of most of the machine inference methods now in use. (Robinson, 1979).

Roughly, resolution works as follows. We want to establish the sequent

$$A'_1, A'_2, ..., A'_n => B' \tag{7.1}$$

(that is, B' is a logical consequence of $A'_1 ... A'_n$ where $A'_1 ...$

$A^{`}_n$ and $B^{`}$ are ordinary sentences in first order logic).

Each sentence $A^{`}_i$ in $A^{`}_1 \ldots A^{`}_n$ can be transformed into a universal clause $A_i$ and $B^{`}$ to an existential clause B. A universal (existential) clause is a disjunction (conjunction) of predications or negations of predications all of whose variables are universally (existentially) quantified. The sequent (7.1) is true if and only if the set of clauses in its clausal transform $\{A_1,...,A_n,\neg B\}$ is unsatisfiable. Resolution proceeds by selecting suitable pairs of clauses from the set and generating a new clause (the resolvent of the pair). The original set is unsatisfiable if and only if the set with the resolvent added is unsatisfiable. The process terminates when an 'empty' resolvent is produced making the final set obviously unsatisfiable.

For resolution systems it is well-known that the strategies by which clauses are selected for resolution play a vital role in determining the pragmatics of such systems and the design of strategies has been an ongoing research activity. Of the systems with any real claim to feasibility a system called Prolog (Kowalski, 1979) has been elaborated over the last decade and has become widely used. It should be stressed that in choosing a selection strategy directed at feasibility, Prolog gives up all claim to completeness: that is, there are logical consequences that it cannot establish. It is also unsound in the sense that it can claim as valid an invalid logical consequence. Prolog has intriguing analogies with Absys (Foster and Elcock, 1969) - an assertative programming system developed in 1968. In what follows we will focus on the issue of incompleteness by comparing some aspects of the two systems. We will finally make some remarks on the problems posed by incompleteness in any serious use of Prolog as a vehicle for a knowledge-based system.

Before proceeding, a remark is probably in order. Prolog is often referred to as a "programming language". We have presented it as a particular procedure for establishing sequenthood in first order logic. How do we reconcile these superficially quite different views?

The first part of the answer is not peculiar to Prolog. Suppose we ask for the sequent $A => G$ to be established, where G contains (existentially) quantified variables $x_1,...,x_m$, say. The resolution sequent procedure terminates with a most general instantiation of $x_1...x_m$ which exhibits an *instance* of the existentially quantified conjunction G which is indeed a consequence of A. We can therefore reinterpret the request "establish that G is a logical consequence of A" as "compute for me the most general instantiations of the variables of G which indeed make G a logical consequence of A".

For example, (and not worrying about a formal syntax), suppose A contains a suitable defining clause for the predicate "grandparent" in terms of the predicate "parent", together with the (degenerate) clauses asserting that "joe is the parent of mary" and that "sue is the parent of joe". We can *compute* a grandparent of mary by asking for the sequent A => grandparent(X,mary) to be established, since, in establishing the sequent, X will be instantiated to "sue" - the value of X we wanted to compute.

The second part of the answer is peculiar to Prolog and systems like it. Prolog uses an even more restricted subset of first order logic. As will be seen below, the particular algorithm used by Prolog to establish sequenthood gives rise to a number of intriguing and potentially helpful computational analogies between Prolog and conventional procedural languages.

7.2. Prolog & Absys: declarative knowledge manipulation systems

Prolog is well-documented: there is an excellent text, (Kowalski, 1979), and numerous short overviews (for example, (Clark and McCabe, 1979), (Warren, Periera, and Periera, 1977)). There is a well-written and comprehensive presentation of Prolog as a programming language, (Clocksin and Mellish, 1981) (with little reference to any connexion with logic!). A fairly detailed description of Prolog is given in Chapter 12.

For these reasons we shall simply note here that a Prolog "program" is a pair [A,G] where A is a set of Horn clauses and G an existentially quantified conjunction of predications. A Horn clause is a universal clause with just one positive predication. A Horn clause "{P, $P_1^*,P_2^*,...,P_m^*$}" can be read as the conditional "P if P_1 and P_2 and and P_m". It can be thought of as a component of a procedure declaration of P, with P the "head" and "P_1 and P_2 and and P_m" the "body" of this component of the procedure declaration. A simple example is the pair of Horn clauses

```
1.  mem(X,[X|L])
2.  mem(X,[Y|L]) if mem(X,L)
```

to inductively axiomatize the predicate "mem" with the intended interpretation of list membership. The term [X|L] is to be interpreted as a list with first member X and remainder list L.

The procedural reading of a Prolog program [A,G] regards the conjunction G as a set of procedure calls to procedures in A. The elaboration of a procedure called G_i in G roughly consists in finding a procedure declaration in A such that a suitable binding of variables to terms makes the head of the procedure declaration in A syntactically identical to the procedure call G_i. G_i in G is then replaced by the body of the relevant procedure declaration and the evaluation process continued in a binding environment (of variables to terms) augmented by the binding used in elaborating the procedure call.

The execution of the procedure calls essentially parallels a linear input resolution strategy. The logic model theoretic and procedural semantics are potentially equivalent in a precise sense, (van Emden and Kowalski, 1976). However, as mentioned in the introduction. for pragmatic reasons Prolog uses a restriction of the linear input strategy for resolut n Essentially, the current executable statement is regarded not as a set, but as a <u>sequence</u> of procedure calls, and A is regarded as a <u>sequence</u> of procedure declarations. Prolog attempts to execute the <u>first</u> of the sequence of calls using the first matching declaration in the sequence of procedure declarations a "depth first" restriction on the strategy. As mentioned, successful matching leads to replacement of the procedure call by the body, if any, of the relevant declaration, and the resumption of the execution cycle with an augmented binding environment determined by the matching. If in attempting to elaborate a particular procedure call no successful matching is

available, then the system backtracks to the last choice point.
The execution ends successfully when the current execution
statement is empty.   This execution strategy makes Prolog
incomplete in the sense that a true sequent A => G is not
necessarily a terminating Prolog program [A,G].   A simple
illustrative example is the program [A,G] where A is the
sequence of clauses (cf the "mem" clauses above).

```
1.  mem(X,[Y|L]) if mem(X,L)
2.  mem(X,[X|L])
```

specifying list membership, and G is

```
mem(a,[a|L]) .
```

The sequent A => G is true but the Prolog evaluator because
of its clause selection strategy persistently uses clause 1 of A
to generate the sequence of execution statements

```
      mem(a,[a|L])
      mem(a,L)
      mem(a,L1)  where L is bound to [X|L1]
      mem(a,L2)  where L1 is bound to [Y|L2]
etc., etc.
```

Unlike Prolog, Absys is not a well-documented system
and only informal accounts are available. (Foster and Elcock,
1969), (Elcock, 1971).   Absys (standing for Aberdeen System)
was designed as an experimental working on-line incremental
compiler for assertions, by the Computer Research Group at the
University of Aberdeen and essentially completed in 1968.

Absys text consists of a conjunction of assertions about
objects and relations holding over them.   The system acts to
construct objects satisfying the conjunction of assertions.   The
written text places no explicit constraints on the order in
which particular operations are performed.   In addition, the
effect of processing an assertion, as in Prolog, depends upon the
binding context in which the assertion is processed.   Thus in
Absys, as in Prolog,

```
L = [X|M]
```

simply asserts that L is a list whose head is X and whose tail
is M. Whether the assertion acts to construct L, or to select X

and M, or simply check that L, X and M satisfy the asserted relation, depends solely on the data or binding environment at the time that the assertion is processed.

In Absys alternatives can be asserted by an explicit disjunction $<<$ a1 or a2 $>>$ where a1 and a2 are conjunctions of assertions. The (implicit) and and or distribute in the usual way so that, for example

a1 $<<$ a2 or a3 $>>$ a4

is equivalent to

$<<$ a1 a2 a4 $>>$ or $<<$ a1 a3 a4 $>>$.

The system attempts to construct data to satisfy each conjunction of assertions, each conjunction notionally constituting a separate (parallel) computation branch. In practice, of course, the non-determinism is handled by appropriate differential record-keeping and backtracking in a similar spirit to Prolog implementations. The distribution of and and or connectives was handled in a way which attempted to minimize duplication of processing. A particular computational branch terminates when unsatisfiability is detected.

A lambda construction allows the expression of functions other than the primitives of the system - the analogy of the procedure declarations of Prolog. Thus, list membership might be specified in Absys by:

```
mem = lambda m,s key s
<< s = [p|s1] and
<< m = p or mem(m,s1) >> >> .
```

The assertion mem(x,[1,2,3]) is equivalent to asserting $<<$ x=1 or x=2 or x=3 $>>$. If in addition we were now to assert mem(x,[2,4,6]), equivalent to $<<$ x=2 or x=4 or x=6 $>>$, then distribution would lead to nine computational branches of which only one, that associated with x=2 would be satisfiable and hence remain active.

The "key" statement in the declaration of "mem" prevents the kind of non-terminating behaviour exhibited in the (admittedly deliberately contrived) Prolog specification of "mem". The "key" statement in effect says "don't elaborate this call of "mem" unless the actual parameter which is to be bound to the indicated formal parameter(s) of "mem" has a value". This prevents a possible attempt to elaborate the recursive call of mem before the conjoined assertion s = [p|st] has been successfully elaborated, and hence prevents the possibility of non-terminating elaboration of mem.

Anticipating Prolog, Absys was provided with a primitive aggregation operator <u>set</u>: it takes as parameters a prototype set element and an assertion and produces the set of prototype elements satisfying the assertion. The assertion is typically a disjunction. The set aggregator initiates the "parallel" computations and then extracts the datum corresponding to the prototype from those computations which terminate successfully (cf. Prolog's extraction of those elements for which the assertion is established to be a logical consequence of the "A" sequence of clauses).

Anticipating Prolog and Planner, Absys negation acts like a degenerate <u>or</u> in that it initiates an independent computational branch but one in which the criteria for termination are reversed in that not(<<a>>), is satisfiable if and only if <<a>> is unsatisfiable (cf. Prolog's interpretation of negation as "not provable").

The main thrust of this thumbnail sketch of Absys, which draws heavily on (Foster and Elcock, 1969), is to bring attention to the fact that Absys, like Prolog, has a declarative reading (semantics) which asserts relations holding over objects. Also like Prolog, it has a uniform evaluation mechanism (inducing a procedural semantics) which attempts to instantiate variables by constants in such a way that the assertions are demonstrably satisfied.

7.3. Primitive goal selection strategies in Absys and Prolog

We have drawn attention to the fact that the Prolog evaluation mechanism is incomplete. What about the Absys evaluation mechanism? In the case of Prolog it is easy to give a precise meaning to the phrase "the Prolog evaluation mechanism is incomplete". As stated in the introduction, we mean that a Prolog program [A,G] can be regarded as expressing the clausal sequent A => G and incompleteness means that there are true segments A => G which are not established as such by the corresponding Prolog program [A,G]. The notion is missing in Absys since Absys does not have a subsuming declarative semantics.   Nevertheless, in an intuitive informal sense Absys fails to meet certain tacit expectations similar to those contained in the notion of the 'incompleteness of Prolog', but for different reasons and in interestingly different ways.

The Absys evaluation mechanism is explained in detail in (Elcock, McGregor, and Murray, 1972).   Absys maintains a list of relations still to be elaborated.   Suppose we activate the first such relation f(x,y,z), say, on this list.   It is expected that the functor f, whether primitive or user-defined, has been defined in such a way that the header f specifies, by means of its "key" statement, a constraint on its argument set which indicates whether or not it is "worthwhile" elaborating the body of f (for example, "plus(x,y,z)" is only worthwhile elaborating if two of its arguments already have values in the domain of "plus"). If the relation is not deemed worth elaborating, then it is "associated" with each of its arguments which are currently uninstantiated variables.   The evaluator now continues processing the list of relations awaiting elaboration.   Suppose, on the other hand, that the relation f(x,y,z) is worth processing in the sense that enough is known about some of the arguments to allow others to be inferred through elaboration of the body of the function. The body is now elaborated and the binding environment necessarily augmented.   The process of changing a variable binding in the binding environment automatically returns any relations associated with that variable to the list of relations still to be elaborated.

Let us illustrate this with a very simple example involving only system functions. Suppose we have the Absys text

$$u+v=16 \text{ and } w*u=v \text{ and } u+10=12$$

and suppose the list of relations is initially processed in this order.   The relation u+v=16 is examined and, for the reasons mentioned, associated with u and v.   The relation w*u=v is now examined and associated with w,u and v.   We now have the association of lists (u: u+v=16; w*u=v); (v: u+v=16;

w*u=v) and (w: w*u=v).   The relation u+10=12 is now examined, elaborated and the binding environment augmented so that u is bound to 2 (that is, 12-10). As a result of this binding to u, the list of relations (2+v=16; w*u=v) associated with u is appended to the list of relations to be elaborated. The relation 2+v=16 is now examined and elaborated and the binding environment augmented so that v is bound to 14, and the list associated with v appended to the list of relations to be elaborated.   This list is now (2+14=16; w*2=14; w*2=14). The first relation is examined, elaborated and found satisfied. The second is examined, elaborated and the binding environment augmented so that w is bound to 7, and the list associated with w appended to the list of relations still to be processed. This list is now (7*2=14; 7*2=14).   Both of these remaining relations are examined, elaborated and found satisfied.   The list of relations to be elaborated is now empty and the (examinable) state of the binding environment reflects what the system has been able to infer from the original conjunction of assertions.

Let us now contrast this with a Prolog evaluation. Suppose we ask Prolog to establish that its "system axioms" imply that there exists a u,v and w such that

$$u+v=16 \ \underline{and} \ w*u=v \ \underline{and} \ u+10=12$$

If the goal conjunction is in this order, then all Prolog implementations of which I am aware would fail at the first relation.   This is because the top-down left-right relation selection-elaboration strategy insists that Prolog determine a successful match for the selected relation and elaborate it or else fail. Now Prolog, like Absys, sensibly says that it is not going to have a system specification of "+" which will allow a matching of u+v=12 involving a potentially infinite set of pairs u,v satisfying the relation: the chance of doing any useful arithmetic this way is slim.   The Edinburgh Prolog, cautious in the true Scots tradition, would insist that all of u,v and w are already instantiated to integers.   IC Prolog from swinging London, like Absys, is happy if two of the three variables are instantiated by integers at the time of elaborating the call. However, IC Prolog still could not cope with the above ordering because of the left-right rule, although it could cope with the logically equivalent conjunction

$$u+10=12 \quad \text{and} \quad u+v=16 \quad \text{and} \quad w*u=v.$$

Indeed, the action of the Absys evaluator could be viewed as dynamically rearranging the order of elaboration of the relations under the influence of the changing binding environment. We are now at the heart of the matter.

7.4. Selection strategies and knowledge systems

Certainly the arithmetic example, of itself, is not very exciting. However, the illustrated problem is quite general. It is that a knowledge manipulation system is likely to have enough to worry about to generate a specification of a consequent under its declarative reading without, at least initially, having to worry about any potential incompleteness of a concomitant procedural reading. For example, the arithmetic relations in the example above might have been generated in that order as a result of a particular parse of the word problem: "Two straight rods laid end to end measure sixteen inches in length. The second rod is longer than the first by a factor "w", and the first rod is the piece that was left after cutting ten inches off a rod one foot long."

Absys would accept the parsed sequence of relations as is. Prolog would need a further stage of processing in which the conjunctions were reordered to meet certain deficiences in the sequent processor.

Although space does not allow an illustration here, Prolog is also sensitive to the interaction of effects due to its incomplete evaluation strategy with effects due to the implementation of the "non-logical" aggregation operators - such as "set-of" mentioned earlier and used to obtain sets of consequences of the knowledge base.

The example above has, of course, been chosen to show Absys to advantage! However, the Absys dynamic data directed elaboration of the conjunction is gained only at the price of more elaborate run-time processing structures. In any case, a naive dynamic data directed flow of elaboration, although elegant in certain well-circumscribed contexts, of itself rapidly runs out of steam. For example, and staying within arithmetic for pedagogic simplicity, much more sophisticated aggregation and solution methods would be necessary to deal with a conjunction of a general set of linear equations in n variables. Even the task of recognizing what aggregations of individual conjuncts, again, say, stemming from a simple parse of a word problem, might lend themselves to reorganization as a specified "higher" relation (for example, the relation "simult-eqs(L)" where L is a list of lists of coefficients obtained from a subset of the conjuncts from the parse, say) is challenging to say the least.

Indeed such aggregation is a central problem of knowledge deployment. Nevertheless, it is likely that flexible dynamically determined selection strategies for evaluation systems will remain an important feature of good knowledge manipulation systems in whatever formalism. The dynamic data directed methods of Absys take one part of the way. The author is currently investigating whether such methods can be extended and embedded in the context of a suitably designed logic programming language.

7.5. Summary

A major problem with particular logic programming languages is that a sequent may be true but not established as such by the system simply because, in the interests of certain notions of efficiency, the sequenthood establishing procedure used by the system is incomplete.

It has been argued that a central issue for Prolog (and for other first order systems) as a vehicle for knowledge representation and use is the dynamic aggregation of and selection of appropriate relations for elaboration. The meta-logical approaches of Bundy (Bundy and Silver, 1981) and others are examples of alternative approaches to similar problems. It might be that, by a suitable superstructure, one could maintain the pragmatic advantages of Prolog (or Prolog-like systems) and yet avoid the sequencing difficulties identified above.

Acknowledgements

The content of this Chapter and its wider context is part of work being conducted under operating grant number A9123 from the Natural Sciences and Engineering Research Council of Canada.

8. Admissible State Semantics for Representational Systems

Jon Doyle

Computer Science Department
Carnegie-Mellon University
Pittsburgh, Pennsylvania 15213

Abstract

Several authors have proposed specifying semantics for representational systems by translating them into logic. Unfortunately, such translations often introduce unnecessary detail and complexity. We indicate how many kinds of informal semantics can be transformed directly into formal semantics of no greater complexity. The key to avoiding the difficulties of logical translations is to recognize the difference between internal and external meanings.

Based on the paper, Admissible State Semantics
for Representational Systems, Jon Doyle, appearing in
COMPUTER, Volume 16, Number 10, October, 1983.

8.1. Introduction - the problem of practical semantics

Although the design of representational systems involves many considerations, such as computational efficiency of the operations and accommodation (at least through front-ends) of the conceptual scheme to those familiar to humans, one of the most important requirements is for a clear semantics.   Just as a slow program may be useless, and just as sermons in one church may bewilder the members of another, one cannot hope for success in representing information about the world if one cannot tell what the representations mean.   Without a clear semantics, one cannot tell if two representations mean the same thing or mean different things.   This prevents judging the correctness of formalizations of one's intuitive knowledge. Similarly, without a clear semantics, one cannot distinguish innocuous, meaning-preserving inferences from inferences which introduce new assumptions or change meanings.

Artificial intelligence has pursued two paths towards formalizing the semantics of representational systems.   Both of these are based on mathematical logic.   In one, the representations themselves are sentences in a logical language, as in PROLOG; in the other, one gives a translation of every representation into a set of sentences in a logical language, as illustrated by (Hayes, 1979) and (Nilsson, 1980).   In either case, the meaning of representations is found by looking at the models of the corresponding set of sentences.

Unfortunately, neither of these paths offers any guarantee that the resulting semantics will be easy to construct or to comprehend.   The source of the difficulty is that many sorts of representations important in artificial intelligence concern self-knowledge of one kind or other, representations of the agent about its own structure and behavior.   Some of these self-representations are purely descriptive or introspective. Some are used normatively as ideal "self-images" to uphold in actual thought and action.   Phrasing such self-representations or their translations in a logical language is not impossible, but usually requires very complex constructions involving convoluted language-metalanguage systems.   This is not theoretically objectionable, but it spells trouble in practice, since extremely complex translations are difficult to comprehend by the designer and user, making translation-based semantics ill-suited to its principal mission. This problem shows up often in artificial intelligence, where many representational systems are described in non-linguistic or non-logical terms and never supplied with formal meanings, even when reasonably clear informal semantics are obvious.

In the following, we indicate how many kinds of informal semantics can be transformed directly into formal semantics of no greater complexity. We avoid the unnecessary burdens of logical formulation and translation by focusing on what is real - the meanings - rather than on their expression within a particular logical language. Translations into logical languages, while theoretically sufficient, are not unique, since many languages can serve if even one can. Yet each logical language introduces peculiarities of its own, details that impede understanding and analysis without affecting the resulting meanings.

The key to avoiding the difficulties of direct logical translation is to recognize the difference between the internal and external meanings of representations.

8.2. Internal and external meanings

Designers of artificial intelligence systems commonly employ two sorts of reference: *external reference*, in which the agent's representations refer (in the designer's mind or by some other means) to objects not immediately "graspable," for example diseases and geological formations; and *internal reference*, in which the agent's representations refer (ostensively or otherwise) to objects immediately graspable and hence in the agent itself. This is reflected in the common focus of artificial intelligence architectures on general manipulations of representations rather than on pure logical deductions. If one has immediate access to an object, one cannot only talk about it, but modify it. With immediate access, if one makes an inaccurate statement, one can either retract it or make it true - both important operations in artificial intelligence systems. On the other hand, without graspability, one can only talk about objects, and cannot quickly modify them to cover one's assertions. This makes deduction an important way of talking about ungraspable objects, since one can say new things without fear of being more wrong than before. The principal novelty of current representational systems relative to traditional systems of deductive logic is their concentration on the use of the relatively neglected tools of internal reference as the basis of self-structuring and self-modifying agents, agents which can state their own intended structure, and then make those statements true if need be.

Putnam and others argue that even supposedly mental objects like human beliefs cannot actually be grasped, and so raise doubts that two sorts of reference exist, doubts that anything can be immediately grasped at all, (Putnam, 1975). The artificial intelligence approach is based on ensuring that some objects are actually grasped by construction. While many representations of the usual knowledge representation systems have external referents, and so do not directly affect the mind (except through mistakes that cause injury or death), many of the information-structuring representations concern mental objects themselves, especially relations between representations. Rather than ask Putnam's question of whether these structural representations *actually* mean what the agent thinks they do, we use the intra-mental relations to *define* the *admissible states* of the agent. The problem of correct implementation of these self-representational specifications is that of implementing the agent so that the states of the implementation are exactly the admissible states, that is, so that the structural representations have exactly their intended meaning. We separate this portion of the meaning of mental components from general ecological meaning by the name *admissible state semantics*, and leave specification of external meanings to the standard tools of model theory.

The method of admissible state semantics is simple, and resembles the usual explanations of intended meanings given by system designers. In both of these, the designer explains the meaning of one representation directly in terms of its relations to other representations in the system. For comparison, the logic translation approach requires that one first translate the initial representation into logic, then find its consequences, and then reverse the translation process to find other representations related to the original one. Since many representational systems involve succinct encodings of notions whose logical translations are very complex, the difficulty of this roundabout logical procedure can be unbearable.

8.3. Admissible state semantics

Admissible state semantics makes several fairly general assumptions about the constitution of agents. These constitutive assumptions involve some "parameters," so one applies the framework by filling in these parameters with the characteristics intended of one's system. The three fundamental parameters are called D, I, and S. We explain these in turn. (These three notions are part of a larger framework developed in (Doyle, 1982) and elsewhere.)

The first constitutive assumption is that every state of the agent can be decomposed into elements drawn from a domain D. Here D is just a set, so each state S is a subset of D, that is, $S \subseteq D$. For most purposes, D is just the set of all possible representations or data structures the system might employ. For example, a logically-structured agent might be characterized by taking D to be the set of all sentences in some logical language; LISP-based agents might require D to be the set of all possible S-expressions; for frame- or unit-structured agents, D can be the set of all possible frames or units; semantic networks likely require D to be the set of all possible nodes and links; and "society of mind" agents can be described using D as the set of all "mental agents" (see (Doyle, 1983)). Note carefully that D is not just the set of all components in some particular state, such as the initial state, but instead the set of all components that might appear in any state, at any time. It is possible, without much trouble, to formalize one's system instead in terms of an increasing sequence of domains (to capture "generated symbols" or other additions), but illustrating that would digress too far from our main purpose here.

The second constitutive assumption is that every element of the domain, every possible state component, represents a specification on the set of states in which it may admissibly occur, and has a meaning or interpretation that sets out these sanctioned states. Formally, we assume an interpretation function $I: D \rightarrow \mathbf{P} \mathbf{P} D$ ($\mathbf{P}$ means power set), so that for each $d \in D$, $I(d) \subseteq \mathbf{P} D$ is the set of potential states sanctioned by d. For example, state components that are indifferent to the states in which they appear (such as representations purely about the external world) can be given the trivial interpretation $I(d) = \mathbf{P} D$ that sanctions all potential states. If the component requires that its appearance always be accompanied by some other components $A \subseteq D$ then one can define $I(d) = \{S \subseteq D \mid A \subseteq S\}$. To forbid the component from occurring with some other components $A \subseteq D$, we can define $I(d) = \{S \subseteq D \mid S \cap A = \varnothing\}$. Of course, these are very simple sorts of interpretations. Sophisticated systems may have some components that play very involved roles in the agent, and these may require very complex interpretations. Note carefully that one is free to use whatever precise (for example, mathematical or logical) language is convenient in defining the interpretations of components. These metalanguages are part of *our* (external) specification of the system, and need have no close relation to the system's own methods of representation. Put another way, we can use logic to characterize the intended behavior of the agent without having to pretend the agent's components and actions are logical sentences and logical inferences. This, as I see it, is the principal advantage of the proposed semantical framework over those based on logical translations. To ease the semanticist's burden even more, we note that when there are several overlapping classes of components with special interpretations, one can specify several separate interpretation functions, one for each class of components, and then intersect them to get the full interpretation function. For example, if A, $B \subseteq D$ each contain related sorts of components, one can define for every $d \in D$

$$I_A(d) = \begin{cases} \cdots & \text{if } d \in A \\ \mathbf{P} D & \text{otherwise} \end{cases}$$

$$I_B(d) = \begin{cases} \cdots & \text{if } d \in B \\ \mathbf{P} D & \text{otherwise} \end{cases}$$

$$I(d) = I_A(d) \cap I_B(d).$$

The third constitutive assumption is that every *admissible state* of the system satisfies the specifications represented by each of its components. We write S to mean the set of admissible states of the agent, and define the class Q of *component-admissible sets* by

$$Q = \{S \subseteq D \mid S \in \cap_{d \in S} I(d)\},$$

so this constitutive assumption is that $S \subseteq Q$. Unfortunately, simple component-admissibility cannot capture some intended ranges of admissible states for agents. For example, the empty set $\emptyset$ is always component-admissible since it has no elements to say otherwise. One might wish to capture other restrictions on the intended states without explicitly representing them by interpretations of components. To allow this, the framework permits definition of S as a proper subset of Q. Note that we can always capture any general restriction except non-emptiness in the components themselves by redefining $I(d)$ as $I'(d) = S$ for every $d \in D$, in which case $Q' = s \cup \{\emptyset\}$. Turning this observation around, if $S = Q$, then all restrictions on states are explicitly represented in the states themselves. This recalls current efforts in artificial intelligence aimed at constructing completely "self-descriptive" systems, but we cannot pursue those here.

In the following examples, we present some semantical specifications using this framework. Unfortunately, demands for brevity limit what we can present here. More detailed and comprehensive treatments of major artificial intelligence systems are in preparation.

8.4. Example: semantic networks

Many systems represent information in so-called semantic networks. One of the fundamental sorts of information encoded in these representational systems concerns the "inheritance" of information by one concept from another. If we look for logical translations of these systems, the temptation is strong to formulate inheritance as implication, since everything derived about one concept can be derived in one further step about any concept it implies. Unfortunately for the simplicity of logical translations, many uses of inheritance in artificial intelligence have nothing to do with implication, but instead concern simple economy in writing down information. One often sets up inheritance relations not to indicate any common referents of descriptions, but as cheap ways of constructing one description in terms of its differences, both positive and negative, from another. For example, if we already have a description of lions, we can quickly construct a description of tigers by declaring that the two descriptions are the same, except (say) that tigers look different and live in India. Here we save rewriting all the information about being mammals, quadrupeds, furred, and so on, yet do not state that all tigers are lions, nor even that some tigers are lions. We just say "ditto." Considerable investigation still continues on what notions of inheritance are practically useful and theoretically important in general and in specific cases. We add nothing to those debates here, but instead illustrate how the semantical framework introduced above allows designers of such systems to state their intended conceptions of inheritance exactly and independently of how they implement those conceptions.

To give perhaps the most trivial example possible, suppose we choose to represent concepts by LISP atomic symbols with property lists, and intend that any concept with an **IS-A** property should also have every property of the concepts listed under the **IS-A** property. Formally, we let D be the set of all LISP S-expressions, take $S = Q$, and define I so that $I(d) = \mathbf{P} D$ if d is not an atomic symbol. We write $p(a) = x$ to mean that the atomic symbol a has x as the value of its p property. With this notation, we specify the interpretation of each atomic symbol a by

$$I(a)=\{S \subseteq D | \forall b \in \textbf{IS-A}(a) \ \ \forall p \neq \textbf{IS-A} \ \ p(b) \neq NIL \supset p(b)=p(a)\}.$$

That is, except for the **IS-A** property itself, which must be treated differently in this representation, the inheriting concept must have all the properties of its ancestor. Since the ancestor imposes similar conditions on states, inheritance is "transitive"

in every admissible state.   Of course, no one would ever want
to use such a simple-minded system: its limitations are obvious.
But we can extend the same methods to more interesting
representational systems.

Consider SRL, the "schema representation language" of
Wright and Fox   (Wright and Fox, 1982).   One important
feature of SRL is the definability of special classes of
inheritance types within the representation system itself.   While
the full language is too large to present here, we can focus on
one typical feature which illustrates how one might begin to
formally specify the internal semantics of all of SRL.   For this
fragmentary analysis, we take D to be the set of all possible
SRL "schema" data structures.   The precise extent of this set
does not matter for this example.   Indeed, we use little more
than the resemblance of schema to the simpler property-list
data-structures discussed above, and so do not do justice to SRL
proper.   The focus of our attention is the "inclusion-spec
inheritance schema."   An inheritance schema describes a class of
inheritance relationships, and inclusion-specs are generalizations
of **IS-A** relationships.   Wright and Fox display the form of
inclusion-spec schemata as

```
{{inclusion-spec
        DOMAIN : < restriction >
                default : all
         RANGE : < restriction >
                default : all
          TYPE :
                default : value
                range : (SET (OR slot value))
          SLOT : < restriction >
                default : all
         VALUE : < restriction >
                default : all
     CONDITION :
                default : T
                restriction : (OR T < predicate >)}}
```

They explain this schema as follows.   Every inheritance
schema has two slots called SCHEMA1 and SCHEMA2 whose
fillers are the schemata to be related by the defined inheritance
relationship. The inclusion-spec has a number of additional slots
which, taken together, describe exactly which sorts of
information should be transferred from SCHEMA1 to

SCHEMA2. DOMAIN and RANGE may be filled with predicates on schemata limiting the force of the inclusion-spec to pairs of schemata satisfying the respective restrictions. CONDITION is in addition a general predicate that must be satisfied for the inclusion-spec to transfer information. The TYPE slot indicates whether only slots, or slots and their values are to be transferred. The SLOT slot allows transfers to be restricted to a subset of SCHEMA1's slots, and the VALUE slot can restrict the sorts of values passed to SCHEMA2. In this way, the inheritance schema encodes a general statement about information transfer in the agent, and one uses the schema by filling in the ranges of some of the implicit quantifiers and referents of some of the explicit names. Use of a schema to state this specification rather than an arbitrary sentence of logic implicitly limits the user to specifications which the system implementor decides can be feasibly computed. To formally specify the semantics of SRL with just this one sort of relation schema, we need only define $I(d) = \mathbf{P}\ D$ when d is anything other than an inclusion-spec, and define the cases for an inclusion-spec d analogously to the property-list example above, perhaps by

$$
\begin{aligned}
I(d) = \{S \subseteq D \mid\ & apply(d.\text{DOMAIN}(S),\ d.\text{SCHEMA}!1(S)) = \textsf{T} \\
& \&\ apply(d.\text{RANGE}(S),\ d.\text{SCHEMA2}(S)) = \textsf{T} \\
& \&\ eval(d.\text{CONDITION}(S)) = \textsf{T} \\
& \&\ \forall s\ \in d.\text{SCHEMA1}.slots(S) \\
& [apply(d.\text{SLOT}(S),s) = \textsf{T} \supset s\ \in \\
& \qquad\qquad\qquad\qquad d.\text{SCHEMA2}.slots(S) \\
& \&\ d.\text{TYPE}(S) = \textsf{value} \supset \\
& \qquad \forall v\ \in\ d.\text{SCHEMA1}.s.values(S) \\
& \qquad [apply(d.\text{VALUE}(S)),v) \supset v\ \in \\
& \qquad\qquad\qquad d.\text{SCHEMA2}.s.values(S)]]\}.
\end{aligned}
$$

By doing enough honest work in defining these subsidiary functions (which we cannot pretend to here), we can continue in this way to give meanings to other sorts of SRL schemata as well.

8.5. Example: k-lines

To illustrate the applicability of admissible state semantics to non-linguistic structures for agents, we consider some elements of Minsky's (Minsky, 1980) K-line theory of memory. For Minsky, the mind is composed of a set of "mental agents." Each mental agent can be either active or inactive, and states of mind are simply sets of active mental agents. We identify the set of mental agents with the domain D of the agent, and consider sets in Q to be the admissible sets of active mental agents, that is $S = Q$.

The two specific sorts of mental agents we formalize here are K-lines and cross-exclusion networks. K-lines are mental agents that, when activated, cause the activation of some set of other mental agents. We formalize this by interpreting each K-line mental agent KL in terms of the set A of mental agents to which it is connected, so that

$$I(KL) = \{S \subseteq D \mid A \supseteq S\}.$$

Cross-exclusion networks are somewhat more complicated. Cross-exclusion networks are sets of mental agents which are mutually inhibitory. Further, cross-exclusion networks facilitate "conflict resolution" by disabling or ignoring all members if two or more manage to become active despite their mutual inhibitions. This disabling allows activation of "higher-level" mental agents which can consider and resolve the conflict. We might formalize this by letting CXN be a mental agent representing a cross-exclusion network, $B = \{b_1, ..., b_n\}$ be the set of mutually inhibiting members, $C = \{c_1, ..., c_n\}$ be indicators of which competitor wins out, and CXN^* be a mental agent representing the existence of an externally forced conflict. To get the desired behavior, we define

$$I(CXN) = \{S \subseteq D \mid [CXN^* \notin S] \supset B \subseteq S\},$$

$$I(b_i) = \{S \subseteq D \mid [S \cap (C - \{c_i\}) = \emptyset] \supset c_i \in S\}$$

for each i, and assume the existence of a "watchdog" WD such that

$$I(WD)=\{S \subseteq D \mid [\exists i \neq j \leqslant n \; c_i, c_j \in S] \supset CXN^* \in S\}.$$

With these interpretations, we can capture the meanings or functions of mental agents without having to dissect them.

8.6. Conclusion

We have indicated the internal meanings of a variety of representational systems without translating representations into a logical language. Unfortunately, demands for brevity limit the scope of this paper, and we have had to omit treatment of virtual state information and action specifications. But as a final remark, we note that the proposed semantical framework provides a starting point for investigating Smith's (Smith, 1982) representational hypothesis. According to Smith, many workers in artificial intelligence suppose that in any "interesting" computational agent, the representational elements of the agent's structure can be viewed propositionally, and that the computations made by the agent depend purely on the form, not on the content, of these elements. Such propositional perspectives on the structure of agents may seem quite elusive if we look at non-linguistic structures like K-lines, but the preceding framework offers tools for reconstructing the propositional structure of non-linguistic agents. For example, if $I(e) = I(e_1) \cap I(e_2)$, one might think of e as the statement e_1 and e_2. Similarly, if I is defined as the intersection of several restricted interpretation functions $I_1, \ldots, I_n$, one can view the domains of nontriviality of these functions as the "syntactic classes" of the agent's language. Even so, one may not find this reconstructed "language" looking anything like a full first-order logical language. What the current framework suggests, I think, is that one can make sense of the formality condition of the representational hypothesis without worrying too much about linguistic re-representability of the agent's structure. This brings us back to the initial proposal of this paper, that there are easier ways to give exact semantics to representational systems than translations into logic.

Acknowledgments

I thank Joseph Schatz for valuable advice.   This research was supported by the Defense Advanced Research Projects Agency (DOD), ARPA Order No. 3597, monitored by the Air Force Avionics Laboratory under Contract F33615-81-K-1539. The views and conclusions contained in this document are those of the author, and should not be interpreted as representing the official policies, either expressed or implied, of the Defense Advanced Research Projects Agency or the Government of the United States of America.

9. Accelerating Deductive Inference: Special Methods for Taxonomies, Colours and Times

Lenhart K. Schubert
Mary Angela Papalaskaris
Jay Taugher

Department of Computing Science
University of Alberta
Edmonton, Alberta T6G 2H1

Abstract

Deductive reasoning in a question answering system could in principle be left entirely to uniform inference methods such as resolution or natural deduction. However, more efficient special methods are needed for determining certain kinds of relationships which people seem to grasp 'without thinking'. These include relationships among types (such as person, girl, and computer), among parts (such as Canada, Alberta, and Alaska), among colours (such as brown, tan, and orange), and among times (such as the times of the Apollo 11 mission, the first moonwalk, and the first space shuttle launch). We outline special graphical and geometric methods for determining such relationships efficiently. The times required are often nearly constant and the storage costs linear in the number of relevant facts stored. Such special methods can be combined straightforwardly and uniformly with a general deduction algorithm.

Based on the paper, Determining Type, Part, Color,
and Time Relationships, L. Schubert, M. Papalaskaris, and J. Taugher,
appearing in COMPUTER, Volume 16, Number 10, October, 1983.

9.1. Introduction

At the University of Alberta, we are trying to construct a system with enough commonsense knowledge, and fluency in English, to be able to answer simple questions about a wide range of mundane subjects.[19]   We would like the system to respond quickly, and to remain structurally comprehensible, no matter how large or varied its knowledge base. Thus our emphasis has been on the generality of both the knowledge representation and of the way in which knowledge is organized for efficient selective access (Schubert, Goebel, and Cercone, 1979), (Covington and Schubert, 1980), (deHaan, 1986).

We will be concerned here with several kinds of inference problems, problems which arise constantly in question-answering processes and, without special handling, can absorb large computational resources.   One kind requires determining how two types of things are related, for example, whether "person" subsumes "girl", or whether "girl" is incompatible with "computer"; others require determining similar taxonomic or ordering relationships among parts of objects, colours, or times. These relationships are of fundamental importance in our perception and conception of the world, and it seems likely that we are specially equipped to deal with them efficiently. To match our cognitive skills, AI systems will need analogous special methods.

The special methods we shall describe are designed to supplement a deductive question-answering algorithm which is now operational (deHaan, 1986), (deHaan and Schubert, 1986). The algorithm draws on a base of logical propositions organized as a semantic net. The net permits selective access to the contents of individual 'mental worlds' and narratives, to sets of entities of any specified type, and to propositions involving any specified entity and classified under any specified topic. For

---

[19]Questions are at present posed logically, the English front end being incomplete. Our approach to parsing, interpretation, and generation of English is described in (Schubert and Pelletier, 1982), (Schubert, 1982), (Schubert, 1984), (Bailes, 1986).

example, if the story "Little Red Riding Hood" is inserted into the net (in logical form), the set of all propositions concerned with the wolf's appearance can be separately and efficiently retrieved. More narrowly, just the propositions concerned with the wolf's colour (a subtopic of appearance) can be selected. Using other topical categories, propositions describing feeding episodes, character traits, and so on, of the wolf or of any other particular or generic concept can be efficiently accessed.

The net syntax permits storage of arbitrary first-order or higher-order formulas, but the deductive algorithm requires stored propositions to be in clause form. (The input routines which convert quantified, arbitrarily connected first-order formulas into clauses also permit modal operators such as "necessarily" and "believes", generating a type of modal clause form; however, the deductive algorithm currently does not deal with modal operators.) The choice of clause form was not motivated by any prior commitment to resolution, but rather by the requirements of the topical classification algorithm on the one hand and the objective of minimizing equivalence inferencing' (for example, inferring $A \rightarrow \neg B$ from $B \rightarrow \neg A$) on the other. Nevertheless, this choice of canonical form has made it natural to rely on resolution as the main inference rule.

The deductive algorithm for answering yes-no questions concurrently tries to refute the clauses corresponding to the given question (for a "no" answer) and the clauses corresponding to its negation (for a "yes" answer). The resolution control strategy incorporates set-of-support and unit preference, but unlike standard strategies, trades off resolving against retrieval of additional information, and generally restricts resolving to pairs of clauses lying on a common path in a concept hierarchy and classified under the same topic. Most importantly for present purposes, it provides for the use of special methods to simplify clauses and to resolve and factor them.

We have described our system as a semantic net. In doing so, we are not speaking from a particular camp. We believe that the issues we are addressing are bound to arise in any general knowledge representation sooner or later, whether it is based on semantic nets, frames, scripts, production systems, or anything else. These nominally disparate formalisms have much in common and are in the process of converging further; for example, all incorporate a predicate-logic-like propositional language, all provide ways of 'clustering' information so that the information brought to bear on a given task at a given time can be sharply limited, and all have (or are to be furnished with) property inheritance mechanisms.

9.2. Recognizing type relationships

We believe that by steering our inference algorithm along 'vertical' paths in type hierarchies and keeping it topically focused, we have done about as much as can be done to ease the computational burden of any general inference algorithm. By radically limiting the set of propositions allowed into the reasoning mill at any time, our strategy helps to prevent the combinatorial explosions which are apt to bring the mill to a halt.

This is not enough for fast question answering, however. For, if all possible derivations of the answer to a question are long, then any general reasoning strategy will probably do a great deal of searching before finding one, even when working with a small set of propositions.

It turns out that standard deductive derivations of the answers to many simple questions are indeed rather long. Consider the question

Whom does Mary love?

and assume that its logical form[20] is

$$?\exists x[[x \; person] \; \& \; [Mary \; loves \; x]].$$

The desired answer is the set of persons Mary is known to love. Now suppose that the system finds, by retrieval of information about Mary under the topic "emotional attitudes" that Mary loves John, and also that she loves her prize orchid

---

[20]We use predicate infix form as an aid to readability, with the predicate symbol following its first argument and followed by the remaining arguments, if any.

plant. It remains to confirm that John is a person (and therefore a suitable answer) while the orchid is not. The former subproblem is not too taxing, assuming that the system has the facts

$$[\text{John boy}],$$

$$\forall x \, [[x \text{ boy}] \rightarrow [x \text{ person}]]$$

at its disposal, and these are selected as relevant. Showing that the orchid is not a person, though, is harder than it ought to be. The following sort of inference chain is required (where o is the beloved orchid):

```
1. [o orchid]                                            known
2. ∀x[[x orchid]  →  [x soft-stemmed-plant]]             known
3. [o soft-stemmed-plant]                                from 1,2
4. ∀x[[x soft-stemmed-plant]  →  [x plant]]              known
5. [o plant]                                             from 3,4
6. ∀x[[x person]  →  [x creature]]                       known
7. ∀x[[x creature]  → ¬[x plant]]                        known
8. ∀x[[x person]  → ¬[x plant]]                          from 6,7
9. ¬[o person]                                           from 5,8
```

This is not a worst-case example; if, for example, Mary also loves her piano, more steps will be required to rule it out as a candidate answer, assuming that "creature" leads upward to "living-thing" in the taxonomy of types, while "piano" leads to "musical-instrument", hence to "artifact", and hence to "nonliving-thing", known to preclude "living-thing".

Subproblems of this kind arise constantly in question-answering processes and, without special handling, can absorb large computational resources. Yet one feels that subproblems such as establishing the non-personhood of an orchid should not detain the reasoning system significantly.

In essence, we wish to be able to perform type compatibility checks for pairs of type concepts quickly. For example, we should be able to confirm the truth of [o plant] or the falsity of ¬[o creature] instantly once [o orchid] has been stored. In other words, we should be able to evaluate certain literals quickly. Similarly, we should be able to 'resolve' the pair of formulas

```
[o orchid]
```

¬[x person] v [x creature]   (= 6, in clause form)

directly to obtain ¬[o person]; likewise, we should be be able to 'resolve' the pair of formulas

[o orchid]
¬[x creature] v ¬[x plant]   (= 7, in clause form)

directly to obtain ¬[o creature]. Note that the first example of generalized resolving is based on the incompatibility of "being an orchid" and "being a creature", while the second is based on the incompatibility of "being an orchid" and "not being a plant", that is, the <u>subordination</u> of "being an orchid" by "being a plant".

With such methods, proofs such as 1-9 above could be 'short-circuited', reducing them to a single step. The potential usefulness of evaluation and generalized resolving is apparent in all of the special domains we consider. This has been a recurrent theme in the knowledge representation and deduction literature (for example, (Papalaskaris and Schubert, 1982), (Brachman, Fikes, and Levesque, 1983), (Stickel, 1983)); much the same idea has motivated the design of sortal logics for AI purposes (for example, (McSkimmin and Minker, 1979), (Walther, 1983), and (Stickel, 1983) offers a unified view of evaluation and generalized resolving, under the rubric "theory resolution" (see section 9.6)).

An obvious method for determining type relations is to pursue upward paths in the type graph -- which we assume to be set apart from other information in the net in any case -- until the paths intersect. If the point of intersection coincides with the point of origin of one of the paths, then the concept at that point of origin is superordinate to the other; (for example, paths from "girl" and "creature" will intersect at "creature", so that "creature" is superordinate to "girl"). In all other cases the concepts are incompatible. (Or are they?...see below). This idea can be implemented as graph algorithms (for example, (Fahlman, 1979)) or as special theorem proving strategies (for example, (Bundy, Byrd, and Mellish, 1982), (Tenenberg, 1985), (Rich, 1985)).

Two comments are in order about such methods. First, it is not always clear in graphical approaches what the intended interpretation of type graphs is.   In particular, it is often unclear whether concepts lying on divergent branches of a graph are to be regarded as incompatible. For example, if there are separate arcs running upward from "plant" and "creature" to "living-thing", are we entitled to conclude that no plant is a creature? If yes, then by the same token, if there are arcs running upward from "novelist" and "poet" to "writer", can we conclude that no novelist is a poet? Moreover, the subcategories of a concept node may or may not be regarded as jointly exhaustive, and this affects what may be inferred. For example, if a microbe is known to be a living thing but not a plant, then the conclusion that a microbe is a creature is warranted just in case the subcategorization of living things into plants and creatures is interpreted as being exhaustive.   Such issues can be clarified by relating type graphs to standard logical representations.

The second comment is that step-by-step tracing of superordination relationships may be a rather clumsy solution to our problem, in that constant-time methods may be possible. For example, by precomputing the transitive closure of an acyclic type graph, we could achieve constant-time testing of subtype-supertype relationships (although we would rather avoid the quadratic storage costs this method can entail).   Our own method, though closely related to path intersection methods, entirely avoids path traversals and (under certain assumptions) determines type relationships in constant time.

Type graphs specifying arbitrary subordination chains and incompatibilities can be defined quite conveniently in terms of a single partitioning relation § such that

$$[T \ \S \ T_1 \ ... \ T_k]$$

means that type concept T is partitioned into the k mutually incompatible, jointly exhaustive subtypes $T_1,...,T_k$. The possibility that a partitioning is non-exhaustive can be taken care of by introducing a remainder type T_k denoting all things of type T not covered by $T_1,...,T_{k-1}$. T_k may happen to denote the null concept (= universally false predicate).[21]   When subtypes are not considered incompatible, this can be expressed by means of multiple partitioning assertions.   For example, the following says that novelists and poets are necessarily writers, without making any commitment about possible incompatibility:

$$[\text{writer} \ \S \ \text{novelist T}], \ [\text{writer} \ \S \ \text{poet T'}],$$

where T and T' are the remainder categories (T = λx [[x writer] & $\neg$[x novelist]], and similarly for T'). Sets of such partitioning assertions can be drawn as graphs, as illustrated in Figure 9-1 (discussed more fully below).   The named nodes represent type concepts, while each T-shaped connection from a superordinate node to a set of subordinate nodes represents a $\S$-assertion.

The graph in Figure 9-1 is a <u>hierarchy</u>, having a unique root (viz., the most general type of concept covered by the hierarchy) and just <u>one</u> partitioning assertion subdividing each of its nonterminal nodes.

In general, a given set of $\S$-assertions certainly need not form a hierarchy, but may define an arbitrarily complex graph. It would be gratifying indeed to have an efficient algorithm for testing concept compatibility and subordination in this general case (where an efficient method is one which requires linear storage and at worst linear time relative to the number of nodes and $\S$-assertions of a graph).   Unfortunately, the prospect of finding such an algorithm is very slim, since doing so would require solving the famous unsolved problem "P=NP?" affirmatively (Schubert, 1979).

Accordingly we have sought methods which, though limited in theory, work well for the kinds of taxonomies we are actually able to construct. In particular, the following is a simple type checking scheme we have implemented.   The

---

[21]We would like to interpret types related by $\S$ as <u>necessarily</u> incompatible, <u>necessarily</u> subordinate to the head type, but <u>not</u> <u>necessarily</u> jointly exhaustive (only as a matter of fact). Thus [ape $\S$ gibbon orangutan chimpanzee gorilla] is true, even though there are conceivable types of apes coinciding with none of the four actual types. However, we will not be concerned with modal logic herein.

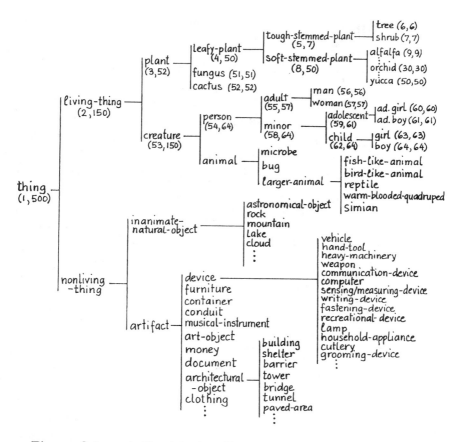

Figure 9-1: A Partitioning Hierarchy for Physical Objects.

Each vertical bar corresponds to a partitioning of a type of
object into subtypes; for example, [living-thing § plant
creature]. Some of the 'number brackets' based on preorder
numbering of the hierarchy are shown. These allow
determination of subordination and exclusion relationships in
constant time. For example, "orchid" is subordinate to "plant"
since (30,30) is included in (3,52), and incompatible with
"person" since (30,30) and (54,64) are disjoint.

partitioning graph for types is first decomposed into a set of
partitioning hierarchies. The hierarchies are allowed to intersect,
but each type concept is assumed to participate in just a few
of them. This assumption is based on attempts to sketch

taxonomies of physical objects, virtual objects (shadows, rainbows, reflections, ...), regions (borders, interiors, holes, ...), substances, events, perceptual/conceptual entities (thoughts, fears, pains, ...), symbolic/linguistic entities (words, musical scores, equations, ...), socio-political entities (families, committees, nations, ...), and a few other 'ontological categories'. In the case of physical objects (Figure 9-1), we can see no reason for having more than one major hierarchy, but in the case of substances, for example, we can construct two alternative, equally natural hierarchies, based respectively on naively scientific criteria (for example, plant substance versus animal substance), and on the 'normal states' of substances (for example, solid versus fluid) (Figure 9-2). The hierarchies intersect at the level of specific substances (leaf nodes), although we have drawn them separately and omitted much of their lower-level structure for the sake of clarity. It is perhaps possible to classify substances in still another way, namely according to their normal role or use (for example, foods, solvents, building materials, explosives, etc.), but beyond that, there seem to be few plausible alternatives.

Each concept has attached to it a short list of hierarchy indicators, where each hierarchy indicator consists of an identifier for a hierarchy to which the concept belongs along with the concept's 'number bracket' relative to that hierarchy. The number bracket consists of the preorder number of the node and the maximal preorder number among its descendants in the hierarchy (refer again to Figure 9-1). It is easy to show that if one node is an ancestor of another, its number bracket (regarded as an interval) contains that of the other. If neither is an ancestor of the other, the number brackets are disjoint.[22]

---

[22]See, for example, (Aho, Hopcroft, and Ullman, 1983) for a discussion of preorder traversal of trees. An alternative scheme is to number leaf nodes left-to-right, and to label non-leaf nodes with the minimal and maximal leaf numbers they dominate. The advantage of preorder numbering is that each terminal and non-terminal node is indexable by a single number. For sufficiently small hierarchies with bounded fanout one could also use bit string representations of nodes (for example, x0000, x0001, x0010, ... for the successors of a node x), with the advantage that lowest common ancestors could be easily determined.

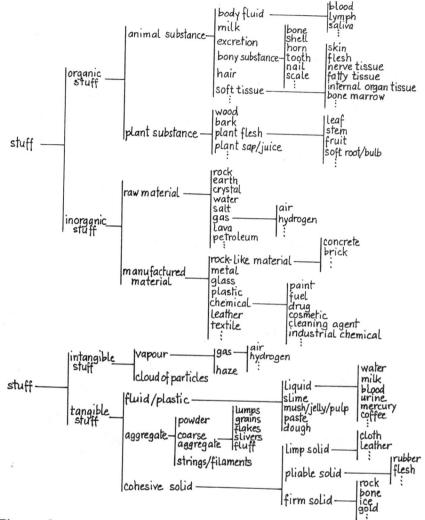

Figure 9-2:   Alternative Partitioning Hierarchies for Substances.

The first is based on 'naively scientific' criteria, and the second on 'normal states' of substances. A third hierarchy based on 'uses or roles' of substances could be added.

Thus, given two concepts, their relationship can be checked by scanning their lists of hierarchy indicators for a common hierarchy identifier, and if one is found, checking whether either of the corresponding number brackets includes the other. If yes, then one concept is superordinate to the other and if no, they are incompatible. If no common hierarchy is found, the result of the check is "unknown relationship". This is a constant-time operation if lists of hierarchy indicators contain just a few elements in most cases, as we have assumed.

This algorithm is very fast, and unlike some of the more ad hoc graphical methods makes provably sound decisions. However, like those methods it is incomplete. Consider for example the "body fluid" node and the "liquid" node in the first and second hierarchies of Figure 9-2 respectively. If we imagine both hierarchies to be completed so that they terminate within a common set of leaf nodes (the lowest-level substance types), then the set of leaves reachable from "body fluid" will presumably be a subset of the set of leaves reachable from "liquid". Thus a 'smart' algorithm could pronounce "body fluid" subordinate to "liquid", whereas ours returns "unknown relationship".

In the next section we sketch such 'smart' algorithms for parts graphs (which are much like type graphs), but for type compatibility checking our present method may be adequate. The reason lies in the fact that the general inference algorithm is not dependent on the §-graph algorithm <u>alone</u> for its type information. For example, the fact that concept A is a special case of concept B will presumably be available as an assertion indexed under the "generalization" topic for A, even though no §-assertion links the two concepts. Such assertions allow the <u>general</u> inference algorithm to make up for the gaps in the graph algorithm. The point is that the special graphical methods are intended only to <u>accelerate</u> the general inference algorithm at the core of the system, not to supplant it. In this respect our design philosophy differs from that in systems like KL-TWO, in which a logically weak (but computationally efficient) core is augmented with specialized extensions, such as a terminological component, to meet the needs of intended applications (Vilain, 1985).

9.3. Recognizing part-of relationships

Suppose that the on-board computer of a manned spacecraft has detected a valve failure. Question: is the valve part of the life support system? In a reasoning system entirely dependent on general rules of inference, this might be difficult to answer. For a positive answer, an inference chain which progresses from part to superordinate part may have to be constructed, and if the inference mechanism treats part-of assertions like all others, this may involve a good deal of combinatorial searching. Indeed, not only sets of superordinate assertions forming such chains need to be explored in general; for, as we shall see shortly, a part-of relation may be implicit in a collection of assertions about parts structure even though no such chain exists.

The part-of structure of an object can be represented in essentially the same way as a taxonomy of concept types. We introduce an object partitioning relation P, with

$$[x \ P \ x_1 \ ... \ x_k]$$

expressing that object x is (exhaustively) partitioned into parts $x_1, \ ..., \ x_k$. If we simply want to assert that x has a part y, we can do so by writing

$$[x \ P \ y \ z],$$

where z is possibly the empty part.

Figure 9-3 shows a partial human anatomy, naively conceived, in the form of a P-graph. It subdivides the body into head, neck, trunk and limbs (enumerated separately) and also specifies a skeleton as part of the body, subdivided into skull, spine, ribcage, pelvis and the bones of the four limbs. Also, note that each division of the skeleton is linked to its appropriate body segment.[23]

The algorithms sketched for type graphs could be used here to determine the truth values of such formulas as

```
[cranium-of-John part-of head-of-John] or
[trachea-of-John part-of bowel-of-John],
```

assuming that a sufficiently complete P-graph had previously been established for John. (The assumption would be more

---

[23]The figure glosses over some logical niceties concerning the interpretation of <u>generic</u> nodes such as "pelvis" and "left-leg".

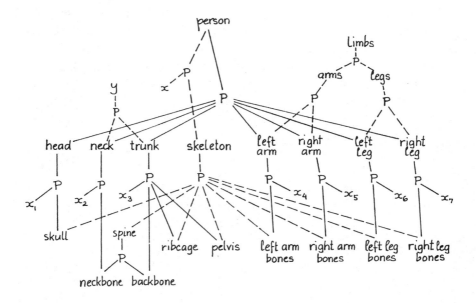

Figure 9-3:   The Upper Levels of a Partitioning Graph
for the Human Body.

Each P-token represents a partitioning assertion dividing the
node to which it is linked above into the nodes to which it
is linked below. The solid lines define a partitioning
hierarchy, and the broken lines define three additional,
superimposed hierarchies.

plausible for an object whose structure is unique, such as a
country. For uniformly structured objects like people the
algorithms could serve to evaluate more general formulas, such
as

    [(s x) part-of x]

where s is a function which, for any person x, picks out x's skull, that is,

$$\forall x[[x \text{ person}] \Rightarrow [(s \ x) \text{ skull-of } x]].)$$

Similarly the algorithms could be used to detect the incompatibility of pairs of formulas such as

```
[x pelvis-of John] and
[x left-leg-of John].
```

Additional types of generalized resolving facilitated by partitioning graphs are mentioned in section 9.6.

   This would short-circuit many proofs, but would also fail to short-circuit many others. Consider, for example, the question "Is the spine part of y?", where y is the combination of trunk and neck, as specified in the graph. This question is similar to the question about the malfunctioning spacecraft valve, and poses just the sort of problem we alluded to. The response would be "unknown", since "spine" and y do not lie in a common hierarchy; yet the graph certainly allows the inference that the spine is part of y, since there is a P-assertion which divides the spine exhaustively into neckbone (cervical vertebrae) and backbone, and these have upward paths to y. Similarly, the question may be asked whether the spine is part of the limbs, and again the response would be "unknown" since "spine" and "limbs" lie in no common hierarchy; yet a negative answer can be deduced from the graph, as the reader can verify.

   A realistic human anatomy would, of course, be far more complicated, particularly if it delineated not only structurally or geometrically well-defined parts, but also the functionally cohesive subsystems, such as the digestive system, cardiovascular system, nervous system, and so on. The interplay of structural and functional views would lead to further 'tangling' of subhierarchies of the sort already evident in Figure 9-3.

   The complexity of parts graphs in comparison with type graphs has led us to seek more powerful methods for them. In view of the "P=NP?" obstacle to the discovery of efficient methods for unrestricted graphs, we have sought to define classes of graphs allowing greater structural freedom than strict hierarchies, yet amenable to fast, complete inference. One such class is the class of <u>closed</u> graphs. Roughly, a closed graph consists of at least one main hierarchy, along with any number of additional hierarchies such that all downward paths from nodes of these hierarchies terminate at leaves of the main hierarchy. Nodes are subdivided into those which are known to denote nonempty parts and those which are potentially empty 'remainder' parts. (It is the possibility of empty parts which makes the generalization from hierarchies to closed graphs nontrivial.)

The graph of Figure 9-3 very nearly satisfies the requirements for closed graphs. The solid lines define the main hierarchy, while the broken lines define additional superimposed hierarchies. Note that all downward paths terminate at leaves of the main hierarchy, save one: the (null) path from x ends at a leaf node, namely x, not belonging to the main hierarchy. Since x intuitively represents the soft tissue of the body (that is, body minus skeleton) and x1 represents the soft tissue of the head, x2 the soft tissue of the neck, and so on, the graph could easily be closed by adding the P-assertion

[x P x1 x2...x7].

Closed P-graphs appear to provide much of the flexibility required for representing part-of structures, yet permit reasonably efficient, complete inference of part-of and disjointness relationships. For nodes which do not lie in the main hierarchy, the inference algorithms work by 'projecting' these nodes into the main hierarchy (or some other common hierarchy). For example, in Figure 9-3 the projection of "spine" into the main hierarchy is the set of nodes S = {neckbone, backbone}, for y it is Y = {neck, trunk}, and for "limbs" it is L = {left arm, right arm, left leg, right leg}. The algorithm for checking "part-of" would conclude that "spine" is part of y since all members of S have ancestors in Y. The algorithm for checking disjointness would conclude that "spine" is disjoint from "limbs", since the members of S have no ancestors in L, and vice versa (for details see (Schubert, 1979)).

While these methods require linear time in the worst case, it is clear that nearly constant expected time is assured if the graph can be decomposed into hierarchies such that no node belongs to more than a few hierarchies and the nodes being compared usually belong to a common hierarchy. Under these conditions separate preorder numbering of the component hierarchies can be used much as in the case of type hierarchies; the main refinement is that projection into the main hierarchy (or into some other common hierarchy) is tried as a last-ditch strategy before an "unknown" response is given.

The restrictions on P-graphs can be relaxed still further without running into the "P=NP?" problem. In particular, we can define a <u>semi-closed</u> P-graph as one which is either a closed P-graph, or a semi-closed P-graph with another semi-closed P-graph attached to it by one of its main roots. Intuitively, such graphs allow for 'entirely unrelated' partitionings of the same entity. Complete and reasonably efficient inference algorithms for such graphs are given in (Papalaskaris and Schubert, 1981), and proved correct in (Papalaskaris, 1982).

9.4. Recognizing colour relationships

Imagine a witness to a bank robbery being questioned about the colour of the get-away car. His impression was that the car was tan, and he is asked "Was the car brown?". Clearly the answer should be affirmative (for example, "Yes, tan"), and this answer could easily be deduced from

```
10. [c tan],
11. ∀x[[x tan] => [x brown]].
```

If the question had instead been "Was the car maroon?", a negative answer could have been inferred from 10, 11,

```
12. ∀x[[x maroon] => [x red]],    and
13. ∀x[[x red] => ~[x brown]]
```

in four proof steps.

These examples follow the pattern of the type and part-of inferences exactly, and suggest that some sort of colour hierarchy or graph should be used to eliminate searching. In fact, the 11 basic colour terms of English could be introduced via the type partitioning

14. [coloured § red orange yellow green blue purple
pink white black grey brown],[24]

and 11 could be reformulated as something like

15. [brown § tan rust midbrown chocolate ...],

and similarly for 12, allowing either of the above questions to be answered by simple hierarchy methods.

However, a series of complications has led us away from graphical methods towards geometric methods. First, partitionings like 15 are inaccurate since shades like tan, midbrown, and chocolate probably overlap. More accurate characterizations require partitioning these shades into overlap and non-overlap parts. Shades like turquoise and lime, which straddle boundaries between basic colours would also have to be subdivided, adding to the proliferation of partitionings. Second, when we attempted to deal with 'hedged' colour relations, such as the statement that lime is sort of yellow and also sort of green, we realized that the colour partitioning graph would at least have to be augmented with adjacency and/or apart-from relations (see below). But even these additions would leave us totally unequipped to deal with other kinds of colour properties and relationships, such as lightness, purity, saturation, complementarity, and the warm/cool distinction. Geometric representations, on the other hand, offered a handle on all of these problems. If colours could be represented as simple regions in some colour space, all their properties and relationships could be 'read off' their parametric representations.

With this objective in mind, we undertook a search for a structurally simple and theoretically complete colour space. We were at first drawn to representations of colours in terms of

---

[24]We regard it as a reasonable claim that every (uniform) colour is at least a marginal instance of one of these basic colours. The claim that no colour instantiates more than one of the basic colours can be defended as well. Suffice it to say that a question answering system could well hold 14 (and in particular the disjointness of colours 14 entails) to be true, yet avoid applying the basic colour terms to their marginal cases, for pragmatic reasons.

three 'orthogonal' primaries, partly because the human visual system employs three kinds of receptors selectively sensitive to different wavelengths (though their frequency response is rather broadband -- see (Kay, 1981)), and partly because a colour cube can be contrived so that it has some very pleasing regularities. (Our version had the six basic colours of the rainbow, along with black and white, at its eight corners.) However, colour cubes are deficient in two respects. First, they are theoretically incapable of representing all perceptually distinct shades of colour (see (Judd and Wyszecki, 1963); this may seem surprising, in view of the wide commercial use of three-colour schemes). In addition, the regions corresponding to the English colour terms are rather complex, obliquely bounded polyhedrons, making region comparison computationally awkward.

Our ultimate choice was a cylindrical representation, arrived at by imagining any colour to be composed of some amount of a pure, monochromatic colour, plus certain amounts of black and white. Thus one dimension runs through the continuum of rainbow hues, arranged in a circle and arbitrarily scaled from 0 to 12; the second (radial) dimension parameterizes the amount of black present as

$$\text{purity} = \text{pure colour}/(\text{pure colour} + \text{black}),$$

which decreases from 1 to 0 as black is added; and the third (axial) dimension parametrizes the amount of white present as

$$\text{dilution} = \text{white}/(\text{pure colour} + \text{black} + \text{white}),$$

which increases from 0 to 1 as white is added (see Figure 9-4).

This model is similar to certain models well-known to colour theorists, (Birren, 1969a), (Birren, 1969b), and like them covers the full range of perceptible shades.[25] It appears to be unique, however, in that it renders each English colour term simply as a region bounded by six coordinate surfaces (defined by three pairs of upper and lower bounds on hue, purity and

---

[25] The 'saturation' and 'lightness' parameters used in these models do not coincide with purity and dilution.

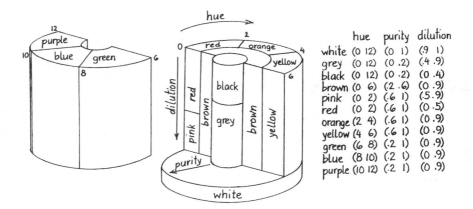

	hue	purity	dilution
white	(0 12)	(0 1)	(.9 1)
grey	(0 12)	(0 .2)	(.4 .9)
black	(0 12)	(0 .2)	(0 .4)
brown	(0 6)	(.2 .6)	(0 .9)
pink	(0 2)	(.6 1)	(.5 .9)
red	(0 2)	(.6 1)	(0 .5)
orange	(2 4)	(.6 1)	(0 .9)
yellow	(4 6)	(.6 1)	(0 .9)
green	(6 8)	(.2 1)	(0 .9)
blue	(8 10)	(.2 1)	(0 .9)
purple	(10 12)	(.2 1)	(0 .9)

Figure 9-4:   The eleven basic colours in a colour space.

The eleven basic colour in a (hue, purity, dilution) colour space (with the cool shades 'lifted away'). Purity decreases as black is added to a pure colour, and dilution increases as white is added to it.

Purity = pure colour/(pure colour + black),
Dilution = white/(pure colour + black + white).

The numerical values have been chosen on purely intuitive grounds. They could be quite drastically altered without affecting the results of the algorithms based on the model, as long as the region <u>adjacency</u> relationships are not changed.

dilution). In the other models we are aware of, the boundaries are more irregular.[26]

---

[26]Some adjustments to the simple regions of Figure 9-4 may be required. Perhaps part of the "brown" region separating "red" from "black" should be maroon or purple. We have attempted to investigate this point empirically using the colour graphics of a Jupiter terminal, but the range of available colours, impressive as it seemed at first, was insufficiently subtle to resolve the issue.

With this colour geometry it is possible to check any desired relationship between pairs of colour regions, such as inclusion, overlap, adjacency, and separation (apart-from) in a small, fixed number of comparisons. Moreover, it is easy to define non-basic terms such as turquoise, maroon, beige, scarlet, and so on, as regions bounded (like basic colour regions) by coordinate surfaces. Colour properties such as lightness, purity, etc., and relations such as complementarity are computable in fairly obvious ways.

Up to this point, we have tacitly assumed that the colour cylinder would contain explicit representations of all colours for which a compatibility check would ever be required. We can relax this assumption, allowing for the possibility that certain non-basic colours are understood only in terms of their qualitative relation to the basic colours. For example, turquoise might be said to be greenish-blue, or what amounts to roughly the same thing, both sort of blue and sort of green.

This calls for extension of our special methods, as is evident from the following variant of the 'robbery' example. Suppose the witness recalls the colour of the car as lime, and the questioner asks whether its colour was turquoise. The incompatibility of these descriptions is clear (though of course the accounts of different eye-witnesses can easily differ to this extent). Let us first see how the incompatibility could be detected by unaided deductive inference, the only knowledge about "lime" being that it is sort of yellow and sort of green and about "turquoise" that it is sort of green and sort of blue. The key to the proof of incompatibility is that nothing can be both sort of yellow and sort of blue, because yellow and blue are 'apart-from' each other (being separated by green):

```
16. [c lime]                                              known
17. ∀x[[x lime] => [x (sort-of yellow)]]                  known
18. [c (sort-of yellow)]                                  from 16,17
19. [c turquoise]                                         hypothesis
20. ∀x[[x turquoise] => [x (sort-of blue)]]               known
21. [c (sort-of blue)]                                    from 19,20
22. [yellow apart-from blue]                              known
23. ∀AB[∃x[[x (sort-of A)] & [x (sort-of B)]]
                   => ~[A apart-from B]]                  known
24. ∀x[~[x (sort-of yellow)] v
                   ~[x (sort-of blue)]]                   from 22,23
25. ~[c (sort-of blue)]                                   from 18,24
```

26. contradiction   from 21,25

The second-order features here are of no importance - they could be suppressed by treating colours as individuals related to objects via a relation "x has colour y". The apart-from' relation is stronger than mere incompatibility since it entails the existence of an intervening colour which separates the two colours. To see that mere incompatibility would be insufficient, consider the problem of checking "lime" and "olive green" (instead of "lime" and "turquoise") for compatibility. "Lime", we may say, entails "sort of yellow" and "sort of green", while "olive green" entails "sort of green" and "sort of brown". But since "yellow", "green" and "brown" are mutually adjacent colours, rather than being 'apart-from' each other, we cannot infer incompatibility on the basis of these entailments. (We may still be able to infer incompatibility in some other way, for example, on the basis of relative lightness or purity.)

We would like to replace inordinately long proofs like the above by methods which directly infer a contradiction from assertions like 18 and 21. In (Papalaskaris and Schubert, 1982) and (Papalaskaris, 1982) we describe a tabular addendum to the cylinder model which allows incompatibilities between pairs of hedged or unhedged, negated or unnegated colour predicates (like those in 18 & 21) to be detected without proof. If the colour predicates are A and B (assumed to be non-equivalent), the method consists of first classifying the relation between A and B as one of "apart", "adjacent", "overlapping" (with neither colour region including the other), "centre-included" (that is, inclusion without boundary contact), or "edge-included", using the colour cylinder. Then this classification, along with the hedging and sign information and the classification of A and B as basic or non-basic is used to judge incompatibility by table look-up. For example, ~A and B are judged incompatible just in case A is basic and B is (edge- or centre-) included in A; (thus ~brown and tan are incompatible); (sort-of A) and (sort-of B) are judged incompatible just in case A and B are apart; (thus sort-of yellow and sort-of blue are incompatible); ~A and (sort-of B) are judged incompatible just in case A is basic and B is centre-included in A; (thus ~red and sort-of scarlet are incompatible);

and ~(sort-of A) and (sort-of B) are judged incompatible just in case A is basic and A and B overlap or B is included in A: (thus ~(sort-of yellow) and lime are incompatible).

These judgements can be understood by interpreting "sort-of" as an operator which <u>expands</u> a colour region with coordinate bounds (x_i, y_i), $i \in \{1,2,3\}$, into one with coordinate bounds $(x_i - d, y_i + d)$, where $d = (y_i - x_i)/4$ (that is, each interval is expanded to one and one-half times its original size). Coordinate intervals for non-basic colours are assumed to be at most half as large as for basic colours. For a one-dimensional visualization of this account see (Papalaskaris, 1982).[27]

9.5. Recognizing time relationships

Did the first moonwalk by an astronaut precede the first space shuttle launch? Most people will be able to answer this question quickly and easily in the affirmative. The answer will perhaps be based on the feeling that the first moonwalk occurred many years ago, while the shuttle program only became operational in recent years. More details than that may be recalled, of course: that the Apollo 11 mission took place in 1969, and the first shuttle launch in 1981, for example, and perhaps even more specific dates. Clearly question answering systems knowledgeable about events will likewise have to be able to store and recall approximate or exact event times.

The ability to retain absolute time information is not enough, however, since people easily recall the time <u>order</u> of connected sequences of events even in the absence of such information. The point can be made by way of any familiar fairy-tale. Did Little Red Riding Hood meet anyone before arriving at her grandmother's cottage? The answer is "the wolf", of course. Now consider how this answer might be arrived at.

---

[27]In (Papalaskaris, 1982) d is in effect assumed to be $(y_i - x_i)/2$, so that interval sizes are doubled by "sort-of". This is probably excessive. For example, the "sort of yellow" region probably should not reach all the way to the centre of the "green" region; similarly, "sort of lime" and "sort of turquoise" probably should be "apart-from" each other, rather than adjacent.

One possibility is that the story is scanned' from the beginning
forward until both LRRH's encounter with the wolf and her
arrival at the cottage have been retrieved, in that order.
However, this does not seem very plausible psychologically, and
certainly would be a clumsy strategy computationally,
especially for long narratives. More likely, events which fit
the pattern "LRRH encounters character x" are recalled
associatively (and this is something that can be duplicated very
nicely with our concept-centred, topic-oriented retrieval
mechanism). Presumably, this will include not only the first
encounter with the wolf, but also the fateful second encounter,
as well as the ultimate encounters with the gamekeeper and
with grandmother. Similarly, LRRH's arrival at the cottage
would be retrieved associatively. The remaining problem is then
to sort out the pre-arrival encounters from the post-arrival
encounters.

Much as in the case of type, part-of, and colour
inference, special methods are needed here, so that the general
reasoning system will not lapse into combinatory search in
determining time order. Moreover, as before we would prefer
constant-time checks to linear searches of story lines. (In this
respect, we would like to improve on heuristic methods such as
those of (Kahn and Gorry, 1977)).

Partitioning graphs which partition time intervals, and in
which the left-to-right order of subintervals is interpreted as
their time order, are a possibility. We found that this
representation makes a mountain out of a molehill, however.
We have remarked before that the problem of extracting part-
of relationships from an arbitrary § or P-graph is intractable
unless P=NP. But the corresponding problem for time intervals
of determining whether one interval lies within another (given
positive, non-disjunctive time ordering information only) is
linearly solvable. All we have to do is to represent all time
intervals in terms of their beginning and end points, and insert
a directed arc for each pair of time points whose order is
known explicitly. The resultant graph is an acyclic digraph
(except for re-entrant time travel stories), and any ordering
relation implicit in it can be extracted by tracing from one
point to the other, a linear operation relative to the number of
edges of the graph.

Unfortunately, no methods are known for extracting ordering relationships from arbitrary acyclic digraphs in sublinear time without incurring non-linear storage cost. (However, see (Kameda, 1975) for a constant-time method for certain restricted kinds of planar acyclic digraphs.) Rather than investing effort in this research problem, which would have limited pay-off in any case given that we would also like to introduce absolute times and durations (or bounds thereon), we have proceeded pragmatically.

Roughly, the idea behind our scheme is to try to assign numeric values (pseudo-times, so to speak) to time points in their time order, when this order is known. To the extent that this is possible, the time order of two time points can be checked in constant time by comparing their pseudo-times.

Figure 9-5 (a) illustrates the kind of time graph determined by a narrative. Nodes denote time instants, and are numbered in the order of addition to the graph. Also the pseudo-times (which are incremented in steps of 1000 when not bounded above) are shown alongside the nodes. Typically narrative events correspond to pairs of time nodes, such as 1 & 2, 3 & 4, etc. Figure 9-5 (b) shows one possible sequence of event relationships which would give rise to the time graph of Figure 9-5 (a). The graph consists of a collection of time chains, each with its own pseudotime sequence. A time chain is a linear graph plus, possibly, transitive edges. Note that the link from node 3 to node 4 becomes a transitive edge of the initial time chain when nodes 9-13 are inserted. In the figure different node shapes are used for the different time chains; actually, this distinction is made by associating a metanode with each chain and maintaining a metagraph showing the interconnections between chains (shown as broken links). The metagraph for Figure 9-5 (a) is shown in Figure 9-5 (c).

As an example of the use of such a graph, suppose that the time order of nodes 7 and 16 is to be checked. Upon determination that 7 and 16 belong to different chains, the metagraph would be searched by a depth-first recursive algorithm to determine a valid path from 7 to 16 or 16 to 7. This would yield the cross-chain path which runs from the 'square' metanode to the 'round' metanode via link (8,3) and from there to the 'hexagonal' metanode via link (4,15). Since

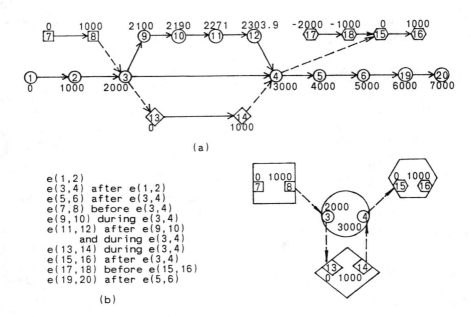

Figure 9-5:   Time graph for a narrative.

(a) Time graph for a narrative. The numbers within the nodes record the narrative sequence, that is, the order in which the nodes were added. The numbers beside the nodes are pseudo-times, used for checking time order within a time chain. The four distinct node shapes distinguish the four time chains in the graph. The link from node 3 to node 4 becomes a transitive edge of the original time chain when nodes 9-12 are inserted. The pseudo-times at nodes 9-12 progress in intervals equal to one tenth of the remaining pseudo-time interval (that is, 1/10 the pseudo-time at node 4 less the last-assigned pseudo-time).

(b) Possible sequence of event relationships giving rise to the graph in (a). Note that event e(11,12) is inserted so that it occurs both after e(9,10) and during e(3,4). This is actually the most common case in story understanding, since events are usually reported one after another, but within a pre-established time frame.

(c) Metagraph for the graph in (a). The large metanodes correspond to entire time chains and are connected by the 'cross-chain' links that occur in the time graph.

the pseudotime of node 7 is less than that of node 8, and the pseudotime of node 15 is less than that of node 16, the answer

"7 before 16" can be returned.

Obviously time-checks restricted to one chain require only one comparison, while the worst-case computation time for time checks across chains is proportional to the number of chain-to-chain connections. This number is typically much smaller than the total number of links in the time graph, as far as we can tell from sample time graphs for newspaper stories several paragraphs long, a fairy-tale (Little Red Riding Hood), excerpts from Hemingway's The Old Man and the Sea, and from a book of European history. Moreover, it appears that the temporal inference problems that arise in story understanding and question answering typically involve only nodes belonging to the same chain; this is because the causal connections of interest (which correlate with time order) are usually quite direct.

We have extended the time representation and algorithms to allow for upper and lower bounds on absolute node times and on arc durations, whenever these are available (Taugher, 1983); cf. (Allen and Kautz, 1985). Bounds on absolute node times are specified as 6-tuples of the form (year month day hour minute second). For example,

$$(1984\ 10\ d\ 12\ 0\ 0) \leqslant t \leqslant (1984\ 10\ d\ 13\ 0\ 0)$$

establishes some day d in October 1984, 12:00 noon, as a lower bound on t, and 1:00 pm of the same day as an upper bound. Note that unspecified constants are permissible in time bounds. Bounds are comparable if they are identical or have identical initial segments followed by distinct numbers. Upper and lower bounds on arc durations are uniformly specified in seconds (possibly fractional).

Optimal bounds on node times and arc durations are maintained by constraint propagation; in essence, upper bounds are propagated backward and lower bounds forward. The constraints used are inequalities relating the bounds associated with pairs of nodes connected by an arc. For example, if (l_1, u_1), (l_2, u_2) are the lower and upper bounds on nodes 1 and 2 respectively, and (l, u) the lower and upper bounds on the duration of the arc from 1 to 2, then the inequalities

$$l_2 - u \leqslant t_1 \leqslant u_2 - l$$

must be satisfied (among others).

The time graphs and associated algorithms provide a basis for fast computation of a wide variety of temporal properties and relationships of events, including time order, overlap, inclusion (during), duration, exact or approximate time of occurrence, and exact or approximate elapsed time between events; all of these are easily expressed in terms of the order of time points marking beginnings and ends of events, actual time bounds on these time points, and bounds on actual time intervals separating them.

We have tested the time-order algorithm (implemented in Pascal) on a set of time relations hand-extracted from "Little Red Riding Hood". The time graph consisted of 290 time points, with 21 metanodes and 33 cross-chain links. Question answering for the ordering of random pairs of time points required 30 milliseconds of CPU time on the average on a VAX 11/780. Randomly generated graphs gave very similar results, and showed the expected linear dependence on the size of the metagraph. (Details are provided in (Taugher and Schubert, 1986)).

It is interesting to compare our approach with that of Allen (Allen, 1983). Allen's interval-based representation is somewhat more flexible -- not because it is interval-based, but rather because it admits certain kinds of disjunctions, such as

e before or after e',

not expressible as conjunctions of time point relations. However, as Vilain & Kautz (Vilain and Kautz, 1986) show, the price paid for this extra flexibility is NP-hardness of temporal inference. Vilain & Kautz also note that when only a conjunction of relations using $<$, $\leqslant$, $=$, $\neq$, $\geqslant$, and $>$ over a set of n time points is allowed, determining the consistency of the conjunction is an $O(n^3)$ time, $O(n^2)$ space operation.

We find that these bounds can be reduced to $O(n^2)$ and $O(n)$ respectively when n is taken to be the number of relationships in the given conjunction, rather than the number of time points. Moreover, our own algorithms allow us to check the consistency of a conjunction of n relations based on $\leqslant$ in $O(mn)$ time and $O(n)$ space, by building up a time graph progressively, with a resultant metagraph of size m. For each relation, we check whether the current graph returns "yes", "no", or "unknown": in the first case, the relation is redundant, in the second it is inconsistent with those already present, and in the third it can be consistently added to the graph. As m may be quite small compared to n, our method can be significantly faster.[28]

9.6. Combining general and special methods

In motivating the special methods proposed above, we mentioned <u>literal evaluation</u> and <u>generalized resolution</u> as two ways in which special methods can be used to accelerate a general deduction algorithm. We will now spell out this interaction in a little more detail for a resolution-based system (like ours), and comment on generalized factoring, subsumption, and tautology elimination in such a setting.

As we have remarked, literal evaluation and generalized resolution are special cases of what Stickel (Stickel, 1983), (Stickel, 1985) calls "theory resolution". The idea in theory resolution is the following. Suppose that clauses c_1, c_2, ..., c_n respectively contain non-null subclauses c_1', c_2', ..., c_n' which are (collectively) inconsistent with some separately assumed theory (for example, a taxonomic theory consisting of assertions about the relationships between types). Then we can infer (c_1-c_1') v (c_2-c_2') v...v (c_n-c_n'). Actually, this describes <u>total</u> theory resolution; a more general version still, called <u>partial</u> theory resolution, allows unit clauses to be added to the clauses c_1', ..., c_n' to achieve inconsistency, the disjunction of whose negations must then be added to the resolvent as a <u>residue</u>. When the c_i' are unit clauses, theory resolution is said to be <u>narrow</u>.

Evaluation of a literal with result "false" can thus be viewed as narrow theory resolution with n=1, and generalized

---

[28]The fact that Vilain & Kautz permit additional relations (of which all but $\leqslant$ and $\neq$ are redundant) turns out to make no difference to the asymptotic upper bounds.

resolving as narrow theory resolution with n=2. It is clear that from this very general perspective, there can in principle be arbitrarily many special methods for any nontrivial domain, geared towards recognition and rapid elimination of arbitrarily complex sets of clauses c_1', ..., c_n'. (For any nontrivial theory there are, after all, arbitrarily complex sets of statements inconsistent with it.) Thus we cannot expect to provide an exhaustive enumeration of deductive shortcuts applicable in taxonomic, colour, or temporal reasoning, even if we confine ourselves to narrow theory resolution with $n \leqslant 2$. What we can do is to list more systematically the kinds of generalized resolving that 'fall out' naturally from the specialized representations we have proposed.

In connection with concept taxonomies, we illustrated two variant forms of generalized resolution. One depended on the incompatibility of two atoms (that is, predicates plus arguments) and the other on subordination of one atom by another (and hence incompatibility of the subordinate atom with the negation of the superordinate one). Incompatibility and subordination of atoms likewise are the key to generalized resolution in the other special domains, as well as to generalized factoring, subsumption testing, and tautology elimination.

In the case of atoms involving 2-place predicates such as "part-of", "skull-of" or "before", there are several ways in which incompatibility or subordination can arise. We can generally classify these ways as 'direct' and 'indirect', but the details depend on the particular predicates involved.

First, atoms can be 'directly' incompatible, or in a relation of subordination, as a result of their predicates being incompatible or in a relation of subordination. Examples are

[x skull-of y], [x spine-of y],

and

[x part-of y], [x skull-of y].

Such cases are analogous to examples involving 1-place predicates, such as "person" and "orchid", or "plant" and "orchid". Generalized resolution in such cases requires that both arguments of one atom be unified with the arguments of the other.

But in addition, incompatibility or subordination can arise 'implicitly' as a result of relationships between the arguments occurring in atoms. For example,

$$[x \text{ part-of } c], [x \text{ part-of } c']$$

are incompatible (despite the identity of their predicates) if x is known to be nonempty and c and c' are known to be disjoint parts (that is, if they lie on different branches of a parts hierarchy). Note that only the first arguments need to be unified in this case. Generalized resolving yields the residue $[x \text{ empty}]$, which reduces to the null clause if x is known to be nonempty. For the same pair of atoms, the first subordinates the second if c' is known to be part of c (that is, if c' is a descendant of c in a parts hierarchy). In this case the negation of the first atom 'resolves' against the second atom to yield the null clause.

Another case of indirect incompatibility is illustrated by the atoms

$$[x \text{ part-of } c], [c' \text{ part-of } x],$$

where c and c' are known to be disjoint parts. In this case the first argument of the first atom must be unified with the second argument of the second atom, and 'resolving' yields $[c' \text{ empty}]$.

An additional case of subordination is illustrated by the atoms

$$[c \text{ part-of } x], [c' \text{ part of } x],$$

where c' is known to be part of c. In this case the second arguments need to be unified, and the negation of the first atom 'resolves' against the second atom to yield the null clause.

For 2-place time relations between moments of time, there are somewhat fewer useful ways of generalizing resolution than in the case of part relations. First, the only cases of 'direct' incompatibility and subordination are trivial ones, not requiring a time graph, such as

$$[t \leq t'], [t \geq t'],$$

or

$$[t \leq t'], [t = t'].$$

In the first example, generalized resolving yields residue $[t = t']$, while in the second example, generalized resolving of the negation of the first atom against the second atom yields the null clause.

Second, there appear to be only 3 useful kinds of 'implicit' incompatibility or subordination. These are illustrated by the following pairs of atoms:

$$[t \leq c], [c' \leq t]$$

$$[c \leq t], [c' \leq t]$$

$$[t \leq c'], [t \leq c]$$

where in all 3 cases $[c \leq c']$ is presumed known (that is, obtainable from the time graph). In the first example, residue $t=c=c'$ can be inferred; in the second and third examples, the null clause is obtained from the negation of the first atom together with the second atom.

This completes our inventory of potentially useful kinds of generalized resolving facilitated by our special methods for parts and times. (About evaluation, and about generalized resolving for types and colours, we provided sufficient detail in earlier sections.) We wish to mention, finally, that just as resolving can be generalized based on recognizing incompatibility or subordination among atoms, so can factoring, subsumption testing, and tautology elimination. The following are examples of clauses and corresponding generalized factors, patterned on the above examples of generalized resolving:

```
[x animal] v [x wolf] .....................        [x animal]
¬[x person] v [x wolf] .................        ¬[x person]
¬[x skull—of y] v [x spine—of y] ...      ¬[x skull—of y]
[x part—of y] v [x skull—of y] .........       [x part—of y]
¬[x part—of c] v [x part—of c'],
    where c, c' are disjoint ..      ¬[x part—of c] v [x empty]
[c part—of x] v [c' part—of x],
    where c' is part of c ...........        [c' part—of x]
```

When $c \leq c'$:

$$\begin{array}{l} \neg[t \leqslant c] \vee [c' \leqslant t] . . \neg[t \leqslant c] \vee [t=c] \quad (i.e., \quad [c \leqslant t]) \\ [c \leqslant t] \vee [c' \leqslant t] \quad \ldots \ldots \ldots \quad [c \leqslant t] \\ [t \leqslant c'] \vee [t \leqslant c] \quad \ldots \ldots \ldots \quad [t \leqslant c'] \end{array}$$

Subsumed literals and tautologous disjunctive pairs of literals follow similar patterns. For example,

$$[x \; wolf] \; \text{subsumes} \; [x \; animal]$$

and

$$\neg[x \; wolf] \vee [x \; animal]$$

is tautologous (in a generalized sense). We leave further details to the reader, but should remark that elimination of a clause one of whose literals evaluates to "true" is tantamount to subsumed clause elimination. For example, eliminating a clause containing [c animal], where c is known to be a wolf, amounts to eliminating a clause subsumed by [c wolf].

In short, then, the special methods we have described provide a basis for constant-time or near constant-time simplification and generalized resolution, factoring, subsumption testing and tautology elimination in the taxonomic, colour, and temporal domains.

9.7. Concluding remarks

We have shown that much combinatory reasoning in a question answering system can be short-circuited by the use of special graphical and geometrical methods.

The domains we have considered -- types, parts, colours and times -- do not quite exhaust those for which special methods seem essential. In particular, part-of relationships are only one aspect of the structure of physical (and other) systems, and more powerful modelling methods are needed for rapid inference of static and dynamic relationships. For example, people intuitively sense the 'faulty physics' in

He put a bunch of roses in the wine glass,

perceiving with their 'mind's eye' that the roses won't stay put (whereas violets might). A good deal has been written on whether image-like representations are psychologically real and theoretically necessary, but that is not at issue here (see Chapter 15, this volume, for more on this). What is at issue is computational efficacy, and it seems clear that the methods of symbolic logic, though no doubt capable in principle of predicting the behaviour of physical systems, need to be supplemented with special modelling methods in order to reach conclusions within reasonable times. The various expert systems incorporating models of toy blocks, electronic circuits, weight-and-pulley assemblies and so forth will point the way, although the often complex and deformable objects of the real world (like plants, coats, and people) may require methods different from those of the popular microworlds. If sufficiently powerful 'analog' models can be developed for physical objects, these may obviate the need for parts graphs such as our P-graphs, just as the colour cylinder obviated the need for colour §-graphs.

Beyond this, we do not foresee having to devise too many more special representations, as long as we are concerned with question answering of a general nature only, and not with expert consultation (for example, on programming, mathematics, or economic forecasting). In fact, even specialized expertise may often require no more than re-deployment of spatio-temporal modelling skills. For example, expertise in symbol manipulation (as required for symbolic logic, mathematics, and programming) may well rest in part on spatio-temporal visualization, and in part on linguistic skills (parsing, pattern matching) which are of course presupposed in a question answering system.

10. Knowledge Organization and Its Role in Temporal and Causal Signal Understanding: The ALVEN and CAA Projects

John K. Tsotsos
Tetsutaro Shibahara

Department of Computer Science
10 King's College Rd.,
University of Toronto,
Toronto, Ontario, Canada M5S 1A4

Abstract

This paper describes the ALVEN and CAA projects. These projects share many basic concepts particularly with respect to the representation of knowledge and to the hypothesize and test nature of the control strategy. They both deal with temporally rich data interpretation tasks. However, they focus on very different aspects of interpretation. ALVEN processes images of a time-varying sequence in a real-time fashion (although not in real time), while CAA considers an entire signal, as if time were a second spatial dimension. ALVEN deals with the assessment of the performance of the human left ventricle from an X-ray image sequence, while CAA considers the causal relationships of the electrophysiology of the human heart and the resulting electrocardiogram signal, and tries to detect and classify anomalies of rhythm. The contributions of these works lie in the elucidation of a representation and control structure for the knowledge-based interpretation of time-varying signals.

Based on the paper, Building Knowledge-Based Systems,
J. Mylopoulos, T. Shibahara, and J. Tsotsos, appearing in COMPUTER,
Volume 16, Number 10, October, 1983.

10.1. Introduction

The development of the ALVEN and CAA systems represents a long-term research effort over the past ten years. The basic approach involves exploiting frame-based representations for interpretation. Frames are organized into a semantic network, and a control strategy has been developed that is driven by those organizational axes. ALVEN uses the generalization/specialization, aggregation/decomposition, similarity and temporal axes, while CAA adds a causal dimension to this set. The remainder of this paper will discuss several aspects of the two systems, with the bulk of the discussion devoted to the CAA system. Details on ALVEN have appeared in several previous publications (Tsotsos, 1984), (Tsotsos, 1985). All of the examples presented in section 10.2 are from the ALVEN system, and examples from the CAA system all appear in section 10.5. The discussions in sections 10.2 and 10.3 summarize features that the two systems have in common.

10.2. The representational scheme

10.2.1. Knowledge packages: classes

Packaging up knowledge leads to a modular representation, with all the advantages of modularity, particularly the enhancement of clarity and flexibility. Most knowledge package representation schemes borrow strongly from (Minsky, 1975). Our frames are called classes and borrow much from the Procedural Semantic Networks formalism (PSN) of (Levesque and Mylopoulos, 1979). A class provides a generalized definition of the components, attributes and relationships that must be confirmed of a particular concept under consideration in order to be able to make the deduction that the particular concept is an instance of the prototypical concept. Classes also have embedded, declarative control information, namely exceptions and similarity links. These features will be described shortly. Note that there is a distinction between the "prerequisites" of the class (those components that must be observed in order to instantiate the class) and the "dependents" of a class (those components that must be derived on instantiation). Dependent slots carry their own computation information. Classes exhibit large grain size, and translating their contents to rules would require many rules. An obvious advantage over the rule scheme is that elements that conceptually belong together are packaged together into a class, with some control information included. Other frame-based schemes for medical consultation systems include the MDX system (Chandrasekaran et al, 1979) and CADUCEUS (Pople, 1982).

10.2.2. Knowledge organization

When confronted with a large, complex task, "divide and conquer" is an obvious tactic. Task partitioning is crucial; however, arbitrary task sub-division will yield structures that are unwieldy, unnecessarily complex or inappropriately simple. Furthermore they have poorly defined semantics, lead to inefficient processing, and lack clarity and perspicuity. Within the existing representational repertoire, there exist two common tools for domain sub-division and organization, namely the IS-A relationship (or generalization/ specialization axis), and the PART-OF relationship (or the part/whole axis or aggregation/decomposition). (Brachman, 1979), (Levesque and Mylopoulos, 1979), (Brachman, 1982) provide discussions of their properties, semantics and use. The IS-A, or generalization/ specialization relationship, is included in order to control the level of specificity of concepts represented. IS-A provides for economy of representation by representing constraints only once, enforcing strict inheritance of constraints and structural components. It is a natural organizational scheme, and provides a partial ordering of knowledge concepts that is convenient for top-down search strategies. In conjunction with another representational construct, SIMILARITY, IS-A siblings may be implicitly partitioned into discriminatory sets. The PART-OF or aggregation relationship allows control of the level of resolution represented in knowledge packages and thus the knowledge granularity of the knowledge base. It provides for the implementation of a divide-and-conquer representational strategy, and it forms a partial ordering of knowledge concepts that is useful for both top-down and bottom-up search strategies. Concept structure can be represented using slots in a class definition. The slots form an implicit PART-OF relationship with the concept. Representational prototypes (classes) are distinguished from and related to tokens by the INSTANCE-OF relationship. Instances must reflect the structure of the class they are related to; however, partial instances are permitted in association with a set of exception instances, or the exception record, for that class. In addition, a third type of incomplete instance is permitted, namely the potential instance or hypothesis. This is basically a structure that conforms to the "skeleton" of the generic class, but that may have only a subset of slots filled, and has not achieved a certainty high enough to cause it to be an instance or partial instance. Details on the precise semantics of IS-A, PART-OF and INSTANCE-OF may be found in (Levesque and Mylopoulos, 1979).

10.2.3. Multi-dimensional levels of detail

The term "level of detail" seems to denote different things to different people. In most schemes, it is used to express problem decomposition only (Nilsson, 1971). We present two separate views of abstraction "level". These views are related to the fact that all concepts have both IS-A and PART-OF relationships with other concepts. Thus, the level of specificity of detail can be controlled by, or examined by traversing, the IS-A hierarchy, while the level of resolution of detail (decomposition in other schemes) is reflected in the PART-OF hierarchy. In (Patil et al, 1982), only the decomposition view of level is present, while in CADUCEUS, (Pople, 1982), it seems that the level of specificity is employed and level of resolution is restricted to causal connections. In (Wallis and Shortliffe, 1982) rule complexity is used, which may be likened to our view of level of resolution; however, its use is restricted to explanation.

10.2.4. Time

Several interacting mechanisms are available for the representation of temporal information. This multi-pronged approach differs from other schemes that embody a single type of construct for handling temporal information. The complexity of time necessitates several special mechanisms. Our approach differs from others (Allen, 1981), (Mead and Conway, 1980), in that we have been motivated by problems in signal analysis rather than in representing natural language temporal descriptions and their inherent ambiguity and vagueness. It is not clear, for example, what kind of control strategy can be employed along with Allen's scheme of temporal representation. Fagan (Fagan, 1980) is concerned with a temporal interpretation situation. However, there are a number of issues, primarily in control, that are not considered by his system, VM:

- using the rule-based approach, only a data-driven recognition scheme is incorporated, and thus, VM cannot instigate a search for temporally expected events;

- the handling of noise is not formalized, but is rather ad hoc;

- the complexity of temporal relationships among rules seems limited, and arbitrary groupings of temporal events and their recognition are not addressed;

- expectations in time are table-driven, and no distinction is made between them and default values or expected ranges. Expectations in ALVEN are computed from such information, but current context is taken into account as well, so that expectations are tailored for the task at hand;

- partial satisfiability of temporal event groupings cannot be handled.

In addition, Long and Russ also address the problem of time-dependent reasoning (Long and Russ, 1983). Their scheme is closer to Fagan's than to ours. The control is data-driven exclusively; we have already highlighted the deficiencies of this approach as a general reasoning scheme. Their representation of time, however, shares some similarities with ours in that both points and intervals are used, and special meaning is assigned to the variable "now".

A brief description of the representation of time used by ALVEN follows. A TIME_INTERVAL class is defined that contains three slots, namely, start time, end time and duration. This class can then be included in the structure of any other class and would define its temporal boundaries and uncertainty in those values. Using those slots, the relations before, after, during, etc., (similar to (Allen, 1981)) are provided. In constraint or default definition, sequences of values (or ranges of values) may be specified using an "at" operator, so that in effect a piecewise linear approximation to a time-varying function can be included. In this case, of course, constraint evaluation must occur at the proper point in time. Tokens of values such as volume or velocity for which use of this operator is appropriate, have two slots, one for the actual value and the other for the time instant at which that value is true. The time instant slot is a dependent slot whose value is set to the value of the special variable "now" (current time slice). Note that this kind of mechanism could easily be expanded if required to multi-dimensional functions.

Finally, arbitrary groupings of events can be represented. The set construct (which may be used for any type of class grouping, not only for events), specifies elements of a group, names the group as a slot, and has element selection criteria represented as constraints on the slot. (Patil et al, 1982) describe a version of temporal aggregation similar to ours, but do not seem to have a time-line along which selection of values can occur, nor do they distinguish between aggregations of events and sequences of measurements.

Since knowledge classes are organized using the IS-A and PART-OF relations, their temporality is as well. By constructing a PART-OF hierarchy of events, one implicitly changes the temporal resolution of knowledge classes (as long as simultaneous events are not the only ones considered). For example, suppose that the most primitive events occur with durations on the order of seconds. Then groupings of those may define events that occur with durations in the minute range, and then groupings of those again on the order of hours, and so on. Events whose durations are measured using months can be so built up. Yet, many kinds of events cannot be so decomposed, and there is no requirement that all events have such a complete decomposition. Those events however, are not left hanging, since they will also be related to others in the knowledge base via the IS-A relationship. The control scheme makes use of the temporal resolution with respect to sampling rates and convergence of certainties.

In the following examples, first the TIME_INTERVAL class is shown, followed by the class for the concept of SEQUENCE, followed by a constraint on volume of the left ventricle from the normal left ventricle class, showing the use of the "at" mechanism for both default and constraint definition.

example 1

```
class TIME_INTERVAL with
prerequisites
    st : TIME_V such that [st >= 0];
    et : TIME_V such that [et >= st];
dependents
    dur : TIME_V with dur ← et − st;
end $
```

example 2

```
class SEQUENCE is-a MOTION with
prerequisites
    motion_set : set of MOTION such that [
        for all m : (MOTION such that
            [m element-of motion_set])
          verify [
            m.subj = self.subj,
            ~find m1 : MOTION where [
            m1 element-of motion_set,
            (m1.time_int.st during m.time_int or
            m.time_int.st during m1.time_int) ],
```

```
        find m2 : MOTION where [
           m2 element-of motion_set,
           (m.time_int.st = m2.time_int.et or
           m2.time_int.st = m.time_int.et ) ] ] ,
        card(motion_set) > 1,
        strict_order_set(motion_set,time_int.st) ] ;

  dependents
     first_mot : MOTION with
        first_mot ← earliest_st(motion_set) ;
     last_mot : MOTION with
        last_mot ← latest_st(motion_set ;
     time_int : with time_int ←
        ( st of TIME_INTERVAL with st ←
        first_mot.time_int.st ,
        et of TIME_INTERVAL with et ← last_mot.time_et );

  end $
```

example 3

```
volume : VOLUME_V with
     volume ← (vol of VOLUME_V with
        vol ← (minaxis.length  now ) ** 3
        default(117  m.systole.time_int.st,
                 22  m.systole.time_int.et,
                 83  m.diastole.rapid_fill.time_int.et,
                100  m.diastole.diastasis.time_int.et,
                117  m.diastole.atrial_fill.time_int.et)
        such that [
     volume  m.diastole.time_int.et >= 97
        exception [TOO_LOW_EDV with volume ← volume ],
     volume  m.diastole.time_int.et <= 140
        exception [TOO_HIGH_EDV with volume ← volume ],
     volume  m.systole.time_int.et >= 20
        exception [TOO_LOW_ESV with volume ← volume],
     volume  m.systole.time_int.et <= 27
        exception [TOO_HIGH_ESV with volume ← volume] ] ,
     time_inst of VOLUME_V with time_inst ← now ) ;
```

10.2.5. Exceptions and similarity relations

The recording of exceptions to slot filling and constraint matching has proven to be valuable. Exceptions are classes in their own right, with slots to be filled on instantiation, that is, when raised. Each slot constraint (or group of constraints) of a class may have an associated exception clause. This clause names the type of exception that would be raised on matching failure, and provides a definition for filling the exception's slots, since these slot fillers identify the context within which the exception occurred and play an important role in the determination of the action to take on the exception. Each slot has an implicit exception associated with it for cases where a slot filler cannot be found. Exceptions are used in two ways: 1) to record the matching failures of current hypotheses, recording the failures of the reasoning process; and 2) to assist in directing system attention to other, perhaps more viable, hypotheses. The prototypical exception class is shown below along with one of its specializations, followed by an example from a stroke volume slot. Other examples have already appeared.

example 1

```
class EXCEPTION with
dependents
   subj : PHYS_OBJ ;
   time_int : TIME_INTERVAL ;
   source_type : CLASS ;
   source_id : INTEGER ;
end $
```

example 2

```
class TOO_MUCH_MOTION is-a EXCEPTION with
dependents
   seg : STRING ;
   disp : LENGTH_VAL with disp ←
            (len of LENGTH_VAL with
        len ← dist(subj.centroid ⊕ source_id.time_int.st,
               subj.centroid  source_id.time_int.et ) ,
        time_inst of LENGTH_VAL with time_inst ← now) ;
end $
```

example 3

```
stroke_vol : VOLUME_V with
         stroke_vol ← (vol of VOLUME_V with
            vol ← self.volume  m.diastole.time_int.et −
                          self.volume
      ⊕ m.systole.time_int.et
               default(95) such that [
```

```
vol >= 70
    exception [LOW_STROKE_VOLUME with
        volume  <-  vol ],
vol <= 120
    exception [HIGH_STROKE_VOLUME with
        volume  <-  vol ]  ] ,
time_inst of VOLUME_V with time_inst  <-  now) ;
```

Similarity measures that can be used to assist in the selection of other relevant hypotheses on hypothesis matching failure are useful in the control of growth of the hypothesis space. These measures usually relate classes that together comprise a discriminatory set, that is, only one of them can be instantiated at any one time. As such, they relate classes that are at the same level of specificity of the IS-A hierarchy, and that have the same IS-A parent classes. Similarity links are components of the frame scheme of (Minsky, 1975), and a realization of SIMILARITY links as an exception-handling mechanism is presented in (Tsotsos et al, 1980) based on a representation of the common and differing portions between two classes. This view is contrasted with the sets of competitors described for the ABEL system (Patil et al, 1982). In that formulation, the level of specificity of the competing set is not represented. Similarity links enable explicit discussion of class comparisons, not only between the connected classes, but also by traversals of several links (Gershon, 1982). Thus, they are an element of embedded declarative control, and add a different view of class representation, thereby enhancing redundancy of the representation. The three major components of a SIMILARITY link are the list of target classes (given first), the "similarities" expression,[29] and finally the "differences" expression, the time-course of exceptions that would be raised through inter-slot constraints of the source

---

[29] A similarities expression indicates the important common portions between the source and target classes - during interpretation, the target classes are not active when the SIMILARITY link is being evaluated. Thus, in time-dependent reasoning situations, the components of the target class that are the same as in the source class before activation of the SIMILARITY link, or that the source class may not care about that have already 'passed in time', can be verified using the similarities expression.

class or in parts of the source class.   There is an implicit conjunction of the differences in the exception record, while the similarities form a disjunction.   Many SIMILARITY links will be shown in subsequent examples.

10.2.6. Partial results and levels of description

Partial instances are permitted with an accompanying exception record.   More importantly, since instance tokens are produced for each verified hypothesis, and since hypotheses maintain the organization exhibited by the classes that they are formed from, interpretation results also exhibit the same structure.   That is, there are levels of description that may examined as appropriate by a user.

It is important to realize that the instantiation of a hypothesis is achieved only when its certainty has reached a threshold value.   (The thresholds are not set in an ad hoc fashion, but rather depend on a number of factors relating to the context of interpretation and knowledge structure - see (Tsotsos, 1984) for details).   Thus, even though not all components of a hypothesis have been verified, instantiation may still take place if that hypothesis has significantly more successes than its competitors over the same time period.   This would then create a partial instance, including the verified components, the final certainty, and a set of exception records specifying what was not observed.

10.3. The interpretation control structure

ALVEN and CAA employ hypothesize-and-test as the basic recognition paradigm.   The activation of a hypothesis sets up an internal goal that the class from which the hypothesis was formed tries to verify itself.   However, activation of hypotheses proceeds along each of five dimensions concurrently, and hypotheses are considered in parallel rather than sequentially.   These dimensions are the same class organization axes that are described above.   Specifically, we define: **goal-directed** search to be movement from general to specialized classes along the IS-A dimension, the goal being to find the appropriate sub-class definition for the data in question; **model-directed** search to be movement from aggregate to component classes along the PART-OF dimension; **temporal** search to be a specific form of model-directed search in that a temporal ordering among components controls the time of activation; **failure-directed** search to be movement along the SIMILARITY dimension; and **data-directed** search to be movement from components to aggregates of components upwards along the PART-OF dimension. For a given set of input data, in a single time slice, activation is terminated when none of the activation mechanisms can identify an un-activated viable hypothesis. Termination is guaranteed by virtue of the finite size of the knowledge and the explicit prevention of re-activation of already active hypotheses. The activation of one hypothesis has implications for other hypotheses as well, as will be described below. Because of the multi-dimensional nature of hypothesis activation, the "focus" of the system also exhibits levels of attention. That is, in its examination, the focus can be stated according to desired level of specificity or resolution (the two are related), discrimination set, or temporal slice. The control structure is illustrated in Figure 10-1.

Each newly activated hypothesis is recorded in a structure that is similar to the class whose instance it has hypothesized. This structure includes the class slots awaiting fillers, the relationships that the hypothesis has with other hypotheses, and an initial certainty value determined by sharing the certainty with the hypothesis that activates the new hypothesis.

In other aspects, the systems differ and these differences are highlighted in upcoming sections of this paper.

10.4. The ALVEN project

10.4.1. Overview

The ALVEN project was an experiment in the design of a framework for the integration of time into high level (attentive) vision. The key elements are an organization of knowledge along several axes, including time; several search modes facilitated by the knowledge organization; a hypothesize-

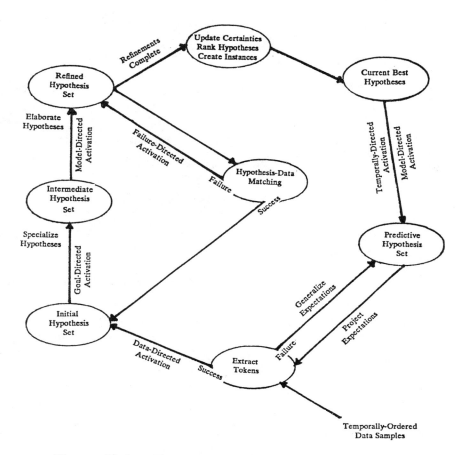

Figure 10-1:   The Interpretation Control Structure.

and-test reasoning framework; and a temporal cooperative process, driven by the knowledge organization, for hypothesis ranking. The major aspects of the cooperative process, namely, the definition of consistency, process neighbourhoods, initial certainties, compatibility factors, are all defined in terms of the knowledge organization. Iterations are tied to temporal measurements, and this allows temporal sampling to be discussed quantitatively. A qualitative analysis that includes hypothesis response rise and fall times is presented in addition to guidelines for setting compatibilities such that performance is appropriate. The scheme subsumes previous relaxation methods in that iterations are performed in time for either dynamic or static situations, and because the structure over which the cooperative process operates is allowed to change with time. It is further shown that the dimensions of knowledge organization, IS-A, PART-OF, SIMILARITY and Temporal Precedence, have uses far beyond their desirable structuring and access properties, and that they play important other roles in a knowledge based interpretation scheme. The application domain was chosen because of its rich temporal nature.

The evaluation of left ventricular (LV) performance by computer from cine representations of LV dynamics is a difficult and long-studied problem. A large number of heuristics have been proposed for measuring shape changes (Brower and Meester, 1981), following anatomical landmarks (Slager, 1979), computing segmental volume contributions (for a comparison, see (Gerbrands et al, 1979)), etc., all performing with varying degrees of success, but being applied independently of each other. Although such heuristics are indeed valuable quantitative measures, we propose that their limited performance is due to two key considerations: 1) it is unlikely, given the complexity of the domain of LV dynamics and the amount of training that a clinical specialist in this area receives, that any single heuristic can capture all the important facets of the evaluation and be successful in all applications; 2) the heuristics are purely quantitative in nature, contrasting with the fact that clinicians, and for that matter humans in general, deal in qualitative or descriptive terms combined with numerical quantities. That is, relational quantities are necessary components of the interpretation process, while numerical ones are secondary. The key here is that a computer system that is to solve the difficult problems present in the domain of LV dynamics interpretation must integrate the above mentioned numerical heuristics as well as consider the symbolic processing aspects of the interpretation. We distinguish our approach from those whose goal is to provide some intermediate visual representation that must still be subjectively interpreted by a clinician (the work described in (Hoehne et al, 1980) is a particularly good example of such a representation). Our goal is to perform this interpretation in much the same way as the clinician does, and to do it in an objective and consistent manner.

In (Aiello, 1983), three incarnations of the PUFF system were compared, each with the same knowledge, but different control schemes. The result of the comparison was that for PUFF's specific problem domain, expectation-driven (what is called model-driven below) was the best strategy, yet it too had drawbacks. Its analysis was strongly influenced by the initial hypothesis, was not able to recover from bad initial states, and moreover could not respond to all input data, only that which was required by the model. The control scheme of ALVEN does not rely on a single mechanism. We recognize that a single scheme may not be adequate for all situations, and thus several interacting dimensions are included. Specifically, our control scheme does not suffer from the above-mentioned drawback, because of its incorporation of model-driven, data-driven and lateral failure-driven search, reflecting traversals of the knowledge base along the IS-A, PART-OF or SIMILARITY dimensions.

Matching is defined as successful if all slots that should be considered for filling are filled and no matching exceptions are raised. Otherwise, the match is unsuccessful. Using this binary categorization of matching, and the relationships amongst hypotheses, a certainty updating scheme based on relaxation processes (Zucker, 1978) is used. Details of this scheme appear in (Tsotsos, 1984), and the definition of temporal relaxation is considered as one of the major contributions of the ALVEN project. Basically, hypotheses that are connected by knowledge organizational relationships that imply consistency support one another, and those linked by relationships that imply inconsistency compete with one another by removing support. The IS-A relationship is in the former group, while the SIMILARITY relationship is in the latter group. The focus of the system is defined as the set of best hypotheses, at each level of specificity, for each set of structural components being considered in the given time slice. The focus, due to the slow change of certainties inherent in relaxation schemes, exhibits inertia, or procrastination, that is, it does not alter dramatically between certainty updates. Both global and local consistency is enforced through the contributions of hypotheses to one another via their organizational relationships.

Examples of the ALVEN system have appeared previously and thus will not be repeated here (Tsotsos, 1985). The results were very satisfactory. Each analysis produced by ALVEN was completely consistent with the reports that radiologists produce for those films. The major difference is in detail. ALVEN produces very detailed descriptions at a number of levels of abstraction. The information that is produced is beyond the capability of analysis by human observation. Moreover, it seems that most of the quantities computed are beyond the capability of the science of cardiology to incorporate into routine patient care. It is encouraging that we can make predictions for quantities and analyses that may also advance the state-of-the-art of heart patient care.

10.4.2. LV dynamics knowledge and its representation

Although there is still much work to be done in the determination of the knowledge of LV dynamics, much can be found in current literature which can be incorporated into our formalism. Two examples will be given. This knowledge is used as a starting point for knowledge base construction only. Moreover, although the exact numerical quantities may differ between imaging techniques, the **qualitative** descriptions do not.

In the series of papers by Gibson and his colleagues, (for example (Doran et al, 1978), (Gibson et al, 1976)), several investigations were carried out that determined quantitative aspects of specific LV motions. In the second paper quoted, the segmental motions of the LV during isovolumic relaxation were examined in normal and ischemic LVs using echocardiography in order to determine dynamic differences between these two cases. Without describing technical details of their method, we will briefly summarize their findings. They discovered that in normal LVs an outward wall motion of 1.5 - 3.0 mm. could be present in any region during isovolumic relaxation. In abnormal cases, that is, patients with coronary artery disease, affected areas show inward motion, 2mm. or more for posterior or apical segments, and any at all for anterior regions, and non-affected areas, due to a compensatory mechanism, may exhibit an increased outward motion of up to 6mm. over normal. The key feature to note here is that the description given does not have a mathematical form at all - it is a combination of quantitative and qualitative measures. The term "outwards" does not specify any precise direction as long as the motion of the segment is away from the inside of the LV. It is not impossible to set up a mathematical model of this; however, the model will be both cumbersome and will bury the pertinent facts in its equations, so that inspection by a non-sophisticated user becomes impossible. The knowledge class for this information (and more) follows:

```
class N_ISORELAX is-a NO_VOLUME_CHANGE with
prerequisites
    subj : N_LV   such that [

            (find ant_mot : NO_TRANSLATION where [
                ant_mot.subj = self.subj.anterior ,
                ant_mot.time_int = self.time_int
                ]
            or
            find ant_mot : OUTWARD where [
                ant_mot.subj = self.subj ,
                ant_mot.time_int = self.time_int ,
                dist(ant_mot.subj.centroid
                    ❷ ant_mot.time_int.st,
                    ant_mot.subj.centroid
                    ❷ ant_mot.time_int.et) < 3
                exception [TOO_MUCH_MOTION with seg
                    ← "anterior" ,
                        direction ← "outward",
                    disp ← dist(ant_mot.subj.centroid
                    ❷ ant_mot.time_int.st,
                    ant_mot.subj.centroid
                    ❷ ant_mot.time_int.et) ]
                ]
            ) exception [TOO_MUCH_MOTION with seg ←
                "anterior", ❷ direction ← "inward"] ,

            (find post_mot : NO_TRANSLATION where [
                post_mot.subj = self.subj.posterior ,
                post_mot.time_int = self.time_int
                ]
            or
            find post_mot : INWARD where [
                post_mot.subj = self.subj ,
                post_mot.time_int = self.time_int ,
                dist(post_mot.subj.centroid
```

```
      ⊖ post_mot.time_int.st,
      post_mot.subj.centroid
      ⊖ post_mot.time_int.et) < 2
        exception [TOO_MUCH_MOTION with seg
          ← "posterior",
          direction ← "inward",
      disp ← dist(post_mot.subj.centroid
        ⊖ post_mot.time_int.st,
      post_mot.subj.centroid
        ⊖ post_mot.time_int.et) ]
  ]
  or
  find post_mot : OUTWARD where [
    post_mot.subj = self.subj ,
    post_mot.time_int = self.time_int ,
    dist(post_mot.subj.centroid
      ⊖ post_mot.time_int.st,
        post_mot.subj.centroid
          ⊖ post_mot.time_int.et) < 3
      exception [TOO_MUCH_MOTION with seg
        ← "posterior",
      direction ← "outward",
      dist(post_mot.subj.centroid
        ⊖ post_mot.time_int.et,
          post_mot.subj.centroid ]
            ⊖ post_mot.time_int.et) ] ]
) ,

(find ap_mot : NO_TRANSLATION where [
    ap_mot.subj = self.subj.apical ,
    ap_mot.time_int = self.time_int
    ]
  or
  find ap_mot : INWARD where [
    ap_mot.subj = self.subj ,
    ap_mot.time_int = self.time_int ,
    dist(ap_mot.subj.centroid
      ⊖ ap_mot.time_int.st,
        ap_mot.subj.centroid
          ⊖ ap_mot.time_int.et) < 2
        exception [TOO_MUCH_MOTION with seg
          ← "apical",
          direction ← "inward",
      disp ← dist(ap_mot.subj.centroid
        ⊖ ap_mot.time_int.st,
          ap_mot.subj.centroid
            ⊖ ap_mot.time_int.et) ]
    ]
  or
  find ap_mot : OUTWARD where [
    ap_mot.subj = self.subj ,
```

```
                    ap_mot.time_int = self.time_int
                    dist(ap_mot.subj.centroid
                      ⊖ ap_mot.time_int.st,
                        ap_mot.subj.centroid
                          ⊖ ap_mot.time_int.et) < 3
                      exception [TOO_MUCH_MOTION with seg
                        ←  "apical"
                        direction ←  "outward",
                        disp ←  dist(ap_mot.subj.centroid
                          ⊖ ap_mot.time_int.st,
                            ap_mot.subj.centroid
                              ⊖ ap_mot.time_int.et) ] ]
          )
        ] ;

dependents
    time_int :  with time_int ←  (dur of TIME_INTERVAL with
                    dur ←  default(0.093*(30/(0.8*HR)))  )
                such that [
                  time_int.st \(>= 0.24*(30/(0.8*HR)) ,
                  tim_int.et \(<= 0.43*(30/(0.8*HR)) ,
                  time_int.dur \(>= 0.08*(30/(0.8*HR)) ,
                  time_int.dur \(<= 0.12*(30/(0.8*HR))
                    exception [TOO_LONG_ISORELAX]
                  ] ;


similarity links

    sim_link1 : ISCH_AP_ISOVOL_RELAX
      for differences :
          d1 : TOO_MUCH_MOTION where [
                seg = "apical" ,
                direction = "inwards" ,
                time_int = ap_mot.time_int ];

          d2 : TOO_MUCH_MOTION where [
                seg = "anterior" ,
                direction = "outwards" ,
                disp < 9 ,
                time_int = ant_mot.time_int ];

          d3 : TOO_MUCH_MOTION  where [
                seg = "posterior" ,
                direction = "outwards" ,
                disp < 9 ,
                time_int = post_mot.time_int ]; ;


    sim_link2 : ISCH_ANT_ISOVOL_RELAX
      for differences :
```

```
        d1 : TOO_MUCH_MOTION where [
              seg = "anterior" ,
              direction = "inwards" ,
              time_int = ant_mot.time_int ];

        d2 : TOO_MUCH_MOTION where [
              seg = "apical" ,
              direction = "outwards" ,
              disp < 9 ,
              time_int = ap_mot.time_int ];
        d3 : TOO_MUCH_MOTION where [
              seg = "posterior" ,
              direction = "outwards" ,
              disp < 9 ,
              time_int = post_mot.time_int ]; ;

  sim_link3 : ISCH_POST_ISOVOL_RELAX
      for differences :
        d1 : TOO_MUCH_MOTION where [
              seg = "posterior" ,
              direction = "inwards" ,
              time_int = post_mot.time_int ];
        d2 : TOO_MUCH_MOTION where [
              seg = "anterior" ,
              direction = "outwards" ,
              disp < 9 ,
              time_int = ant_mot.time_int ];
        d3 : TOO_MUCH_MOTION where [
              seg = "apical" ,
              direction = "outwards" ,
              disp < 9 ,
              time_int = ap_mot.time_int ]; ;
```

The definition states that for a normal isovolumic relaxation phase to be recognized, normal motions for each segment must be present. There are three main clauses in the definition. The first defines the expected normal motion of the anterior segment, the second for the posterior segment and third for the remaining segment, the apical one. So for example, in the first clause, the definition reflects Gibson's characterization: the anterior segment during this phase, must either not display any translational movement, or could display an outward motion of displacement less than 3 mm. A larger displacement than this in the outwards direction would be recorded as the exception TOO_MUCH_MOTION, with specific additional contextual information recorded as well. In the matching of class definitions to actual observed motions, matching failures are recorded as exceptions. If the anterior segment were displaying motion and it were not outwards, then it must be inwards and this fact, too, would be recorded as an exception. The dependent portion specifies relevant timing information for the temporal placement of the phase within the left ventricular cycle. *HR* is in units of beats/sec. so that the right hand side of the timing expressions is in units of number of images. Also, using the information derived from (Gibson et al, 1976), the similarity links provide definitions of the constraints that must be found if a possible ischemic segment is to be recognized. Note that only the connections to possible ischemic states detectable by considering only the characteristics of the isovolumic relaxation phase, are included above; a set of similarly formed constraints would have to be present for other disease states as well, for those cases where the isovolumic relaxation phase plays a role in their definition. "sim_link2" relates the normal phase to the motion of an abnormal apical segment exhibiting the effects of ischemia. This, according to Gibson's definition, is shown by either the apical region itself having too much inward motion during this phase, and/or one of the other regions (posterior or anterior) exhibiting too much outward motion during the phase. Note that the set of differences does not define a necessary set; any one of the conditions is sufficient.

It should be clear that the above is not complete; it requires the remainder of the definitions for the other phases and motions since the entire definition of each class of LV motion is defined as a hierarchy of abstraction, each level adding more detail to the previous one. Some of the types of information that are represented are volume changes where known for normal phases, ejection fractions, for example; measures of degrees of abnormalities, derived heuristically; and others.

A second body of knowledge of the form necessary for interpretation can be found in (Fujii et al, 1979). In this research eight different clinical cardiac disease states have been investigated with the intent of discovering posterior wall motion differences and similarities among the diseases, as well as global LV characteristics. The diseases are pericarditis, congestive cardiomyopathy, hypertrophic cardiomyopathy, valvular aortic stenosis, aortic insufficiency, mitral stenosis, mitral insufficiency, and systemic hypertension. Normal LV's were also studied. The measurements made for each of the above LV states are stroke volume, rapid filling volume, slow filling volume, atrial filling volume, the percent filling for each of the previous three phases with respect to the stroke volume, posterior wall excursion in total, and for each of the three phases of diastole, as well as the percentage excursion in each phase, diastolic posterior wall velocity, rapid filling rate, LV end diastolic dimension, and ejection fraction. It is, of course, difficult to verify their results. However, they are important - they provide at least a starting point for the further elaboration and verification of such detailed dynamic information. In addition to the large amount of numerical information that has been derived, the significant findings have had attached to them qualitative descriptors - such as whether or not this quantity should be higher or lower than in the normal case. This is rather fortunate from our point of view: the representational formalism that we have designed can handle description via common components and differences very well, and uses such information to advantage during the decision phases of the interpretation. It should be clear from the previous example how such information would be included into the representation, and this fact alone raises another important advantage of this scheme. The addition of information into a mathematical model may require a complete re-definition of the model. In our case, information is easily inserted, as long as one understands the semantics of the representation.

10.5. The CAA project

10.5.1. Overview

The objective of the CAA (Causal Arrhythmia Analysis) system is to establish a framework for the recognition of time-varying vital signals of a complex repetetive nature, such as electrocardiograms (ECGs). The CAA system uses a causal model of the physiological entity so that observed abnormalities of the temporality or morphology of the signal are explained by referring to the corresponding abnormalities of causal events and relationships in the entity model.

In the domain of electrocardiology, this causal reasoning process is especially important because the domain involves causal and temporal knowledge about the cardiac conduction system with which cardiologists analyze clinical observations (ECGs) and thereby provide diagnostic interpretations of abnormal events in the underlying physiological mechanism of the heart. The recognition problem of ECG rhythm disorders, is interesting, above all, because the overall performance of existing ECG programs (for example, IBM Bonner's program) is at most 80% reliable for abnormal ECGs (Hagan et al, 1979) and we believe a basic reason for this unreliability is that current systems lack underlying physiological knowledge to handle the complexity inherent in cardiac rhythms. The ECG wave identification is much complicated by its "antenna" nature of receiving only the aggregated electrical activity of the heart; that is, there is no simple correspondence between signal features and individual electrical discharges in the heart.

Our approach to the problem of building such a system is to construct a knowledge base stratified by several distinct knowledge bases (KBs) from different perspectives of the domain. Its control structure, therefore, supports a guiding mechanism between corresponding concepts in different KBs as well as another guiding mechanism between causally related concepts in each KB. In our representational terms, the former mechanism uses **projection links** and the latter uses **causal links**, and these links together contribute to the generation of hypotheses and the decision of overall interpretations in the recognition of ECG signals. This approach also integrates several established AI techniques. The system inherited the basic control framework from the ALVEN system, and other techniques such as the attention mechanism for specialization and aggregation, which is supported by the implementation of similarity links (Minsky, 1975) and the exception handling mechanism. The hypothesize-and-test paradigm is used as in ALVEN and other systems like PIP (Szolovits and Pauker, 1978) and HEARSAY-II (Mostow and Hayes-Roth, 1978). The knowledge organization method is based on the IS-A, PART-OF, and INSTANCE-OF hierarchies as used in the PSN formalism.

To prove the efficacy of our methods, a prototype system has been designed and implemented using a frame-input PSN system on Franz LISP (Shibahara et al, 1983), (Shibahara, 1985). The prototype with a limited size of knowledge base is being tested and so far has yielded satisfactory results.

10.5.2. Representation of causal connections

Causality may be viewed in various aspects. Rieger and Grinberg distinguished **one-shot causality** where the cause event(s) is required only at the start of the effect event(s) from **continuous causality** where the continuous presence of the cause is required to sustain the effect (Rieger and Grinberg, 1976).

CAA causal links are based on two features of causal connections: first, they specify the existential dependency of an affected event on its causative event(s); second, they impose temporal constraints between causative and affected events. Thus, the affected events cannot occur without the occurrence of the corresponding causative events, with effects temporally following their causes. Since we are interested in representing the dependencies of causal connections among events more precisely, we look at causality from the viewpoint whether a causal influence is internal to a subject or whether it influences other distinct subject(s). One-shot causal links, therefore, are specialized into the following:

1. **Transfer**: the subject of the event normally completes the current event and proceeds to the following event.

2. **Transition**: the subject is forced to terminate its current event and proceed to a new event.

3. **Initiation**: the causative event, due to a given subject, triggers a new event of another subject.

4. **Interrupt**: the causative event, due to a given subject, interrupts and forces the termination of an

event by another subject.

5. **Causal-block**: the causative event of a subject fails to influence an event of another subject due to a blockage of the causal flow.

The above CAA causal links include implicit temporal constraints; thus, causal structures are described more qualitatively without specifying time coordinate values.

Causal events are aggregated at several levels involving arbitrary number of causal links. However, causal links themselves remain atomic lest the semantics of causal connections should become ambiguous.

10.5.3. Use of causal links

To interpret real ECG signals, the knowledge base must contain causal knowledge about normal and abnormal connections among cellular events, which produce particular ECG tracings in the observable signal domain. We represent such causal activities using CAA causal links. Figure 10-2 illustrates a typical ECG tracing for a normal cardiac cycle in (a), its electrical conduction path in an anatomical diagram in (b), and the corresponding causal conduction model with causal links in (c).

In this causal model, short symbols like E0a are used to denote one of four basic events (phases) in a small portion of the cardiac conduction system. These phases are "depolarization" [symbol a], "under-repolarization" [symbol b], "partial-repolarization" [symbol c], and "full-repolarization" [symbol d]. Such basic phase events are successively aggregated into "cycle", "activity", "beat", and "beat-pattern" events in the physiological event component knowledge base to describe more global and complex causal structures.

Note that causal links across beat events (not shown) are TRANSITIONs and INTERRUPTs except pace-making parts (normally, the SA-Node) because the overall oscillation of the conduction system is controlled (or triggered) by such self-oscillating cells. Also, since the current model is rather devoted to supraventricular arrhythmias, the bundle branches are

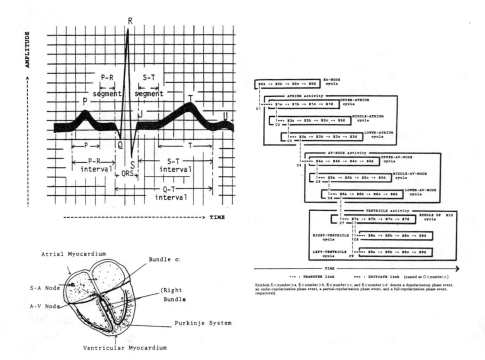

Figure 10-2: A Typical ECG Tracing for a
Normal Cardiac Cycle
included in the ventricles.

10.5.4. Recent research related to causality

ABEL and CADUCEUS are recent medical expert systems
that use causal notions. The ABEL system provides multiple

levels of descriptions of medical hypotheses and hierarchically organizes disease structure (Patil, 1981). In the CADUCEUS system, which analyzes differential diagnoses and causal graphs of diseases, Pople proposes sophisticated control links for efficient decision making (Pople, 1982).   In spite of the sophistication in expressing causal mechanisms in ABEL and CADUCEUS, these systems do not seem to provide a means to construct a recognition system of time-varying signals, due to the weakness in the representation of precise timing context among events.

Causality has been recently approached from the standpoint of "qualitative reasoning" (Forbus, 1984), (Kuipers, 1984), (De Kleer and Brown, 1984).   In this regard, Long's work must be noted (Long, 1983).   He introduced qualitative times to describe the causal relations that might or must have taken place. He proposed four causal templates that give an extension of "continuous causality", while our causal links are specialized in "one-shot causality". We have taken a different approach, because original signals are given to the system as real-valued data, and the use of some quantitative analysis is inevitable at the measurement level, so that unnecessary ambiguity is avoided, as Kunz noticed in his AI/MM system (Kunz, 1983).

Based on the methods of multivariate analysis Blum approached causality statistically (Blum, 1982).   However, our problem domain includes mostly exact causal relationships. Therefore, we limit the use of statistical standards to the estimation of inherently spontaneous variables such as event durations.

10.5.5. Representation of domain knowledge

Figure 10-3 exemplifies the use of a class frame and causal links.   (The dot "." notation is used to specify the component of the referred slot.)   This normal activity of the ventricles is decomposed into three cycle events: bundle-of-his-cycle-event, right-ventricle-cycle-event, and left-ventricle-cycle-event. Two INITIATE links represent the conductions from the bundle of His to the left and the right ventricles, respectively.

Note that the information related to the class itself (in this case, the subject part name and the activation type) is given as the instantiation of a metaclass ACTIVITY-CONCEPT.

```
class VENT-ALL-MATURE-FORWARD-ACTIVITY
    is-a VENT-ACTIVITY;
    instance-of ACTIVITY-CONCEPT instantiated-with
                        subject:    VENTRICLE;
                        activation: FORWARD;;
with  components
    bundle-of-his-cycle-event: BHIS-MATURE-CELL-CYCLE;
    right-ventricle-cycle-event: RV-MATURE-CELL-CYCLE;
    left-ventricle-cycle-event: LV-MATURE-CELL-CYCLE;
    bhis-rv-delay: NUMBER-WITH-TOLERANCES
            calculate := /* delay set-up expression */;
    bhis-lv-delay: NUMBER-WITH-TOLERANCES
            calculate := /* delay set-up expression */;
causal-links
    bhis-rv-propagation:    INITIATE
    causative-starting-event: bundle-of-his-cycle-
                        event.depolarization-phase-event;
    initiated-event:  right-ventricle-cycle-
                        event.depolarization-phase-event;
    delay: bhis-rv-delay;;
    bhis-lv-propagation:    INITIATE
    causative-starting-event: bundle-of-his-cycle-
                        event.depolarization-phase-event;
    initiated-event:  left-ventricle-cycle-
                        event.depolarization-phase-event;
    delay: bhis-lv-delay;;
end
```

Figure 10-3:   Class Frame for Normal Activity
of the Ventricles

Let us examine how the IS-A and the PART-OF principles contribute to the organization of the CAA knowledge base. We take a look at the QRS and QRST waveforms in the ECG waveform KB as examples.

First, the QRST waveform consists of the QRS complex and the T wave; thus, the corresponding class QRST-COMPOSITE-WAVE-SHAPE has the generic PART-OF structure with major components shown in Figure 10-4(a). This generic QRST waveform is specialized into several QRST waveforms in Figure 10-4(b), along its IS-A hierarchy. Let us pick one component from the STANDARD-QRST-COMPOSITE-SHAPE.

NORMAL-QRS-COMPLEX is such a component and this class is itself included in the IS-A hierarchy of the QRS waveforms as in Figure 10-4(c). The orthogonality of IS-A and PART-OF hierarchies is shown in Figure 10-4(d), since STANDARD-R-WAVE-SHAPE is a component of STANDARD-QRS-COMPLEX-SHAPE, and, at the same time, it is included in a local IS-A hierarchy of R-WAVE-SHAPE.

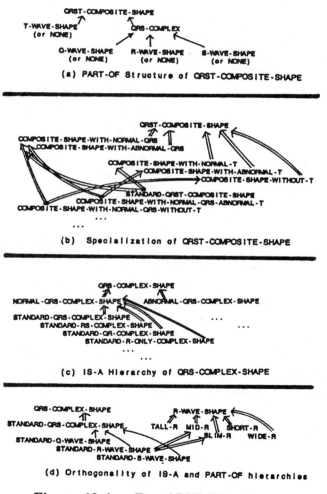

Figure 10-4:   The QRST Waveform.

Similarly, various IS-A and PART-OF hierarchies are defined in the physiological KB. Such organizational hierarchies not only contribute to the clarification of the interdependency among domain concepts but also provide guiding knowledge for the recognition process, as discussed later.

Statistical information, commonly used in medical reasoning systems, has particular importance when insufficient information is available about the disease status of a patient (Szolovits and Pauker, 1978). In our case, the recognition system uses statistical standards to produce expectations of unknown attributes of events and to estimate consistencies (goodness-of-fit) of hypotheses. Since statistical standards about a class are not the attributes of any particular instance of the class but the attributes of the class itself, such standards could be defined in appropriate metaclasses and instantiated as properties of the class itself. In other words, event statistics are good examples of meta-knowledge or "knowledge about knowledge", and such knowledge is organized along the INSTANCE-OF axis. In fact, to provide "mean" and "standard-deviation" values to all the physiological phase events, CAA has the metaclass CELL-PHASE-CONCEPT shown in Figure 10-5(a):

In Figure 10-5(a), default functions, MEANFUNC and DEVFUNC, are generic functions that are supposed to generate the mean and standard deviation about durations of phase events. Such statistical standards about phases are function procedures of "subject", "maturity", "phase", and a state variable HR$ (heart rate). Therefore, such a standard, for example, a mean value, is given by the expression "(mean subject maturity phase HR$)" in a particular phase event class (Figure 10-5(b)). In the evaluation of this expression, the slot-names such as "mean" and "subject" are replaced by real properties of the class, such as "MEANFUNC" and "SA-NODE". This is considered as the tailoring process of the general "mean" expression to the definitional context of this event; that is, such statistics may change to fit into each event hypothesis. On the other hand, HR$ is a global variable that reflects the current state of the model, where hypotheses are being instantiated; in other words, such global variables are used to make statistical standards sensitive to the current recognition context. Heart rate, blood pressure and breathing rate are examples of dynamic or time varying global variables, while age-group, sex, race, and types of medications are static global variables. Obviously, the default functions, MEANFUNC and DEVFUNC, may be replaced by

```
metaclass CELL-PHASE-CONCEPT
with components
        subject:   HEART-PORTION;
        maturity: DEGREE-OF-MATURITY;
        phase:    PHASE-NAME;
        mean:     EXPRESSION default MEANFUNC;
        deviation: EXPRESSION default DEVFUNC;
end
```

(a)

```
class SAN-COMP-DEP-PHASE
 instance-of  CELL-PHASE-CONCEPT
   instantiated-with
   subject: SA-NODE;
   maturity: COMPLETE;
   phase:  DEPOLARIZATION;
   mean: ;/* default is MEANFUNC */
   deviation: ; /* default is DEVFUNC */
 is-a PROTO-EVENT
 with
  components
  consistency: NUMBER;
  start-time: NUMBER-WITH-TOLERANCES; /* inherited */
  end-time: NUMBER-WITH-TOLERANCES;   /* inherited */
  duration: NUMBER-WITH-TOLERANCES
        such-that NON-NEG-CONSTR:
          [NOT [GT 0 VALUE$.central-value]]; /* inherited */
  constraints
  duration-estimation:
    (DURATION-ESTIMATE start-time end-time duration
      (mean subject maturity phase HR$)
      (deviation subject maturity phase HR$));
end
```

(b)

Figure 10-5:   (a) A Metaclass to Describe Phase-Concepts'
Own Properties
(b) A Phase Class as an Instance
of CELL-PHASE-CONCEPT

any ad hoc functions if necessary.

The role of the function DURATION-ESTIMATE is similar to that of causal links, in that the equation "end-time = start-time + duration" is used to estimate any unknown values among them. In this case, however, the standard mean and deviation values of the duration must be explicitly supplied for the calculation of the consistency (or reasonableness) of the estimated duration value, based on physiological knowledge.

10.5.6. Knowledge-base stratification and projection links

Due to our causal model approach, we distinguish two subdomains: the ECG morphological (shape) domain and the electrophysiological domain. Therefore, the knowledge base of the whole system is stratified by the ECG waveform KB and the physiological event KB. Our idea of stratifying a knowledge base resembles Rich's "overlays", since it provides different perspectives to the problem (Rich, 1981). In our method, however, the linking mechanism between different KBs is biased to recognition purposes.

Projection links have been introduced into the CAA system to relate corresponding concepts in distinct domain KBs. In our model based approach, such links are essential, since they relate temporal and/or morphological abnormalities in waveforms to corresponding abnormalities in physiological causal structures.

The diagram in Figure 10-6 illustrates a projection link that defines the correspondence between the corner point information of a normal QRST waveform and the timings of a normal activity event of the ventricles. This projection link must be defined in the class frame of the normal QRST waveform.

For recognition, the most important aspect of projection links is that they provide guiding paths to map concepts across differently organized KBs and support the synchronization of recognition activities in different domains. In our system, projections from established waveform hypotheses result in the basic data set (hypotheses) in the underlying event domain, on which the recognition of causal events works.

10.5.7. Recognition strategies and control

Signals are processed by three functional modules in the following order:

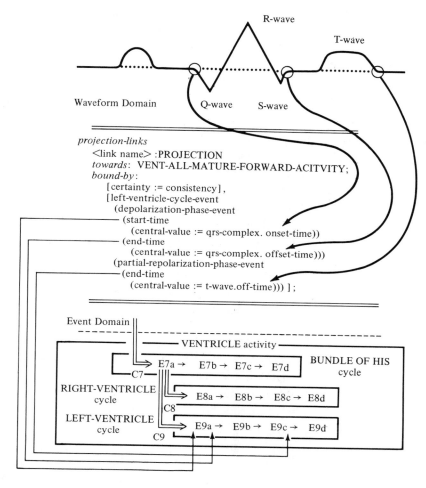

Figure 10-6:   A Projection Link

1. The **peak-detection module** extracts wave segments and slopes from sampled ECG input signals and emits peak tokens with the measured parameters. This module uses the syntactic method given by Horowitz (Horowitz, 1975) based on piecewise linearization and parsing techniques using a context-free grammar.

2. The **waveform analysis module**, for each cardiac cycle, forms waveform hypotheses on the peak tokens and refines the hypotheses to describe the

given set of tokens best. Once established, such
hypotheses are projected into the physiological event
domain to form their corresponding event
hypotheses.

3. The **event analysis module** accepts projected events
as a starting data set and generates rhythm event
hypotheses in a more global context of time to
elucidate rhythm abnormalities in the underlying
cardiac conduction system. Since most physiological
events do not have observable counterparts
(waveforms), the event analysis module produces
expectations of unknown events, using the causal
knowledge of the conduction system and statistical
standards of events. If the system encounters a
lack of information because of missing waves, it
may request the peak-detection module to search for
such missing tokens based on the expectation of
such waves.

Our recognition strategy is based on the hypothesize-and-
test paradigm, in particular, the attention mechanisms of
ALVEN. The focus-of-attention mechanism makes recognition
(hypothesis formation) proceed from the generic to the specific
along IS-A class hierarchies downward. When a class hypothesis
succeeds, a focusing action is taken by choosing and
hypothesizing an arbitrary specialized class of the successful
class. When a current hypothesis fails, the change-of-attention
mechanism chooses alternative hypotheses through similarity
links, examining the similarity and the difference between
classes.

Let us examine how the above specialization-and-
aggregation process works for QRST waveforms (see Figure
10-6). After all peaks are detected and measured, the
waveform analysis module chooses groups of consecutive
prominent peaks with high amplitude and steep slope as
anchoring shapes. These anchoring shapes are candidates for
QRST-COMPOSITE-SHAPE. The wave analysis for an anchoring
shape starts with hypothesizing the class QRST-COMPOSITE-
SHAPE on the prepared set of basic peak tokens. This class is

the most generic for all the shapes composed of Q, R, S, and T waves and only requires the existence of any QRS complex wave as the sole component; thus, this component class, which is again the most generic class for QRS complex waves, is hypothesized, and its instantiation follows, using the prepared Q, R, and/or S wave tokens. If there are no Q, R, or S wave tokens, the hypothesis of QRS-COMPLEX-SHAPE fails, and so does QRST-COMPOSITE-SHAPE. As the second step, one of the specialized QRST composite wave classes under QRST-COMPOSITE-SHAPE is hypothesized, and all its attributes are tested; that is, an attempt is made to instantiate the slot tokens. Since all the specialized classes are connected by similarity links, the system may choose the next appropriate hypothesis using exceptions raised by test results and finally reach the valid hypothesis for the given anchoring shape. The test procedure for each attribute slot, however, triggers an independent process for recognizing the token of the slot. For example, class STANDARD-QRST-COMPOSITE-SHAPE has a slot named qrs-complex and this slot is defined by class NORMAL-QRS-COMPLEX which is an IS-A parent class to classes STANDARD-QRS-COMPLEX-SHAPE, STANDARD-QR-COMPLEX-SHAPE, STANDARD-RS-COMPLEX-SHAPE, and STANDARD-R-ONLY-COMPLEX-SHAPE. Thus, the previous QRS wave slot token of the generic QRST-COMPOSITE-SHAPE must be specialized along the IS-A hierarchy of QRS-COMPLEX-SHAPE, and this process also uses the same procedure in order to reach the most refined QRS complex shape hypothesis. With such a specialized QRS wave token and a separately specialized T wave token, the second step decides the most appropriate hypothesis among QRST composite shapes for the given set of wave tokens.

Similarly, but independently, in the physiological event domain, the specialization-and-aggregation process starts with the most generic beat pattern and eventually provides several specialized patterns as probable overall interpretations.

The recognition starts with establishing hypotheses in the waveform domain. The projection mechanism maps such established hypotheses into the event domain, preparing a set of basic event hypotheses, which are treated like data in the event recognition process.

256 The Knowledge Frontier:

A beat pattern (rhythm) is a complex time-varying event aggregated from more local events such as beats, activities, cycles, and phases. Causal links in such an aggregated event imply connections among its component events. Thus, once projections are made to some of these components, the system can produce expectations of unknown components from the known components. Therefore, when the system hypothesizes such an aggregated event, it looks ahead or looks back for its component events, which are causally linked to "already-established" component events. Most frequently, causal links are used to locate the temporal positions of "to-be-expected" events by their inherent temporal constraints. This expectation is made by the following basic equality implicitly imposed over starting or ending times of participating events:

<effect-time> = <cause-time> + <delay-period>.

Let us look at the above mechanisms in a small but clear case where a QRST composite wave is seen but the P wave has not been recognized for the current wave group.

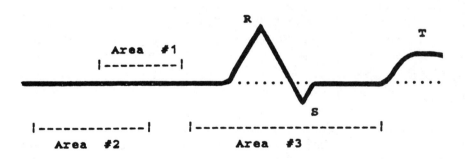

Figure 10-7: The Case and the Interval "Area #1"

Figure 10-7 illustrates the case. The interval "Area #1" is the probable area where a P wave would appear if the beat is a normal sinus-pacing beat. To estimate such an area under a particular beat hypothesis is important, since the peak-detection module may search for a P wave intensively in this area, again.

The area is estimated using the projection and the

expectation mechanisms in the following fashion:

1. A hypothesis of NORMAL-QRST-COMPOSITE-SHAPE is established.

2. A projection to a normal ventricle activity event (Figure 10-6) is undertaken, as follows:

   a. The onset and offset times of the QRS complex are bound to the starting and ending times of the depolarization phase of the left ventricle. The off-time of the T wave is bound to the ending time of the partial-repolarization phase. These phase events are generated immediately, and two other phase events are expected by three TRANSFER causal links and event statistics. Thus, the left ventricle (LV) cycle event is generated.

   b. By the INITIATE causal link to the Bundle of His (BHIS) and subsequent TRANSFER links, the BHIS cycle event is generated. Also, by the INITIATE link from the BHIS to the right ventricle (RV), the RV cycle event is generated.

   c. With the above three cycle events, the projection to the normal ventricle activity event is completed.

Expectation of AV-Node activity, Atrium activity, and SA-Node activity under a hypothesis of the normal sinus-pacing beat (Figure 10-2(c)) is carried out as follows:

   a. The INITIATE link C7 is invoked to expect phase E6a; then E6b, E6c, and E6d phases are expected by three TRANSFER links· and, finally, the lower AV-Node cycle event is

generated.   Similarly, using C6 and C5
INITIATE links, the middle and upper AV-
Node activity events are generated. Thus, the
AV-Node activity event is formed with these
component cycle events.

b. Starting with the INITIATE link C4, the
atrium activity event is expected in the same
way as above, and, next, the SA-Node cycle
event is expected.

c. A hypothesis of the normal sinus-pacing beat
is completed.

Under this hypothesis, the on-time and the off-time of
the P wave correspond to the starting time of the upper-atrium
cycle and the ending time of the lower-atrium cycle,
respectively. Therefore, the search area for a probable P wave
is given as the interval between these times (for example, from
110 +/- 16ms to 40 +/- 15ms before the QRS complex). The
request of the search for the P wave is fed back to the peak-
detection module to repeat the detection with different
sensitivity parameters.

The above CAA expectation mechanism is characterized by
the following features:

(1) The expectation is made from the known to the
unknown, forward or backward in time, and upward or
downward in a PART-OF class structure.

(2) The expectation proliferates to make a closure of
temporal and/or structural dependencies and complete the
PART-OF structure of the hypothesis.

Projections are made in the following fashion:

(1) Projections may be made between differently
structured classes, as seen in Figure 10-6.

(2) To eliminate unnecessary instantiations of projections,
any projected class is instantiated only when a current global
hypothesis requests the class as a component.

To recognize a periodic or successive arrhythmia, its
repetitive behavior is defined by the recursive definition of
beat-pattern frames. By such a frame, recognition may proceed

one beat to the next along the time axis instantiating successive beats to form the beat-pattern.

In the process of forming beat-patterns, causal links between adjacent beats allow the system to verify the causal relationship that governs the pace-making mechanism on a beat-to-beat basis. The overall consistency of a beat-pattern is calculated based on the consistencies of these causal links and beat components.

As well as the causal consistency among beats, overall characteristics and tendencies are observed and used to recognize individual arrhythmias. For this purpose, most beat-pattern classes include a component that monitors the changes of variables from one beat to another. A typical example is to monitor the change of the R-R interval or the P-R interval.

In arrhythmia beat-patterns, similarity links must also be defined to relate beat-patterns that have some features in common and handle situations where one or more matching exceptions have been raised. Figure 10-8 shows ECG wave configurations that correspond to three different AV-Block arrhythmia patterns and the matching exceptions used by similarity links. Such similarity links between repetitive beat-patterns enable the system to switch beat-pattern hypotheses from one pattern to its alternatives [according to the exceptions raised during the instantiation of the pattern hypothesis.]

The recognition of particular arrhythmia patterns such as the above AV-Block beat-patterns must be initiated by more general classes in the IS-A hierarchy they belong to. The most generic class for repetitive arrhythmias is REPETITIVE-RHYTHM-PATTERN, and this class is immediately specialized according to the heart rate into one of three rate-specific classes: FAST-RHYTHM-PATTERN, MODERATE-RHYTHM-PATTERN, and SLOW-RHYTHM-PATTERN. If we assume a normal heart rate between 60 and 100 beats per minute, MODERATE-RHYTHM-PATTERN is selected And one of its more specialized classes must again be chosen. Normally, the first choice is NORMAL-SINUS-RHYTHM-PATTERN, because it represents the most generic rhythm that has only NORMAL-SINUS-PACING-BEATs. If any abnormality is found in the recognition of such normal beats, other rhythm pattern(s) are triggered through a similarity link, which detects the

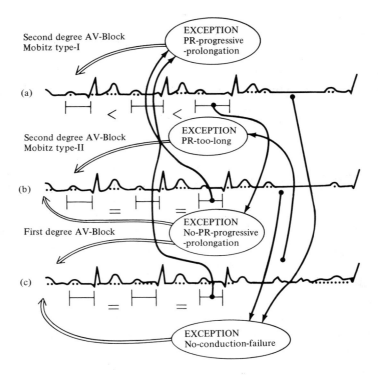

Figure 10-8:   ECG Wave Configurations

abnormality.   For the cases of AV-Blocks, an exception must be raised by the prolongation of the atrium-ventricle-interval in the recognition of one of component beats. Then the similarity link which contains this exception condition triggers a rhythm pattern AV-PROLONGED-RHYTHM-PATTERN, which is the immediate IS-A class of the above three AV-Block beat pattern classes.

To   recognize   particular   arrhythmia   patterns,   the specialization-and-aggregation process must be initiated with the most   generic   class   for   repetitive   arrhythmias.   The   final interpretation, therefore, is given by a set of all survived beat-patterns with overall consistency factors.   The consistency is calculated using event statistics and a test-score function, which is similar to a fuzzy constraint in (Zadeh, 1983a).

10.6. Conclusions

Our basic conclusions lie in the claim that frame-based representations are appropriate for complex time-varying signal interpretation tasks. We have presented aspects of representation, knowledge organization and control, that have led to successful implementations of two systems, ALVEN and CAA, that deal with temporally rich medical signal domains. In the case of CAA, a further contribution was described, namely the deep model of the heart's electrophysiology, and a mechanism, projection, was presented that allows for relating signal characteristics to conceptual entities responsible for generating those signals. A final basic claim is that it is not the frame nature of the knowledge representation per se that has been responsible for the success of these systems, but rather the relationships of the frame organization, that is, the IS-A, PART-OF, INSTANCE-OF, SIMILARITY, and Temporal Precedence relations, that drive the control. These relationships drive the control structure as well as provide desirable knowledge structure.

Acknowledgements

The applications to cardiology would not have been possible without the constant support and encouragement of E. Douglas Wigle, Chief of Cardiology, Toronto General Hospital. Dominic Covvey, Peter McLaughlin, Menashe Waxman, Robert Burns, Peter Liu, and Maurice Druck, all of the Division of Cardiology at Toronto General Hospital at the time, provided much useful guidance and data. The first author is a Fellow of the Canadian Institute for Advanced Research.

11. SNePS Considered as a Fully Intensional Propositional Semantic Network

Stuart C. Shapiro
William J. Rapaport

Department of Computer Science
University of Buffalo
State University of New York
Buffalo, New York 14260

Abstract

SNePS, the Semantic Network Processing System, is a semantic network language with facilities for building semantic networks to represent virtually any kind of information, retrieving information from them, and performing inference with them. Users can interact with SNePS in a variety of interface languages, including a LISP-like user language, a menu-based screen-oriented editor, a graphics-oriented editor, a higher-order-logic language, and an extendible fragment of English.

This article discusses the syntax and semantics for SNePS considered as an intensional knowledge representation system and provides examples of uses of SNePS for cognitive modelling, database management, pattern recognition, expert systems, belief revision, and computational linguistics.

11.1. Introduction

This chapter presents a formal syntax and semantics for SNePS, the *Semantic Network Processing System* (Shapiro, 1979b).[30] The syntax shows the emphasis placed on SNePS's *propositional* nature. The semantics, which is based on Alexius Meinong's theory of intentional objects (the objects of thought), makes SNePS's *fully intensional* nature precise: as a fully intensional theory, it avoids possible worlds and is appropriate for AI considered as "computational philosophy" - AI as the study of how intelligence is possible - or "computational psychology" - AI with the goal of writing programs as models of *human* cognitive behavior. We also present a number of recent AI research and applications projects that use SNePS, concentrating on one of these, a use of SNePS to model (or construct) the mind of a cognitive agent, referred to as CASSIE (the *C*ognitive *A*gent of the *S*NePS *S*ystem-an *I*ntelligent *E*ntity).

11.1.1. The SNePS environment

A semantic network is a data structure typically consisting of labeled nodes and labeled, directed arcs. SNePS can be viewed as a semantic network language with facilities for

1. building semantic networks to represent virtually

---

[30]This research was supported in part by the National Science Foundation under Grant No. IST-8504713 and SUNY Buffalo Research Development Fund grants No. 150-9216-F and No. 150-8537-G (Rapaport), and in part by the Air Force Systems Command, Rome Air Development Center, Griffiss Air Force Base, NY 13441-5700, and the Air Force Office of Scientific Research, Bolling AFB, DC 20332 under contract No. F30602-85-C-0008 (Shapiro). We wish to thank Michael Almeida, James Geller, João Martins, Jeannette Neal, Sargur N. Srihari, Jennifer Suchin, and Zhigang Xiang for supplying us with descriptions of their projects, and Randall R. Dipert, the members of SNeRG (the SNePS Research Group), and three anonymous reviewers for comments and discussion.

any kind of information or knowledge,

2. retrieving information from them, and

3. performing inference with them, using SNIP (the
   SNePS Inference Package) and path-based inference.

Users can interact with SNePS in a variety of interface
languages, including: SNePSUL, a LISP-like SNePS User
Language; SENECA, a menu-based, screen-oriented editor;
GINSENG, a graphics-oriented editor; SNePSLOG, a higher-order-
logic language (in the sense in which PROLOG is a first-order-
logic language) (McKay and Martins, 1981), (Shapiro, McKay,
Martins, and Morgado, 1981); and an extendible fragment of
English, using an ATN parsing and generating grammar
(Shapiro, 1982). see Figure 11-1.

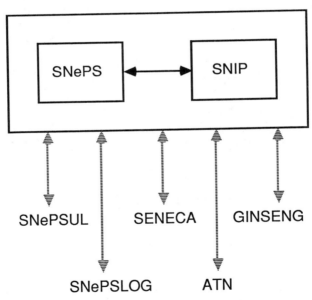

Figure 11-1:   SNePS, SNIP and Their User Interfaces.

SNePS, SNIP (the SNePS Interface Package) and their user
interfaces. When the arcs, case frames, and ATN grammar are
those of SNePS/CASSIE, then the system is being used to
model CASSIE. When the arcs are for the database (see
Section 11.4.1), then the system is being used as a database
management system, etc.

SNePS is the descendent of SAMENLAQ (Shapiro, Woodmansee, and Kreuger, 1968) (Shapiro and Woodmansee, 1969) and MENTAL (Shapiro, 1971b), (Shapiro, 1971c). It was developed with the help of the SNePS Research Group at Indiana University and at the University at Buffalo. The current version is implemented in Franz LISP and runs on VAX 11/750s and 780s in the Department of Computer Science at Buffalo. An earlier version was implemented in ALISP on a CDC Cyber 730; and an updated version is being implemented in Common LISP on Symbolics LISP machines, TI Explorers, and a Tektronix 4406. There are additional installations at other universities in the U.S. and Europe.

11.1.2. SNePS as a knowledge representation system

Some researchers, for example, (Levesque and Brachman, 1985), view a knowledge representation (KR) system as a subsystem that manages the knowledge base of a knowledge-based system by storing information and answering questions. In contrast, we view SNePS as the entire knowledge-based system, interacting with a user/interlocutor through one of its interfaces. Of course, the user/interlocutor could be another computer program using SNePS as a subsystem, but that is not the way we use it.

A basic design goal of SNePS and its ancestors was to be an environment within which KR experiments could be performed, that is, to be a semantic network at the "logical" level, to use Brachman's term (Brachman, 1979), see Section 11.5, below. This has been effected by providing a rather low level interface, SNePSUL. Using SNePSUL, a KR designer can specify a syntax: individual arc labels and sets of arc labels (or case frames) that will be used to represent various objects and information about them. It is also the designer's obligation to supply a semantics for these case frames. As is the case for any provider of a language or "shell", we cannot be responsible for what use others make of the facilities we provide. Nevertheless, we have our own preferred use.

In this chapter, we try to do two things. First, we try to provide an understanding of SNePS and of some of the uses to which it has been put. Second, and most importantly, we present our own preferred use: this is to use SNePS, with a particular set of arc labels and case frames, and a particular parsing/generating grammar for a fragment of English, as (a model of) the cognitive agent, CASSIE. We shall refer to SNePS with these arcs, case frames, and grammar as SNePS/CASSIE. SNePS/CASSIE forms CASSIE's mind and stands as our current theory of KR at the "conceptual" level (cf. Section 11.5, below, and (Brachman, 1979)). The purpose of the central part of this paper is to present this theory by explaining the entities represented by structures in SNePS/CASSIE, by giving a formal syntax and semantics for those structures, and by showing and explaining a sample conversation with CASSIE.

11.1.3. Informal description of SNePS

Regardless of the intentions of a KR-system designer, SNePS, as a KR formalism, provides certain facilities and has certain restrictions. The facilities (for example, for building, finding, and deducing nodes) are best understood as those provided by SNePSUL, but we shall not give a complete description of SNePSUL here. [For an example, cf. Section 11.4.1, below; for details, see (Shapiro, 1979b).] The restrictions, however, are important to understand, because they distinguish SNePS from a general labelled, directed graph and from many other semantic network formalisms.

SNePS is a *propositional* semantic network. By this is meant that all information, including propositions, "facts", etc., is represented by nodes. The benefit of representing propositions by nodes is that propositions about propositions can be represented with no limit. (In the formal syntax and semantics given in Section 11.3, the propositions are the nodes labelled 'm' or 'r'.)

Arcs merely form the underlying syntactic structure of SNePS. This is embodied in the restriction that one cannot add an arc between two existing nodes. That would be tantamount to telling SNePS a proposition that is not represented as a node. There are a few built-in arc labels, used mostly for rule nodes. *Paths* of arcs can also be defined, allowing for *path-based* inference, including property inheritance within generalization hierarchies [see Section 11.3.4, below; cf. Shapiro (Shapiro, 1978), (Srihari, 1981), and (Tranch, 1982).] All other arc labels are defined by the user, typically at the beginning of an interaction with SNePS, although new labels can be defined at any time.

For purposes of reasoning, propositions that are asserted in SNePS must be distinguished from those propositions that are merely represented in SNePS but not asserted. This could happen in the case of a proposition embedded in another (for example, "Lucy is rich" embedded in "John believes that Lucy is rich"). SNePS interprets a proposition node to be asserted if and only if it has no arcs pointing to it.[31]

Another restriction is the *Uniqueness Principle:* There is a one-to-one correspondence between nodes and represented concepts. This principle guarantees that nodes will be shared whenever possible and that nodes represent intensional objects.[32] We next consider the nature of these objects.

11.2. Intensional knowledge representation

SNePS can be used to represent propositions about entities in the world having properties and standing in relations. Roughly, nodes represent the propositions, entities, properties, and relations, while the arcs represent structural links between these.

SNePS nodes *might* represent *extensional* entities. Roughly, extensional entities are those whose "identity conditions" (the conditions for deciding when "two" of them are really the "same") do not depend on their manner of representation. They

---

[31] This is not really a restriction of SNePS, but of SNIP (the SNePS Inference Package) and path-based inference.

[32] In (Maida and Shapiro, 1982) this name was given to only half of the Uniqueness Principle as stated here: "each concept represented in the network is represented by a unique node" (page 291).

may be characterized as those entities satisfying the following rough principle:

Two extensional entities are equivalent (for some purpose) if and only if they are identical[33]

For example, the following are extensional:

```
the Fregeon referent of an expression;
physical objects;
sentences;
truth values;
mathematical objects such as:
    sets,
    functions defined in terms of their input-output
        behavior (that is, as sets of ordered pairs),
    n-place relations defined in terms of sets of
        ordered n-tuples.
```

Although SNePS *can* be used to represent extensional entities in the world, we believe that it *must* represent *intensional* entities. Roughly, intensional entities are those whose identity conditions *do* depend on their manner of representation. They are those entities that satisfy the following rough principle:

Two intensional entities might be equivalent (for some) purpose without being identical (that is, they might really be two, not one).

Alternatively, intensional entities may be characterized as satisfying the following five criteria:

1. They are non-substitutible in referentially opaque contexts.

2. They can be indeterminate with respect to some properties.

3. They need not exist.

---

[33]that is, if and only if "they" are really one entity, not two

4. They need not be possible.

5. They can be distinguished even if they are necessarily identical (for example, *the sum of 2 and 2* and *the sum of 3 and 1* are distinct objects of thought).

For example, the following are intensional:

```
the Fregean sense of an expression;
concepts;
propositions;
properties;
algorithms;
objects of thought, including:
    fictional entities (such as Sherlock Holmes),
    non-existents (such as the golden mountain),
    impossible objects (such as the round square)
```

Only if one wants to represent the relations between a mind and the world would SNePS also have to represent extensional entities [cf. (Rapaport, 1976), (Rapaport, 1978), (McCarthy, 1979)]. However, if SNePS is used just to represent a mind - that is, a mind's model of the world-then *it does not need to represent any extensional objects.* SNePS can then be used either to model the mind of a particular cognitive agent or to build such a mind - that is, to *be* a cognitive agent itself.

There have been a number of arguments presented in both the AI and philosophical literature in the past few years for the need for intensional entities. (Castaneda, 1974), (Woods, 1975), (Rapaport, 1976), (Rapaport, 1985a), (Brachman, 1977), (Routley, 1979), cf. (Rapaport, 1984a), (Parsons, 1980), cf. (Rapaport, 1985b)). Among them, the following considerations seem to us to be especially significant:

Principle of Fine-Grained Representation:

The objects of thought (that is, intentional objects) are intensional: a mind can have two or more objects of thought that correspond to only one extensional object.

To take the classic example, the Morning Star and the Evening Star might be distinct objects of thought, yet there is only one extensional object (viz., a certain astronomical body) corresponding to them.

Principle of Displacement:

> Cognitive agents can think and talk about non-existents:
> a mind can have an object of thought that corresponds to
> no extensional object.

Again to take several classic examples, cognitive agents can think and talk about fictional objects such as Santa Claus, possible but non-existing objects such as a golden mountain, impossible objects such as a round square, and possible but not-yet-proven-to-exist objects such as theoretical entities (for example, black holes).

If nodes only represent intensional entities (and extensional entities are not represented in the network), how do they link up to the external, extensional world? In SNePS/CASSIE, the answer is by means of a LEX arc (see syntactic formation rule SR.1 and semantic interpretation rule SI.1 in Section 11.3.3, below): the nodes at the head of the LEX arc are *our* (the user's) interpretation of the node at its tail. The network without the LEX arcs and their head-nodes displays the *structure* of CASSIE's mind [cf. (Carnap, 1967), Section 11.14].

A second way that nodes can be linked to the world is by means of sensors and effectors, either linguistic or robotic. The robotic sort has been discussed in (Maida and Shapiro, 1982). Since so many AI understanding systems deal exclusively with language, here we consider a system with a keyboard as its sense organ and a CRT screen as its only effector.

Since the language system interacts with the outside world only through language, the only questions we can consider about the connections of its concepts with reality are questions such as:

> Does it use words as we do?
> When it uses word w, does it mean the same thing as
>   when I use it?
> When I use word w, does it understand what I mean?

The perceptual system of the language system is its parser/analyzer - the programs that analyze typed utterances and build pieces of semantic network. The motor system is the generator - the programs that analyze a section of the semantic network and construct an utterance to be displayed on the CRT. One crucial requirement for an adequate connection with the world is simple consistency of input-output behavior. That is, a phrase that is analyzed to refer to a particular node should consistently refer to that node, at least while there is no change in the network. Similarly, if the system generates a certain phrase to describe the concept represented by a node, it should be capable of generating that same phrase for that same node, as long as nothing in the network changes. Notice that it is unreasonable to require that if a phrase is generated to describe a node, the analyzer should be able to find the node from the phrase:: The system might know of several brown dogs and describe one as "a brown dog"; it could not be expected to find that node as the representation of "a brown dog" consistently.

If we are assured of the simple input-output consistency of the system, the main question left is whether it uses words to mean the same thing as we do. It is the same question that we would be concerned with if we were talking with a blind invalid, although in that case we would assume the answer was 'Yes' until the conversation grew so bizzare that we were forced to change our minds. As the system (or the invalid) uttered more and more sentences using a particular word or phrase, we would become more and more convinced that it meant what we would mean by it, or that it meant what we might have described with a different word or phrase ("Oh! When you say 'conceptual dependency structure', you mean what I mean when I say 'semantic network'."), or else that we *didn't* know what was meant, or that it was not using it in a consistent, meaningful way (and hence that the system (or invalid) did not know what it was talking about). As long as the conversation proceeds without our getting into the latter situation, the system has all the connections with reality it needs.

11.3. Description of SNePS/CASSIE

In this section, we introduce CASSIE, and give the syntax and semantics for SNePS/CASSIE in terms of a philosophical theory of mental entities inspired by Alexius Meinong's Theory of Objects.

11.3.1. CASSIE - A model of a mind

SNePS nodes represent the objects of CASSIE's thoughts - the things she thinks about, the properties and relations with which she characterizes them, her beliefs, her judgments, etc. [cf. (Maida and Shapiro, 1982), (Rapaport, 1985a)]. According to the Principle of Displacement, a cognitive agent is able to think about virtually anything, including fictional objects, possible but non-existing objects, and impossible objects. Any theory that would account for this fact requires a non-standard logic, and its semantics cannot be limited to merely *possible* worlds. (Otherwise, it could not account for impossible objects. This accounts for the difficulties David Israel has in providing a possible-worlds semantics for SNePS (Israel, 1983), (cf. (Rapaport, 1985a)). Theories based on the Theory of Objects of the turn-of-the-century Austrian philosopher-psychologist Alexius Meinong are of precisely this kind.

For present purposes, it will be enough to say that Meinong held that psychological experiences consist in part of a psychological *act* (such as thinking, believing, judging, wishing, etc.) and the *object* to which the act is directed (for example, the object that is thought about or the proposition that is believed). Two kinds of Meinongian objects of thought are relevant for us:

1. The *objectum*, or object of "simple" thoughts: Santa Claus is the objectum of John's act of thinking of Santa Claus. Objecta are the meanings of noun phrases.

2. The *objective*, or object of belief, knowledge, etc.: that Santa Claus is thin is the objective of John's

act of believing that Santa Claus is thin. Objectives are like propositions in that they are the meanings of sentences and other sentential structures.

It is important to note that objecta need not exist and that objectives need not be true. [For details, see: (Meinong, 1904), (Findlay, 1963), (Rapaport, 1976), (Rapaport, 1978), (Rapaport, 1981), (Rapaport, 1982), (Castaneda, 1974), (Castaneda, 1975a), (Castaneda, 1975b), (Casteneda, 1975), (Castaneda, 1977), (Castaneda, 1979), (Tomberlin, 1984), and (Routley, 1979); cf. (Rapaport, 1984a), (Parsons, 1980); cf. (Rapaport, 1985b), (Lambert, 1983); cf. (Rapaport, 1986a), (Zalta, 1983).]

This is, perhaps, somewhat arcane terminology for what might seem like AI common sense. But without an underlying theory, such as Meinong's, there is no way to be sure if common sense can be trusted. It is important to note that not only are all represented things intensional, but that they are all objects of CASSIE's mental acts; that is, they are all in CASSIE's mind (her "belief space") - they are all intentional. Thus, even if CASSIE represents the beliefs of someone else (for example, John's belief that Lucy is rich, as in the conversation in the next section), the objects that she represents as being in that person's mind (as being in his "belief space") are actually CASSIE's representations of those objects - that is, they are in CASSIE's mind.

11.3.2. A conversation with CASSIE

Before giving the syntax and semantics of the case frames employed in representing CASSIE's "mind", we present a conversation we had with her. An ATN parser/generator (Shapiro, 1982) was used to parse the English input into SNePS and to generate the SNePS structures in English. User input is on the lines beginning with the :-prompt; CASSIE's output is on the lines that follow. (Execution and garbage-collection times have been edited out for clarity.)

```
: Young Lucy petted a yellow dog
I understand that young Lucy petted a yellow dog

: What is yellow
```

a dog is yellow

: Dogs are animals
I understand that dogs are animals

: Who petted an animal
young Lucy petted a yellow dog

: Lucy is sweet
I understand that young Lucy is sweet

: Lucy is a girl
I understand that sweet young Lucy is a girl

: Girls are people
I understand that girls are people

: What was petted by a person
a yellow dog was petted by sweet young Lucy

: The dog is named Rover
I understand that Rover is a yellow dog

: What was petted by a person
yellow Rover was petted by sweet young Lucy

: John believes that Lucy is rich
I understand that John believes that Lucy is rich

: Who is rich
I don't know.

: Who is sweet
young Lucy is sweet

: John believes that Lucy is old
I understand that John believes that rich Lucy is old

: John is a boy
I understand that John is a boy

: Boys are people
I understand that boys are people

: Dogs are pets
I understand that dogs are pets

: For every p and d if p is a person and d is a pet then p
       loves d
I understand that for every d and p, if p is a person
and
    d is a pet

```
      then p loves d

    : Who loves a pet
    sweet young Lucy loves yellow Rover
    and
    John loves yellow Rover
```

11.3.3. Syntax and semantics of SNePS/CASSIE

In this section, we give the syntactic formation rules (SR) and semantic interpretations (SI) for the nodes and arcs used in this interaction, together with some other important ones. We return to a more detailed examination of the interaction in the next section. What we present here is our current model; we make no claims about the completeness of the representational scheme. In particular, we leave for another paper a discussion of such structured individuals as the golden mountain or the round square, which raise difficult and important problems with predication and existence. [For a discussion of these issues, see (Rapaport, 1978), (Rapaport, 1985a).]

Information is represented in SNePS by means of *nodes* and *arcs*. Since the meaning of a node is determined by what it is connected to in the network, there are no isolated nodes. Nodes that only have arcs pointing *to* them are considered to be unstructured or *atomic*. They include:

(A1) *sensory* nodes, which represent interfaces with the external world (in the examples that follow, they will represent words, sounds, or utterances);

(A2) *base* nodes, which represent constant individual concepts and properties;

(A3) *variable* nodes, which represent arbitrary individuals (cf. (Fine, 1983)) or arbitrary propositions.

Molecular nodes, which have arcs emanating *from* them, include:

(M1) *structured individual* nodes, which represent structured individual concepts or properties (that is, concepts and properties represented in such a way that their internal structure is exhibited; see the discussion of structured information in (Woods, 1975));

(M2) *structured proposition* nodes, which represent

propositions; those with no incoming arcs represent
beliefs of the system.[34] (Note that structured
proposition nodes can also be considered to be
structured individuals.) Proposition nodes are either
atomic (representing atomic propositions) or are
rule nodes. Rule nodes represent deduction rules
and are used by SNIP (the SNePS Inference Package) for
node—based deductive inference.[35]

For each of the three categories of molecular nodes (structured individuals, atomic propositions, and rules), there are *constant* nodes of that category and *pattern* nodes of that category representing arbitrary entities of that category.

The rules labeled 'SR', below, should be considered as syntactic formation rules for a *non-linear* network language. The semantic interpretations, labeled 'SI', are in terms of Meinongian objecta and objectives, which are intentional objects, that is, objects of thought. Since intentional objects are intensional, our Meinongian semantics is an *extensional* semantics over a domain of *intensional* entities (Meinongian objects).

We begin with a few definitions.[36]

Definition 1

A node *dominates* another node if there is a path of directed

---

[34]There is a need to distinguish structured proposition nodes with no incoming arcs from structured individual nodes with no incoming arcs; the latter, of course, are not beliefs of the system. This is handled by the syntactic formation rules and their semantic interpretations. There is also a need to distinguish between beliefs of the system and those propositions that the system is merely contemplating or "assuming" temporarily [cf. (Meinong, 1983)]. We are currently adding this capability to SNePS by means of an *assertion* operator ('!').

[35]For details, see (Shapiro, 1977), (Shapiro, 1978), (McKay and Shapiro, 1980), (McCarty and Sridharan, 1981), (Shapiro and McKay, 1980), (Shapiro, Martins, and McKay, 1982), (Martins, 1983a).

[36]These are actually only rough definitions; the interested reader is referred to (Shapiro, 1979b), Section 2.1, for more precise ones.

arcs from the first node to the second node.

Definition 2

A *pattern* node is a node that dominates a variable node.

Definition 3

An *individual* node is either a base node, a variable node, or a structured constant or pattern individual node.

Definition 4

A *proposition* node is either a structured proposition node or an atomic variable node representing an arbitrary proposition.

SR.1 If "w" is an English word and "i" is an identifier not previously used, then

is a network, w is a sensory node, and i is a structured individual node.

SI.1 i is the Meinongian objectum corresponding to the utterance of w.

SR.2 If either "t_1" and "t_2" are identifiers not previously used, or "t_1" is an identifier not previously used and t_2 is a temporal node, then

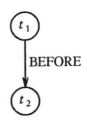

is a network and t_1 and t_2 are *temporal* nodes, that is individual nodes representing times.

SI.2 t_1 and t_2 are Meinongian objecta corresponding to two time intervals, the former occurring before the latter.

SR.3 If i and j are individual nodes, and "m" is an identifier not previously used, then

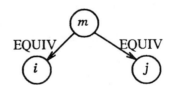

is a network and m is a structured proposition node.

SI.3 m is the Meinongian objective corresponding to the proposition that Meinongian objecta i and j (are believed by CASSIE to) correspond to the same actual object. (This is not used in the conversation, but is needed for fully intensional representational systems; cf. (Rapaport, 1978;RAPA84b) and (Castaneda, 1974;CAST75b) for analyses of this sort of relation, and (Maida and Shapiro, 1982) for a discussion of its use.)

SR.4 If i and j are individual nodes and "m" is an identifier not previously used, then

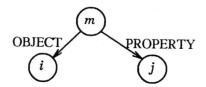

is a network and m is a structured proposition node.

SI.4 m is the Meinongian objective corresponding to the proposition that i has the property j.

SR.5 If i and j are individual nodes and "m" is an identifier not previously used, then

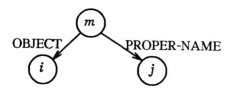

is a network and m is a structured proposition node.

SI.5 m is the Meinongian objective corresponding to the proposition that Meinongian objectum i's proper name is j. (j is the Meinongian objectum that is i's proper name; its expression in English is represented by a node at the head of a LEX-arc emanating from j.)

SR.6 If i and j are individual nodes and "m" is an identifier not previously used, then

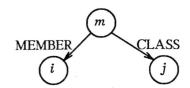

is a network and m is a structured proposition node.

SI.6 m is the Meinongian objective corresponding to the proposition that i is a (member of class) j.

SR.7 If i and j are individual nodes and $"m"$ is an identifier not previously used, then

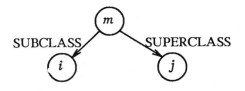

is a network and m is a structured proposition node.

SI.7 m is the Meinongian objective corresponding to the proposition that (the class of) is are (a subclass of the class of) js.

SR.8 If i_1, i_2, i_3 are individual nodes, t_1, t_2, are temporal nodes, and $"m"$ is an identifier not previously used, then

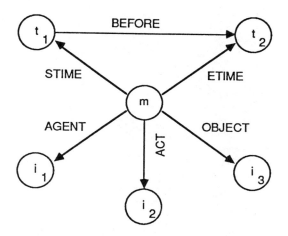

is a network and m is a structured proposition node.

SI.8 m is the Meinongian objective corresponding to the proposition that agent i_1 performs act i_2 to or on i_3 starting at time t_1 and ending at time t_2, where t_1 is before t_2.

It should be noted that the ETIME and STIME arcs are optional and can be part of any proposition node. They are a provisional technique for handling the representation of acts and events; our current research on temporal representation is much more complex and is discussed in Section 11.4.7, below.

SR.9 If m_1 is a proposition node, i is an individual node, j is the (structured individual) node with a LEX arc to the node, believe, and "m_2" is an identifier not previously used, then

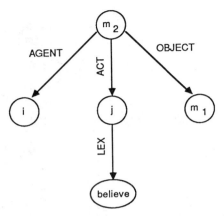

is a network and m_2 is a structured proposition node.

SI.9 m_2 is the Meinongian objective corresponding to the proposition that agent i believes proposition m_1.

Two special cases of SR.9 that are of interest concern *de re* and *de dicto* beliefs; they are illustrated in Figure 11-2 and Figure 11-3. [For details, see (Rapaport and Shapiro, 1984) and (Rapaport, 1984b), (Rapaport, 1986b).]

SR.10 If $m_1, \ldots, m_n$ are proposition nodes ($n \geqslant 0$), "i" and "j" are integers between 0 and n, inclusive, and "r" is an identifier not previously used, then

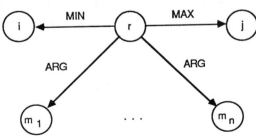

is a network, and r is a rule node.

SI.10 r is the Meinongian objective corresponding to the proposition that there is a relevant connection between

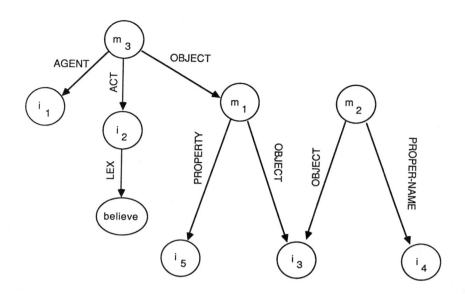

Figure 11-2:   Meinongian Objective - *de re* Reading

m_3 is the Meinongian objective corresponding to the proposition that agent i_1 believes *de re* of objectum i_3 (who is believed by CASSIE to be named i_4) that it has the property i_5.

propositions $m_1, \ldots, m_n$ such that at least i and at most $i(j)$ of them are simultanenously true.

Rule r of SR/SI.10 is called *AND-OR* and is a unified generalization of negation $(i = j = 0)$, binary conjunction $(i = j = 2)$, binary inclusive disjunction $(i = 1, j = 2)$, binary exclusive disjunction $(i = 0, j = 1)$, etc.

SR.11 If $m_1, \ldots, m_n$ are proposition nodes (n $\leqslant$ 0), is an integer between 0 and n, inclusive, and "r" is an identifier not previously used, then

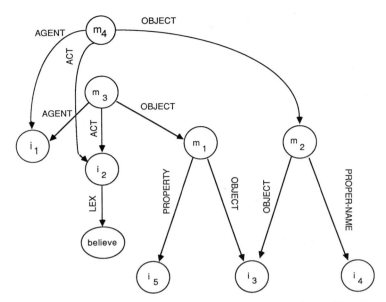

Figure 11-3:   Meinongian Objective - *de dicto* Reading

m_4 is the Meinongian objective corresponding to the proposition that agent i_1 believes *de dicto* that objectum i_3 (who is believed by i_1 to be named i_4) has the property i_5.

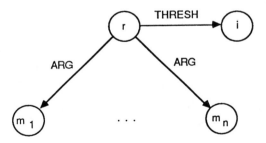

is a network, and r is a rule node.

SI.11 r is the Meinongian objective corresponding to the proposition that there is a relevant connection between propositions m_1, ... , m_n such that either fewer than i of them are true or they all are true.

Rule r of SR/SI.11 is called *THRESH* and is a generalization of the material biconditional ($i = 1$).

SR.12 If $a_1, \ldots, a_n, c_1, \ldots, c_j,$ and $d_1, \ldots, d_k$ are proposition nodes $(n \geq 1; j, k \geq 0; j + k \geq 1)$, "$i$" is an integer between 1 and n, inclusive, and "r" is an identifier not previously used, then

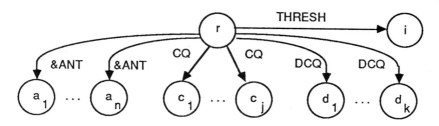

is a network, and r is a rule node.

SI.12 r is the Meinongian objective corresponding to the proposition that the conjunction of any i of the propositions $a_1,$ $\ldots, a_n$ relevantly implies each c_l $(1 \leq l \leq j)$ and relevantly implies each d_l $(1 \leq l \leq k)$ for which there is not a better reason to believe it is false.

SR.13 If $a_1, \ldots, a_n, c_1, \ldots, c_j,$ and $d_1, \ldots, d_k$ are proposition nodes $(n, j, k \geq 0)$, and "r" is an identifier not previously used, then

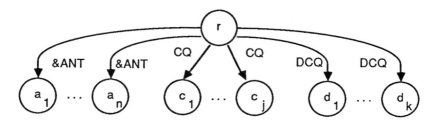

is a network, and r is a rule node.

SI.13 r is the Meinongian objective corresponding to the proposition that the conjunction of the propositions $a_1, \ldots, a_n$ relevantly implies each c_l $(1 \leq l \leq j)$ and relevantly implies each d_i $(1 \leqslant l \leqslant k)$ for which there is not a better reason to believe it is false.

The d_i are *default* consequences, in the sense that each is implied only if it is neither the case that CASSIE already believes *not* d_l nor that *not* d_i follows from non-default rules.

SR.14 If $a_1, \ldots, a_n, c_1, \ldots, c_j,$ *and* $d_1, \ldots, d_k$ are proposition nodes $(n \geqslant 1: j, k \geqslant 0; j + k \geqslant 1)$, and "$r$" is an identifier not previously used, then

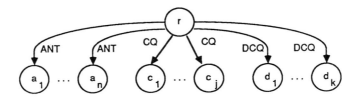

is a network, and r is a rule node.

SI.14 r is the Meinongian objective corresponding to the proposition that any a_i, $1 \leqslant i \leqslant n$, relevantly implies each c_l $(1 \leqslant l \leqslant j)$ and relevantly implies each d_l $(1 \leqslant l \leqslant k)$ for which there is not a better reason to believe it is false.

SR.15 If m is a proposition node, and "r" is an identifier not previously used, then

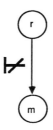

is a network, and r is a rule node.

SI.15 r is the Meinongian objective corresponding to the proposition that there is no good reason for believing proposition m.

SR.16 If r is a rule node as specified by SR.10-SR.15, and r dominates variable nodes v_1, ... , v_n, and, in addition, arcs labeled "AVB" go from r to each v_i, then r is a quantified rule node.

SI.16 r is the Meinongian objective corresponding to the proposition that the rule that would be expressed by r without the AVB arcs holds after replacing each v_i by any Meinongian object in its range.

SR.17 If r is a rule node as specified by SR.10-SR.15, and r dominates variable nodes v_1, ... , v_n, and, in addition, arcs labeled "EVB" go from r to each v_i, then r is a quantified rule node.

SI.17 r is the Meinongian objective corresponding to the proposition that the rule that would be expressed by r without the EVB arcs holds after replacing each v_i by some Meinongian object in its range.

SR.18 If a_1, ... , a_m and c are proposition nodes; v_1, ... , v_l are variable nodes dominated by one or more of a_1, ... , a_m, c; "i", "j", and "n" are integers $(0 \leqslant i \leqslant j \leqslant mn)$; and "$r$" is an identifier not previously used; then

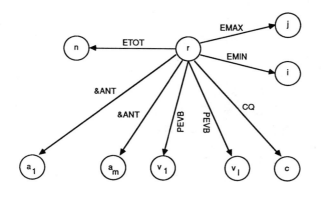

is a network, and r is a rule node.

SI.18 r is the Meinongian objective corresponding to the proposition that, of the n sequences of Meinongian objects which, when substituted for the sequence $v_1, ... , v_l$, make all the a_i believed propositions, between i and j of them also satisfy c. (For further details on such numerical quantifiers, see (Shapiro, 1979c).)

11.3.4. The conversation with CASSIE, revisited

In this section, we shall review the conversation we had with CASSIE, showing the network structure as it is built – that is, showing the structure of CASSIE's mind as she is given information and as she infers new information. (Comments are preceded by a dash.)

```
: Young Lucy petted a yellow dog
I understand that young Lucy petted a yellow dog

 - CASSIE is told something, which she now believes. Her
   entire belief  structure is shown in Figure 11-4 (a).
   The node labeled "now" represents the current time, so
   the petting is clearly  represented as being in the past.
   CASSIE's response is "I understand that" appended to her
   English description of the proposition just entered.


: What is yellow
a dog is yellow

 - This response shows that CASSIE actually has some
   beliefs; she  did not just parrot back the above
   sentence.

: Dogs are animals
I understand that dogs are animals

 - CASSIE is told a small section of a class hierarchy.

: Who petted an animal
young Lucy petted a yellow dog

 - CASSIE can answer the question using the class
   hierarchy, because, prior to the conversation,
   the inheritance rule
```

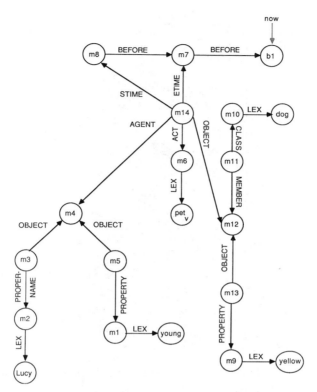

Figure 11-4:   Fragment of CASSIE's Belief Structure

Fragment of CASSIE's belief structure after being told
that young Lucy petted a yellow dog.

```
(def-path class (compose class (kstar
                (compose subclass- superclass))))
```

was given to SNePS. This rule says that the CLASS arc is
implied by the path consisting of a CLASS arc followed
by zero or more occurrences of the two-arc path
consisting of the converse SUBCLASS arc followed by the
SUPERCLASS arc [see (Shapiro, 1978), (Srihari, 1981)].
The dog was called "a yellow dog" rather than "a yellow
animal" because the redundant CLASS arc is not built.
Figure 11-5 shows the current state of
CASSIE's belief structure about the dog's classification
and color.

: Lucy is sweet
I understand that young Lucy is sweet
```
```

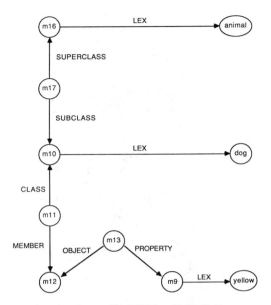

Figure 11-5:   CASSIE's Belief Structure

CASSIE's belief structure about the dog's classification
and color. (Node m12 represents the dog.)

- CASSIE's response shows that she identifies this
  Lucy with the previous Lucy.

: Lucy is a girl
I understand that sweet young Lucy is a girl

- The beginning of a class hierarchy for Lucy. Notice
  that all the adjectival properties of Lucy are mentioned.

: Girls are people
I understand that girls are people

- More of the class hierarchy is given.

: What was petted by a person
a yellow dog was petted by sweet young Lucy

- Again, the proposition is retrieved using the CLASS
  inheritance rule. The answer is expressed in the
  passive voice because of the way the question was
  asked.

: The dog is named Rover
I understand that Rover is a yellow dog

- 'the dog' refers to the only dog CASSIE knows about, who is now given a name.

: What was petted by a person
yellow Rover was petted by sweet young Lucy

- This is exactly the same question that was asked before. It is answered differently this time, because the dog now has a name, and CASSIE prefers to describe an individual by its name when it has one.

: John believes that Lucy is rich
I understand that John believes that Lucy is rich

- At this point in our development of CASSIE, she interprets 'believes that' contexts to be *de dicto*, so she assumes that the Lucy that John has in mind is a different one from the Lucy that she knows. Figure 11–6 shows CASSIE's beliefs about the two Lucies.

: Who is rich
I don't know.

- CASSIE knows no one who is rich. She only believes that *John* believes that someone (whom she believes that he believes to be named 'Lucy') is rich. The answer is 'I don't know', rather than 'no one is rich', because CASSIE doesn't use the closed-world hypothesis.

: Who is sweet
young Lucy is sweet

- This question is asked merely to demonstrate that Lucy is able to answer a "who is <property>" question when she has relevant beliefs.

: John believes that Lucy is old
I understand that John believes that rich Lucy is old

- Even though CASSIE assumes that John knows a different Lucy than she knows, she assumes that all John's beliefs about "Lucy" are about the same Lucy.

: John is a boy
I understand that John is a boy

- This and the next two inputs are given to establish more of the class hierarchy and

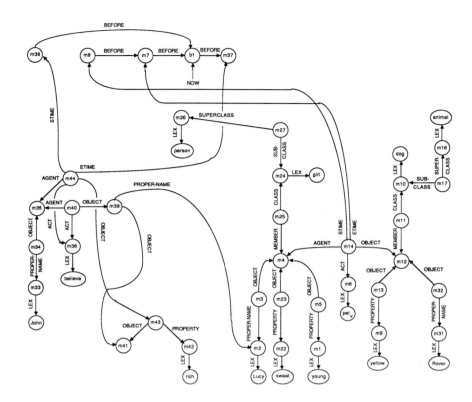

Figure 11-6:   A Fragment of the Network

A Fragment of the network after CASSIE is told that
John believes that Lucy is rich, showing CASSIE's beliefs
about the two Lucies.

to make it clear that when CASSIE answers
the last question of this session, she is
doing both path—based reasoning and node—
based reasoning at the same time.

I understand that boys are people

: Dogs are pets
I understand that dogs are pets

: For every p and d if p is a person and d is a pet then p
    loves d

I understand that for every d and p, if p is a person and
d is a pet

- Figure 11-7 shows how this node-based
  rule fits into the class hierarchy. This is, we
  believe, equivalent to the integrated TBox/ABox
  mechanism proposed for KRYPTON
  [(Brachman, Fikes, and Levesque, 1983),
  (Brachman, Gilbert, and Levesque, 1985)].

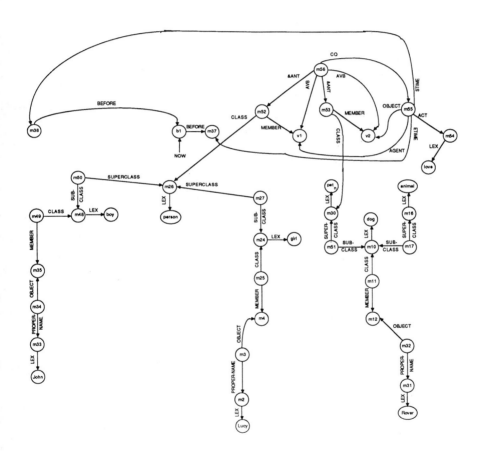

Figure 11-7: A Node-based Rule in a Class Hierarchy

: Who loves a pet
sweet young Lucy loves yellow Rover
and

John loves yellow Rover

– The question was answered using path–based inferencing
  to deduce that Lucy and John are people and that Rover
  is a pet, and node–based inferencing to conclude that,
  therefore, Lucy and John love Rover.

– The full network showing CASSIE's state of mind at the
  end of the conversation is given in Figure 11–8.

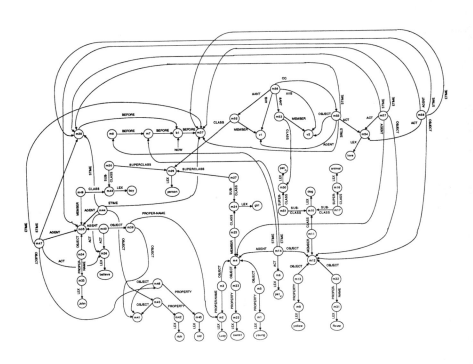

Figure 11-8:   CASSIE's Beliefs at the End of the Conversation

11.4. Extensions and applications of SNePS

In this essay, we have been advocating the use and interpretation of SNePS networks to model (the beliefs of) a cognitive agent. SNePS, however, is of much wider and more general applicability. In this section, we give examples of recent and current research projects using SNePS in belief-revision, as a database management system, for developing several expert systems, and for representing temporal information in narratives. Even though most of these uses of SNePS do not explicitly involve a cognitive agent, it should be noted that in each case the asserted nodes can be treated as "beliefs" of the system: beliefs about the database, beliefs about the various domains of the expert systems, beliefs about linguistics, etc.

11.4.1. SNePS as a database management system

SNePS can be used as a network version of a relational database in which every element of the relational database is represented by an atomic node, each row of each relation is represented by a molecular node, and each column label (attribute) is represented by an arc label. Whenever a row r has an element e in column c, the molecular node representing r has an arc labeled c pointing to the atomic node representing e. Relations (tables) may be distinguished by either of two techniques, depending on the particular relations and attributes in the relational database. If each relation has an attribute that does not occur in any other relation, then the presence of an arc labeled with that attribute determines the relationship represented by the molecular node. A review of the syntax of the CASSIE networks will show that this technique is used there. The other technique is to give every molecular node an additional arc (perhaps labeled "RELATION") pointing to an atomic node whose identifier is the name of the relation. Table 11-1 shows the Supplier-Part-Project database of (Date, 1981, p 114). Notice that the SNAME and STATUS attributes only occur in the SUPPLIER relation; PNAME, COLOR, and WEIGHT only occur in the PART relation; JNAME only occurs in the PROJECT relation; and QTY only occurs in the SPJ relation. Figure 11-9 shows the SNePS network for part of this database.

Table 1: SUPPLIER

S#	SNAME	STATUS	CITY
s1	Smith	20	London
s2	Jones	10	Paris
s3	Blake	30	Paris
s4	Clark	20	London
s5	Adams	30	Athens

Table 2: PART

P#	PNAME	COLOR	WEIGHT	CITY
p1	nut	red	12	London
p2	bolt	green	17	Paris
p3	screw	blue	17	Rome
p4	screw	red	14	London
p5	cam	blue	12	Paris
p6	cog	red	19	London

Table 3: PROJECT

J#	JNAME	CITY
j1	sorter	Paris
j2	punch	Rome
j3	reader	Athens
j4	console	Athens
j5	collator	London
j6	terminal	Oslo
j7	tape	London

Table 4: SPJ

S#	P#	J#	QTY
s1	p1	j1	200
s1	p1	j4	700
s2	p3	j1	400
s2	p3	j2	200
s2	p3	j3	200
s2	p3	j4	500
s2	p3	j5	600
s2	p3	j6	400
s2	p3	j7	800
s2	p5	j2	100
s3	p3	j1	200
s3	p4	j2	500
s4	p6	j3	300
s4	p6	j7	300
s5	p2	j2	200
s5	p2	j4	100
s5	p5	j5	500
s5	p5	j7	100
s5	p6	j2	200
s5	p1	j4	1000
s5	p3	j4	1200
s5	p4	j4	800
s5	p5	j4	400
s5	p6	j4	500

Table 11-1:   Tables **Supplier Part Project** and **SPJ**

Many database retrieval requests may be formulated using the **find** command of SNePSUL, the SNePS User's Language. The syntax of **find** is **(find r_1 n_1 ... r_m n_m)**, where r_i is either an arc or a path, and n_i is either a node or a set of nodes (possibly the value of a nested call to **find**). The value of a call to find is the set of all nodes in the network with an r_1 arc to any node in the set n_1, an r_2 arc to any node in

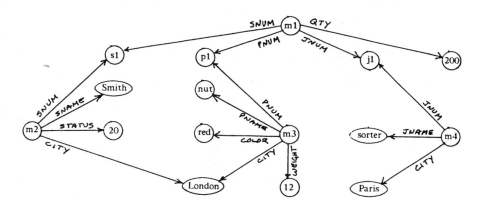

Figure 11-9:   Fragment of SNePS Network for the
Supplier-Part-Project Database.

the set n_2, ... , and an r_m arc to any node in the set n_m. Free
variables are prefixed by "?". An infix '-' sign between **finds**
represents the set difference operator.

The session below shows some of the queries from (Date,
1981); pp 141-142 translated into **find** commands, and the
results on the database shown above.   (In each interaction,
comments are preceded by semicolons, user input follows the
'*'-prompt, and SNePS responses are on succeeding lines.
Execution and garbage collection times have been edited out for
clarity.)

```
; Get full details of all projects in London.
* (dump (find jname ?x city London))
(m18 (city (London)) (jname (tape)) (jnum (j7)))
(m16 (city (London)) (jname (collator)) (jnum (j5)))
(dumped)

; Get SNUM values for suppliers who supply project J1
; with part P1.
* (find snum- (find jnum j1 pnum p1))
(s1)

; Get JNAME values for projects supplied by supplier S1.
```

```
* (find (jname- jnum jnum- snum) s1)
(console sorter)

; Get S# values for suppliers who supply both projects
; J1 and J2.
* (find (snum- jnum) j1 (snum- jnum) j2)
(s3 s2)

; Get the names of the suppliers who supply project J1
; with a red part.
* (find (sname- snum snum-)  (find jnum j1 (pnum pnum-
      color) red))
(Smith)

; Get S# values for suppliers who supply a London or Paris
;      project with a red part.
* (find snum- (find (jnum jnum- city) (London Paris)
                    (pnum pnum- color) red))
(s4 s1)

; Get P# values for parts supplied to any project by
;      a supplier in the same city.
* (find pnum- (find (jnum jnum- city) ?city (snum snum-
      city) ?city))
(p5 p4 p1 p2 p6 p3)

; Get J# values for projects not supplied with any red part
;      by any London supplier.
* ((find jnum- ?x)-(find jnum- (find (pnum pnum- color) red
                                (snum snum- city) London)))
(j6 j5 j2)

, Get S# values for suppliers supplying at least one part
; supplied by at least one supplier who supplies at least
; one red part.
* (find (snum- pnum pnum- snum snum- pnum pnum- color) red)
(s3 s4 s2 s5 s1)

; Get J# values for projects which use only parts which are
;      available from supplier S1.
* ((find jnum- (find qty ?q))
   - (find (jnum- pnum) (find pnum- ?r) - (find (pnum- snum)
     s1)))
nil
```

11.4.2. Address recognition for mail sorting

A research group led by Sargur N. Srihari is studying address recognition techniques for automated mail sorting (Srihari, Sargur, Jonathan, Palumbo, Niyogi, and Wang, 1985).

Computer determination of the sort-destination of an arbitrary piece of letter-mail from its visual image is a problem that remains far from solved. It involves overcoming several sources of ambiguity at both the spatio-visual and linguistic levels: The location of the destination address has to be determined in the presence of other text and graphics; relevant address lines have to be isolated when there are irrelevant lines of text in the address block; the iconic shapes of characters have to be classified into words of text when numerous types of fonts, sizes, and printing media are present; and the recognized words have to be verified as having the syntax and semantics of an address.

Spatial relationships between objects are essential knowledge sources for vision systems. This source extends naturally to the postal-image understanding problem, because of strong directional expectations. For example, the postage mark is usually above and to the right of the destination address, and the return address is usually to the left of the postage. A semantic network is a natural representation for geometric relations.

An envelope image is segmented into blocks, and a SNePS network is built that represents the geometric relations between blocks and information about the relative and absolute area occupied by each block. A preliminary set of geometric relations are the eight compass points. Relative area occupancy is expressed as the percentage of each block that falls in each of nine equal rectangular subdivisions of the envelope image, and absolute area is given in terms of the number of pixels covered by each block. The program constructs an exhaustive representation of all the geometric relations present in the image. Given the image produced by an initial segmentation procedure, a rough, intuitive output, shown in Figure 11-10 with some arc labels removed for clarity) was produced.

Future work in this area includes refinement of the data structure to represent more information more efficiently and the addition of inferencing capabilities whose objective is to present the control structure with tentative decisions about the address block based only on the information provided by the initial segmentation.

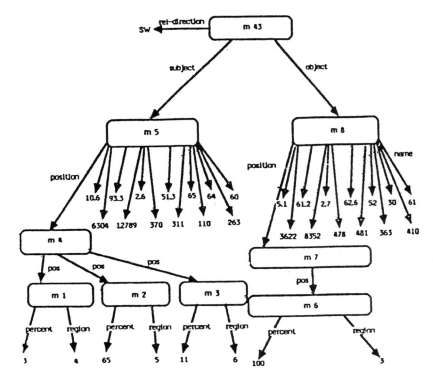

Figure 11-10:   SNePS Network Representation of Initial
                     Segmentation of Envelope Image
                     (from Srihari, Hull et al. 1985)

11.4.3. NEUREX

The NEUREX project (Cheng, 1984), (Xiang and Srihari,
1985), (Xiang, Srihari, Shapiro and Chutkow, 984"), (Suchin,
1985) is a diagnostic expert system for diseases of the central
and peripheral nervous systems; it also deals with information
about neuroaffectors, neuroreceptors, and body parts. SNePS is
used to represent spatial structures and functions
propositionally. Entities are represented topologically by means
of proposition nodes expressing an entity's shape, position, etc.,
and spatial relations are represented by proposition nodes

expressing adjacency, connectivity, direction, etc. This approach integrates structural and functional neuroanatomical information. Moreover, the representation is both propositional and analog. For the peripheral nervous system, there are nodes representing such propositions as that, for example, a sequence of nerve segments are linked at junctions, and that the whole sequence forms a (peripheral) nerve; the network that is built is itself an analog representation of this nerve (and ultimately, together with its neighbors, of the entire peripheral nervous system). See Chapter 15 for further discussion of analog representations. For the central nervous system, there are coordinates in the network representation that can be used to support reasoning by geometrical computation or graphical interfaces.

As one example, the network of Figure 11-11 can be used by the system to determine which muscles are involved in shoulder-joint flexion, using the SNePS User Language request

```
(find (ms- cn) (find jt shoulder-joint mv flexion)),
```

which returns the following list of four nodes:

```
(deltoid pectoralis_major_clavicular_head
coracobrachialis biceps_brachii)
```

Furthermore, rules, like that shown in Figure 11-12, can be employed and can even include probabilistic information. (Note that node r in Figure 11-12 is the SNePS implementation of the IF-THEN rule; cf. (SR.13).)

11.4.4. Representing visual knowledge

The goal of the Versatile Maintenance Expert System (VMES) project is to develop an expert maintenance system that can reason about digital circuits represented graphically (cf. (Shapiro, Srihari, Geller, and Taie, 1986;SSTG86)). A similar perspective on the need for visual knowledge representation is taken by Tsotsos and Shibahara (Chapter 10) and Havens and Mackworth (Chapter 16). The representation is not pixel-oriented; this is a project in visual knowledge representation integrated with more traditional conceptual and propositional knowledge representation. The graphical form of

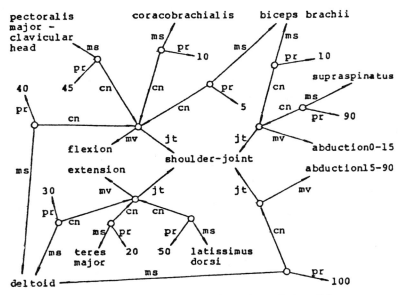

Figure 11-11:   Four of the Shoulder-Joint Movements

Four of the shoulder-joint movements with musscles involved
and their contribution to each relevant movement. (Meaning
of the arc labels: jt=joint; mv=movement; ms=muscle;
cn=contribute; pr=percentage.) (From Xiang and Srihari 1985)

an object is a LISP function that, when evaluated, draws the
object on the screen.   Propositional nodes express information
about (1) the relative or absolute position of the object and (2)
attributes of the object.   Visual knowledge can also be
distributed among nodes in traditional hierarchies: for example,
the knowledge of how to display a particular hammer may be
stored at the level of the class of hammers; the knowledge of
how to display a person may be distributed among the nodes
for heads, arms, etc.

For example, Figure 11-13 shows a set of three assertions.
Node   m233   represents   the   assertion   that   the   object
TRIANGLE-1 is 100 units to the right and 20 units below the
object SQUARE-1. The MODALITY arc permits the selection of
different modes of display; here, we want to display
TRIANGLE-1 in "functional" mode.   Node m220 states that
every member of the class TRIANGLE displayed in functional
mode has the form DTRIANG associated with it. Finally, node
m219 asserts that TRIANGLE-1 is a TRIANGLE.

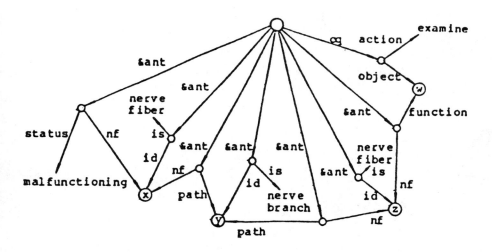

Figure 11-12:   SNePS Network for a NEUREX Rule. .
(From Xiang and Srihari 1985)

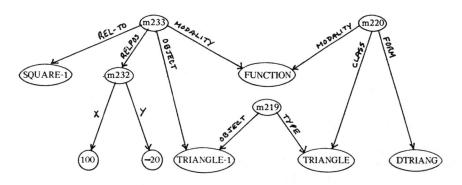

Figure 11-13:   SNePS Network in VMES for the Form
and Relative Position of TRIANGLE-1.

Figure 11-14 contains four assertions, of which node
m246 is the most complex. It links the object GATE-1 to an
absolute position at 100/400 and to the class of all AND-gates.
Node m244 asserts that GATE-1 is a part of BOARD-1. Node

m248 asserts that INP1-GATE1 is a PART-OF GATE-1 and belongs to the class AINP1. The label 'PART' actually stands for "has part". Node m239 links the attribute BAD to GATE-1. Every attribute belongs to an attribute class, and the arc ATTRIBUTE-CLASS points to the class STATE.

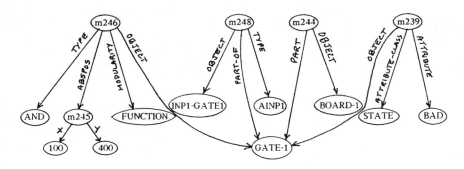

Figure 11-14:   SNePS Network in VMES for the Location, Structure, and State of GATE-1.

11.4.5. SNeBR: A belief revision package

The SNePS Inference Package has been extended by João Martins to handle belief revision – an area of AI research concerned with the issues of revising sets of beliefs when a contradiction is found in a reasoning system. Research topics in belief revision include the study of the representation of beliefs, in particular how to represent the notion of belief dependence; the development of methods for selecting the subset of beliefs responsible for contradictions; and the development of techniques to remove some subset of beliefs from the original set of beliefs. (For an overview of the field, see (Martins, 1987).)

SNeBR (*SNe*PS *B*elief *R*evision) is an implementation in SNePS of an abstract belief revision system called the Multiple Belief Reasoner (MBR), which, in turn, is based on a relevance logic system called SWM (after Shapiro, Wand, and Martins)

(Shapiro and Wand, 1976), (Martins, 1983b), (Martins, 1983a), (Martins and Shapiro, 1984), (Martins and Shapiro, 1986a), (Martins and Shapiro, 1986b), (Martins and Shapiro, 1986c). SWM contains the rules of inference of MBR and defines how contradictions are handled. The only aspect of SWM relevant to this description concerns the objects with which MBR deals, called *supported wffs*. They are of the form

$$A \mid t, o, r$$

where A is a well-formed formula representing a proposition, t is an *origin tag* indicating how A was obtained (for example, as a hypothesis or as a derived proposition), o is an *origin set* containing *all* and *only* the hypotheses used to derive A, and r is a *restriction set* containing information about contradictions *known* to involve the hypotheses in o. The triple t, o, r is called the *support* of the wff A. The origin tag, origin set, and restriction set of a wff are computed when the wff is derived, and its restriction set may be updated when contradictions are discovered.

MBR uses the concepts of context and belief space. A *context* is any set of hypotheses. A context determines a *belief space*, which is the set of all the hypotheses defining the context together with all propositions derived exclusively from them. The propositions in the belief space defined by a given context are characterized by having an origin set that is contained in the context. At any point, the set of all hypotheses under consideration is called the *current context*, which defines the *current belief space*. The only propositions that are retrievable at a given time are the ones belonging to the current belief space.

A contradiction may be detected either because an assertion is derived that is the negation of an assertion already in the network, or because believed assertions invalidate a rule being used (particularly an AND-OR or a THRESH rule; see (SR/SI.10-11)). In the former case, the contradiction is noted when the new, contradictory, assertion is about to be built into the network, since the Uniqueness Principle guarantees that the contradictory assertions will share network structure. In the latter case, the contradiction is noted in the course of applying the rule. In the former case, it may be that the contradictory assertions are in different belief spaces (only the new one being in the current belief space). If so, the restriction sets are updated to reflect the contradictory sets of hypotheses, and nothing else happens. If the contradictory assertions are both in the current belief space (which will be the case when one of them is a rule being used), then, besides updating the restriction sets, the user will be asked to delete at least one of the hypotheses underlying the contradiction from the current context. Management of origin sets according to SWM guarantees that, as long as the current context was originally not known to be contradictory, removal of any one of the hypotheses in the union of the origin sets of the contradictory assertions from the current context will restore the current context to the state of not being known to be inconsistent.

11.5. Knowledge-based natural language understanding

Jeannette Neal has developed an AI system that can treat knowledge of its own language as its discourse domain, (Neal, 1985). The system's linguistic knowledge is represented declaratively in its network knowledge base in such a way that it can be used in the dual role of "program" to analyze language input to the system and "data" to be queried or reasoned about. Since language forms (part of) its domain of discourse, the system is also able to learn from the discourse by being given instruction in the processing and understanding of language. As the system's language knowledge is expanded beyond a primitive kernel language, instructions can be expressed in an increasingly sophisticated subset of the language being taught. Thus, the system's language is used as its own metalanguage.

The kernel language consists of a relatively small collection of predefined terms and rewrite rules for expressing syntax and for expressing the mapping of surface strings to the representation of their interpretations.

The knowledge representations include representations for surface strings and for relations such as: (a) a lexeme being a member of a certain lexical category, (b) bounded string B being in category C and this phrase structure being represented by concept N. (c) a structure or parsed string expressing a certain concept, and (d) one phrase structure being a constituent of another structure.

In order to talk about both the syntax and semantics of language, the network representations distinguish between a word or string and its interpretation. In one experiment, the statements

> (1)   A WOMAN IS A HUMAN
> (2)   'WOMAN' IS SINGULAR

were input to the system. The first makes a claim about women; the second makes a claim about the *word* 'woman'. Nodes m40 and m50 of Figure 11-15, respectively, represent the propositions expressed by these statements. The concept or class expressed by 'WOMAN' is represented by node b22; the entity represented by node b22 is a participant in the subset-superset proposition expressed by (1). However, in the representation of (2), the word 'WOMAN' itself is the entity having the property SINGULAR.

Additional statements, such as:

> (R) IF THE HEAD-NOUN OF A NOUN-PHRASE X
>   HAS NUMBER Y, THEN X HAS NUMBER Y.

were input to the system to demonstrate the use of a subset of English as its own metalanguage in building up the system's language ability from its primitive predefined language. Figure 11-16 illustrates the representation of the system's interpretation of rule (R) as well as the representation of certain linguistic relations. Node m87 represents the proposition that some bounded string represented by variable node v4 is in the category HEAD-NOUN, and this phrase structure is represented by variable node v3. Node m88 represents that the phrase structure represented by node v3 is a constituent of v1, which represents a NOUN-PHRASE structure. (In this figure, the AVB arcs have been eliminated for clarity; cf. (SR/SI.16).) As soon as any rule such as (R) is parsed and interpreted, it is immediately available for use in subsequent processing. Thus, the system is continuously educable and can use its language as its own metalanguage.

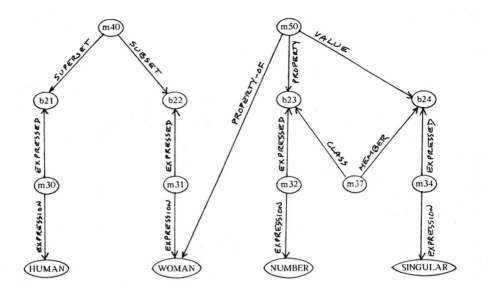

Figure 11-15:   Representation of the Interpretation of
Statements About Linguistic and Non-
linguistic Entities.

11.5.1. Temporal structure of narrative

Michael Almeida is using SNePS in the development of a
system that will be able to read a simple narrative text and
construct a model of its temporal structure   (Almeida and
Shapiro, 1983), (Almeida, 1986).   This project uses an event-
based, rather than a proposition-based, approach: that is,
intervals and points of time are associated with events
represented as objects in the network rather than with the
propositions that describe them.   The temporal model itself
consists of these intervals and points of time related to one
another   by   such   relations   as   BEFORE/AFTER,
DURING/CONTAINS, etc.

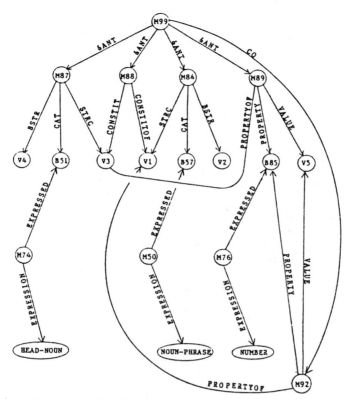

Figure 11-16: SNePS Net for Rule (R) (From Neal, 1985)

The representation of the following short narrative,

> John arrived at the house. The sun was setting.
> He rang the bell; a minute later, Mary opened
> the door.

is shown in Figure 11-17. The ARG-PRED-EVENT case frame
asserts that the proposition consisting of the argument pointed
to by the ARG-arc and the predicate pointed to by the PRED-
arc describes the event pointed to by the EVENT-arc. Notice
that the predicates are classified into various types. This
information plays an important role in the temporal analysis of
a text.

NOW is a reference point that indicates the present
moment of the narrative; it is updated as the story progresses
through time. NOW is implemented as a variable whose
current value is indicated in Figure 11-17 by a dotted arrow.

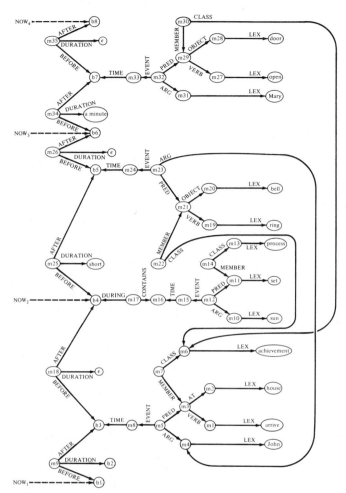

Figure 11-17:   SNePS Network for a Short Narrative.

Subscripts are used in the figure to show the successive values of NOW.

The BEFORE-AFTER-DURATION case frame is used to indicate that the period of time pointed to by the BEFORE-arc temporally precedes the period of time pointed to by the AFTER-arc by the length of time pointed to by the DURATION-arc.   These durations are usually not known precisely. The value <epsilon> stands for a very short interval; whenever an event occurs in the narrative line, it has the effect of moving NOW an interval of <epsilon> beyond it.

The DURING-CONTAINS case frame is used to indicate that the period of time pointed to by the DURING-arc is during (or contained in) the period of time pointed to by the CONTAINS-arc. Notice that the progressive sentence, "The sun was setting", created an event that contains the then-current NOW. If the system knows about such things as sunsets, then it should infer that the event of the sun's setting also contains John's arrival, his ringing of the bell, and probably also Mary's opening of the door.

11.6. Conclusion: SNePS and SNePS/CASSIE as Semantic Networks

We shall conclude by looking at SNePS and SNePS/CASSIE from the perspective of Brachman's discussions of structured inheritance networks such as KL-One and hierarchies of semantic network formalisms (Brachman, 1977, Brachman, 1979).

11.6.1. Criteria for semantic networks

Brachman offers six criteria for semantic networks:

A semantic network must have a *uniform notation*. SNePS provides some uniform notation with its built-in arc labels for rules, and it provides a uniform procedure for users to choose their own notation.

A semantic network must have an *algorithm for encoding information*. This is provided for by the interfaces to SNePS, for example, by the parser component of our ATN parser-generator that takes English sentences as input and produces SNePS networks as output.

A semantic network must have an *"assimilation"* *mechanism* for building new information in terms of stored information. SNePS provides for this by the Uniqueness Principle, which enforces node sharing during network building. The assimilation is demonstrated by the generator component of our ATN parser-generator, which takes SNePS nodes as input and produces English output expressing those nodes: Our conversation with CASSIE illustrated this the node built to represent the new fact, 'Lucy is sweet', is expressed in terms of the already existing node for Lucy (who had previously been described as young) by 'young Lucy is sweet'.

A semantic network should be *neutral* with respect to network formalisms at higher levels in the Brachman hierarchy. SNePS is a semantic network at the "logical" level, whereas SNePS/CASSIE is at the "conceptual" level. SNePS is neutral in the relevant sense; it is not so clear whether SNePS/CASSIE is. But neutrality at higher levels may not be so important; a more important issue is the reasons why one formalism should be chosen over another. Several possible criteria that a researcher might consider are: *efficiency* (including the ease of interfacing with other modules; for example, our ATN parser-generator has been designed for direct interfacing with SNePS), *psychological adequacy* (irrelevant for SNePS, but precisely what SNePS/CASSIE is being designed for), *ontological adequacy* (irrelevant for SNePS/CASSIE-see below), *logical adequacy* (guaranteed for SNePS because of its inference package), and *natural language adequacy* (a feature of SNePS's interface with the ATN grammar).

A semantic network should be *adequate* for any higher-level network formalism. SNePS meets this nicely: KL-One can be implemented in SNePS (Tranch, 1982).

A semantic network should have a *semantics*. We presented that in Section 11.3. But it should be observed that there are at least two very different sorts of semantics. In SNePS, nodes have a meaning *within the system* in terms of their links to other nodes; they have a meaning *for users* as provided by the nodes at the heads of LEX arcs. Arcs, on the other hand, only have meaning within the system, provided by node- and path-based inference rules (which can be thought of as procedures that operate on the arcs). In both cases, there is an "internal", system semantics that is holistic and structural: the meaning of the nodes and arcs are not given in isolation, but in terms of the entire network. This sort of "syntactic" semantics differs from a semantics that provides links to an external interpreting system, such as a user or the "world" - that is, links between the network's way of representing information and the user's way. It is the latter sort of semantics that we provided for SNePS/CASSIE with respect to an ontology of Meinongian objects.

11.6.2. SNePS and SNePS/CASSIE vs. KL-One

SNePS and SNePS/CASSIE can be compared directly to KL-One. Unlike KL-One, which is an *inheritance*-network formalism for representing concepts, instances of concepts, and properties and relations among them, SNePS is a *propositional*-network formalism for representing propositions and their constituents (individuals, properties, and relations).

Nevertheless, SNePS can handle inheritance. We have already seen an example of inheritance by *path*-based inference in the conversation with CASSIE. In that example, inheritance could also have been accomplished through node-based inference by, for example, representing 'dogs are animals' as a universally-quantified rule rather than by a SUBCLASS-SUPERCLASS case frame. That is, where an inheritance network might express the claim that dogs are animals by a single arc (say, a subclass-arc) from a dog-node to an animal-node, SNePS could express it by a proposition (represented by node m17 in Figure 11-5.).

One advantage of the propositional mode of representation and, consequently, of the second, or *rule*-based, form of property inheritance is that the proposition (m17) expressing the relationship can then become the objective of a proposition representing an agent's belief or it can become the antecedent or consequent of a node-based rule. In some inheritance networks, this could only be done by choosing to represent the entire claim by either the dog-node, the animal-node, the subclass-arc, or (perhaps) the entire structure consisting of the two nodes and the arc. The first two options seem incorrect; the third and fourth either introduce an anomaly into the representation (since arcs can then point either to nodes or to other arcs or to structures), or it reduces to what SNePS does: SNePS, in effect, trades in the single arc for a node with two outgoing arcs. In this way, the arcs of inheritance networks become information-bearing nodes, and the semantic network system becomes a propositional one.

Second, KL-One uses "epistemologically primitive links".

But why does KL-One use the particular set of links that it does, and not some other set; that is, what is the ontological justification for KL-One's links?   There have been many philosophical and logical theories of the relations of the One to the Many (part-whole, member-set-superset, instance-concept, individual-species-genus, object-Platonic Form, etc.).   KL-One's only motivation seems to be as a computationally efficient theory that clarifies the nature of inheritance networks; but it does not pretend to ontological or psychological adequacy. Indeed, it raises almost as many questions as it hopes to answer. For example, in KL-One, instances of a general concept seem to consist of *instances* of the attributes of the general concept, each of which instances have *instances* of the values of those attributes.   But this begs important philosophical questions about the relations between properties of concepts (or of Forms, or of ...) and properties of individuals falling under those concepts (or participating in those Forms, or ...; some of these issues are discussed in (Brachman, 1983), but not from a philosophical point of view):   Are they the same properties? Are the latter "instances" of the former?   Are there such things as concepts (or Forms, or ...) of properties?   And do instance nodes represent individuals?   Do they represent individual concepts?   [cf. (Brachman, 1977): 148.]

Now, on the one hand, SNePS/CASSIE's arcs are also taken to be "primitive"; but they are justified by the Meinongian philosophy of mind briefly sketched out above and explored in depth in the references cited.   On the other hand, SNePS's arcs, by contrast to both SNePS/CASSIE's and KL-One's, are not restricted to any particular set of primitives. We believe that the interpretation of a particular use of SNePS depends on the *user's* world-view; the user should not be required to conform to *ours*.

And, unlike KL-One, the entities in the ontology for SNePS/CASSIE are not to be taken as representing things in the world: SNePS/CASSIE's ontology is an *epistemological ontology* [cf. (Rapaport, 1985a), (Rapaport, 1985b), (Rapaport, 1986a)] consisting of the purely intensional items that enable a cognitive agent to have beliefs (about the world). An epistemological ontology is a theory of what there must be in order for a cognitive agent to have beliefs (about what there is).

12. Representing Virtual Knowledge Through Logic Programming

Veronica Dahl

Laboratory for Computer and Communications Research
School of Computing Science
Simon Fraser University
Burnaby, British Columbia, CANADA V5A 1S6

Abstract

The idea of representing knowledge through logic programming is examined in simple, non-technical terms. We show how to represent problem-solving and database systems knowledge in terms of logical descriptions of facts and rules. These facts and rules describe a general context or world and allow for appropriate inferences to be drawn automatically, triggered by the statement of a specific problem in the world described. Thus, problem-solving and database consultation can be mostly viewed as side-effects of merely stating the problem to be solved of the data to be retrieved, and letting a hidden theorem-prover make the necessary inferences from a logic-programmed representation of the world.

Based on the paper, Logic Programming as a
Representation of Knowledge, Veronica Dahl, appearing in COMPUTER,
Volume 16, Number 10, October, 1983.

12.1. Introduction

The idea that logic could serve as a programming language (Kowalski, 1974), (van Emden, 1977) was put to practical use around 1972 in the form of Prolog, (Colmerauer, 1973b) (Roussel, 1975). It has proved extremely valuable in many ambitious and diverse computational areas, including natural language processing, deductive databases, robotics, symbolic integration, and expert systems.

Logic has traditionally provided a firm conceptual framework for representing knowledge, as it can formally deal with the notion of logical consequence. The introduction of Prolog has made it possible to represent knowledge in terms of logic and also to expect appropriate inferences to be drawn from it automatically.

In Prolog, knowledge is expressed straightforwardly in terms of *facts* and *rules* for computing further facts; and whatever logical consequences follow from them are available to the user upon request. These consequences can be viewed as virtual knowledge: not explicitly present, but deducible. The deductions necessary to this are performed by the Prolog interpreter, and hidden from the user. Thus, logic programming not only provides a highly formalized while practical context for representing knowledge, but also provides the machinery for processing that knowledge in an automatic fashion.

Because of this amalgamation of declarative and procedural notions, a parallel can be drawn with PSN (see Chapter 10, this volume), which tries to integrate semantic networks and procedural notions. Kowalski has described semantic networks as a particular case of logic programming, and presented extended semantic networks as an alternative notation for it (Kowalski, 1979). Logic programming, although not specifically suited for heuristic knowledge, has proved to be an excellent tool for expert systems development (Dahl and Sambuc, 1976).

This article illustrates and explores the ideas of logic programming with respect to two central representational issues; problem-solving knowledge and database knowledge. The technical aspects of both subjects have been covered elsewhere (Kowalski, 1979) (Dahl, 1982); this explanation uses simple, nontechnical terms.

12.2. Representing knowledge in Prolog

We can express knowledge in Prolog in terms of either facts or rules. The basic units for building facts or rules are *predications*, that is, expressions that say simple things about the individuals in our universe. For instance, the piece of information "Sweetie likes Rover" is represented

$$likes(Sweetie, Rover).$$

Classes of individuals, which we would introduce in English through words such as "everyone," "anything," "somebody," etc., must make use of variables. For instance, "Everyone is liked by its/her/his mother" can be represented

$$likes(mother(x), x).$$

Predications, in short, are represented by a predicate name (for example, "likes") followed by a list of arguments. Each argument can be

1. the <u>name</u> of an individual, also called a constant (for example, "Sweetie," "Rover");

2. a <u>variable</u> (for example, "x"); or

3. a <u>functional</u> <u>expression</u> (for example, "mother(x)").

Functional expressions can be thought of as names for those individuals who are in the corresponding functional relation to their arguments; for example, mother(x) is a name for the individual who happens to be the mother of x. We can represent a fact simply by writing a predication followed by a period:

$$likes(Sweetie, Rover).$$

Prolog will take this as an assertion that the predication holds in the world we are trying to describe.

Rules, on the other hand, have the general form

$$P_1 \text{ if } (p_2 \text{ and } P_3 \text{ and } \dots \text{ and } P_n)$$

where the P_i stand for predications and the parentheses are generally omitted. For instance, the general rule that Rover likes everyone who likes him can be stated

likes(Rover,y) if likes(y,Rover).

Prolog will take a rule as stating that if all the conditions P_2, P_3, ..., P_n hold, then the conclusions P_1 holds. If the rule contains any variables, it is taken to apply for all their possible values. Thus, in a world in which our only individuals were Rover and Sweetie, writing the rule

likes(Rover,y) if likes(y,Rover).

would amount to writing the two rules

likes(Rover,Rover) if likes(Rover,Rover).

likes(Rover,Sweetie) if likes(Sweetie,Rover).

These rules are called *instances* of the more general rule above. (Notice that the first of the two rules, if applied while trying to prove that Rover likes himself, can lead to an infinite loop. Skillful programming makes as much of a difference in Prolog as in any other language.)

The individuals who constitute the world are the ones we have referred to in our facts and rules either directly through their identifying names (for example, Rover) or indirectly through functional expressions (for example, mother(x) can denote mother(Sweetie), or mother(mother(Rover)), etc., in a world in which the only constants are Rover and Sweetie). Facts containing variables are likewise taken to stand for all their possible instances.

Given knowledge about a certain domain or world, we usually have alternative ways of representing it through facts and rules. For instance, the piece of information "everyone is liked by its/his/her mother" could also be represented

likes(x,y) if mother(x,y)

(that is, if x is the mother of y, then x likes y). Here we are using a binary predication instead of a functional expression to represent the relationship "mother" between two individuals.

Whatever representation is chosen, it must remain consistent throughout the whole description and querying of our knowledge. Each individual represented should have a unique name.

We can represent more information with predications than we can with functions. For instance, if we take uncle(x,y) to mean x is the uncle of y, we can easily describe a world where a person has two uncles:

uncle(Tom, Mary).

uncle(John, Mary).

If, however, the only means of referring to somebody's uncle is a functional expression of the form uncle(x), then we can only name one uncle for each individual, since uncle(Mary) denotes a unique individual in the universe.

12.3. Asking for inferences - virtual knowledge

Once a set of facts and rules has been defined to Prolog, we can use Prolog to check whether our assumptions about the world described are consistent with the description. We can even ask Prolog to find information that can be deduced from those facts and rules. This is done ·by writing a query, an expression of the form

P_1 and P_2 and...P_n?

where the P_i are predications.

For instance, given the world description

```
(1) likes(Sweetie, Rover).
(2) likes(mother(x), x).
(3) likes(Rover, y) if likes(y, Rover).
(4) likes(Rover, Tim).
```

we can verify that Sweetie does indeed like Rover by writing the query

likes(Sweetie, Rover)?

to which Prolog will print some indication of agreement, such as "yes" or "no" (in this case "yes").

If we want to obtain information about who likes Rover, we can write

likes(z, Rover)?

This causes Prolog to find instances of the above predication that make it true. It finds the answers

```
z = Sweetie
z = mother(Rover).
```

To ask about who Rover likes, on the other hand, we query

likes(Rover,z)?

This causes Prolog to find the answers

```
z = Sweetie
z = mother(Rover)
z = Tim.
```

The way Prolog makes these deductions is of no concern to the user, but to form a clear intuitive picture of what is going on we can imagine that each program is automatically expanded with all those instances of its facts and rules that are relevant to our query. Thus, the query "likes(Rover, z)?" would use the following instances of our facts and rules:

```
(5) likes (mother(Rover), Rover).
(6) likes (Rover, mother(Rover)) if
          likes(mother(Rover), Rover).
(7) likes(Rover, Sweetie) if
          likes(Sweetie, Rover).
```

With respect to this extended, more explicit world description, the answer z = mother(Rover) follows from (5) and (6). The answer z = Tim follows trivially from (4).

Here are two more possible queries and their answers:

```
likes(x, Rover) and likes(Rover, x)
     [Who likes and is liked by Rover?]

x = Sweetie
x = mother(Rover)

likes(x, y)?            [Who likes whom?]

x = Sweetie, y = Rover
```

```
x = mother(Rover), y = Rover
x = Rover, y = Sweetie
x = Rover, y = mother(Rover)
x = Rover, y = Tim.
```

In short, Prolog answers a query

$$P_1 \text{ and } P_2 \text{ ... and } P_n?$$

by taking each P_i in turn and trying to find it among the
expanded facts and rules, either as a fact or as the left-most
predication of a rule. If found among the facts, Pi is
considered proven. If it appears in a rule of the form

$$P_i \text{ if } Q_1 \text{ and } Q_2 \text{ ... and } Q_m,$$

then Prolog simply tries to prove each and all of Q_1, ..., Q_m in
the same fashion. Any variable instances adopted for the
expansions needed are remembered and thus form the answers
required.

Users can specify alternative proof paths for a predication
P_i simply by giving several rules like the one above. For
instance, we can give Prolog the following two ways of
proving that a person is someone else's parent:

```
parent(x,y) if mother(x,y).
parent(x,y) if father(x,y).
```

Facts, rules, and queries can be augmented with control
and input/output specifications. Through these specifications we
can, for instance, instruct Prolog to find and print one, several,
or all of the possible answers. Rather then dwell on them here,
let's just say that queries may look more like the following
example:

likes(x,y) and write(x) and write(y)?[37]

The names we choose for variables are local to each fact,
rule, or query. Thus, in the above query, x stands, in both of

---

[37]Some Prolog versions (for example, DEC 10) automatically print values for
variables in a query, but other input/output and control features are more
difficult to automatically embed in the language.

its occurrences, for the same individual in our world, but it is totally unrelated (except for coincidence) to the variable also named x in fact (2). This corresponds to our intuitive notion of what words like "everyone" mean. If we say "everyone invited showed up" and "everyone not invited was offended," we are clearly referring to distinct groups of individuals in each case, although in both sentences we introduce them through the same word, "everyone."

12.4. Representing problem-solving knowledge

The logic programming methodology can be used for describing and retrieving general knowledge about the world, for describing our knowledge about traditional computational tasks, and even for describing less commonplace problem-solving tasks that for the time being are considered within the artificial intelligence field. Since Prolog is essentially a programming language, and since problem solving is still largely dependent on our human intuitions, which are often hard to explain and formalize, there is no general recipe for a "best" use of Prolog in problem solving. But I will try to illustrate some of the flexibility that Prolog offers by considering the pathfinding approach to problem solving.

In this approach we represent a problem domain as a world with a set of actions that transform that world from one state to another. A particular problem is then specified by describing an initial state and a desired goal state, and the problem solver is expected to find a path, that is, a sequence of actions, leading from the initial state to the goal state.

Consider the following situation, for example. A farmer, a wolf, a goat, and a head of cabbage are all on the north bank of a river, and the problem is to transfer them to the south bank. The farmer has a rowboat in which he can take only one passenger at a time. The goat cannot be left with the wolf, and the cabbage, which counts as a passenger, cannot be left with the goat.

Since there are four individuals in our world, we can represent a state of the world though a predication

$$state(x,y,z,v),$$

which expresses that the farmer is on bank x, the wolf on
bank y, the goat on bank z, and the cabbage on bank v. (The
order of the arguments is arbitrary, but once chosen must be
respected throughout the formulation). The possible values for
the variables are either "north" or "south".

Using this predication, the initial and final states can be
respectively represented

```
(1) state(north, north, north, north).
(2) state(south, south, south, south)?
```

Figures 12-1 and 12-2 represent states (1) and (2), respectively.
Now let us try to express the passage from one state to
another. Unconstrained by safety requirements, this consists of
rules like

```
(3) state(y,y,g,c) if state(x,x,g,c) and opposite(x,y)
```

If the farmer and the wolf can be on the same bank x while
the goat and cabbage are on banks g and c, respectively, and if
the opposite of bank x is y, then it is possible to reach the
state in which the farmer and wolf are on the opposite bank y
while the goat and cabbage remain where they were.

Figure 12-1:   Initial State.

Notice that rule (3) represents a whole set of transitions,
for instance those shown in Figure 12-3.   Rules like (3) are

Figure 12-2:   Desired State.

called recursive, since they define a predication in terms of another with the same predicate name (in this case, "state"). The "opposite bank" relationship can be rendered by

```
(4) opposite(north, south).
(5) opposite(south, north).
```

Now let's define the conditions under which a state can be reached safely. We know that the goat and wolf (or goat and cabbage) are safe if they are on the same bank as the farmer or if they are on opposite banks. We will use a predication

$$\text{safe}(x, y, z)$$

to express that the position x and y of two conflicting individuals (the goat and the wolf or the goat and the cabbage) are safe with respect to the farmer's position, z. We have

```
(6) safe(x,x,x).
(7) safe(x,y,z) if opposite(x,y).
```

We can now use the "safe" predication to define when a state is acceptable. We take f to be the farmer's position, w the wolf's, etc., and we have

Figure 12-3:   Two examples of state transitions in the goat,
cabbage, wolf problem, unconstrained by
safety requirements.

(8) acceptable(f,w,g,c) if safe(g,w,f) and
safe(g,c,f).

Rule (3) now becomes

(3.1) state(y,y,g,c) if state(x,x,g,c) and
opposite(x,y) and acceptable(y,y,g,c).

We can now complete our formulation by adding the

following rule:

```
(3.2) state(y,w,y,c) if state(x,w,x,c) and
      opposite(x,y) and acceptable(y,w,y,c).
(3.3) state(y,w,g,y) if state(x,w,g,x) and
      opposite(x,y) and acceptable(y,w,g,y).
(3.4) state(y,w,g,c) if state(x,w,g,c) and
      opposite(x,y) and acceptable(y,w,g,c).
```

Although this formulation is still not directly executable in most Prolog versions[38], it illustrates the expressive strength of nondeterminism. There need be little commitment regarding which rule to choose; the theorem prover will try the alternatives given and automatically backtrack upon failures.

More sophisticated plan formation problems may require keeping track of several conditions that hold in a given state. In such problems, information about which conditions hold should not be confined to the arguments of a state predication. Instead we can use Kowalski's formulation, (Kowalski, 1979), name states by functional expressions, and use a predication

$$holds(assertion, state)$$

to describe that information through as many facts and rules as necessary. This approach allows us to treat states more generally. We can, for instance, have a rule stating that every assertion that holds in a state s also holds in a state immediately succeeding s, with a few explicitly specified exceptions.

12.5. Representing database knowledge

Databases are a particularly attractive application area for logic programs, and some of the advantages have already been exemplified. The following list makes them even more explicit.

---

[38]Efficiency calls for some evaluation function to guide the search. Moreover, some way of avoiding loops should be provided, for example, the (procedural) requirement that a state be not only acceptable but as yet unvisited.

1. Facts and rules can coexist in the description of any relationship. (See the description of "likes" given earlier.)

2. Recursive definitions are allowed. (See "state" definitions.)

3. Multiple answers to the same query are possible, as noted earlier. This feature is usually referred to as nondeterminism.

4. There is no input/output role distinction for a predication's arguments. Thus, the same Prolog description of a relationship can be queried for the values of any argument or combination of arguments, given fixed values for all the others. (See sample queries for "likes.")

5. Inference takes place automatically.

These features have important implications for database applications. Because facts and rules can be used, no separate deductive component is needed unlike most conventional database system. Moreover, since recursive rules and alternative answers are allowed, very clear, concise, and nonredundant descriptions of the data at hand can be arrived at. Because of the non-distinction between input and output, any argument or combination of arguments can be chosen for retrieval, whereas conventional databases must name and control different paths to make this possible. Finally, the fact that answers are automatically extracted from the data description by a user-invisible inference procedure results in a great degree of data independence; not only is the user allowed to represent data in higher level, human-oriented terms rather than in terms of bits, pointers, arrays, etc., but he/she/it is also spared the effort of describing the operations used to retrieve it. These operations are implicit in the Prolog inference mechanisms, which are capable of giving an operational meaning to the purely descriptive facts and rules used.

12.6. Limitations

As pointed out by Elcock in Chapter 7, Prolog's basic inference strategy may result in failure to prove a query that would be provable if differently ordered. In many cases, reordering the query itself is not enough, as it may, in turn, generate inconveniently ordered subqueries. However, our work on applications of logic programming to expert knowledge (Dahl and Sambuc, 1976) resulted in useful extensions that are now being incorporated into Prolog itself (for example, a set constructing predicate). Notable among these is dynamic query reordering on the basis of statically user-defined priorities for predications. For example, a predication "price(x,y)" that calculates the price y of an assemblage x can be given maximum priority if x is known, and a prohibitively low priority otherwise.

Variations of this idea have been incorporated into Prolog versions, and into other database interrogation systems. Marseille's Prolog 2 has a primitive predication allowing the user to postpone the evaluation of a predication according to run-time conditions.

Still, careful programming is needed, whether for recognizing which predications need to be postponed under which conditions, or for ensuring termination (cf. Elcock's list membership example, or our river crossing problem formulation). Current research into concurrent versions of Prolog, for example, see (Shapiro, 1983), seems a promising approach to the latter problem.

12.7. Conclusions

Logic programming, with its multifaceted nature, has proved a useful approach to knowledge representation. It is, in fact, much more than a mere representation scheme. It is both a formalism for representing knowledge and a mechanism to compute further (virtual) knowledge. In another article, (Dahl, 1982), useful extensions were described that were implemented for database system development. This research was coupled with investigations into natural language queries that could be automatically translated into Prolog. (Dahl, 1981). A three-valued logic was used to detect false presuppositions, in a different way than that surveyed in Webber (Chapter 4, this volume). Basically, presuppositions in this system translate into conditions of an "if" formula, which are automatically checked for satisfaction against the database. Failed presuppositions induce a third logical value ("undefined") upon the "if" formula they belong to. Our investigation of Spanish and French queries resulted in a system that was later adapted to Portuguese (H. Coelho and L. Pereira) and to English (F. Pereira and D. Warren) and served as a starting point for further research in this area. (Warren and Pereira, 1982) (Dahl and McCord, 1983).

Research into Prolog-related issues is currently very active and quite promising. This article is intended to enhance these efforts by filling the need for a tutorial presentation of the main issues involved in knowledge representation through logic programming.

Acknowledgments

This work was completed with PRG grant 42406 and NSERC operating grant A2436. I am indebted to the reviewers for their helpful comments.

13. Theorist: A Logical Reasoning System for Defaults and Diagnosis

David Poole
Randy Goebel
Romas Aleliunas

Logic Programming and Artificial Intelligence Group
Department of Computer Science
University of Waterloo
Waterloo, Ontario, Canada N2L 3G1

Abstract

We provide an introduction to Theorist, a logic programming system that uses a uniform deductive reasoning mechanism to construct explanations of *observations* in terms of *facts* and *hypotheses*. *Observations, facts,* and *possible hypotheses* are each sets of logical formulas that represent, respectively, a set of observations on a partial domain, a set of facts for which the domain is a model, and a set of tentative hypotheses which may be required to provide a consistent explanation of the *observations*.

Theorist has been designed to reason in a fashion similar to how we reason with and construct scientific theories. Rather than monotonically deduce theorems from a fixed logical theory, theorist distinguishes *facts* from *hypotheses* and attempts to use deduction to construct consistent theories for which the *observations* are logical consequences. A prototype, implemented in Prolog, demonstrates how diagnosis, default reasoning, and a kind of learning can all be based on the Theorist framework.

13.1. Introduction

Prolog is the *generic* resolution-based logic programming language. Its formulas consists of *facts*, for example, *father(randy,kari)*, *rules*, for example, *parent(P,C) if father(P,C)*, and *queries*, for example, *parent(P,kari)?* Facts and rules comprise Prolog *assertions*, and are used to answer queries. Here the example fact and rule can be used to provide the answer that one parent of *kari* is *P=randy*.

As explained in the paper by Dahl (Chapter 12, this volume), this class of logical formulas is called Horn clauses, and is appropriate as a representation language when the domain description requires no incomplete or negative knowledge. From this view, Prolog is an implementation of a proof procedure for a simple logic, where knowledge about the world is specified in terms of Horn Clauses, variables are universally quantified, and answers are logical consequences of the knowledge.

There are, of course, other ways to view Prolog. It can be seen as

- a programming language, with pattern matching procedure calls and a backtracking control structure;

- a database language used to specify relations which are either stored or derived;

- a question-answering system, where queries and bodies of clauses are treated as questions to be answered by heads of clauses. A clause is viewed as an assertion which means "to answer a question matching the head, answer the questions provided by the body."

Prolog is rather successful at these, and much research is being done to make it efficient for each of these uses. In fact, in any extension one might consider, it is desirable to retain these views and the efficiency with which Prolog provides them.

13.2. Prolog as a representation system

A serious deficiency of Prolog as a representation system is that answers are often not just logical consequences of our knowledge. For example,

- non-monotonic reasoning uses generalised knowledge, as long as it is consistent. New knowledge can then "remove" things previously deduced;

- diagnosis is not just finding what follows from our knowledge. A diagnosis is not a logical consequence of our observations about a patient. In fact exactly the opposite is the case: it is the observations that should be shown to be logical consequences of our knowledge and the diagnosis;

- learning by forming models of the world is, again, not just finding out what follows from what we know. The scientific method suggests that we build up theories about the world which are to be empirically verified;

- even many mundane tasks like filling out an income tax form require us to make uniform choices about how we declare some income. Your final tax payable is not just a logical consequence of your income, but how you choose to declare various kinds of income and deductions.

This paper suggests a way to solve all of these problems within a uniform framework. The proposed method is an extension to pure Prolog, and can exploit the implementation technology of current Prolog systems.

13.3. The Theorist framework

Here we provide an overview of the Theorist framework, in order that the following explanation of appropriate task

domains is clear. Theorist is a system for representation and
reasoning. The current representation language is the clausal
form of first order logic. A typical theorist knowledge base
consists of a collection of formulas classified as *possible
hypotheses* (Δ), *facts* (F), and *observations* (G) (see Figure
13-1). The Theorist reasoning strategy attempts to accumulate
consistent sets of facts and instances of hypotheses as
explanations for which the observations are logical consequences.

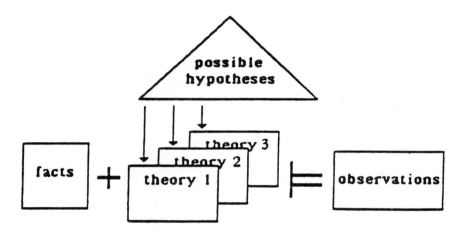

Figure 13-1:   "The Theorist framework"

The three formulae we use are

- F - the set of formulae we know are true in the
  world we are trying to represent. We assume that
  these are consistent (the intended interpretation
  being a model).

- Δ - the set of possible hypotheses. These are things
  we are prepared to accept as part of an explanation.
  By allowing these to be defaults we get default
  reasoning, to let these be possible diseases or
  malfunctions we get diagnosis, and by letting these
  be generalisations of the observations or laws
  derived from the observations then we get learning.

- G - the set of observations to be explained.

A theory is a subset of the possible hypotheses which are consistent, and imply the observations. More formally, we say G is *explainable* if there is some subset D of Δ such that

$F \cup D \models G$ and
$F \cup D$ is consistent

D is said to be a *theory that explains* G. D should be seen as a "scientific theory" (Popper, 1958) (Quine and Ullian, 1978).

The following sections show how by considering Δ in different ways we can form a unifying framework for many AI reasoning problems.

The following syntax will be used for facts and defaults (all examples in this paper work with our current Theorist prototype).

:*fact* <*clause*>;
:*default* <*name*><*clause*>;

where <*clause*> is a clause as in Prolog, (except that the symbol $n(a)$ is used to represent the true negation of a, see below). The first line above means that the clause is an element of F; the second means that for every instance of the name, the clause is a member of Δ (that is, each instance of the clause can be used in a theory). The name is used as a way to refer to the default, as well as a way to specify which variables are significant in making instances of possible hypotheses.

13.4. Tasks appropriate for the Theorist framework

13.4.1. Nonmonotonic reasoning - reasoning with default and generalised knowledge

The notion of default reasoning is ubiquitous in common-sense reasoning, and is manifest in all our reasoning from inconsistent and incomplete information. The default logic of

Reiter (Reiter, 1980) formalizes the notion of default rules in a logic that uses a non-monotonic reasoning strategy to draw conclusions from defaults that are consistent with an intended model. We have shown (Poole, 1984) how defaults can be seen as possible hypotheses to be used in a theory to explain the answers.   These possible hypotheses are pieces of knowledge which can be used as long as they are consistent with everything else. This was the initial intuition behind Reiter's defaults. Note that we have translated defaults not as probability statements, or statements of "typically", but rather as things we are prepared to accept in an explanation.

Tweety the non-flying bird is the most common example of the inadequacy of monotonic reasoning from consistent facts. "birds fly" and "Tweety is a bird" suggests that "Tweety can fly". However subsequent observations like "Tweety is a penguin," and "Penguins can't fly" reveals the first inference to be too eager.   While this example explains why logical consequence is alone an inadequate model of common-sense reasoning, there are many natural task domains where the same phenomenon arises.

Theorist handles this by treating the defaults that we want to use as possible hypotheses. Any answer derived from the default has the explicit dependency on the theory which we cannot show is inconsistent.

Figure 13-2 is a dialogue with Theorist that shows how Theorist can do the above reasoning.   Lines that begin with a bold-face command indicate user inputs.   The syntax "n(X)" means "¬ X." Note that there is a consistent explanation for *flies(tweety)* because *flies(tweety)* can be initially explained by the theory *birdsfly(tweety)*, but when we add the fact that tweety is an emu, that theory is no longer consistent, as its negation can be proven.   We can then no longer explain tweety flying.

13.4.2. Diagnosis

Most current *rule-based* diagnosis systems use knowledge of the form

observation and knowledge of situation → problem

```
Welcome to Theorist 0.1
type "help;" for help
good luck
:default birdsfly(X) flies(X) <- bird(X);
:fact n(flies(X)) <- emu(X);
:fact bird(tweety);
:explain flies(tweety);
yes
Theory: [birdsfly(tweety)]
Answer: []
:fact emu(tweety);
:explain flies(tweety);
no
:quit;
```

Figure 13-2: "Default reasoning in Theorist 0.1"

to express knowledge about the potential cause of an observation. For example, the medical diagnosis system MYCIN (Buchanan and Shortliffe, 1984) expresses its knowledge in terms of rules of the form

$$symptom \rightarrow disease \ [CF]$$

where *CF* is a *certainty factor* in the interval $[-1,1]$ that represents a subjective evaluation of the rule's quality. The diagnosis task consists of matching rule *symptoms* and observed symptoms, accumulating the conclusions suggested by relevant rules, and ranking the conclusions by a simple arithmetic function on certainty factors.

This rule-based approach has a number of problems:

1. There is the philosophical problem of what the certainty factors mean. What does it mean for a rule to be correct? Is there a way of looking at a rule independently of the whole system?

2. There is the pragmatic problem obtaining the certainty factors. The only methodology we have is to guess, and then tune the system when unintuitive answers result. We can then never be

sure that our rule base was correct, unless we have checked all combinations.

3. Only an assignment of certainty factors to labels is produced. If we desire a deeper explanation of a problem, we require a theory from which the observed symptoms can be deduced. An "explanation" is a consistent grouping of possible hypotheses; the Mycin system cannot generate such groupings of hypotheses.

4. The rules above are the wrong way around: diseases result in symptoms, rather than symptoms resulting in diseases.

The rule-based representation encodes the *methodology* of the diagnostician instead of knowledge about diseases. The certainty factors are partly a record of experience (what has been previously observed) and partly a representation of belief about the relationship between symptoms and diseases.

Theorist uses an alternative formulation of the rules, viz.,

$$\text{problem} \rightarrow \text{observation}$$

where knowledge is expressed in terms of problems and the observations that consequently arise. For example, the medical diagnosis task would use rules of the form

$$\text{disease} \rightarrow \text{symptom}$$

to encode the observable symptoms of diseases. This form of representation is more appropriate for expressing text book knowledge of diseases, as it records what is known without any requirement for heuristic measures like certainty factors.

The possible hypotheses then are the diseases and possible malfunctions that we are prepared to accept in a diagnosis. We can allow for inaccurate knowledge by the use of defaults. Thus the diagnosis then becomes a theory of diseases and defaults on these diseases which then explain the observations.

The example in Figure 13-3 shows how Theorist can be used for diagnosis. The set of *possible hypotheses* which we are prepared to accept as part of an explanation are the patient

```
:fact aching(elbow) <- tennis-elbow;
:fact aching(hands) <- dishpan-hands;
:fact aching(X) <- arthritis joint(X);
:fact joint(elbow);
:fact joint(hands);
:fact joint(knee);
:fact plays-tennis <- tennis-elbow;
:default patient-has-tennis-elbow tennis-elbow;
:default patient-has-dishpan-hands dishpan-hands;
:default patient-has-arthritis arthritis;
:default patient-has-meningitis meningitis;
:askable plays-tennis;
:explain aching(elbow) aching(hands);
Is plays-tennis true? (give negative instances)
yes;
yes
Theory: [patient-has-dishpan-hands,patient-has-tennis-elbow]
Answer: []
:retry;
yes
Theory: [patient-has-arthritis]
Answer: []
:retry;
no
:askable aching(X);
:explain aching(elbow) aching(hands);
Is aching(elbow) true? (give negative instances)
unknown;
Is aching(hands) true? (give negative instances)
unknown;
yes
Theory: [patient-has-dishpan-hands,patient-has-tennis-elbow]
Answer: []
:retry;
Is aching(knee) true? (give negative instances)
no;
no
:quit;
```

Figure 13-3:   "Diagnosis in Theorist 0.1"

has tennis elbow, patient has dishpan hands, patient has
arthritis, or patient has meningitis. The *observations* are
symptoms; that some part is aching, or that the patient plays

tennis. This information can be offered as observations in the request for an explanation, or by answering Theorist's questions. In Figure 13-3, the first emboldened "explain" command asks Theorist to explain how a patient could have aching hands and an aching elbow. By using a general deduction system, the system generates the possible explanatory theories:

```
1) patient has dishpan hands and tennis elbow, and
2) patient has arthritis.
```

While attempting to construct a consistent explanation, Theorist can ask relevant questions that may help reject an explanation. This can be accomplished through application of the deduction machinery to try to prove that the theories are inconsistent. Again, in Figure 13-3, an emboldened "askable" command informs Theorist that it may query the user about whether or not some body part is aching. In the subsequent request to explain "aching(hands) and aching(elbow)," Theorist asks the user about aching hands and elbow. The "unknown" response forces Theorist to continue it's construction of an explanation based only on the observations and facts. Near the end of Figure 13-3, the first explanation for "aching hands" and "aching elbow" is "dishpan hands and tennis elbow", as in the first case. In other words none of the user responses made any difference in determining the first possible explanation. However, when asked to consider another possible explanation by requesting a "retry", Theorist again prompts with the question "Is aching(knee) true?" Having already received "unknown" responses about hands and elbows, Theorist is asking about other body parts in order to attempt to refute the possible hypothesis "patient-has-arthritis." The response "no" provides the necessary information; arthritis is refuted, so no other explanations are possible. This corresponds to empirically checking a scientific theory by allowing it to make predictions, and then modifying the theory if the facts do not correspond with the predictions.

13.4.3. Learning as theory construction

Figure 13-3 shows that there may be multiple consistent theories that provide an explanation for a given set of observations. In general, one expects that the "best" explanation for the diagnostic problem is the *most specific theory* (within the constraint of having the knowledge, and the desire to discriminate between different more specific theories). That is, we would prefer an explanation like "The observations are a consequence of bronchial pneumonia" rather than a less specific explanation like "The observations are a consequence of a respiratory disorder." The motivation for preferring the most specific explanation is the desire to provide the most appropriate treatment. We (Jones and Poole, 1985) have described a way to do a hierarchical diagnosis based on Theorist and this notion of the best theory.

If we are interested in the accumulation of rules to explain new observations, then the most specific of a number of consistent theories is not what we desire. Rather we expect the *most general theory* to be more interesting, as it presumably may account for more observations. This is precisely the intuition behind Carbonell, Michalski and Mitchell's explanation of how one recognizes improvement within the *knowledge acquisition* form of machine learning: "A person is said to have learned more if his knowledge explains a broader scope of situations, is more accurate and is better able to predict the behavior of the physical world.", (Carbonell, Michalski, and Mitchell, 1983).

The notion of theory construction is used in several models of machine learning, for example, (Hayes-Roth, 1983) (Lenat, 1983) (Langley, Bradshaw, and Simon, 1983) where the major emphasis is on strategies for generating and using *useful* hypotheses. For example, Hayes-Roth concentrates on heuristics for controlling a theory building mechanism. In fact, with Theorist as a basic foundation, Hayes-Roth's five heuristics for dealing with refuted hypotheses amount to strategies for controlling the way in which Theorist backtracks (*retraction, avoidance*) or modifies selected hypotheses (*exclusion, assurance, and inclusion*). A cursory analysis suggests that distinguishing theory revision by hypothesis modification and theory revision by hypothesis deletion will clarify the differences that Hayes-Roth notes.

Notice that Theorist suggests nothing about where hypotheses come from or how they should be employed. This, we claim, is the essence of learning research; Theorist merely offers a foundation on which to experiment with various strategies of theory construction and maintenance, in the same way that Prolog provides a basic logical foundation for programming reasoning strategies.

13.4.4. User modelling as theory maintenance

A fundamental problem in the development of more sophisticated computer-mediated learning is the maintenance and use of user models (Sleeman and Brown (eds), 1982). For example, a program that is helping a child to learn arithmetic will only be able to deal with that child's specific problems if the program maintains a model of the child's performance. Current approaches to user modelling, for example, (Brown, Burton, and de Kleer, 1982), (Goldstein and Burton, 1982) coincide in their emphasis on the construction and maintenance of *evolving* models of a user. The essence of intelligent computer-aided instruction is to improve a user's understanding of a subject area by revealing misconceptions that exist in that user's current model of the domain. The foundation of both Goldstein's WUSOR-I program and Brown et al.'s SOPHIE programs is the maintenance of a "theory" that is consistent with what has been observed by the program, or understood by the user.

For example, SOPHIE uses a theory construction procedure to show its user how to debug a faulty electronic circuit. An important aspect of SOPHIE is to teach a debugging strategy by interactively refining a theory of the faulty component. The strategy, briefly summarized, is to refine a model of the faulty circuit by proposing hypotheses and then verifying hypotheses by making measurements. Hypothesis formation in SOPHIE proceeds in three stages:

1. examine each observation and propose a list of

hypotheses which explain it;

2. simulate each hypothesized fault to verify that it accounts for the circuit measurements; and

3. instantiate partially specified hypotheses and test their consistency.

The Theorist framework simplifies this process: measurements are the *observations* to be explained, *facts* correspond to general knowledge about the circuit, and *possible hypotheses* correspond to potential explanations for the observed behaviour. Again, as in learning by theory construction, note that Theorist does not provide any expertise about forming hypotheses, nor does it suggest any method for preferring one consistent explanation over another. However, it does provide a logical system for constructing consistent explanations regardless of domain, which frees the ICAI system designer to concentrate on domain issues (for example, the expertise required for hypothesis generation and selection), pedagogical issues (for example, the management of user interaction and participation), and the development of concepts for relating different explanations that a user might believe (for example, of one explanation being a refinement of another).

13.4.5. Choices in mundane tasks

Even government bureaucracy relies on a style of reasoning that requires one to pursue multiple paths of reasoning based on different original hypotheses. For example, Revenue Canada's 1985 Instalment guide for individuals explains

You may determine the amount of your instalment payments of Income Tax for 1985 by one of three methods...choose the method that will result in the lowest possible quarterly remittance. [Revenue Canada 1985]

In this situation, the collection of *possible hypotheses* include

three different methods for determining the quarterly income
tax payments:

1. base the instalment on the 1984 taxes and estimated
   deductions in 1985, and none of the following
   apply: you reside outside of Canada, you received
   income from a source outside of Canada, you have
   rental or self-employment income, you have forward
   averaging income, you have a share purchase credit
   or a scientific research tax credit, you have claimed
   a business investment tax credit or employment tax
   credit.

2. base the instalment on the 1984 taxes and estimated
   deductions in 1985, and at least one of the above
   exceptions apply;

3. base the instalment on the 1985 estimated income
   and deductions.

The *facts* include all the regular rules about how income
and deductions are manipulated to produce an estimate of the
instalment payment. *Observations* would include income and
deduction data from 1984 and 1985. Clearly one would like
Theorist to construct the three possible explanations, and select
the one in which the instalment estimate was least.

13.5. Representation and reasoning in theorist

Given the semantics of Theorist we want to now show
how it can be implemented, based on a Prolog-technology
deduction system. We will show how we can implement this
in Prolog, but we plan to implement it at the same
implementation level as Prolog, using the advances being made
in logic programming implementation techniques.

13.5.1. Extending Horn clauses to full first order logic

Unfortunately we cannot directly use a Prolog implementation, as Horn clause logic is alone inadequate for the deductive basis of Theorist. Semantically, this is because Horn clause theories are always consistent, that is, there is always a true interpretation for any set of Horn clauses. Pragmatically this is because Horn clause theories can never derive the negation of a formula; one can never show a Horn clause theory to be incorrect. For this, we need to add negation. With negation, we also get disjunction, as $x \subset \neg y$ is the same as x **or** y.

The resulting representation language is simply the full first order form of clausal logic. The current Theorist prototype will accept, as assertions, any formula of the form

$$L_1 \text{ or } L_2 \text{ or } ... \text{ or } L_n <- L_{n+1} \text{ and } L_{n+2} \text{ and } ... L_{n+m}$$

where each L_i is an arbitrary literal. While we have chosen this simple language as the basis for representation in Theorist, we recognize the advantage of providing representation structures that are suggestive of the manner in which a user conceives his application domain. Therefore, an extension currently being considered is the addition of descriptions, (Goebel, 1985). This extension will provide the Theorist user with the ability to refer to individuals and set by their properties, and to assert relations on such descriptions.

13.5.2. Reasoning as the construction of consistent theories

The semantics of Theorist allow us to directly implement a deduction system by treating validity as derivability. The construction of consistent explanations is done in two steps. Each step uses a first order theorem prover, and so each step is only semi decidable. The combination makes explainability completely undecidable. This corresponds to never being really able to show our beliefs are correct and consistent, or that scientific theories can be shown to be the correct theory.

As explained above, each user "*explain G*" command initiates a procedure that attempts to find a consistent theory to explain the observations G. Mirroring the semantics given above, we seek a procedure that can select a subset D of Δ such that

$F \cup D \vdash G$ and
$F \cup D$ is consistent

The first step, and first use of the first order proof procedure, is to try to prove G, using elements of F and Δ as axioms. The strategy in step one is to use a goal-directed, backward theorem-prover that will generate subgoals that can be used to select relevant hypotheses from the set Δ. We then make D those elements of Δ actually used in the proof. As we have previously noted, the intelligent selection of hypotheses is a major problem (below we describe a simple strategy that is similar to the way in which Prolog considers assertions in the construction of an SLD[39] proof tree).

The second step also requires the use of a first order proof procedure. To verify that a subset D of Δ together with the facts is consistent, we attempt to show that

$F \cup D \neg \vdash \neg d$

for each $d \in D$. We assume that the set F' of facts is consistent (that is, the intended interpretation is a model for F), so that we need only verify the consistency of each hypothesis used in the explanation. Notice that the second step requires the use of a *complete* first order proof procedure, and that, like the previous step, the computation is semidecidable. Note, however, that if no defaults were used, and the

---

[39]SLD-resolution stands for SL-resolution for Definite clauses. The SL stands for Linear resolution with Selection. If P is a program, G a goal, and R a computation rule, then the SLD proof tree for $P \cup \{G\}$ via R is defined as follows: (1) each node of the tree is a goal (possibly empty); (2) the root node is G; (3) let $\leftarrow A_1,...,A_m,...,A_k$ ($k \geqslant 1$) be a node in the tree and suppose that A_m is the atom selected by R. Then this node has a decendent for each input clause $A \leftarrow B_1,...,B_q$ such that A_m and A are unifiable. The decendent is $\leftarrow (A_1,...,A_{m-1},B_1,...,B_q,A_{m+1},...,A_k)\psi$ where ψ is a most general unifier of A_m and A; and (4) nodes which are the empty clause have no decendents.

knowledge was in the form of Horn clauses, then this system defaults to exactly Prolog.

13.6. Implementing a Theorist prototype in Prolog

Here we show how we can construct a full first order clausal theorem prover in Prolog.

The extension of Prolog to a first order clausal theorem prover is equivalent to Loveland's development of the MESON proof procedure, as based on the *problem reduction* problem solving strategy, (Loveland, 1978). Loveland's development of the resolution-based MESON procedure represents his logical reconstruction of the goal-driven problem solving strategy that reasons by reducing a given goal to a set of "simpler" subgoals. Loveland's departure point is the use of informal rules of the form

$$goal \rightarrow subgoal_1 \ \& \ subgoal_2 \ \& \ ... \ subgoal_n$$

which, of course, have the format of Horn clauses: at most one positive literal when in clause form (recall that $L \rightarrow L_1 \ \& \ L_2 \ \& \ ... \ L_n$ is equivalent to L or$\neg$ L_1 or$\neg$ L_2 or ... or$\neg$ L_n).

A full first order theorem prover based on Prolog has been constructed by Umrigar and Pitchumani (Umrigar and Pitchumani, 1985) and is based on Loveland's description of the MESON procedure. The implementation here is similar, except that we have not implemented any cycle check, nor the mechanism that will produce indefinite answers. We note here that the cycle check used in Umrigar and Pitchumani's F-Prolog system is not correct. See (Poole and Goebel, 1985) for a description of the problems with some of the suggested techniques for eliminating loops in Prolog proofs.

The fundamental idea behind the implementation of a first order theorem prover in Prolog can be understood by considering the following example. Suppose that we are given the propositional clauses

$$a \lor b$$
$$c \rightarrow a$$
$$c \rightarrow b$$

and the goal c. Even if we could state this as Horn clauses, Prolog's response to the goal is "no"; there is no SLD derivation of c, even though it is easy to see that c is valid, given that one of a or b is true. As Loveland explains (see (Loveland, 1978)) what is lacking here is negation as required to express the contrapositive form of the assertions given above. If we augment the above assertions with their *general contrapositives* we get

$$a \lor b$$
$$a \rightarrow \neg b$$
$$b \rightarrow \neg a$$
$$c \rightarrow a$$
$$\neg a \rightarrow \neg c$$
$$c \rightarrow b$$
$$\neg b \rightarrow \neg c$$

The general backchaining strategy will now produce the proof branch

$$c - (c \rightarrow a) - a -)a \rightarrow \neg b) - \neg b - (\neg b \rightarrow \neg c) - \neg c$$

which can be marked as successful by virtue of a *reductio ad absurdum* argument (see (Loveland, 1978) for a full elaboration). That is, during the construction of a proof branch, the proof terminates successfully if the negation of a new subgoal occurs further up the subtree. In other words, the implementation of a full first order theorem prover in Prolog requires

1. the addition of the contrapositive forms of each assertion, and

2. an elaboration of the Prolog search procedure to look for the negation of a newly generated subgoal anywhere earlier in the current proof branch.

Figure 13-4 is a listing of the current implementation of the Theorist proof system in Waterloo UNIX[40] Prolog. Note

---

[40]UNIX is a registered trademark of Bell Laboratories.

that this implementation is only correct when there are no Skolem functions (that is, none of the functions should be interpreted as Skolem functions) and there are no free variables in hypotheses when they are tested for consistency.

Of most interest is the definition of the proof predicate *pr*. The relation *pr(G A D1 D2)* means that the observations G can be proved, with proof tree ancestors A, and initial theory D1 and final theory D2. The first clause for *pr* implements the search of the proof tree ancestors for a contradiction, as described above. The second clause retrieves a fact from the *fact module* and attempts to use that fact to generate a new set of subgoals. The *fact module* is a WUP module that contains a compiled version of user assertions. The compiled version is simply clause form represented as a Prolog list. The contrapositive form of each assertion is formed dynamically by matching the current goal with a literal of the compiled list form, and then returning the negated form and the remaining literals in the list as the new subgoals. The third clause uses an auxiliary relation *default(N G B)* which retrieves the next default or hypothesis from the *hypothesis module* with name N, head G, and body B. As with facts, hypotheses are stored in clause form, and the appropriate form is constructed as necessary; when a literal of the clause form matches the current subgoal, the appropriate body is constructed as the new set of subgoals.

The last two clauses in the definition of *pr* are for permitting the user to declare "Prolog only" predicates, and to initiate a user dialogue based on the declaration of *askable* predicates (see discussion of Figure 13-3 above).

13.6.1. Not parallelism

Note that the definition of the *pr* relation in Figure 13-4 uses the standard Prolog sequential selection of facts to attempt the backchaining construction of a proof for the goal G. As acknowledged above, a simple assertion-order selection of both facts and hypotheses is used to search for a set of hypotheses which, when combined with the facts, supports the derivation of the observations G.

```
% explain(G D) is true when the list of goals G is
    explainable by the facts and the list of consistent
    defaults D
explain(G D) <-
        prall(G [] [] D);
% prall(B A D1 D2) means every element of B can be proven,
    with ancestors A, starting theory D1 and resulting
    theory D2
prall([] A D D);
prall([G|B] A D1 D3) <-
        pr(G A D1 D2)
        prall(B A D2 D3);
% pr(G A D1 D2) means G can be proven, with ancestors A, and
    starting theory D1 and with resulting theory D2
pr(G A D D) <-      % search up tree for negation of
current goal
        neg(G GN)
        member(GN A);
pr(G A D1 D2) <-      % retrieve next fact for expanding
proof tree
        fact(G Body)
        prall(Body [G|A] D1 D2);
pr(G A D1 D2) <-      % get next default/hypothesis for
expanding proof
        default(N G B)
        prusedef(G A N B D1 D2);
pr(G A D D) <-
        prolog(G Module)    % G is defined in Module
        prove(Module G);
pr(G A D1 D2) <-
        askuser(G A D1 D2);
% prusedef(G A N B D1 D2) means G can be proven using
    default name N, body B, previous defaults D1 and
    resulting defaults D2, and ancestors A.
prusedef(G A N B D1 D2) <-
        member(N D1)
        prall(B [G|A] D1 D2);
prusedef(G A N B D1 D2) <-
        not(member(N D1))
        prall(B [G|A] [N|D1] D2)
        neg(G GN)
        not(pr(GN [] D1 D1));
% neg(A B) means A is the negated form of B
neg(n(A) A) <-
        ne(A n(_));
neg(A n(A)) <-
        ne(A n(_));
```

Figure 13-4:   Prolog implementation of Theorist proof system

The   second   portion   of   the   Theorist   computation, consistency verification, is initiated whenever a new default is selected by the third clause of the definition of *pr*. The relation *prusedef* will first determine if the default has been previously used, in which case its consistency has been established and the normal proof procedure can continue. Otherwise, verification of the consistency of the newly considered hypotheses must be attempted by trying to fail to prove the negation of the conclusion suggested by the hypothesis.

In general, every hypothesis considered will spawn a (potentially infinite) computation that attempts to show that the hypothesis is consistent with the current facts and the current partial theory. We speculate that these computations can be pursued in parallel; that they define *not parallelism* which is responsible for the verification of consistency while the hypothesis selection mechanism concurrently generates plausible theories whose consistency is in question.

Note that this idea of *not parallelism* can be seen as equivalent to the idea of using a scientific theory before it has been fully tested, and then fixing up the theory when errors have been found. It also allows us to have the idea of having a set of beliefs which may be inconsistent, but still being able to use these beliefs, and fixing them up when an inconsistency is detected. All of these are consistent with the idea we used before, as a search strategy, and fit in with our logic.

13.7. Status and conclusions

Here we have presented a simple, yet very powerful methodology which unifies many disparate areas of artificial intelligence. The idea is that rather than just doing deduction from our knowledge, we should build 'scientific' theories which can explain the results. A very naive implementation was presented which allows us to play with these ideas. This implementation is a strict extension to pure Prolog, in the sense that if all of the knowledge is in Horn clauses, and no defaults are used, then we get just Prolog.

This approach seems to ask more questions than it answers. It gives us a new way to approach old problems. For example, we claim that learning research should proceed by first asking the question *what does it mean to have learnt something?* We claim the answer to this is to *build a better theory of the world.* So to do research into learning, we claim that we should look at the two issues of when is one theory better than another, and how can we effectively compute the best theory for special cases, or maintain a good theory for the general case. The notion of a best theory will change depending on whether we are using defaults (Poole, 1985) or diagnosis (Jones and Poole, 1985). Much research still needs to be done.

Acknowledgements

We have had fruitful discussions about the concept of Theorist, and theory formation in general, with Ray Reiter, Russ Griener, Michael Genesereth, Bob Hadley, Jim Delgrande, and members of the Logic Programming and AI Group of the University of Waterloo: Robin Cohen, Maarten van Emden, and Marlene Jones. This research has been supported by Natural Sciences and Engineering Research Grant No. A0894.

14. Representing and Solving Temporal Planning Problems

R. James Firby
Drew McDermott

Department of Computer Science
Yale University
New Haven, Connecticut

Abstract

AI planning research has generally been concerned with the advantages and disadvantages of representing temporal planning information as a partially ordered task network. Such a network represents a growing plan as a set of tasks that become more completely temporally ordered as the plan is elaborated. A partially ordered task network is an attractive plan representation because it maintains the flexibility to avoid or take advantage of unexpected task interactions by simply adding appropriate ordering constraints between existing tasks. Unfortunately, a partially ordered network has difficulty representing tasks with properties that depend on precisely what other tasks come before them. How can one keep track of a bank balance in the face of unordered withdrawals and deposits? This paper discusses work done at Yale by Dean and Miller that addresses both the problem of building and maintaining a partially ordered task network and the problem of reasoning about tasks that have order-dependent properties.

The Time Map Manager designed by Dean is a comprehensive system for building a predicate calculus database of assertions that may be true over only certain intervals of time. The database is augmented with a mechanism for representing assertions that persist until contradicted (or "clipped") and with inference rules that assert new facts whenever particular conjunctions of facts are true at the same time. This database can be used to represent tasks and their effects and to dynamically order unordered tasks as the need arises.

The Heuristic Task Scheduler of Miller is an algorithm for finding a consistent temporal order for a set of tasks that have context dependent properties. The tasks to be ordered may have varying durations, varying effects and may contain loops. In addition, tasks may use and alter common resources (such as bank balances) in a wide variety of ways. Constraints on possible orders for the tasks take the form of restrictions on temporal order, task deadlines, and competition for resoursces.

14.1. Introduction

The field of Artificial Intelligence has been concerned from its inception with planning research. The early work of Newell, Shaw and Simon on the GPS system (Newell and Simon, 1972) introduced the idea of means-ends analysis: planning for a goal by applying an operator that will generate the goal and then taking the preconditions of the operator as new goals. GPS was followed by the STRIPS program (Fikes, 1971) of Fikes and Nilsson which recognized that operators could correspond to actions in the world and that changes made by these actions could be represented as facts to be added to and deleted from a world model. From these basic concepts, planning research evolved through several stages to Sacerdoti's influential NOAH system (Sacerdoti, 1975). Until NOAH was developed, planning programs all assumed that the actions being planned were completely ordered in time; when considering a new action, the planner knew those actions planned to come before it and those that would come after. NOAH relaxed this assumption and allowed some actions to remain unordered with respect to others. Final ordering of these actions was put off until it became necessary or advantageous. Working with partially ordered actions gave NOAH the flexibility to overcome many unexpected interactions between plan steps, and to notice when one action fortuitously enabled the preconditions for another. Planning work since NOAH has largely been concerned with representing and reasoning about partially ordered actions in more sophisticated and powerful ways.

Planning can be defined as the process of turning a desired goal or activity into a set of actions that will achieve it in the real world. Goals and activities are high-level problem statements like "wash the car", "build a candlestick" or "fix the TV", and actions are those activities that can be directly executed in the world, such as moving from one point to another, orienting a sensor, or grasping an object. A planner is expected to take in a conjunction of several such goals and produce a detailed plan of action to carry them all out together.

The main thrust of research since NOAH has been toward

a theory in which high-level goals are represented as abstract tasks and the process of planning consists of refining those tasks into simpler and simpler subtasks, until only primitive actions remain.   At each level of refinement all tasks and subtasks have preconditions that must hold before they can be executed, and effects that change the world state after they are executed.   Task refinement is accomplished by the planner manipulating the tasks in two ways.   First, it can expand a task by replacing it with a set of simpler subtasks that will accomplish the same goal.   Second, it can constrain tasks in time to take advantage of situations where task preconditions are already met, or to avoid undesirable interactions between tasks (such as when one task undoes the precondition of another).   The tasks and ordering information that the planner is working with are collectively referred to as a *task network*. A partially ordered task network is one where the final order in which tasks will be executed has not yet been decided.

The principal advantage of planning with a partially ordered task network is that it retains flexibility. In a totally ordered task network, the order in which tasks will be executed is decided early and when an unexpected subtask interaction is found during more detailed planning, changing task order to avoid the interaction is difficult. Furthermore, because the task order is fixed, opportunities to use fortuitously generated subtask preconditions are difficult to seize.   A partially ordered task network, on the other hand, leaves the planner free to arrange tasks in ways that avoid bugs or use opportunities as they arise.   The major difficulty with planning in a partial order is keeping the task network consistent.   Each task changes the state of the world through its effects so keeping track of which facts are true over which intervals becomes complicated when the order of the tasks is not pinned down.

A second difficulty with partially ordered task networks arises when reasoning about tasks with context-dependent properties.   Keeping track of a bank balance over time (to guarantee it never goes below zero) requires knowing all of the deposits and withdrawals made to the account.   In fact, to monitor the value of the account balance at all times, the order of the deposits and withdrawals must also be known because the value of the balance after a transaction depends on the state it was in before the transaction. If some transactions are unordered with respect to others the bank balance cannot be known precisely.

Any solution to these problems of planning with partial orders must address the often conflicting issues of computational efficiency and expressive power. A planner cannot hope to reason about context-dependent effects if the knowledge structures it uses cannot represent them. A partially ordered task network must allow for a rich and detailed set of potential interactions between tasks. Unfortunately, the more complex that the network becomes the more difficult it is to keep it consistent. Every new type of task interaction represented requires another dimension that must be considered when making planning decisions. This paper describes: two practical knowledge representation systems that address different but complimentary aspects of the partially ordered task network representation. To help focus the discussion, each system is described as a tool to use in building and maintaining a partially ordered task network for planning. The interesting issue however, is the kind of knowledge each system can represent and manipulate while remaining a working program.

The two systems described below were constructed by Thomas Dean and David Miller as part of a Yale University project to explore issues in planning. The first section of the paper discusses a system developed by Dean called the Time Map Manager (Dean, 1985). The Time Map Manager is designed to perform most of the processing required to build a partially ordered task network and keep it temporally consistent. The second part of the paper describes Miller's work: a system called the Heuristic Task Scheduler (Miller, 1985) designed to enable context sensitive reasoning about a set of tasks. The conclusion of the paper discusses the differences between the two systems and suggests ways that they might be used to complement one another.

14.2. The Time Map Manager

A time map is a representation of the tasks, ordering constraints and task effects that make up a partially ordered network. The Time Map Manager, or TMM (Dean, 1985), is a system for building and reasoning about partially ordered time maps. The TMM allows a task to be elaborated into more detailed subtasks, while keeping previous elaborations and ordering decisions undisturbed. At its most basic, the TMM ensures that the preconditions for one task are not endangered by the effects of another as new effects and ordering constraints are added to the time map. At its most advanced, the TMM rearranges tasks to take advantage of existing preconditions and warns of unexpected, dangerous interactions between the effects of unrelated tasks.

The most important contribution of the TMM to planning is the way that it integrates a task and effect representation with predicate calculus database mechanisms for reasoning about that representation over time. This section of the paper describes the representation language used by the TMM along with the interface it provides for inquiring about and constraining the tasks and effects it represents.

The time map that the TMM maintains is a temporally scoped predicate calculus database. In fact, the TMM is a general system for building and maintaining such a database, but the discussion in this paper will focus on those aspects of the database and TMM that are most relevant to planning. Each task and effect in the planning problem is represented in the time map database as a proposition that holds true over some interval of time, although the exact ordering of the time intervals needs not be known. Ordering and absolute time constraints (like deadlines) on the tasks and effects are represented with additional assertions to the database. Planning decisions are based on queries made to the database to determine when effects are expected to be true.

Discussion of the TMM begins with an overview of how a predicate calculus database is used for the storage and retrieval of timeless facts and for doing simple deduction. Then the representation used to temporally scope formulae is introduced so that facts can be asserted to be true over only certain intervals of time. The deductive mechanisms of the database are also extended to make use of the temporally scoped facts. Finally, specialized temporal projection mechanisms supplied by the TMM for reasoning about task networks are described.

14.2.1. A Predicate Calculus Database

The Time Map Manager uses a temporally scoped predicate calculus database implemented in the DUCK language (McDermott, 1985). A predicate calculus database consists of a set of formulae along with methods for adding new formulae and making inquiries about the formulae already there. The TMM makes sure that as formulae are asserted or removed from its database no inconsistencies arise that go unnoticed.[41] The notation used for formulae in the database follows DUCK syntax which has a standard Lisp-like form. Basic assertions to the database take the form of predicates:

$$(predicate\text{-}name\ arg_1\ arg_2\ arg_3\ \dots\ )$$

where the predicate name is any symbol and the arguments are functions, literals or variables. Variables are denoted by symbols prefixed with a "?" and in database assertions are universally quantified. In practice, most formulae are ground assertions containing no variables. Some examples of valid formulae are:

```
(ON BLOCK1 TABLE)
(OCCASION (MACHINE-STATUS LATHE1 BUSY) ?OCC1)
(DISTANCE (BEGIN ?OCC1) (END ?OCC1) 5 7)
(ON ?X TABLE)
```

Adding new formulae to the database is done using the TMM function ASSERT which takes a predicate, or conjunction of predicates, as its argument. The small blocks world description found in Figure 14-1 can be set up with the single

---

[41]That is, all inconsistencies detectable by the TMM are noticed. There are certain classes of interaction between temporally scoped propositions that cannot be detected and these are discussed later in the paper.

assertion:

```
(ASSERT (AND (ON A B)
             (ON B TABLE)
             (ON C TABLE)))
```

Formulae added to the database using ASSERT are timelessly true: they are taken to be true at all times.

```
(ON A B)
(ON B TABLE)
(ON C TABLE)
```

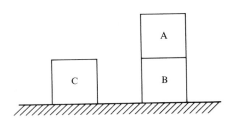

Figure 14-1:   A Simple Database

Information is extracted from the database using the TMM function FETCH. This function takes a single argument that represents a formula to be looked up in the database. The fetch formula, or pattern, can be any predicate or conjunction of predicates and it may contain variables. Variables used in fetch patterns are assumed to be existentially quantified. For example, the following query can be used to find out if anything is on *B* in the database of Figure 14-1:

```
(FETCH (ON ?X B))
```

This query might be read, "Does there exist an *X* such that *(ON X B)* holds?" If there are no assertions in the database that match the query, FETCH returns *NIL*. If there are assertions that match the query, FETCH returns an answer that holds a set of variable bindings that unify the query pattern with the assertion. In the example above, an answer would be returned saying that the fetch succeeded with *?X* bound to *A*.

The variable bindings are captured in a data structure called an ANS that records the "environment" surrounding the answer to a query. As another illustration, the query:

```
(FETCH (AND (ON A ?Z)
            (ON ?Z TABLE)))
```

made to the database in Figure 14-1 will return an ANS recording that *?Z* unifies with *B*.

There often will be more than one formula in the database that matches the pattern in a query. The function call *(FETCH (ON ?X TABLE))*, made to the sample database above, will find that two blocks are on the table. To deal with this situation, FETCH returns a list of answers, each an ANS containing an environment with one set of bindings. Thus, *(FETCH (ON ?X TABLE))* returns one ANS holding the binding *(?Z=B)* and another holding *(?Z=C)*. The TMM, through DUCK, supports several coding constructs for referring to the environments kept in ANS structures. The most commonly used construction is:

```
(FOR-EACH-ANS
    list of ANS structures
    code using environment)
```

The code in the *FOR-EACH-ANS* is executed repeatedly , once in the environment of each ANS in the list supplied. For example, to enlarge the database to include the fact that every block on another block is not on the table, the following code could be used:

```
(FOR-EACH-ANS
    (FETCH (AND (ON ?X ?Y)
                (NOT (= ?Y TABLE)))))
    (ASSERT (NOT (ON ?X TABLE))))
```

The ASSERT function is executed in the environment of every ANS returned by the fetch and the variable *?X* in the asserted formula is bound to according to each environment in turn.[42]

---

[42]The DUCK language supports several other special forms for executing code in the environment of an ANS. The more important ones are *FOR-ANS* and *FOR-FIRST-ANS* which do the obvious things.

The idea that an environment is saved in each ANS is important. When an environment is built by a query, it contains not only variable bindings as discussed above, but also a set of data dependencies that specify which features of the database must remain true for the variable bindings to remain valid. Consider executing the previous *FOR-EACH-ANS* on the database in Figure 14-1. The query will match the single assertion *(ON A B)* and the ANS returned will contain the variable bindings *(?X=A)* and *(?Y=B)*. However, because these bindings are only valid as long as *A* is on *B*, the ANS will also contain the dependency data that all assertions made within its environment must depend on the assertion *(ON A B)* being in the database. In the example, the assertion *(ON A B)* supports the assertion *(NOT (ON A TABLE))*. All assertions in the database with valid support are said to be *in* (or believed true) and all assertions that have had some of their supporting assertions removed are said to be *out* (no longer believed true). Whenever any of the support for an assertion goes *out*, the data dependencies that set up the support automatically make the assertion go *out* as well. As long as assertions are made within the environments of the answers that they rely on, the TMM will automatically maintain the truth of the assertions by keeping track of those that are *in* and those that are *out*. If the assertion *(ON A B)* is ever signalled to be *out*, then *(NOT (ON A TABLE))* will go *out* as well. The user can respond to such automatic changes through the use of signal functions that are executed when selected assertions go *out*.

Along with simple ground assertions, the database can contain logical implications to be invoked at either assertion or fetch time. Implications invoked at assertion time are called forward chaining rules. A forward chaining rule consists of a pattern and a formula. When an assertion is made to the database that matches the rule pattern, the rule formula is asserted automatically. Forward chaining rules take the form:

```
(-> pattern
    formula)
```

which might be read, "*pattern* implies *formula*". Consider adding to the database that any block on the table is not higher than the table. One way to do it is with the code:

```
(FOR-EACH-ANS
    (FETCH (ON ?X TABLE))
    (ASSERT (NOT (HIGHER-THAN ?X TABLE))))
```

However, this code can only act on blocks already on the table. If more blocks are placed on the table in the future, the code must be executed again. A better way is to make the fact into a forward chaining rule:

```
(ASSERT (-> (ON ?X TABLE)
            (NOT (HIGHER-THAN ?X TABLE))))
```

which asserts that all blocks currently on the table are not higher than the table, and which will continue to make the same assertion for all blocks put on the table in the future. Assertions made by forward chaining rules are made within the environment created by matching their pattern. Therefore, variable bindings from the match are used and data dependencies are set up to keep the asserted formula valid.

Phrasing an implication as a forward chaining rule has the advantage that the implied formulae are added directly into the database without explicit action on the part of the user. However, the very fact that forward chaining rules add assertions can cause the database to grow enormously. Furthermore, the data dependencies set up by the assertions can cause a lot of work to be done when the database is changed. To help avoid an explosion of ground assertions and data-dependencies in the database, it is often appropriate to include an implication as a backward chaining rule. Backward chaining rules are used only at fetch time, and take the form:

```
(<- pattern-sought
    subgoal-pattern)
```

which might be read, "*subgoal-pattern* implies *pattern-sought*." Whenever the *pattern-sought* is used as a conjunct in a query pattern, the *subgoal-pattern* can be used instead. For example, the forward chaining rule in the previous paragraph can be rephrased as the backward chaining rule:

```
(ASSERT (<- (NOT (HIGHER-THAN ?X TABLE))
            (ON ?X TABLE)))
```

If a query is ever made that asks for a block not higher than the table, a block can be sought that is on the table. Using a backward chaining rule means that the formula *(NOT (HIGHER-THAN ?X TABLE))* never explicitly appears in the database, and data-dependencies for it need not be set up until it is actually used. This trades database space and dependency update time for longer query times.

14.2.2. Adding Basic Concepts of Time

The classic problem with using traditional predicate calculus databases for planning is that they assume that their contents are timelessly true. For propositions that represent tasks or effects, this assumption is clearly false, and planners based on such a database are forced to spend a lot of time and trouble working around it. If the truth of a proposition changes during the period the planner is reasoning about it, then the planner must erase or reassert it. This sort of database manipulation is inappropriate because it makes it difficult to reason about temporal deadlines or delays and it conflates change of belief with change of the world.

The proper way to correct these deficiencies is to turn the predicate calculus database into a true time map by incorporating a metric representation of time. The TMM uses the occasion as its basic temporal concept. An occasion consists of a formula and the interval of time over which it holds true. Each formula in the database that is not true forever must be expressed as an occasion. Occasions are represented as predicates in the database and take the form:

(OCCASION occasion-type name)

where *occasion-type* is a formula and *name* is a unique label for making reference to the occasion in other formulae. In practice, *name* is always a variable and when the occasion is first asserted the variable is bound to a unique identifier assigned by the TMM. As an example, consider the database of blocks built with the assertion:

```
(ASSERT (AND (OCCASION (ON A B) ?OCC1)
             (OCCASION (ON B TABLE) ?OCC2)
             (OCCASION (ON C TABLE) ?OCC3)))
```

This database represents exactly the same world as the one built earlier using timeless formulae. The three occasions represent three facts required about the blocks, but the intervals over which the facts are true has not been declared. Therefore, all three formulae might be true at any time.

To constrain the interval that an occasion represents, and to link many occasions together in time, temporal relationships between occasions must be specified. Only a single type of constraint is needed to represent all temporal relationships between occasions, and it takes the form:

```
(DISTANCE point1 point2 lo hi)
```

When a predicate of this type is added to the time map database, it asserts that the temporal distance between *point1* and *point2* must lie in the "fuzzy interval" between *lo* and *hi*. To specify distance constraints between occasions, the occasion end points are referenced using the functions BEGIN and END. For example:

```
(ASSERT (AND (OCCASION (ON A B) ?OCC1)
             (OCCASION (ON A C) ?OCC2)
             (DISTANCE (BEGIN ?OCC1) (END ?OCC1) 250 300)
             (DISTANCE (END ?OCC1) (BEGIN ?OCC2) 10 10)))
```

states that the fact *(ON A B)* is true throughout an interval that is 250 to 300 temporal units long and the fact *(ON A C)* begins to be true exactly 10 units after *(ON A B)* ends.

The TMM supports the notion of relative as well as absolute temporal constraints by allowing the four symbols *pos-tiny*, *neg-tiny*, *pos-inf* and *neg-inf* to be used as interval sizes in distance constraints. The first two symbols stand for the smallest positive and negative distances possible and the last two stand for the largest positive and negative distances possible. Using these symbols and forward chaining rules, qualitative constraints like those that follow can be defined:

```
(-> (BEFORE ?OCC1 ?OCC2)
```

```
          (DISTANCE (END ?OCC1)
                    (BEGIN ?OCC2) *pos-tiny* *pos-inf*))

    (-> (DURING ?OCC1 ?OCC2)
        (AND (DISTANCE (BEGIN ?OCC2)
                       (BEGIN ?OCC1) *pos-tiny* *pos-inf*)
             (DISTANCE (END ?OCC1)
                       (END ?OCC2) *pos-tiny* *pos-inf*)))

    (-> (BEGINS-DURING ?OCC1 ?OCC2)
        (AND (DISTANCE (BEGIN ?OCC1)
                       (BEGIN ?OCC2) *pos-tiny* *pos-inf*)
             (DISTANCE (BEGIN ?OCC2)
                       (END ?OCC1) *pos-tiny* *pos-inf*)))
```

The first of these rules states that one occasion comes before another only if it ends before the other begins. The second rule says that one occasion occurs during another only if it starts and finishes entirely between the begin and end points of the other. The third example says that an occasion starts during another if its begin point comes between the other's begin and end points.

As a brief example to illustrate the use of occasions and constraints, consider the following set of assertions. In this and later examples, the symbol *ref* is used to represent an arbitrary point in time from which the distance to other points is measured; usually it corresponds to "now."

```
(ASSERT (AND (OCCASION (ON B TABLE) ?OCC1)
             (DISTANCE (BEGIN ?OCC1) (END ?OCC1) 100 100)
             (DISTANCE (BEGIN ?OCC1) *ref* 0 0)
             (OCCASION (ON C TABLE) ?OCC2)
             (DISTANCE (BEGIN ?OCC2) (END ?OCC2) 100 100)
             (DISTANCE (BEGIN ?OCC2) *ref* 0 0)
             (OCCASION (ON A B) ?OCC3)
             (DISTANCE (BEGIN ?OCC3) (END ?OCC3) 40 45)
             (DURING ?OCC3 ?OCC1)
             (OCCASION (ON A C) ?OCC4)
             (DISTANCE (BEGIN ?OCC4) (END ?OCC4) 40 45)
             (DURING ?OCC4 ?OCC2)
             (BEFORE ?OCC3 ?OCC4)))
```

The time map built with these assertions represents the situation where block *A* is moved from block *B* to block *C* about 45 time units after a reference point. A diagrammatic representation of this time map is shown in Figure 14-2. Occasions are shown as thick horizontal bars, and thin arrows are used to show ordering constraints between their end-points. Occasion end-points that do not have explicit ordering constraints between them are unordered with respect to each other unless an ordering is forced by explicit constraints that do exist.

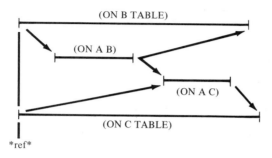

(ON B TABLE)

(ON A B)

(ON A C)

(ON C TABLE)

ref

Figure 14-2:   A Simple Blocks World Time Map

The use of occasions and distance constraints often leads to a time map containing temporally scoped assertions that are ambiguously ordered with respect to one another. In Figure 14-2 it is clear which occasions occur over the same interval of time, and what order occasions at different times come in. In contrast, dropping the last distance constraint used to build that time map gives Figure 14-3, which shows a time map where it is not known whether *(ON A B)* comes before *(ON A C)* or vice versa. Indeed, both facts may be true at the same time. This property of representing partially ordered databases of occasions is what gives the TMM its power as a tool for solving planning problems.

Most temporal features needed to reason about planning can be easily represented using occasions and distance constraints. For instance, consider translating the following ideas into TMM propositions:

```
"A block that is on another block is supported."
"The output bin of the lathe contains a candlestick."
"The car is red."
```

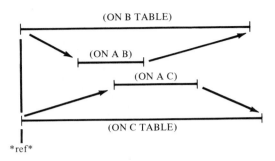

Figure 14-3:   A Partially Ordered Blocks World Time Map

The first statement might be represented as a rule that says
that whenever an occasion of type *(ON ?A ?B)* is asserted
another occasion of type *(SUPPORTS ?B ?A)* should be
asserted to overlap it exactly.   It would make no sense for one
occasion to extend before or after the other.   On the other
hand, the second statement suggests the inference that the lathe
was running some time before the candlestick arrived in the
output hopper; a *(RUN LATHE)* occasion should exist that
ends just when the candlestick arrives in the output bin.
Finally, the third phrase can be represented as an occasion that
begins with the building of the car and extends indefinitely
into the future.   Methods for representing these types of
statement and inference are discussed in the rest of this section
of the paper, along with the mechanisms required to deal with
the complications of allowing partially ordered occasions.

14.2.3. Events and Persistences

Occasions   and   distance   constraints   are   the   general
mechanisms used by the time map to represent predicates that
are only true over specific intervals of time.   When working
on planning problems, it is useful to make a conceptual
distinction between two kinds of occasions: events and
persistences.   An event is an occasion that corresponds to an

action under the control of the planner. For example, moving a block from one place to another, starting or stopping a lathe, and examining a hopper to see if it is full are all reasonable events. On the other hand, a persistence is a fact that becomes true in the world and stays true until another event changes it. For example, the facts that one block is on another, that the lathe is running, or that the hopper is full will tend to persist indefinitely. The distinction between events and persistences is designed to capture the naive causal notion that things remain the same unless they are actively altered. Figure 14-4 illustrates the situation that events and persistences are meant to deal with. The event *(START LATHE)* causes the fact *(LATHE-STATUS RUNNING)* to become true, and it persists indefinitely. In general, event occasions correspond to the planning notion of a task and persistence occasions correspond to the notion of an effect. Events will usually be known to occur over finite intervals of time,while persistences will extend indefinitely into the future.

```
(ASSERT (AND (OCCASION (START LATHE) ?OCC1)
             (DISTANCE (BEGIN ?OCC1) (END ?OCC1) 2 3)
             (OCCASION (LATHE-STATUS RUNNING) ?OCC2)
             (BEGINS-DURING ?OCC2 ?OCC1)))
```

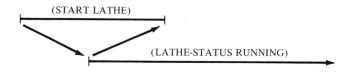

Figure 14-4:   An Event and a Persistence

To support temporal reasoning about events and persistences, the TMM treats persistence occasions differently from regular occasions. A persistence occasion is allowed to extend indefinitely into the future, but if another persistence is asserted that contradicts it, the earlier one is automatically "clipped" to end just before the point where they would overlap. More precisely, the TMM uses the following rule of persistence to keep the time map consistent:

> When two contradictory occasions are required to overlap in the time map, the TMM constrains the one that begins earlier to end before the other one begins.

For example, it might be the case that grasping a block causes it to be held and therefore it should no longer be considered to be on any other block. If we have the simple time map shown in Figure 14-5a and assert that (*PICKUP A*) will occur 45 units after *ref* and will cause (*HOLD A*), then the time map in Figure 14-5b should be generated where (*ON A B*) has been automatically clipped.

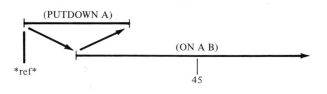

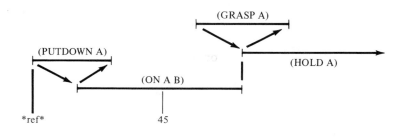

Figure 14-5:   An Example of Clipping a Persistence

The TMM is told that a class of persistence occasions is to be clipped by another using the special predicate CLIPS. In particular, the clipping of (*ON A B*) discussed above requires the assertion:

```
(ASSERT (CLIPS (HOLD ?X)
```

```
(ON ?X ?Y)))
```

which says that whenever an occasion of type *(HOLD ?X)* is asserted to come after the beginning of an occasion of type *(ON ?X ?Y)*, then that occasion should be clipped to end before *(HOLD ?X)* begins. A CLIPS assertion is not commutative and has the general form:

```
(CLIPS occasion-type-that-clips
       occasion-type-that-is-clipped )
```

When an assertion is clipped by the TMM, data dependencies are set up so that if the occasion that does the clipping ever goes *out*, the clipped assertion will become unclipped.

Automatic clipping gives the user a great deal of flexibility to rearrange occasions in the time map without fear of generating inconsistencies. However, it is sometimes useful to prohibit an effect from being clipped. For example, if the effect of an event is required by another event later in time, then it is important that the effect not be clipped before the event that uses it begins. Suppose that an event is planned that puts a metal blank in the hopper of a lathe and a later event is planned to run the lathe and turn out a candlestick. Such a situation is shown in Figure 14-6.[43] Clearly, the run lathe event requires the metal blank to be in the hopper, so the clean hopper event must not be allowed to start between them. To prevent unwanted clipping from occurring, a protection is asserted of the form:

```
(PROTECT occasion-name end-point)
```

which says that the occasion with name *occasion-name* is to be protected up until the point *end-point*. For example, adding the assertion:

```
(PROTECT ?OCC4 (END ?OCC2))
```

to the time map in the illustration will prohibit the occasion

---

[43]In this and following examples, the constraints needed to fix the duration of event occasions will be omitted for clarity.

of type *(HOPPER-HOLDS NOTHING)* from beginning
between the time that the occasion of type *(HOPPER-HOLDS
METAL)* starts and the occasion of type *(RUN LATHE)* ends.
In general, the TMM prevents an occasion from being
constrained to overlap an interval where it would clip a
protected persistence. Using protection assertions, events can be
prevented from accidently clobbering the preconditions for other
events.

```
(ASSERT (AND (OCCASION (LOAD-HOPPER METAL) ?OCC1)
             (OCCASION (RUN-LATHE) ?OCC2)
             (OCCASION (CLEAN-HOPPER) ?OCC3)
             (OCCASION (HOPPER-HOLDS METAL) ?OCC4)
             (OCCASION (HOPPER-HOLDS NOTHING) ?OCC5)
             (BEFORE ?OCC1 ?OCC2)
             (BEGINS-IN ?OCC4 ?OCC1)
             (BEGINS-IN ?OCC5 ?OCC3)
             (CLIPS (HOPPER-HOLDS METAL)
                    (HOPPER-HOLDS NOTHING)))))
```

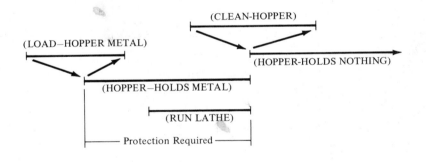

Figure 14-6:   A Time Map Needing a Protection

When using the TMM in planning, tasks are added to the
time map as event occasions and the effects of those tasks are
added as persistences. To keep the time map consistent when
contradictory effects are generated by different tasks, the
offending effects are declared to clip one another. Using
persistences and automatic clipping is a somewhat more general
way of overcoming the planning frame problem than the more
traditional add and delete list. Essentially, a persistence is

believed to be true by the TMM as far into the future as the earliest point (if one exists) where it would be clipped. Thus, there is no difficulty in propagating a fact into the future once it has been asserted, yet many different persistence types can clip it at any time. Also, to keep automatic clipping under control, effects required as preconditions for later tasks can be protected from accidental clobbering through the use of protections.

14.2.4. Temporal Database Queries

Planning relies on the ability to look through the representation of partially ordered time maps to discover when the preconditions for new tasks have been set up by earlier tasks. In addition, the planner needs a method for determining how unordered tasks in the plan can be arranged so that preconditions not already true might be made true and so that newly added tasks do not interfere with preconditions set up previously. The TMM function FETCH introduced earlier is responsible for handling both of these problems.

The TMM function FETCH is considerably affected by the introduction of occasions into the database. When all of the facts in the database were timelessly true, it made perfect sense to ask what blocks were on the table. However, when facts are represented as occasions, database queries must make careful reference to the temporal intervals they are concerned with. In the time map shown in Figure 14-7, what answer should be returned when a query is made asking for the block that is on B? Different blocks are on B at different times. To overcome this problem, queries specify the intervals that concern them using the special fetch pattern TT:

(TT *begin-point end-point occasion-type*)

which asks whether an occasion of type *occasion-type* is true throughout the interval from *begin-point* to *end-point*. Consider the following temporal query made to the database in Figure 14-7:

(FETCH (TT ?BEGIN ?END (ON ?X B)))

which asks for all known intervals where something is on *B*. This query will return three answers, one with *?X* bound to each of the blocks *A*, *C* and *D*. More specific temporal queries can be made by including more conjuncts in the fetch pattern. For example:

```
(FETCH (AND (TT ?BEGIN ?END (ON ?X B))
            (TT ?BEGIN ?END (ON B F))))
```

asks whether an interval exists where both a block is on *B* and *B* is on *F*. The time map in Figure 14-7 gives a single answer to this with binding *(?X=C)*. Similarly, the query:

```
(FETCH (AND (TT ?BEGIN ?END (ON ?X B))
            (TT ?BEGIN2 ?END2 (ON C B))
            (DISTANCE ?END ?BEGIN2 *pos-tiny* *pos-inf*)
            (DISTANCE ?BEGIN ?END 4 *pos-inf*)))
```

will match an interval with a block on *B* that ends before *(ON C B)* begins and is at least 4 time units long. There is again only one answer in the example time map with *?X* bound to *A*.

```
(ASSERT (AND (OCCASION (ON A B) ?OCC1)
             (OCCASION (ON C B) ?OCC2)
             (OCCASION (ON D B) ?OCC3)
             (OCCASION (ON B F) ?OCC4)
             (DURING ?OCC4 ?OCC2)
             (BEFORE ?OCC1 ?OCC2)
             (BEFORE ?OCC2 ?OCC3)))
```

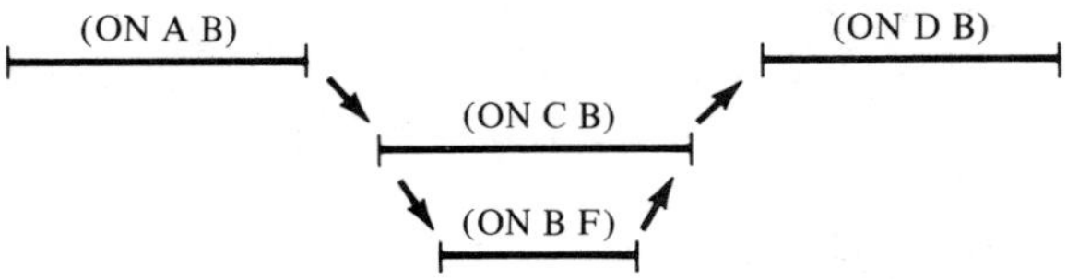

Figure 14-7:   Which Block is on *B*?

In the examples above, the answer that should be returned by each query is clear because the patterns being sought are matched unambiguously in the time map. The answer that should be returned when a query pattern only *might* be matched is less clear. Consider the simple time map in Figure 14-8a. Here an event (*WASH FLOOR*), that will last for 30 time units, is constrained to begin sometime after the point *ref*. What answer should be returned to the query:

```
(FETCH (AND (TT ?BEGIN ?END (WASH FLOOR))
            (DISTANCE *ref* ?BEGIN 15 20)
            (DISTANCE ?BEGIN ?END 20 20)))
```

which asks if there is an interval 20 units long beginning 15 to 20 units after *ref* where the floor is being washed? Since the (*WASH FLOOR*) event is not required to occur over that interval, and yet might occur over that interval, the answer to the query is uncertain. This uncertainty is inherent in time maps containing partially ordered occasions and if the TMM is to return meaningful answers, it must put a broader interpretation on the special form TT. During a fetch, the query pattern (*TT begin end fact*) is taken to mean, "Is it *possible* that *fact* could be true throughout the interval from *begin* to *end*?" Thus, the query above asks if it is possibly true that (*WASH FLOOR*) could be true over the desired interval. To this the answer is unambiguously "yes", and FETCH returns an appropriate ANS structure.

Another complication arises immediately. If a new assertion is made in the environment of the returned ANS, it would become inconsistent if future constraints on (*WASH FLOOR*) force it outside of the desired interval. To avoid this happening, the TMM augments the ANS environment with constraints that, if added to the time map, will guarantee that the answer to the query remains true. These constraints are called abductive premises from their analogy to explanatory assumptions; assuming these premises causes the desired result to follow deductively. FETCH saves abductive premises in the ANS environment so that the database remains untouched by the query. However, when a later assertion is made in the environment of the ANS, the constraints are added to the database as support for the assertion. Then, if any of the assumptions are contradicted and go *out*, invalidating the query answer, the assertion made in the answer environment goes *out* as well. This keeps the database consistent. In the example above, the query will return a single answer that contains the abductive premises that the *(WASH FLOOR)* occasion must begin no later than 20 units after *ref* and must end no earlier than 35 units after *ref*. Making an assertion in the environment of this answer will add these constraints to the database. For example, the following code will generate the time map in Figure 14-8b:

```
(FOR-EACH-ANS
    (FETCH (AND (TT ?BEGIN ?END (WASH FLOOR))
                (DISTANCE *ref* ?BEGIN 15 20)
                (DISTANCE ?BEGIN ?END 20 20)))
    (ASSERT (AND (OCCASION (AVOID FLOOR) ?OCC1)
                 (DISTANCE (BEGIN ?OCC1) ?BEGIN 0 0)
                 (DISTANCE (END ?OCC1) ?END 0 0))))
```

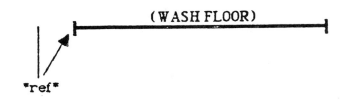

a

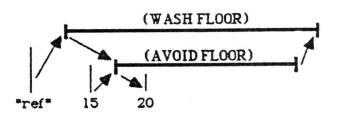

b

Figure 14-8:   A Time Map Before and After an
Abductive Assertion

It is now clear what the time map does when a query is made about a conjunction of occasions that only *may* overlap. Faced with a query involving a conjunction of TT forms, the TMM looks for a set of constraints that can be added to the time map to force the conjuncts to overlap as desired and then returns an ANS containing those constraints as abductive premises. If there is more than one set of constraints that would work, an ANS is returned for each one. When searching for a set of abductive premises, there are only three restrictions that the TMM must obey:

- No existing distance constraints can be violated.

- As persistences are moved around, occasion clipping must be updated to correspond with any new occasion orderings.

- No protected persistence can be clipped.

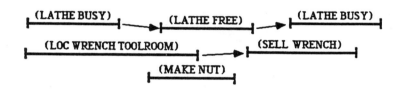

a

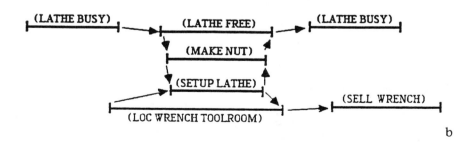

b

Figure 14-9: An Abductive Query and Assertion

As an example, consider the time map in Figure 14-9a. The situation shown represents a task network that includes

selling a wrench, making a nut, and using a lathe for several
things. Suppose that making a nut requires the use of the
lathe and also the use of the wrench. In that case, the
(MAKE NUT) event should be constrained to occur during
both the interval when the lathe is free and the interval when
the wrench is in the toolroom. One way to arrange this is to
set up all of the constraints individually. However, it is often
more useful to make an abductive fetch on the preconditions of
events like *(MAKE NUT)*. Assertions within the environment
of the returned ANS then set up the required ordering
constraints automatically. For instance, the following temporal
query and assertion generate the new time map in Figure
14-9b:

```
(FOR-FIRST-ANS
 (FETCH (AND (OCCASION (MAKE NUT) ?OCC1)
             (TT (BEGIN ?OCC1) (END ?OCC1) (LATHE FREE))
             (TT (BEGIN ?OCC1)
                 (END ?OCC1) (LOC WRENCH TOOLROOM))))
  (ASSERT (AND (OCCASION (SETUP LATHE) ?OCC2)
               (DURING ?OCC2 ?OCC1))))
```

This piece of code asks the TMM whether both the facts
(LATHE FREE) and *(LOC WRENCH TOOLROOM)* can be
made true throughout an interval when the *(MAKE NUT)*
event can take place. If so, then that interval should be seized
and the new event *(SETUP LATHE)* should be added during
it. The Figure shows the constraints from the environment
returned by the fetch that are added to the time map to
guarantee that the appropriate occasions will continue to
overlap.

14.2.5. Chaining Rules in a Temporal Database

An interesting problem in time map management is how
forward and backward chaining rules should be extended to
handle partially ordered occasions. In their most basic form,
chaining rules are unaffected by occasions in the database. For
example, to claim that whenever a block is on something it is
supported, one can simply assert the forward chaining rule:

```
(-> (OCCASION (ON ?X ?Y) ?OCC1)
```

```
(AND (OCCASION (SUPPORTS ?Y ?X) ?OCC2)
     (DISTANCE (BEGIN ?OCC2) (BEGIN ?OCC1) 0 0)
     (DISTANCE (END ?OCC2) (END ?OCC1) 0 0)))
```

This rule adds a "supports" occasion to coincide with every "on" occasion that is asserted. In addition to these original simple forms of chaining, however, temporal information in the database supports several new ideas. Two examples of additional chaining rules supported by the TMM are described below.

One type of augmented forward chaining allowed by the time map is implication from a conjunction of overlapping occasions. This is called basic temporal forward chaining and takes the form:

```
(->T conjunction-of-occasion-types
     occasion-type-to-be-asserted)
```

The syntax is very similar to regular forward chaining except that the pattern being watched for is a conjunction of one or more *occasion types*. For example, the fact that it is noisy when both the lathe and milling machines are running at the same time might be asserted to the database as:

```
(->T (AND (STATUS LATHE RUNNING)
          (STATUS MILLING-MACHINE RUNNING))
     (NOISE-LEVEL HIGH))
```

This rule says that whenever an occasion of type *(STATUS LATHE RUNNING)* overlaps another occasion of type *(STATUS MILL-MACHINE RUNNING)*, a new occasion specifying the noise level as high should be created with precisely the same interval as the overlap. Unlike the abductive database rearranging done by FETCH, temporal forward chaining rules are only activated when the occasions being watched for *must* overlap. In planning, temporal forward chaining rules are most useful for noticing unexpected interactions between the plan steps of different plans. If some plan requires use of the lathe, and another requires the milling machine, the rule above might be included to post a warning about noise level to the time map whenever both end up being used at the same time. Other planning interactions, like smoking while filling the gas tank come to mind as examples where such warnings would be appropriate.

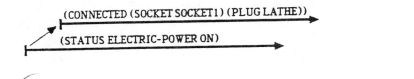

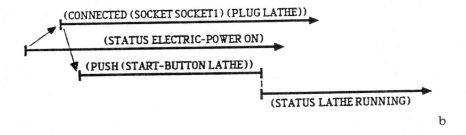

Figure 14-10:   An example of a *PCAUSE*

Another type of forward chaining is designed primarily for describing the physics of a planning domain.   The idea is to have rules that add the effects of events into the database automatically whenever the events are asserted.   Rules for this are called causal forward chaining rules and take the form:[44]

```
(PCAUSE precondition
        event-type
        effect-type)
```

This rule declares that whenever an occasion matching the event type is asserted, and the temporal precondition is true throughout the event interval, a new occasion of the effect

---

[44]The term *PCAUSE* is used to denote a causal forward chaining rule for historical reasons and stands for persistence causation.

type should be created as a persistence that begins when the event ends. For example, the rule:

```
(PCAUSE (AND (CONNECTED (SOCKET ?SOCKET) (PLUG ?MACHINE))
             (STATUS ELECTRIC—POWER ON))
        (PUSH (START—BUTTON ?MACHINE))
        (STATUS ?MACHINE RUNNING))
```

says that if the start button of a machine is pressed while the machine is plugged in and the electricity is turned on, the machine will begin to run. In particular, if this rule resides in the database shown in Figure 14-10a and an occasion of type *(START-BUTTON LATHE)* is asserted, the time map shown in 14-10b will result. As with temporal forward chaining, the preconditions *must* hold over the event interval; the database is not rearranged.

It should be noted that both types of temporal forward chaining rules make reference to occasion types rather than to occasions directly. This follows naturally from the abstraction that occasion and distance assertions exist solely as means of describing the temporal relationships between database formulae. The formulae themselves are represented as occasion types and it is the formulae we care about when doing forward chaining and making queries (using TT). Thus, temporal forward chaining rules must refer to occasion types and the occasion notation need not be mentioned explicitly in the rules.

Temporal forward chaining rules allow a planner to make projections of the future. Basic temporal forward chaining rules allow arbitrary interactions to be inferred from the effects generated by tasks in unrelated subplans, and causal forward chaining rules allow the effects of unordered tasks to change as they are moved around in the time map and the context surrounding them changes. Use of these features and the abductive query mechanisms of FETCH can push many of the decisions required of a planner into the hands of the TMM, which maintains a detailed picture of the expected future.

14.2.6. A Simple Planner Based on the TMM

To illustrate how the abilities of the TMM work together
as planner-building tools, this section of the paper describes a
simple hierarchical planner similar to NOAH (Sacerdoti, 1975).
The planner has three major components: a task network to
keep track of the plan as it is expanded from an initial goal to
a set of primitive actions, a control structure for carrying out
the expansion, and a language for writing down task expansion
plans and their effects on the world.   The task network is
built and managed by the TMM.

As is customary in these situations, the domain used in
this example is that of stacking blocks on a table.[45] The only
primitive action in the domain is *(PUT-ON ?x ?y)* which
moves the block *?x* from wherever it is to the top of *?y*:
either another block or the table. Initial goals for the planner
take the form *(ACHIEVE ?goal)* where *?goal* can be any
conjunction of the states *(ON ?x ?y)* and *(CLEAR ?x)*.
Goals and actions are represented in the TMM as event
occasions, and the states *(ON ?x ?y)* and *(CLEAR ?x)* are
represented as persistences. For instance, the planner might be
given the initial goal *(ACHIEVE (ON A B))*. This would
be placed in the task network as an event occasion, and the
planner's job would be to expand it into a set of *(PUT-ON
?x ?y)* events that transform the current world into one
where the state *(ON A B)* is true.

The language for describing possible expansions for
(ACHIEVE ...) tasks is based directly on the abilities of
the TMM, and consists of the following construction:

```
(PLAN-FOR ?task ?task-type
    (ASSUME reduction assumptions)
    (PLAN   assertion to the time map)
    (PROTECT persistences to be protected))
```

---

[45]The blocks world is used because it is likely to be familiar: the problems
that it poses are well known. It is hoped that the ease with which a blocks
world planner can be built will illustrate the power of the TMM as a planning
tool. Perhaps an example from a richer world would be more enlightening, but
unfortunately it would also take up much more space.

```
(PLAN-FOR ?task (ACHIEVE ?a)
  (ASSUME  (TT (BEGIN ?task) (END ?task) ?a))
  (PLAN    (DISTANCE (BEGIN ?task) (END ?task) 0 0))
  (PROTECT (?a FROM (BEGIN ?task) TO (END ?task))))

(PLAN-FOR ?task (ACHIEVE (AND ?a ?b))
  (ASSUME  ())
  (PLAN    (AND (OCCASION (ACHIEVE ?a) ?occ1)
                (OCCASION (ACHIEVE ?b) ?occ2)
                (DURING ?occ1 ?task)
                (DURING ?occ2 ?task)))
  (PROTECT (?a FROM (END T1) TO (END ?task))
           (?b FROM (END T2) TO (END ?task))))
```

Figure 14-11: Two Basic Expansion Plans

This form states that a valid expansion for a task of type *?task-type*, corresponding to the time map occasion with name *?task*, consists of the occasions and ordering constraints asserted in the PLAN clause. Furthermore, this set of assertions is a valid expansion given that the assumptions in the ASSUME clause are true (and remain true) and given that the effects mentioned in the PROTECT clause are not clipped over the intervals specified. For example, consider the two basic expansions shown in Figure 14-11. The first one says that a task can be accomplished by doing nothing if it is supposed to achieve a state that is already true. The second plan states that one way to expand a conjunction of tasks is to work on them separately and keep the results of both true. The remaining plans needed to describe the blocks world are given in Figure 14-12. All of these plans will be assumed to exist in the TMM database as timeless assertions.

The control structure of this simple planner is also based largely on abilities of the TMM and it works in the following way. First, an unexpanded task is picked out of the task network using a TMM fetch. Tasks are flagged as expanded using assertions of the form *(STATUS-OF task EXPANDED)* where *task* is the unique identifier assigned to the occasion representing the task. When new tasks are asserted, the forward chaining rules below tag them as either

```
(PLAN-FOR ?task (ACHIEVE (CLEAR ?a))
  (ASSUME (AND (TT (BEGIN ?task) (END ?task) (ON ?b ?a))
               (INSTANCE-OF ?a BLOCK)))
     (PLAN (AND (OCCASION (ACHIEVE (ON ?b TABLE)) ?occ1)
                (DISTANCE (END ?occ1) (END ?task) 0 0)))
  (PROTECT ()))

(PLAN-FOR ?task (ACHIEVE (ON ?a TABLE))
  (ASSUME (TT (BEGIN ?task) (END ?task) (ON ?b ?a)))
     (PLAN (AND (OCCASION (ACHIEVE (CLEAR ?a)) ?occ1)
                (OCCASION (PUT-ON ?a TABLE)    ?occ2)
                (BEFORE ?occ1 ?occ2)
                (DISTANCE (BEGIN ?occ2) (END ?occ2) 2 2)
                (DISTANCE (END ?occ2)   (END ?task) 0 0)))
  (PROTECT ((CLEAR ?a) FROM (END ?occ1) TO (END ?occ2))))

(PLAN-FOR ?task (ACHIEVE (ON ?a ?b))
  (ASSUME (INSTANCE-OF ?b BLOCK))
     (PLAN (AND (OCCASION (ACHIEVE (CLEAR ?a)) ?occ1)
                (OCCASION (ACHIEVE (CLEAR ?b)) ?occ2)
                (OCCASION (PUT-ON ?a ?b) ?occ3)
                (BEFORE ?occ1 ?occ3)
                (BEFORE ?occ2 ?occ3)
                (DISTANCE (BEGIN ?occ3) (END ?occ3) 2 2)
                (DISTANCE (END ?occ3)   (END ?task) 0 0)))
  (PROTECT ((CLEAR ?a) FROM (END ?occ1) TO (END ?occ3))
           ((CLEAR ?b) FROM (END ?occ2) TO (END ?occ3))))
```

Figure 14-12:   Plans for the Blocks World Domain

unexpanded or primitive:

```
(-> (OCCASION (ACHIEVE ?a) ?task)
    (NOT (STATUS-OF ?task EXPANDED)))

(-> (OCCASION (PUT-ON ?a ?b) ?task)
    (STATUS-OF ?task PRIMITIVE))
```

After a task needing expansion is retrieved, a plan for
the task is chosen from the set of possible expansion plans
residing in the database for which the ASSUME clause holds true
in the time map. In fact a single TMM query can select an
appropriate plan and check its assumptions. To finally carry
out the task expansion, the PLAN clause of the chosen plan is
asserted to the time map and a persistence of each type

mentioned in the PROTECT clause is located and protected appropriately. In schematic form, this control structure looks like:

```
; Find a task
(FOR-FIRST-ANS (FETCH (AND (OCCASION ?task-type ?task)
                           (NOT (STATUS-OF ?task EXPANDED))
                           (NOT (STATUS-OF ?task
                                           PRIMITIVE))))
  ; Find a plan
    (FOR-EACH-ANS (FETCH (AND (PLAN-FOR ?task ?task-type)
                              (ASSUME ?assumptions)
                              (PLAN    ?plan)
                              (PROTECT ?protections))
                         ?assumptions))
```
Code to choose the "best" plan returned)
```
    (FOR-ANS answer of best plan returned
; Add the plan
        (ASSERT (AND ?plan
;   and protections
                     (STATUS-OF ?task EXPANDED)))
```
(*Loop over each clause in* ?protections
with the form:
```
        (?effect-type FROM ?begin TO ?end)
        (FOR-FIRST-ANS
          (FETCH (AND (OCCASION ?effect-type ?effect)
                      (DISTANCE (BEGIN ?effect)
                                ?begin 0 *pos-inf*)
                      (DISTANCE ?end
                                (END ?effect) 0
                                *pos-inf*)))
          (ASSERT (PROTECT ?effect ?end))))))))
```

Of course, the code for choosing the "best" plan expansion is the heart of a real planner but this discussion will leave that code up to the reader. What is important for purposes of illustration, is how the functionality of the TMM complements any choice of such code.

The only thing left to complete the planner is to specify the effects of each of the task expansion plans. One way to specify these effects is through the use of temporal forward chaining rules. The significant effects in the blocks world domain are captured by the three causal rules in Figure 14-13. The first of these rules states that any task generates the effect it is supposed to. It is the responsibility of a later expansion to insert a primitive task into the time map that actually produces that effect; in the meantime it is just to be assumed. The second two rules give the effects of the primitive task *PUT-ON*. In particular, a *PUT-ON* task always has the effect of a block being on something and, if the block being moved was on another, then that one is now clear. Finally, there are two clipping rules that specify how the *CLEAR* and *ON* effects interact.

```
(PCAUSE T                          (CLIPS (CLEAR ?a)
        (ACHIEVE ?a)                      (ON ?b ?a))
        ?a)
                                   (CLIPS (ON ?a ?b)
(PCAUSE T                                 (CLEAR ?b))
        (PUT-ON ?a ?b)
        (ON ?a ?b))

(PCAUSE (AND (ON ?a ?c)
             (INSTANCE-OF ?c BLOCK))
        (PUT-ON ?a ?b)
        (CLEAR ?c))
```

Figure 14-13:   Blocks World Domain Physics

Armed with the control structure, the task expansion plans, and the blocks world physics outlined above, consider the initial situation shown in Figure 14-14. The planning goal to be achieved is to build the tower described by *(AND (ON A B) (ON B C))*. The first step in constructing a plan for this goal is to add it to the time map as an achieve task with the code:

```
(ASSERT (OCCASION (ACHIEVE (AND (ON A B)
                                (ON B C))) ?OCC1))
```

Setting the control structure described into action expands this task one level using the second plan in Figure 14-11. The resulting time map is shown in Figure 14-15.[46] Note that PCAUSE rules have added the appropriate effects and that the two new tasks, *(ACHIEVE (ON A B))* and *(ACHIEVE*

---

[46]In this and later figures, protected persistences are shown as double lines.

(ON B C)), remain unordered with respect to one another.

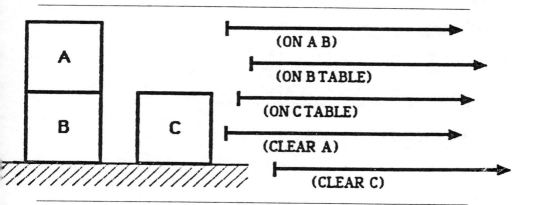

Figure 14-14:   A Simple Blocks World Problem

To further expand the plan for building the tower, a choice must be made as to which of the two unexpanded tasks in Figure 14-15 should be worked on first.   If the task to achieve *(ON A B)* is chosen, it will be expanded into doing nothing because *(ON A B)* is already true in the time map. The result is shown in Figure 14-16a where it can be seen that there is now no way to expand the task to achieve *(ON B C)* since the fact *(ON A B)* is protected over the entire interval that it might fit in.   When a mistake like this is made, there is no recourse but to backtrack and undo the incorrect choice.   Such a control structure is easy to describe and will not be discussed at any length here.   Instead assume that the task to achieve *(ON B C)* is chosen to be expanded first.

When faced with expanding the task *(ACHIEVE (ON B C))* the planner will pick the appropriate plan from those in Figure 14-12. The situation after the plan has been chosen and added to the time map is shown in Figure 14-16b.   Note that once again the PCAUSE rules have the appropriate expansion effects and the result of the new *(ACHIEVE (CLEAR B))* task is the effect *(CLEAR B)*.   In addition, since *(CLEAR B)* would clip the effect *(ON A B)* protected from the *(ACHIEVE (ON A B))* task onward, the TMM has added constraints to force *(CLEAR B)* to begin before it.   Pushing

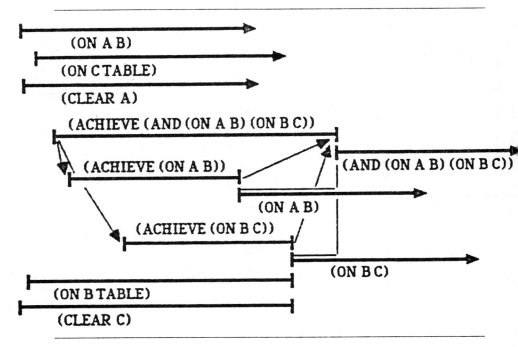

Figure 14-15:   The Time Map after One Expansion

(*CLEAR B*) earlier in this manner results in the task (*ACHIEVE (ON B C)*) being completed before (*ACHIEVE (ON A B)*) is begun. Thus, through the use of clipping and protections, the machinery of the TMM automatically makes a task network ordering decision that would have been difficult for the planner itself to foresee.

Continuing the plan expansion as described will eventually result in a set of primitive actions to construct the desired stack of blocks. This simple control structure and set of plans is sufficient to deal effectively with most blocks world planning issues including those involved in the Sussman anomaly (*that is*, the same problem discussed above but with the initial conditions being (*ON C A*) and (*ON B TABLE*)) where inappropriate initial plan choices can cause some types of planner to do unnecessary work (Sussman, 1975), or, in fact, to fail completely. By extending the control structure of the planner to include backtracking when an expansion step does not work out, the important completeness aspects of Tate's

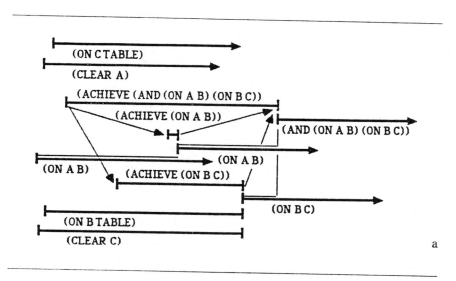

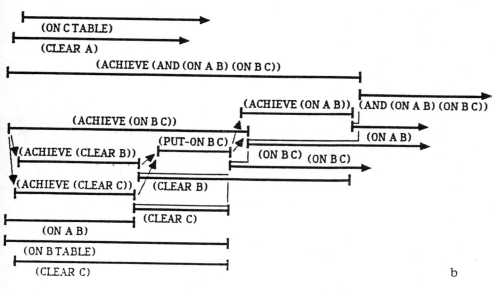

Figure 14-16:   Possible Second Plan Expansions

NONLIN system (Tate, 1977) can also be achieved. Furthermore the ability of the TMM to represent absolute metric constraints like deadlines and "execution windows", and the data-dependency information maintained for each assertion, parallel the temporal and dependency-directed backtracking aspects of Vere's work on the DEVISER planning system (Vere, 1983). These features and the effect projection mechanisms of temporal forward chaining and clipping make the TMM a flexible planner building tool able to represent and reason about the basic problems confronting all systems based on partially ordered task networks.

In the last section of this paper some speculations are made as to how planners based on the TMM can be extended by exploring more than one time map at a time or by using some method to study possible completions of partially ordered time maps at crucial decision points. The next section of the paper describes a Heuristic Task Scheduler that can be used for just such explorations.

14.3. The Heuristic Task Scheduler

Planning with a partially ordered time map has one major shortcoming: it is difficult to detect interactions between tasks when the effects of the tasks depend on the order in which they are executed. Although temporal forward chaining can take care of some situations, interactions still arise that the TMM cannot handle. The most dramatic example of order-dependent interaction comes when the travel time in a plan is important (more generally, the time required to change a resource from the state one task needs to the state the next task needs). The time it takes to travel from the location required by one task to that required by another clearly depends on which comes first, and whether or not other tasks are to come between. There is no way to reason about travel time without making a conjecture about the order tasks will be executed in. Detecting order-dependent interactions between tasks requires exploring the possible orderings that the tasks might take.

The Heuristic Task Scheduler, or HTS (Miller, 1985), is a

planning system designed to look through a set of tasks and arrange them into a linear order that does not produce any undesirable order-dependent interactions. The most interesting contribution that the HTS makes to planning research is the class of task interactions that it can deal with. In particular, because the HTS is always dealing with totally ordered tasks, it can represent both incremental changes to a quantity, like deposits and withdrawals from a bank account, and some forms of continuous change, like the growth of lateral drift during a robot steering task. Furthermore, the HTS can deal with task constraints that depend on which other tasks are to be executed earlier. For instance, a task for crossing the room might be constrained to begin no earlier than 30 minutes after a task to wash the floor, if the floor-washing task is placed before it in time, yet the same task can remain unconstrained if the floor-washing task is placed after it. This type of constraint is difficult to represent in a partially ordered time map because the relative ordering of the tasks involved may remain unknown.

The model of planning based on the use of the TMM assumes that goals will be specified as tasks to perform, and that these tasks are to be refined to more and more detail until only primitive actions remain. At each step in the refinement the TMM-based planner strives to ensure that no detectable interactions occur between tasks that will compromise the correctness of the plan. In contrast, planners based on the HTS do not refine abstract tasks as a group, sorting out interactions as they arise, but rather expand each goal task in isolation and then sorts out interactions by finding a consistent order for the set of all primitive tasks together. The main purpose of the HTS itself is to build a total temporal order for a set of tasks. Thus, it can be used to form the major part of a planner in its own right or it can be used to explore completions of the partial task ordering represented by a time map built with the TMM. The Bumpers robot planner described by Miller (Miller, 1985) is an example of the former use, while the Forbin planner (Firby et. al., 1985) uses the HTS to enforce consistency on a partially ordered time map.

Although the heart of the HTS is the scheduling algorithm, its versatility rests on the types of task interaction

it can deal with. Therefore this section of the paper describes
the Bumpers planning language before going on to discuss the
method used by the HTS to build total task orderings. The
Bumpers language illustrates the different classes of task
interaction that the HTS is capable of reconciling. In
particular, order-dependent effects and continuous change are
described in Bumpers resource declarations, and the various
ways that tasks might depend on each other are detailed in the
task and constraint sections of Bumpers plan declarations.

A Bumpers planning problem consists of a conjunctive set
of goals to be achieved. For each type of goal there is a
library plan describing how to reduce the goal in isolation to a
list of tasks and constraints that will carry it out. When all
goals have been broken down into primitive tasks using these
library plans, Bumpers calls the HTS to create a total order, or
schedule, that includes all of the tasks and does not violate
any of the constraints. The Bumpers representation language
consists of resource declarations that describe how features of
the world can be changed from one state to another, and plan
declarations that specify how goals can be broken down into
tasks that rely on resource states as preconditions.

14.3.1. Describing a Resource

The central concept in this formulation of the planning
problem is that of a *world state*. Unlike the situation with a
partial temporal order, a total task order means that the state
of the world before and after each task can be calculated in
detail. Thus a task can be viewed as a primitive action, or set
of actions, that moves the world from one state to another.
The change in state brought about by a task is mediated
through the use of resources. Intuitively, a resource is a tool
that the planner needs to perform some primitive action but
the concept has been generalized to the point where a state is
completely described just as a collection of resources. A state
is changed by acting on the individual resources that make it
up.

Each resource is an abstract property of the world that,
either directly or indirectly, falls under the control of the

planner. For example, the position of a robot's sonar sensing device would be a resource. To determine the distance to an object the robot must turn the sensor to point at the object and then take a sonar reading. To effectively coordinate tasks that require the sensor to point in different directions, the planner must keep track of its expected direction at all times. Other examples of more abstract resources are position and bank balance.

Resources need not be simple static quantities; the assumption that tasks will be totally ordered during planning allows resources to take on more dynamic properties. Most importantly, a resource can have a method to change itself from one value to another encoded as a plan attached to it. If a task requires that some resource be in a given state as a precondition but the world is in a different state, the plan attached to the resource can be asked what actions are necessary to transform the resource to the state required. For example, a robot's sonar sensor might have a method for pointing itself in a particular direction, and a position resource might have a plan for moving the robot to a particular location.

The Bumpers language requires that each resource be defined before planning begins. A definition describes the way a resource behaves and can be controlled, that is, the *physics* of the resource. A possible sonar sensor resource definition is shown in Figure 14-17. The physics of a resource is described in four parts: three functions that describe its characteristics, and a list of adjustable variables with strategies for their use.

Each of the functions - *POSSIBLE*, *DELAY*, and *PLAN* - take three parameters: the "current" world state, $S1$, the "current" time $t1$, and the desired world state, $S2$. The *POSSIBLE* function returns a boolean value declaring whether or not the resource can change its value from that in the current state to that in the desired state. The *DELAY* function returns an estimate of the time necessary to complete the change, and the *PLAN* function returns a list of primitive actions that will bring the change about in the real world. If during the scheduling process the preconditions for a task require that a resource be in a specific state, the HTS asks these functions if and how the resource can be moved to the

```
(RESOURCE-PHYSICS 'sonar-sensor
  (POSSIBLE (S2 S1 t1)
    T)
  (DELAY (S2 S1 t1)
    (/ (ABS (- (VALUE-IN S2 'sonar-sensor)
               (VALUE-IN S1 'sonar-sensor)))
       ?rotation-rate))
  (PLAN (S2 S1 t1)
    (LET* ((angle (- (VALUE-IN S2 'sonar-sensor)
                     (VALUE-IN S1 'sonar-sensor)))
           (direction (COND ((> angle 0) 'counter-
                                          clockwise)
                            (T            'clockwise))))
      (ACTION 'rotate-sensor direction (ABS angle)
                                       ?rotation-rate)))
  (VARIABLES
    (?rotation-rate
      (VALUES discrete 5 15 45 60)
      (DEFAULT 15)
      (COORDINATION-STRATEGY match-best)))))
```

Figure 14-17:   A Sonar Sensor Resource Definition

state required.   It is possible for these three resource physics
functions to do whatever planning is necessary to effect
complex resource state changes, perhaps even invoking the
whole planning system recursively.

Another important aspect of the physics of a resource is
that it may depend on adjustable parameters called *scheduling
variables*. Scheduling variables are assigned values by the HTS
during scheduling and are represented with the question-mark
notation. The sonar example in Figure 14-17 uses the variable
?rotation-rate, representing the speed that the sensor is
to be rotated.   One can imagine that the sensor should be
rotated at some nominal speed like 15 to keep it from wearing
out, but that in time-critical applications it can be made to
turn much more quickly.   When the HTS is building a
schedule and comes upon a task that requires that the sonar
sensor be pointed in a particular direction, it picks a value for
the rotation rate and consults the *POSSIBLE*, *DELAY* and
PLAN functions as required.   If the chosen value gives
unacceptable results then the HTS is free to choose another

value and try again. For example, if the robot must take a sensor reading within 30 seconds, but at a rotation rate of 15 it will take 60 seconds to point in the correct direction, the rotation rate can be set to 45 and the problem resolved. The HTS assumes that the *DELAY* function is monotonically decreasing with respect to the values it can take on.

```
(VARIABLE
    (name (VALUES {discrete continuous} values)
          (DEFAULT value)
          (COORDINATION-STRATEGY strategies))))
```

Figure 14-18:   The Scheduler Variable Description Schema

Different resources will depend on scheduling variables with different properties, so the resource physics declaration includes a section for describing each one. This *VARIABLE* declaration section takes the form shown in Figure 14-18. The sonar sensor physics in Figure 14-17 shows an example for the variable *?rotation-rate*. The *VALUES* clause declares the variable to be either continuous or discrete, and gives either a range or a list of values that it can take on. Values can be anything compatible with their use in the *POSSIBLE, DELAY,* and *PLAN* functions. The *DEFAULT* gives a value to be used whenever possible, and the *COORDINATION-STRATEGY* suggests a method for choosing a value compatible with other scheduler variables from different resources being changed over the same interval of time. A coordination strategy can be one or more of the following:

- **match-first** - set the variable to have the value that makes its resource reach the desired state at a time as close as possible to, but not later than, the time when the other resources reach their states.

- **match-last** - set the variable to have the value that makes its resource reach the desired state at a time as close as possible to, but not before, the time when the other resources reach their states.

- **match-best** - set the variable to have the value that makes its resource reach the desired state at a time as close as possible to when the other resources reach their states.

When the HTS is building a schedule that requires setting several scheduler variables simultaneously, it uses the coordination strategies suggested to help decide on the values for each one. If variables are found to have conflicting strategies, for instance if there is more than one **match-last**, then variables are assigned their default values until the conflict is resolved.

14.3.2. Describing a Plan

With the concepts of world state and resource in hand, we turn to the Bumpers representation of a plan. A plan is a collection of tasks that will achieve a particular planning goal. Each task is either a single primitive action or a set of such actions, and tasks are linked together using constraints. Constraints take the form of deadlines on specific tasks, task ordering requirements, or conditions under which tasks need not be done. If, starting from the current world state, the tasks in a plan can be arranged so that none of their constraints are violated, the goal of the plan is guaranteed to be achieved. Typical plan goals are traveling across a crowded room, building a car, or doing the laundry.

A sample plan that a robot might use to travel down a hallway is shown in Figure 14-19. The robot is to travel down the hall while glancing occasionally at the wall with its sonar to make sure it isn't drifting off course. Invoking the plan requires three pieces of information: the hall length, the time the goal should be completed, and the distance the robot should keep between itself and the wall. A goal of the form *(FOLLOW-HALL-TO-END 40ft 10:00am 1.5ft)* would index into this plan.

Each plan description requires a section that specifies the resources used by the plan, the tasks that make up the plan,

```
(PLAN-FOR (FOLLOW-HALL-TO-END hall-length finish-time
                                            wall-separation)
    (RESOURCES
      (GLOBAL (position     *varied* continuous)
              (sonar-sensor 45       discontinuous)
              (sonar-sensor 0        discontinuous)
              (drive-motor  on       discontinuous))
      (LOCAL  (lateral-drift
                 (* ?drive-speed (drift-coefficient
                                    ?drive-speed)))))
    (TASKS
      (task1 REPEAT
               (task1.1 (ACTION 'adjust-steering
                                (READ sonar-sensor
                                 distance-to-wall)
                                wall-separation))
             WHEN  (CHANGE 'lateral-drift
                            (/ wall-separation 2))))
      (task2 REPEAT
               (task2.1 (READ sonar-sensor
                              distance-to-hall-end))
             WHILE (> distance-to-hall-end wall-separation)
             WHEN  (CHANGE 'position wall-separation))))
    (CONSTRAINTS
      (DEADLINE task1 finish-time)
      (DEADLINE task2 finish-time)
      (PRECONDITIONS task1.1 (sonar-sensor 45))
      (PRECONDITIONS task2.1 (sonar-sensor 0))
      (MAY-START task2 0.0 (BEGIN task1))
      (IF-SCHEDULED task2 (MAKE-FINISHED task1))))
```

Figure 14-19:   A Plan for Following a Wall Down a Hallway and any constraints on those tasks.

14.3.3. Specifying Plan Resource Use

The *RESOURCES* section of a plan declaration has the basic syntax shown in Figure 14-20.   Resources are broken up into two types: global and local.   A global resource is one that has been specified using a *RESOURCE-PHYSICS* declaration and might be used in many plans, while a local resource is important to only this plan.   In the hallway travel plan, the global   resources   *sonar-sensor.   position.*   and *drive-motor* are used and changed, and the local resource *lateral-drift* must be monitored. The lateral drift or steering error of the robot is related to the speed at which it is traveling and is thus related to the *drive-motor* resource. However, the lateral drift is a result of drive motor use and cannot be independently controlled. Therefore it is not a good candidate for an independent resource and is best described as a quantity to monitor or constrain. A local resource declares such a quantity to be a function of the scheduler variables that it depends on. The function for lateral drift depends on the scheduler variable *?drive-speed* described in the resource physics for *drive-motor*. Whenever the value of lateral drift is required during planning, this function is used to compute the value with the "current" value of *?drive speed*. Local resources always take the form:

```
(local-name function-of-scheduler-variables)
```

```
(RESOURCES
    (GLOBAL
        - resources that will be used by the plan -)
    (LOCAL
        - relationships between scheduler variables that
        are important for this plan only -))
```

Figure 14-20:   The Plan Resource Use Description Syntax

Global resource specifications give the expected value of the resource involved and the times during the plan that the resource will be required. These specifications give the planner some idea of how "heavily" resources will be used during execution of the plan so that it can decide what other plans, if any, it can execute at the same time. For example, no other plan that must change the robot's position can run at the same time as the *FOLLOW-HALL-TO-END* plan because the position resource is in use continuously. On the other hand, a plan that needs to use the sonar sensor might work in parallel with the hall plan because the hall plan only needs the sonar intermittently during its execution.   Global resource specifications take the form

```
(resource-name value time-required)
```

The resource must have been described in a previous resource physics declaration, and its *value* can be either something allowed by that specification or the symbol **varied** which declares that its value will change in an unspecified way during the plan. The *time-required* may be one of the following:

- **continuous** - stating the resource will be required in the given state throughout the plan.

- **discontinuous** - stating the resource will be required in the given state for ,one or more intervals during the plan.

- **start** - stating the resource will be required in the given state near the beginning of the plan.

- **end** - stating the resource will be required in the given state near the end of the plan.

14.3.4. Specifying Plan Tasks

In essence a plan consists of a set of tasks that must be performed to carry out some goal in the world. Each task is a set of primitive actions that can be executed by the planner once they have been coordinated with the other tasks from the same plan, or from other concurrent plans. The *TASKS* section of a plan description specifies the tasks required by that plan and also describes the actions that make up each task. The *TASKS* section itself is a simple list of tasks, with their ordering in the list implying nothing about their actual ordering. Task orderings are given in the *CONSTRAINTS* section of the plan description or are implied by the use of the *PROG* statement described below.

A task is described using the form

```
(task-name task-description)
```

The *task-name* is a symbol to identify the task so that it
may be referred to later in the constraint section of the plan
description. The *task-description* is either a *REPEAT*
statement, a *PROG* statement, or a piece of code that returns a
list of primitive actions. A task that returns a list of
primitive actions is the basic building block of the plan
description, while *REPEAT* and *PROG* statements are ways of
grouping such tasks together. The ability to group tasks
allows constraints to be placed on a group without having to
place the constraints on each task in the group. Furthermore
the *REPEAT* statement declares a set of tasks to be scheduled
repeatedly by the planner and the *PROG* statement specifies a
set of tasks that must be scheduled in the order that they are
described.

```
(task1 PROG
      (task1.1 (ACTION 'pick-up  'dishes))
      (task1.2 (ACTION 'wash     'dishes))
      (task1.3 (ACTION 'put-away 'dishes)))
```

Figure 14-21:   The task of doing the dishes

The syntax of the *PROG* statement is very simple and an
example is shown in Figure 14-21. The basic form is:

```
(task-name PROG
           list-of-tasks)
```

where *list-of-tasks* is a nested list of basic tasks,
REPEAT statements, or more *PROG* statements. The important
feature of a *PROG* task is that the tasks within it must be
scheduled in the order they are given. In Figure 14-21 for
example, the three tasks specified for washing the dishes must
be done in the order they are given; no other order will work.
Thus, a *PROG* statement is shorthand for a list of the tasks
and sufficient explicit constraints to force an order on them.

The *REPEAT* statement has a slightly more complex
syntax than the *PROG* statement because it must specify not

only a set of tasks but also the conditions under which the set should, or should not, be repeated. The basic form of a repeat task is:

```
(task-name REPEAT
          [WHEN test-resource-state]
          [WHILE test-resource-state]
          [TIMES n]
          list-of-tasks)
```

Like a *PROG* task, the tasks that make up a *REPEAT* must be scheduled in the order that they are specified and when the last one is scheduled, the whole set is ready to be scheduled again. This rescheduling continues until one of the tests terminates the loop. The *WHILE, WHEN,* and *TIMES* tests can be placed anywhere within the list of tasks that make up the loop and when one is encountered during scheduling the HTS checks the test to see if the loop should be continued.

```
(task1 REPEAT
       TIMES 2
       (task1.1 REPEAT
                (task1.1.1 (ACTION 'pour '1cup
                                   'vinegar 'coffee-maker))
                WHILE (NOT (= (STATE 'coffee-water-reservoir)
                           'full)))
       (task1.2 (ACTION 'run 'coffee-maker))
       (task1.3 (ACTION 'empty 'coffee-maker)))
```

Figure 14-22:   A Task for Cleaning a Coffee Maker

When a *TIMES* statement is encountered during scheduling the number of times the tasks in the repeat loop have been scheduled is compared to the number of times specified and, if they match, the loop is terminated. When a *WHILE* statement is encountered the specified resource is checked to see if it is currently in the state required. If not, the loop is terminated. Once a loop has terminated, none of its tasks are scheduled again. Examples of the *TIMES* and *WHILE* constructs are shown in Figure 14-22 which shows a way of cleaning a coffee maker by running vinegar through it twice. The inner loop adds vinegar a cup at a time until the coffee maker is full, and the outer loop does the cleaning operation two times.

When the HTS reaches a *WHEN* test it suspends the loop until the specified resource state becomes true. This form of repeat test is used to synchronize iterations of a loop with external states of the world. For example, the tasks in the repeat loop shown in Figure 14-23 are to be rescheduled each time that the lathe shavings bin is full.

```
(task1 REPEAT
       WHEN (= (STATE 'lathe-shavings-bin) 'full)
       (task1.1 (ACTION 'empty 'lathe-shavings-bin)))
```

Figure 14-23:   A Task for Emptying the Lathe Shavings Bin

A *WHEN* test is also used in the hallway following plan shown in Figure 14-19. In the hallway plan, the task for correcting the steering to account for possible robot drift needs to be repeated each time that the lateral drift *changes* by a specific amount. To synchronize repeated tasks with resource changes, the following form is used:

```
(CHANGE resource-name amount)
```

Whenever a *WHEN* statement with a *CHANGE* test is encountered while scheduling, the HTS waits until the specified resource has changed by the appropriate amount before rescheduling the tasks in the loop. Furthermore if the resource specified in the *CHANGE* statement is a global resource, the HTS asks the resource to change itself by the amount given. Thus the *CHANGE* of a local resource is monitored until it becomes true, while the *CHANGE* of a global resource is actively undertaken. This property of the *CHANGE* statement is exploited in the hallway plan, which never explicitly generates any motor-drive actions. Instead all of the actions required are generated implicitly by the *(CHANGE 'position wall-separation)* statement in the second repeat task.

14.3.5. Specifying Plan Constraints

The final part of the plan syntax is the *CONSTRAINTS* section. Constraints are used to guarantee that certain properties will hold in any schedule chosen for the plan's tasks. For example, the hallway following plan consists of two tasks: one to travel down the hallway by repeatedly moving ahead a small amount, and one to occasionally correct the steering for lateral drift. Each of these tasks is a loop that expands into a string of subtasks, and it doesn't matter what order the planner chooses for those subtasks as long as certain constraints are met. In particular there is no point in scheduling a lateral drift correction subtask before any movement subtasks are executed. Similarly, when the end of the hallway is reached, lateral drift corrections should cease. These two constraints, and others, are given in the constraint section of the hallway plan in Figure 14-19.

The plan declaration syntax allows four different types of constraints:

- Task ordering constraints

- Metric time constraints

- Task precondition constraints

- Conditional constraints

Task ordering constraints are used to specify the order in which plan tasks must be scheduled. The use of *PROG* and *REPEAT* statements in the plan imply some ordering constraints, but these implied constraints can be augmented with the specific ordering declarations:

```
(FOLLOWS task2 task1)
(PRECEDES task1 task2)
```

These two declarations are essentially the same, both stating that the task with name *task2* must begin sometime after the task named *task1* ends. An ordering constraint does not require that the following task come immediately after the preceding task, only that it come sometime after. To force a task to come a specified time after another, a metric time constraint should be used.

Metric time constraints are used to fix the execution time of a task, either absolutely in time or relatively with respect to another task. Fixing a task absolutely in time is accomplished with the declaration:

```
(DEADLINE task time)
```

A *DEADLINE* constraint says that the task with name *task* must be finished before the absolute time *time*. Relative metric time constraints are specified with the declaration:

```
(MAY-START task2 delay task1)
```

which says that the task named *task2* may start no earlier than *delay* units of time after the task named *task1* has finished. For example, the following set of constraints states that the floor must be washed and waxed before 3:00 but the floor must dry for at least 30 minutes between the washing waxing:

```
(DEADLINE wax-floor-task 3:00pm)
(MAY-START wax-floor-task 30min wash-floor-task)
```

Often a task cannot be carried out unless a resource, or set of resources, is in a specific state. For instance, taking a sonar reading to see how far away an obstacle is requires the sonar sensor to point toward the front. To declare resource states that must be true before a task can be executed, the *PRECONDITIONS* constraint is used. A precondition constraint has the form:

```
(PRECONDITIONS task
            - resource value pairs -)
```

For example, to put the laundry in the washing machine, the robot must be at the washing machine and the machine must be empty. One way to phrase this is:

```
(PRECONDITIONS load-washing-task
            (position at-washing-machine)
            (washing-machine-status empty))
```

When the planner attempts to schedule a task it checks the value of each resource mentioned as a precondition to see if it is in the correct state and if any resource is not, the planner asks it for a plan to change itself to the desired value. If the robot is not at the washing machine when it is time to load the washing, the position resource must move it there. In this way precondition constraints often implicitly code a large number of primitive actions.

Conditional constraints are used when the exact constraints on a task depend on which tasks are scheduled to come before it. The task of crossing a room would normally have no constraints on it, but if the floor has just been washed, then crossing it may have to be delayed. Conditional constraints take one of the forms:

```
(IF-SCHEDULED task constraint)
(IF-NOT-SCHEDULED task constraint)
```

In the first case the *constraint* only becomes active after the task named *task* has been scheduled, while in the second case the *constraint* is only active before *task* is scheduled. Using these forms the room crossing constraint might be phrased as follows:

```
(IF-SCHEDULED wash-floor-task
   (IF-NOT-SCHEDULED cross-room-task
      (MAY-START cross-room-task 30min wash-floor-task)))
```

When the wash floor task is scheduled, the cross room task is checked and if it has not yet been scheduled, it is constrained to follow the floor washing task by 30 minutes.

In addition to turning other constraints on and off during scheduling, conditional constraints can be used to synchronize the end of *repeat* loops and to make unnecessary tasks disappear. The special constraint forms below do this:

```
(MAKE-FINISHED task)
(MAKE-EVAPORATE task)
```

These forms are used as conditional constraints to be added during scheduling. The *MAKE-FINISHED* form says that the *REPEAT* task named *task* should be terminated immediately. For example, if a *REPEAT* task exists to wash the car every

Friday, but the car is to be sold, the following constraint would ensure that no more car washing subtasks are scheduled after the car is sold:

```
(IF-SCHEDULED sell-car-task
  (MAKE-FINISHED weekly-car-wash-loop))
```

Another example of *MAKE-FINISHED* can be found in the hallway following plan in Figure 14-19.

The *MAKE-EVAPORATE* form is used when executing one task makes another unnecessary. One situation where this arises is when there are two ways of carrying out a particular action. For example, if a message can be sent two different ways, the following constraints will prevent the message from being sent twice:

```
(IF-SCHEDULED send-telegram-task (MAKE-EVAPORATE send-
  letter-task))
(IF-SCHEDULED send-letter-task    (MAKE-EVAPORATE send-
  telegram-task))
```

14.3.6. Producing a Completed Linear Task Ordering

Once the planning problem has been completely specified using Bumpers resource and plan descriptions, it has been reduced to a set of tasks that need to be performed and a set of constraints that need to be obeyed. Now the HTS must make a linear ordering, or schedule, out of the set of tasks without violating any of the constraints. Conceptually, the problem of forming a schedule is quite straightforward: one task is chosen to be first, then tasks are added one at a time with the HTS making sure that no constraints are violated. In practice, constraint violations may not appear until long after the problem task has been added to the schedule and the HTS must back up and undo many choices. This makes task scheduling a search through the space of *all possible* task orderings.

For any reasonably sized problem, an exhaustive search of all possible task orderings is impractical. Therefore the HTS uses a heuristically guided beam search to explore only a portion of the complete problem space. The basic algorithm is to create a set of scheduling "prefixes" (*that is*, totally ordered sets of tasks that could form the first part of a schedule) and add tasks to the end of only the most promising prefixes until a complete schedule is found. Initial prefixes are all tasks that could feasibly come first given the constraints that must be satisfied. Each of these prefixes is rated using a heuristic function, and the most promising few are used to generate a new set of prefixes by adding all feasible second tasks to them. This process continues, always working on only the most promising prefixes from those generated so far, until one prefix includes every task. This final prefix is the completed schedule. Since the "best" prefix is always being added to, the first complete schedule found ought to be a "good" one. To limit the search, the HTS restricts both the number of new prefixes generated by adding a single task and total number of prefixes being considered at any one time. If too many tasks could be the next added to a prefix, only the most promising few are chosen, and if too many prefixes are generated in total, the least promising ones are dropped from the search. This has the effect of making several widely spaced, narrow beam searches through the space of possible schedules.

The use of a beam search limits the amount of work that the HTS must do in the worst case, but often the structure of the task ordering problem itself gives a further reduction in the number of prefixes that need be considered. Two characteristics are of particular importance:

- Many tasks will not be feasible as the "next" task in a scheduling prefix because "current" constraints prohibit them.

- When a scheduling prefix fails because no task is feasible to add next, the reason for the failure may be common to a whole class of prefixes, which can all be ruled out.

Consider the situation where a screw insertion task yet to be scheduled requires a screwdriver, but in the scheduling prefix being examined, a task to sell the screwdriver has already been scheduled. The screw insertion task is not feasible as a candidate to add next because there is no screwdriver; it must be put off until another task can be scheduled that acquires a new screwdriver. Thus the screw insertion task will not generate a new scheduling prefix. Furthermore if no task left to be scheduled acquires a screwdriver, the prefix can never become a complete schedule. In this case the HTS can remove the prefix from future consideration and, in fact, can look through all prefixes currently active and remove any of them that have made the same mistake of scheduling the sell-screwdriver task but not the screw insertion task. Whole pieces of the HTS search space can be trimmed away by noticing that classes of scheduling prefixes are impossible in this way.

A search through only the most promising schedules requires a measure of "promise". The HTS uses four different heuristics to evaluate each prefix it is considering. The heuristics are based on the following considerations:

1. Temporal constraints on when each task must be completed. It is usually better to schedule tasks with early deadlines before those with later deadlines.

2. The *tour time* of the tasks feasible to schedule next. A rough calculation is made to estimate the best order of the feasible tasks to see which order would take the least time. The first task in best order is usually a good candidate to schedule next.

3. Least wasted time. If all of the feasible tasks have temporal constraints on them that would require that some wait time be put in the schedule (for example, if the scheduling prefix is ready for another task at 2:00 PM but all feasible tasks must begin after 3:00), the task that requires the least wait is usually best to add next.

4. A user-defined *schedule evaluation function*. The HTS allows an external function to be defined that takes a scheduling prefix as input and returns a

"rating" of how good it is. The feasible task that generates the best user rating when added on is a possible good candidate to add next.

These heuristics are designed to give an idea of the flexibility that a prefix leaves for scheduling the tasks to follow. The more flexibility that the HTS has, the more likely it is that it will be able to turn a given prefix into a completed schedule. The HTS is always trying to find the shortest schedule possible that does not violate any constraints.

One way of looking at what the HTS does when it creates a linear task order is that it is simulating the execution of tasks as they are added to a prefix. A prefix can be considered to be a list of tasks in the order they should be executed, along with the world state that results after execution of the last one. When the HTS is deciding what unscheduled task to add next, it checks any precondition constraints on the task to see if they are met in the current state. If they are, or if the appropriate resource can change itself to the correct state, then the task is feasible. When one of the feasible tasks is selected and added to a prefix, the world state is updated to reflect the new world state after the task. Thus the HTS is in essence a simulator that keeps track of world state as tasks are arranged into a total order. As long as the world state and task order is always consistent with all constraints, the finished schedule will be guaranteed to work in the simulated world.

14.4. Summary and Conclusions

This paper has presented two different tools that can be used to build conjunctive planners. The Time Map Manager supports a temporal predicate calculus database and the Heuristic Task Scheduler constructs a valid total order for a predefined set of tasks. Although the TMM and HTS are aimed at solving different parts of the planning problem, they have many features in common, and together illustrate the essential aspects and difficulties of representing and reasoning about the knowledge required.

The Time Map Manager allows representation of partially

ordered task networks that include both relative ordering and absolute temporal constraints. Planning tasks become event occasions that may or may not have temporal distance constraints between them. In traditional planning systems, changes that tasks make in the world are usually coded as add and delete lists. The continuous model of time used by the TMM extends this idea by representing task effects as persistence occasions. Persistences extend indefinitely into the future until clipped by contradictory effects. The automatic clipping of persistences enables event occasions to remain partially ordered in time without fear of the time map coming to depict an inconsistent view of the future. The TMM takes advantage of this fact in supporting abductive queries. When the TMM is asked to find temporal intervals where a set of task preconditions is true, it will return answers that include consistent ways of further constraining existing occasions in the time map so that effects already generated satisfy the preconditions. In addition the TMM can keep track of some types of context-dependent task effects through the use of temporal forward chaining rules.

The Heuristic Task Scheduler is designed to reason about complex task interactions by exploring the consistent total orderings that the tasks can be arranged into. Since the HTS is always working with an ever-growing totally ordered task network, constraints between tasks can be made to depend on task order. Tasks can be flagged as unnecessary, constrained arbitrarily in time, or have their preconditions altered by tasks that are scheduled to come before them. The HTS can also monitor resource state values through simulation of both absolute and incremental changes to the resource made by all tasks scheduled so far. Furthermore, resources can be declared to have arbitrary physics and can thus be made to deal with tasks that cause them to begin a continuous change.

The TMM and HTS are both powerful tools for plan representation and manipulation but both also have certain shortcomings. In particular, the TMM has no simple way for representing constraints between tasks that depend on the order in which they will be executed. Making constraints appear automatically for one arrangement of the time map, and then disappear for another, is quite difficult. The TMM also cannot model a resource that can be changed incrementally. Keeping track of a bank balance in a sea of unordered withdrawals and deposits is an extremely hard problem. These two limitations on the TMM stem directly from the desire to allow tasks to remain unordered with respect to one another. Reasoning in detail about order-dependent tasks and incremental resource changes requires speculation on what total task orderings might occur. Another possible difficulty with the TMM is that the general problem of deciding what facts are necessarily true in a partially ordered predicate calculus database has been shown to be NP-hard (Chapman, 1985). The TMM relies on such decisions to maintain consistency, especially when confronted with temporal forward chaining rules. However, "real" planning problems may build time maps that exhibit sufficient inherent structure to keep such decisions tractable in practice.

Unlike the TMM, the HTS is very good at reasoning about incremental resource changes and order-dependent constraints since it is always working with a total task order. Unfortunately the fact that the HTS generates a total task order is also its major shortcoming. If new information is discovered, or another goal is added to the planning problem, the HTS must be called all over again so that a new schedule can be found that incorporates the additional information. This problem follows directly from the need to order tasks completely, as the order eliminates the flexibility to reorder tasks when required. Another potential difficulty is that the HTS does not have a general way of dealing with interaction between continuously changing resources. It is assumed that for the most part changes to the state of one resource are independent of changes to another. More powerful methods of dealing with resource interactions would require research directed at incorporating the ideas being developed in qualitative physics (Hobbs and Moore, 1985).

Several interesting avenues remain for exploring the usefulness of the concepts embodied by the TMM and HTS. In particular, the strengths and weaknesses of the TMM and HTS are seductively complementary: everywhere that the TMM is weak the HTS appears to be strong, and *vice versa*. An obvious course of action is to combine the two. Unfortunately, putting the two together is more difficult than it first appears.

The HTS could be used to turn the time map's partial order of events into a total order once planning with the TMM is complete. This approach will make a complete and powerful planner, but it retains most of the weaknesses of the TMM. Alternatively, the HTS could be called after every change that is made to the time map. With this approach the HTS is essentially a consistency check on the TMM to insure that order-dependent task constraints and incremental resource changes do not cause undesirable interactions. However, to maintain the flexibility of a partially ordered task network, the total order found by the HTS must be thrown away. A good combination of the HTS and TMM must include heuristics both for deciding when to call the HTS so that important interactions are detected in a timely manner, and for deciding how much of the order returned by the HTS to adopt so that flexibility is maintained but the number of times it is called is minimized.

Another direction that this work could be extended is toward a planning system that maintains more than one picture of the future at a time. Many times while planning it is better not to put off ordering decisions in the task network, but rather to "split" the task network into two: one where the required decision went one way and another where the decision went the other way. Then later, when further planning has shown one decision to be superior, the inferior alternative can be thrown away. Planning by refining a time map using the TMM is essentially a search through the space of all possible task networks. The search keeps many options open by allowing ordering decisions to be put off. Splitting the time map at a key decision point allows the space of time maps being searched to be collapsed by the decision without forcing it down a single channel. The TMM supports the notion of time map splitting through the use of "gating objects." A TMM gating object creates a *virtual copy* of the time map that differs from the original map only according to the decision the object represents. How gating objects can best be used is still an open question. In particular, it is not yet known when it is better to make a decision and stick to it and when it is better to split the time map at the decision point and reason about each alternative in some detail.

Acknowledgements

This work was supported in part by the Advanced Research Projects Agency of the U.S. Department of Defense under the Office of Naval Research contracts N00014-83-K-0281 and N00014-85-K-0301.

15. Analogical Modes of Reasoning and Process Modelling

Brian V. Funt

School of Computing Science
Simon Fraser University
Burnaby, British Columbia, CANADA V5A 1S6

Abstract

The nature of analogical representations and analogical processes is discussed from the standpoint of two illustrative parallel processing systems. One uses a diagram as an analogical representation and the other models mental rotation as an analogical process of message passing between neighbors in a collection of locally interconnected processors. It is argued that the effectiveness of both analogical representations and analogical processes follows, in part, from the way symbolic information is coded in a form amenable to parallel processing.

15.1. Introduction to analogical reasoning

If we need to investigate the stability of a collection of objects on the moon, one approach we can take is to model the situation by a collection of similar objects on earth. We can derive quite a large number of predictions about the behavior of the objects on the moon by simply watching the behavior exhibited by our model. Do any of the objects move? If one moves, does it slide or fall? Does it collide with any other objects? Experiments such as removing an object or shaking the table on which they are stacked, yield even more observations.

While many of these accurately reflect what will happen in the corresponding situation on the moon and can be used as valid predictions, sometimes the model will lead us astray. If we observe, for example, that in the model it takes an apple dropped from the top of the leaning tower of Pisa two seconds to hit the ground, the obvious prediction that it will take two seconds for a similar apple to hit the moon from the same height, is clearly false. Because of the difference in gravity and the presence of air friction, our model breaks down. We can still use it, however, if we take these factors into account. Our observations must be properly interpreted (Pylyshyn refers to a semantic interpretation function, (Pylyshyn, 1973)) if we are to obtain valid predictions.

Drawing conclusions from a model, as in the above, is an example of *analogical reasoning*. An analogy exists between the situation on earth and the situation on the moon; and we may use this analogy as the basis on which to draw conclusions. The earth situation is an analog of the moon situation. We do not need to discover the analogy between the two situations in order to use it Someone can simply point it out to us.

While analogical reasoning is common to everyday problem solving - motorists follow road maps, architects make blueprint drawings, aerodynamics engineers run wind tunnels, physicists rely on wave and particle metaphors for light, and programmers once used flowcharts - it has not been common in artificial intelligence systems. The move from the situation of someone making predictions on the basis of the observed behavior of a physical model to that of a computer program manipulating internally represented models clouds the status of analogical reasoning. Similarly, the shift to human use of mental models and the entailed concept of mental imagery is equally problematic. The confusions which arise have resulted in an extended debate within AI and psychology, see (Pylyshyn, 1981), (Kosslyn, 1980).

Attempts to distinguish analogical representations or analogical processes from non-analogical ones are generally susceptible to attack on the basis that once in a computer all formalizations are in some sense equivalent. While most protagonists will admit that such equivalences, based as they are on the universal nature of Turing Machine computations, can blur important distinctions by reducing everything to too low a level common denominator; an adequate definition of the appropriate level for comparison has not been found.

Putting this problem aside for a moment, two good characterizations of "analogical" are those of Sloman (Sloman, 1975) and Shepard (Shepard, 1978). Sloman writes:

> If R is an analogical representation of T, then (a) there must be parts of R representing parts of T, as dots and squiggles on a map represent towns and rivers in a country ... and (b) it must be possible to specify some sort of correspondence, possibly context-dependent, between properties or relations of parts of R and properties or relations of parts of T ...

Shepard's characterization is of an analogical process:

> By an analogical or analog process I mean just this: a process in which the intermediate internal states have a natural one-to-one correspondence to appropriate intermediate states in the external world.

Clearly, the positions, shapes and orientations of the earthbound objects analogically represent, in Sloman's sense, the positions, shapes and orientations of the corresponding objects on the moon; and their tumbling motions constitute an analogical process, with the qualification that Shepard's reference is to internal mental states, something the states of the falling earth objects cannot be construed to be.

When we attempt to implement the falling-objects model in a program, thereby making the states of our model "internal" ones, we run immediately into trouble. A major advantage of our model was that we could make predictions with it, without a detailed understanding of how and why it worked. Before we can write a program capable of making the same predictions, we must, however, have a much more sophisticated knowledge of the physics of the situation. Alternatively, we have the option of designing a system which itself watches objects on earth to make predictions about similar objects on the moon. In the context of a real need to learn about objects on the moon this might be a bizarre proposal; however, as an aspect of a system designed to exhibit intelligent behavior, the ability to manipulate and observe models seems fundamental. Two AI systems demonstrating how analogical reasoning can be incorporated into a computer problem-solving system will be briefly described.

15.2. WHISPER: A program using analogs

The first system, dubbed WHISPER, uses a diagram to predict the collapse of a structure constructed from a set of blocks. The diagram depicting the blocks acts as an analog of the problem situation. Figure 15-1 gives an overview.

The diagram depicting the blocks, in conjunction with the diagram-update transformations, functions as an analog of the problem situation. The transformations represent the kinds of changes that one might make with pencil and eraser to reflect the changing state of affairs as the blocks tumble. Alternatively, we could produce a sequence of new diagrams, never erasing the old ones. To be useful, there must be a strong correspondence between the transformations which can be applied to the diagram and the actions which can occur in the world, as well as the obvious need for similarity between the shapes in the diagram and the shape of the objects they represent. Two examples of WHISPER's diagrams appear in Figure 15-2. The fact that the blocks are rigid bodies restricts the transformations to rotation and translation.

The program "looks at" its diagrams with a parallel-

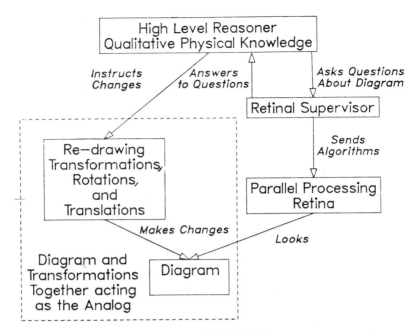

Figure 15-1:   Overview of WHISPER, a system using
analogs in reasoning.

processing "retina". While its design is not intended to model
the human eye, it was inspired, in part, by some of the eye's
most dominant features. Like it, the retina can be fixated at
any location in the diagram, its resolution decreases towards
the periphery, and it is highly parallel. From Figure 15-3 we
can see how the resolution varies. Each of the "circles" (I will
call them bubbles) represents a processor, and it receives input
from the part of the diagram which lies under it. If a line in
the diagram appears anywhere under the bubble then it is
"marked"; otherwise, it remains unmarked. The bubbles, which
are independently executing processors, communicate via
neighborhood-restricted communication links, so the processing is
locally parallel. While this structure could be implemented
with VLSI hardware, the current system relies on a software
simulation of the parallelism. In addition, the diagram is
represented, one might say simulated, by a two-dimensional
integer array.

Referring again to Figure 15-1, we see that the *high level*

Figure 15-2:   Examples of WHISPER's diagrams;
(a) the starting state;
(b) the result of the first predicted event.

reasoner, a program encapsulating the system's knowledge of physics, interacts with the parallel processing component of the retina through the mediating *retinal supervisor*. It directs the parallel computation by broadcasting algorithms to the bubbles which they then all execute. It may collect results and broadcast further algorithms several times before a complete answer, which can be passed back to the HLR, is obtained.

Examples of the type of question that the retinal-supervisor-plus-retina team can respond to are:

- Do shapes A and B touch?

- Is shape C symmetrical about a given axis?

- Where is the center of area of shape D?

- How far can shape E rotate about a given point before it will intersect some other shape?

The algorithms which answer these questions are called the *perceptual primitives*. To avoid the need for object recognition

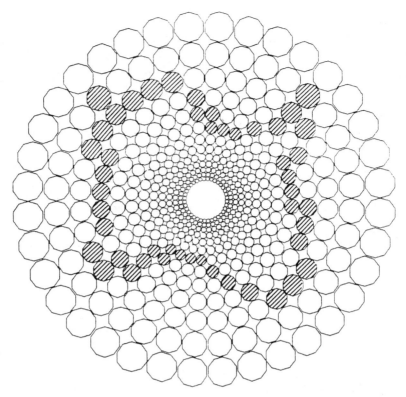

Figure 15-3:   WHISPER's parallel processing retina.

Each "circle" represent a processor. The shaded ones are
processors which are marked to represent the contour of a
two-dimensional object.

primitives, the shapes in the diagram are color coded.

The HLR consists of procedures which reason about the
physical world in commonsense terms such as: 'If a block is
hanging over to Far, it will topple' and 'If a block is on a
slant, it will slide' These procedures call the retinal perceptual
primitives. The perceptual primitives are shape-oriented, domain-
independent operations. To determine that a block is in fact
hanging over too far, the HLR must generate calls to the retina
in terms of shapes and how the shapes make contact, rather
than in terms of blocks and support relationships. It is the
HLR which assigns domain-dependent meanings to the answers
returned from the retina.

To predict the events which ensue from the starting

situation depicted in Figure 15-2. the HLR first ascertains that the topmost object is unstable and will begin to rotate about its rightmost point of contact with the object below it. The object will rotate until it hits the object balanced like a see-saw. To discover that a collision will occur and predict the approximate angle of rotation, a particularly interesting perceptual primitive is invoked. The rotation can be "visualized" directly on the retina if it is first fixated on the center point of the rotation. The visualization algorithm requires every bubble which is marked by the object to send its mark as a message to its nearest neighbor in the direction of the rotation. Because the bubbles are organized with their centers radially aligned, the angle subtended by any two concentrically neighboring processors is constant. Message-passing between neighboring processors therefore corresponds to a uniform rotation about the center of the retina.

Once the collision point has been determined, WHISPER calls the diagram-updating transformations to create a new diagram illustrating the state of affairs which will pertain just as the moving object collides with the balanced one. This is the first in a sequence of "snapshot" diagrams that WHISPER produces. Each shows an event that it predicts will occur, in this first case, the tumbling of the top object. WHISPER predicts the next event in the sequence by looking at the most recent snapshot. Full details are given in (Funt, 1980).

WHISPER can also handle situations involving sliding objects. It cannot, though, easily envision the simultaneous motion of two objects, except by the trick of approximating simultaneity by alternately moving each object by a small amount.

15.3. Observations on the use of analogs

How does WHISPER benefit from its diagrams? A significant aspect of the analogy between the diagrams and the world situation is the correspondence in the shape of regions of empty space. Determining how far an object will travel before it collides with something is equivalent to finding how much empty space there is for it to move through. Partly because of its parallel-processing capability, the retina can quickly spot the areas of empty space in the diagram. An object's motion affects the shape of the surrounding spaces. Very significantly for WHISPER, the changing diagram reflects the changing nature of these spaces in the world.

Many other features of the situation are also self-evident to WHISPER: which is not to say that no computation is involved, but rather that the computations simply involve the retina's perceptual primitives. The features are self-evident in the same sense as they are self-evident to us when we look at the diagram with our eyes. We see at a glance which objects are near one another, places where they touch, and whether or not two objects meet in such a way as to allow an object to slide smoothly from one to the other. The emergence of properties, such as the last one, is another way in which diagrams help simplify WHISPER's problem-solving, and give it more of a commonsense character. Another example of an emergent property of this sort is the way in which two identical right-isosceles triangles, when joined hypotenuse to hypotenuse, form a square. From an appropriate set of geometry axioms, this property could be deduced as a theorem - one might say that it would "emerge" as a theorem - but, although it is a pretty simple theorem, the self-evident nature of simply observing the square in a diagram of the two triangles is lost.

Perhaps it should not be surprising that the deductive method seems more complicated in this situation, since it does, in fact, produce a more general result. A diagram is necessarily particularized. The triangles, and resulting square, are ones with sides of specific length; whereas, the theorem obtained from the axioms is valid for any two triangles of the right-isosceles variety. The diagram acts as a model (in the formal, theoretical sense of that term) of an axiomatic theory. It is only one of many models which satisfy the theory (that is, one for which the axioms hold true). The FOL system's "simulation structures" are used in this way, (Weyhrauch, 1980). Methods of constructing and using "mental models" are discussed by Johnson-Laird (Johnson-Laird, 1980).

While sometimes we obviously need the generality of deduction within a formal theory, formulating a proper axiomatization generally requires quite a degree of insight, as, for example, is the case when axiomatizing programs in order to prove them correct Not only is axiomatization difficult, but in cases such as the famous Monkey and Bananas problem, it is difficult to provide a formalization of the problem which does not at the same time almost give away the answer.

Sometimes an analog allows, as is the case with the earthbound blocks and with WHISPER's diagrams, conclusions to be drawn without first having a complete axiomatization of the situation in hand. The connection between the problem situation, an analog of it, and a theory which formally describes it can be viewed in the following manner. When we axiomatize a situation, S, we abstract its crucial aspects with the intent that S will be one of the models, the "standard" model, satisfying our axioms. A second situation, S', which is an analog of S, will, if the analogy is strong, also be a model satisfying the same set of axioms. While facts true in one model are not necessarily true in all models (that is, they may not be valid theorems of the theory) it suffices, if all we are interested in is what is true in our standard model, for facts true in S' also to be true in S. While the theory describing situations S and S' may exist, in the sense that it could be formulated, we do not need to formulate it. We can use the analog, S', to yield conclusions about S without it. We generally turn to S', rather than S itself, because it is more readily accessible.

15.4. Mental rotation as an analog process

Through an ingenious series of experiments, Shepard and his collaborators (Shepard and Cooper, 1982) have attempted to demonstrate that human subjects mentally rotate their representations of three-dimensional objects at a constant rate or "angular velocity". Their key experiment consists in showing individual subjects two line-drawings of an object in two different orientations (see Figure 15-4), and measuring the time they require to determine that the object is in fact the same. Amongst other controls, some of the trials included dissimilar objects. The main result was that reaction-times were found to be a linearly increasing function of the angular disparity, in three-dimensions, between the two objects. This and other results, led Shepard to describe mental rotation as an analog process of the kind characterized by thegiven in theintroduction.

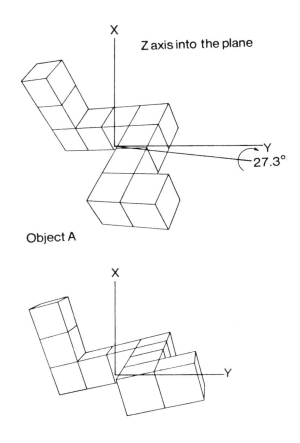

Object A

Object B

Figure 15-4:   Two objects similar to those used in Shepard's mental rotation experiment.

Also shown are the axis and angle of rotation computed by the program described in this paper.

The concept of an analog process entails the notion that the computation itself has characteristics which are analogous to those of the process in the world. We can easily see how a block falling on earth is a "computation" which is analogous to a similar block falling on the moon, but in what sense can a computation be analogous to a rotating object?

The example of WHISPER's visualization primitive hints at an answer to this question. Although it only rotates two-dimensional shapes, the rate of rotation is restricted by the rate of message-passing between neighboring processors. The greater the angle of rotation, the greater the number of message relays required; and this number, in fact, is directly proportional to the angle. The computation also passes through intermediate states which correspond to those of a rotating shape. This contrasts with the obvious, non-analog algorithm based on sequentially transforming the individual points defining the shape by an equation formulated in sines and cosines. The computation time of a trigonometric function clearly does not change appreciably with its argument. A generalization of two-dimensional visualization to the three-dimensional case would provide an analog process model of mental rotation.

Figure 15-5 shows one such generalization which has been tested in a program modeling mental rotation as an analog process, (Funt, 1983). The hexagons represent processors which, as in the case of WHISPER's bubbles, directly communicate only with immediately touching neighbors. The layout does not require that the processor be physically located around a sphere as they are in the figure, but it must maintain the same communication topology. Objects are modelled as if they were inside the sphere of processors. Each processor has the responsibility of representing the shape of that part of the object located within its "cone". It stores the radial distance from the center of the sphere to where the surface intersects the cone. Since each processor knows its own "longitude" and "latitude" (that is, where it would be located if the processors were actually spread around a sphere), the points on the object's surface are maintained in what amounts to a spherical polar coordinate system.

Each processor can keep track of more than one object. The same object in two different orientations will have its corresponding parts represented by different subsets of the processors. Once aligned, two objects can be compared very rapidly in parallel, every processor tests whether its local

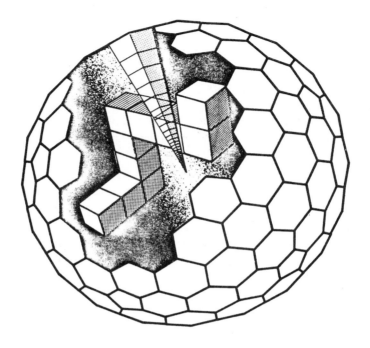

Figure 15-5:   A cut-out view of the sphere of processors
with an object inside of it.

Each processor is responsible for representing the part of the
object within its "cone". One of the 482 cones used in the
simulation is shown.

information about them matches. To align two objects, one
must be rotated into the other. Rotation consists of relaying
information between neighboring processors. The distance
between neighboring processors at the "equator" of the rotation
imposes a constraint on the maximum rate of rotation. A single
rotation step cannot exceed the angle between them, for
otherwise a message would have to travel to a non-neighboring
processor, which it cannot do without being relayed.

The complete object-matching process consists of four
stages. The first is the line-drawing interpretation phase in
which the two drawings are interpreted as three-dimensional
objects and stored in the sphere of processors. For this special

case, a simple algorithm suffices; it will not be described in more detail here. The second stage is determining the appropriate angle and axis of rotation; the third, rotating the object; the fourth, matching. For the second stage, the only one yet to be discussed, an object's physical moments of inertia provide a natural and unique (for non-symmetrical objects) set of axes for it. If two objects are identical, then they will be aligned once their inertial axes are aligned. The angle and axis of rotation required, therefore, are the ones which will rotate one object's inertial axis system into the other's (the ambiguity in how to pair up the axes is resolved by recourse to the objects' third-order moments).

We can easily see that the time required to align and compare two objects will be a linearly increasing function of the angle between them. This is a consequence of three aspects of the model: (i) parallelism, (ii) distributed object representation, and (iii) neighborhood-restricted communication. The rotation process obtains its analog nature from the communication and computational structures of the sphere of processors. Messages flow between processors in a way which is analogous to the way in which the parts of a rotating object move through space. While WHISPER uses an analog (the diagram plus re-drawing transformations) and the mental rotation model is an analog, the two systems nonetheless share a common feature. Both rely on parallel processing. In the case of WHISPER, its parallelism is not crucial, we could still have the diagrammatic analog without it, but for it to be of advantage, the parallelism is essential. The diagrams represent information in a way which is ideally suited to parallel processing. Similarly, the object representation in the rotation model facilitates parallel matching.

An important aspect of analogs and analogical processes is this representation of data in a form amenable to parallel processing. Sequential processing requires concise data formulations. Parallel processing requires widely distributed ones; otherwise only a few processors can be kept busy. It is natural to hypothesize, therefore, that sometimes when people use diagrams they are reformulating information in a manner which makes it accessible to their highly-parallel visual systems.

Similarly, it can be argued that the construction of mental images is a process in which information, stored in a concise form is reformulated into one amenable to parallel processing. Kosslyn argues for a CRT (cathode ray tube) metaphor of mental imagery in which "deep representations" are converted into "surface images" which "occur in a spatial display medium (Kosslyn, 1980)." Parallel processing structures can act as the display medium. For example, if line-segments were to be used as a concise representation of a shape, then the retinal supervisor could broadcast them to the retinal processors. Each processor would then independently determine which lines it lies on and mark itself accordingly. The retinal "image" thus constructed would be identical to that which would have been obtained by fixating on a diagram.

15.5. Conclusions

The use of analogs in reasoning and analog processes are closely related topics. Both involve correspondences between the behavior of an external situation and a model of that situation. In the case of an AI problem-solving system like WHISPER, the model may be internal or external, and the correspondences are exploited to yield conclusions about the situation. Describing a phenomenon, such as mental rotation, as an analog process, on the other hand, is to assert that correspondences exist between the structure of the internal model and that of the external situation. As we have seen in the particular case of the parallel rotation model, the correspondence is between message flow and object motion.

Acknowledgements

This work was supported by the Natural Sciences and Engineering Research Council of Canada under grant A4322.

16. Representing and Using Knowledge of the Visual World

William Havens and Alan Mackworth[†]

Department of Computer Science
University of British Columbia
Vancouver, British Columbia, Canada V6T 1W5
[†] Fellow, Canadian Institute for advanced Research

Abstract

Methodology for the representation of knowledge is a fundamental aspect of research in Computational Vision. The properties of objects and the relationships among objects must be represented for a given task domain and the representation must also support efficient processes of recognition and search. These twin criteria for evaluating knowledge representations are called *descriptive adequacy* and *procedural adequacy* respectively and are applicable to both early visual processing and high-level visual recognition. All vision requires knowledge representations which exhibit both descriptive and procedural adequacy. Here, we examine the knowledge representations which have been used in high level vision. In particular, well-understood network consistency representations are shown to have a number of inherent limitations. We propose the use of schemata as a unifying representational formalism. Mapsee2, a recent experimental system using this representation, is used to illustrate the advantages of schema-based techniques.

Based on the paper, Representing Knowledge of the Visual World, William Havens and Alan Mackworth, appearing in COMPUTER, Volume 16, Number 10, October, 1983.

16.1. Introduction

The central issue in Artificial Intelligence is the representation and use of knowledge. That underlying theme unifies areas as diverse as natural language understanding, speech recognition, story understanding, planning, problem solving and vision. In this article, we focus on how computational vision systems represent knowledge of the visual world. Current methodologies will be examined under two criteria: *descriptive adequacy*, the ability of a representational formalism to capture the essential visual properties of objects and the relationships among objects in the visual world, and *procedural adequacy*, the capability of the representation to support efficient processes of recognition and search.

A major theme in computational vision has been the distinction between the methodology of *image analysis* (or early vision) and *scene analysis* (or high-level vision). Briefly, image analysis can be characterized as the science of extracting from images useful descriptions of lines, regions, edges and surface characteristics up to the level of Marr's **primal** *sketch*. (Marr, 1982). It is generally assumed that image analysis is domain-independent and passive, that is, *data-driven*. Scene analysis attempts to recognize visual objects and their configurations. It is domain dependent and *goal-driven*, motivated by the necessity of identifying particular objects expected to be present in a scene.

These distinctions should be seen not as a strict dichotomy but as a spectrum. In fact, all visual perception is domain dependent and must be simultaneously both a data and goal-driven process. Image analysis theories make assumptions about the processes of image formation and transmission, such as, surfaces are opaque and smooth almost everywhere, light travels in straight lines, and the transmission medium is transparent. Such constraints on visual processing are evolutionarily valid for our world and usually reliable. This knowledge consists of constraints, compiled from the invariant properties of objects and surfaces and the physics of imaging. These constraints are projected onto our mammalian vision hardware.

If we adopt this unifying view of computational vision,

then what is needed is a representation adequate for representing all visual knowledge. We enumerate some general properties of such a representation:

1. Visual knowledge must be structured to reflect its natural organization. That organization is tree-like, from general constraints valid for almost all visual domains to very specialized constraints associated with specific object instances and their configurations. The only alternative to such an organization is to employ many specialized vision systems with a *homunculus* switching among them.

2. The knowledge representation must be modular. Knowledge about a particular visual entity, from image pixels, to surfaces, to physical objects, must be localized in the representation.

3. The relationships and interactions among modules must be well-defined and limited. The increasing complexity of Artificial Intelligence systems necessitates such a regimen to make them understandable, predictable, and modifiable.

4. The processes that operate on knowledge modules must be local to those modules. Knowledge about a visual domain includes both knowledge of *what*, called *declarative knowledge*, and knowledge of *how*, called *procedural knowledge*, (Winograd, 1975). For efficient vision systems, both are necessary.

5. Search of the knowledge base is necessary for visual perception. Perception is a non-deterministic process. A single intensity value for each pixel confounds information about surface irradiance, surface reflectance, orientation, and depth. Each pixel is under-constrained in its local interpretation, (Mackworth, 1983). Only by searching for a global interpretation consistent with every local constraint can the ambiguity be removed.

6. Neither purely data-driven search nor goal-driven search is alone adequate. It is generally accepted that a knowledge representation must support and integrate both, (Havens, 1983), (Rumelhart and Ortony, 1976). For data-driven processing to work, the domain assumptions that are almost universally valid should be applied uniformly in early vision, as Marr and others have advocated, (Marr, 1982), (Barrow and Tenenbaum, 1978). Marr has also argued that these techniques may allow the extraction of domain independent descriptions up to the level of the 2.5-D sketch. However, the exact boundary between domain-independent and domain-dependent visual processes is not an issue. Visual perception occupies a spectrum of domain-specificity and generality.

Early vision is data-driven but must access higher knowledge structures efficiently, and, given the principles outlined above, it seems clear that high-level visual processes must be able to establish parameters for and control the attention of lower-level processes.

In this paper, we outline a methodology of scene analysis. We assume an organization of early vision as described in (Marr, 1982), (Barrow and Tenenbaum, 1978), (Woods, 1983). A number of deficiencies in current methodology are identified. We discuss the new schema-based knowledge representations that are a response to these problems. To illustrate our arguments, examples are taken from *Mapsee2*, a recent schema-based scene analysis system.

16.2. Progress in high-level vision

The necessity of adequate representations for visual knowledge has been a constant theme in high-level vision. The very early work of Roberts, (Roberts, 1965), established the research paradigm that has persisted for twenty years. Roberts' system consisted of two programs: an image analysis program that constructed a line drawing which served as input to his scene analysis program. From a grey-scale image the image analysis line finder constructed a line drawing using spatial differentiation, clipping and line following techniques. The scene analysis program assumed that the visual world consisted of instances of three primitive polyhedra: a cube, a wedge and a hexagonal prism. These primitives were allowed to be scaled, translated and rotated. Composite objects were constructed of instances of the primitives glued together.

The scene analysis program iterated through a cycle of four processes: cue discovery, model invocation, model verification, and model elaboration, (Mackworth, 1978). A variety of topological image cues were used to index into the set of primitive models, finding candidate matches without exhaustive analysis-by-synthesis. The model fragment thus invoked was then subjected to metrical tests to judge its fit to the image. If a successful partial fit was obtained then the appearance of the rest of the model was predicted in the image. A good match between that prediction and the image indicated a successful model hypothesis. The predicted appearance of the model was then used to produce a new line drawing of the scene with that portion of the scene deleted from the image. The cycle then repeated until all of the image had been accounted for.

Although limited, Roberts' program provided a major impetus to computational vision research. He introduced:

1. Explicit models of three-dimensional geometric objects.

2. The use of composition to represent complex scenes as a configuration of their parts.

3. The reliance on image cues derived directly from the image to invoke scene models.

4. An active model of perception as a cyclic recognition process.

The *blocks world* remained the focus of vision research for the subsequent decade. A detailed analysis of the most important contributions is given in (Mackworth, 1977). The

Huffman-Clowes labelling scheme was a crucial breakthrough. The key idea was that edge types (convex, concave and occluding) in the scene domain can be determined from image domain evidence (junction shapes) and the scene domain coherence rule that an edge cannot change its type from one end to the other. In the cue-model paradigm, a junction shape acts as a cue for a number of corner models in the scene domain. This local ambiguity can be globally reduced by enforcing the edge object coherence rule between adjacent corners. Extending these ideas, Waltz, (Waltz, 1975), made two contributions. He extended the descriptive adequacy of this scheme by allowing additional edge types such as cracks and shadows. He enhanced the procedural adequacy by introducing a filtering algorithm that removed local inconsistencies before constructing global solutions. He gave some experimental evidence that this could be more efficient than backtracking.

Mackworth, (Mackworth, 1975), generalised the filtering algorithm to a class of formal network consistency algorithms for problems in which a set of variables have to be instantiated in associated domains while satisfying a set of binary constraints. Usually the domains are specified extensionally as a finite set of labels or values, but the techniques will also work on intensionally specified domains. It has been shown that the time complexity of the Waltz filtering algorithm is linear in the number of constraints, (Mackworth and Freuder, 1982). In the blocks world application there is a constraint for each scene edge and the constraint graph is planar so the number of constraints is linear in the number of variables where each variable corresponds to a corner.

The constraint-based approach to knowledge representation in vision has been applied to other visual domains. Mapsee, (Mackworth, 1977), interpreted freehand geographical sketch maps. In this world, image lines or chains could be scene roads, rivers, bridges, mountains, towns, lakeshores or seashores while image regions could be land, lake or ocean. The constraint approach used these entities as the objects to be instantiated while the models were derived from scene domain knowledge of how the objects can interact. For example, a T-junction of two image chains could be a road junction or a river junction or a river going under a bridge, *et cetera*. The models were thus n-ary constraints on the objects and the network consistency algorithms were generalised to cope with that extension.

16.3. The complexity barrier

The computational paradigm introduced by Roberts and developed by others is now mature. It has resulted in a uniform representational framework for encoding and manipulating knowledge about the visual world. Unfortunately, network consistency has reached its inherent limitations. It does not easily scale upwards to more complex domains and exhibits a number of shortcomings:

1. The objects defined in the representation correspond only to primitive scene entities. Complex scene interpretations must be expressed solely as atomic labels for these primitive objects. In order to represent abstract high-level scene interpretations, they must be projected onto the low-level label sets of the objects. Consequently, abstract interpretations are represented only implicitly and must be reconstructed from the low-level interpretations after the recognition process has terminated.

   As well, by projecting abstract interpretations onto the label sets of the objects, the size of these label sets grows exponentially with the complexity of the scene domain. This phenomenon was a major obstacle in Waltz's research. We conclude that objects at the lowest level of description in a system are not appropriate hooks for attaching high-level interpretations.

2. The models are impoverished. Each model is represented as a relation over the label sets of a small number of neighbouring objects in the

network and, therefore, can only express local
constraints on the scene. No explicit descriptions of
the structural relationships appearing in the overall
scene are represented. Instead, they are implicit in
the relations themselves.

3. The *extension* of the label set for each object has
been represented explicitly. Network consistency
methods proceed by deleting from the label set of
each object any label that does not satisfy every
model constraining that object. Any deleted label
cannot be part of a global scene interpretation.
Label sets are usually represented explicitly as a list
of atoms, each naming a particular interpretation.
Furthermore, each individual label must be
considered independently, even though many of the
labels in a given label set share a partial common
interpretation. More efficient, *intensional*
representations for interpretations are needed.

4. A *compiler* must be constructed to compute the
label sets for each type of object in the system.
This compiler, given a suitable description of the
semantics of the scene domain, considers
exhaustively all possible scene configurations and
represents those configurations in the label sets of
the primitive objects.

For example, Waltz used a compiler suggested
previously by Huffman. It considered every
topologically invariant view of all possible
intersections of three surface planes (trihedral
vertices) from all possible lighting directions and
projected these interpretations onto the label sets of
the resulting picture junctions. Although Waltz was
eminently successful in the limited domain of toy
blocks under simplified assumptions about lighting
and shadows, constructing semantic compilers for
significantly more complex domains is not feasible.

5. Network consistency relies on a single level of cues

and models.   Cues are image properties computed *context-free* from the input image.   Once discovered, they are used to invoke appropriate models directly. Since each model depicts relationships among objects at a single level of abstraction, its semantics must be tied closely to the invoking image cue. Therefore, models for high-level abstract scene relationships are not possible.   Attempts at using low-level image cues to invoke high-level models have been disappointing, (Barrow and Tenenbaum, 1975).   What is needed is a hierarchy of cues and models.   Low-level, context-free cues should be used to invoke low-level scene models and high-level *context-sensitive* cues, which have been computed as a result of recognition, should be used to invoke high-level models, (Mackworth and Havens, 1981), (Mackworth, 1976).

6. Procedural knowledge is absent.   Network consistency employs a uniform constraint propagation control structure to guide the search process.   Although its performance is often more efficient than parallel or automatic backtrack search, (Mackworth and Freuder, 1982), no procedural knowledge specific to the scene domain is used. What is needed are procedures, called *methods*, (Havens, 1978), (Bobrow and Winograd, 1977), attached to each model which can efficiently guide the search process for instances of the model. These methods must be able to use a combination of data-driven and goal-driven techniques.

7. A correct segmentation of the input image is necessary.   Erroneous cues resulting from a poor segmentation will inevitably invoke inappropriate models leading to improper or empty scene interpretations.   The problem can be ameliorated by a conservative initial segmentation that is designed to invoke only appropriate models.   The resulting partial interpretations can then be used in a *cycle of*

perception, (Mackworth, 1976), to refine the parameters of the segmentation in a context-sensitive way. However, this approach appeals to a control mechanism which is external to the basic methodology itself. Furthermore, for complex imagery, there may be no appropriate segmentation strategy that yields sufficient "correct" cues to drive the interpretation process. The disappointing performance of classification and region growing algorithms for interpretation illustrates this phenomenon.

Of these seven shortcomings, the first four can be considered descriptive adequacy issues while the last three concern procedural adequacy.

16.4. Achieving descriptive adequacy

In response to the shortcomings discussed above, we have been exploring schemata as a knowledge representation for visual knowledge. There is currently great interest in the theoretical properties of schema-based systems, (Havens, 1985). The representation has been discussed variously in the literature as *frames,* (Minsky, 1975), (Winograd, 1975), *scripts,* (Schank, 1975), *plans,* (Abelson, 1975), *units,* (Bobrow and Winograd, 1977), and *schemata,* (Bartlett, 1932), (Rumelhart and Ortony, 1976), (Havens, 1983), and the effectiveness of the methodology in computational vision has recently been demonstrated in a number of systems, (Hanson and Riseman, 1978), (Glicksman, 1982).

Our own experiments with schemata have resulted in a program called *Mapsee2,* (Mackworth and Havens, 1981). The program automatically interprets hand-drawn sketch-maps of cartographic scenes, producing a hierarchical structural description of the scene. An example input sketch interpreted by Mapsee2 is shown in Figure 16-1. The image is a sketch map of the Lower Mainland in the Vancouver area. It depicts a large waterbody on the left, the Strait of Georgia, and the mainland on the right. Three islands in Howe Sound are indicated in the upper left of the sketch. On the mainland, the cities of Vancouver, North Vancouver, West Vancouver, and Surrey are represented by the dense "squiggly" lines. North of the cities in the map, the North Shore Mountains can be seen. The cities are connected by roads which cross the Fraser River at various points and cross Burrard Inlet at the Lions' Gate Bridge. Some features of the Vancouver area have been stylized in this map to conform with the symbols understood by the system.

Figure 16-1: "Lower Mainland of British Columbia"

The sketch map domain was chosen for the following reasons:

- Sketch maps capture in a simple form fundamental problems in representing and applying visual knowledge.

- Techniques for understanding maps have application in interpreting real imagery. In particular, sketch maps have been used to guide the cooperative interpretation of aerial photography. (Glicksman, 1982).

- By using the same task domain, the capabilities of schema-based systems can be compared directly with the well understood properties of network consistency methodology.

The knowledge base used in Mapsee2 is a network of schema models. Each model represents a *class* of objects, providing a description of the generic properties of every member of the class and specifying the possible relationships of the class with other schemata in the network. When a schema is used to represent a particular scene object, known or hypothesized to exist in a given sketch map, the class is used to generate a schema *instance*. For example, Figure 16-2 shows an instance of the class, *Geo-System*. This instance, named *Geo-System-3*, represents the Vancouver metropolitan area in the sketch map. The instance contains a number of defining properties including: a *Labelset*, indicating that the instance has been interpreted both as a *Landmass* and the *Mainland*, a set of relations with other schema classes (indicated in bold type), and a set of components, which are also schema instances.

Schemata represent complex scene interpretations as specific compositions of simpler schemata, forming a *composition hierarchy*. The recognition of a complex scene object is achieved by recursively recognizing its component parts so that the internal constraints of its schema are satisfied. Figure 16-3 shows the composition hierarchy used in Mapsee2.

In this hierarchy, each node is a schema class and the arcs between nodes depict relations between schemata. Looking downward the arcs represent *composition* whereas in the upward direction they represent its inverse relation, *part-of*. The intuitive interpretation of the hierarchy is that a cartographic *World* is composed of some number of geographic systems, called *Geo-Systems*, which are in turn composed of combinations of *River-Systems, Road-Systems, Mountain-Ranges,*

SCHEMA	
Type:	Instance
Class	**Geo-System**
Name	Geo-System-3
Labelset	{ Landmass, Mainland }
Part-of	**{ World }**
Composition	**{ River-System, Road-System, Town, Shore, Mountain-Range }**
Components:	
World	World-1
Road-Systems	{ Road-System-1 }
River-Systems	{ River-System-1, River-System-2 }
Shores	{ Shore-2, Shore-8, Shore-9 }
Towns	{ Town-1, Town-2, Town-3, Town-4 }
Mountain-Ranges	{ Mtn-Range-1, Mtn-Range-2, Mtn-Range-3, Mtn-Range-4 }
Chains	{ C3, C4, C5, C6, C7, C29, C27, C19, C30, C32, C33, C31, C25, C26, C20, C21, C34, C35, C38, C39, C41, C42, C43, C24, C28, C22, C23, C36, C37, C40, C45, C17, C8, C9, C10, C11, C12 }
Regions	{ R1, R2, R3, R10, R11, R12, R13, R14, R15, R16, R17, R18, R19, R20, R22, R23 }

Figure 16-2:   "A Geo-System Schema Instance"

Shorelines, and *Towns.* Each of these are, in turn, composed of simpler sub-schemata finally terminating in the primitive input sketch lines, called *Chains,* and the "empty space" *Regions* bounded by the chains. Conversely, the hierarchy can be viewed as a *part-of hierarchy* representing, for example, that *Town* schemata are component parts of both *Geo-Systems* and *Road-Systems.*

Schemata provide an important improvement in descriptive adequacy over network consistency and related representations. To substantiate this claim, in this section we examine how schemata overcome the first four of the objections outlined above. In Section 16.5 (*Achieving Procedural Adequacy*), the remainder are discussed.

(1) *The distinction between models and objects is unnecessary.* Instead, schemata are models for scene objects at various levels of abstraction. The interpretation of a scene is

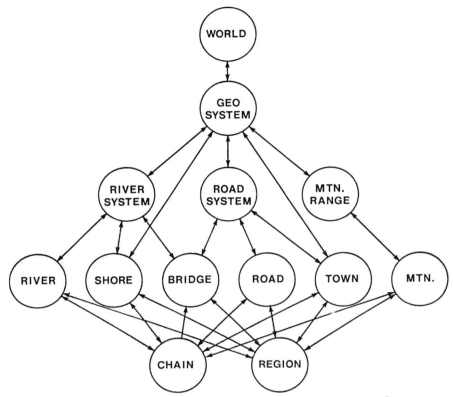

Figure 16-3:   "Mapsee2 Composition Hierarchy"

expressed as a structural network of schema instances instead
of being projected onto atomic labels for primitive objects. The
interpretation is represented explicitly and need not be
reconstructed from the labels. For example, Mapsee2 produces
a network description of the Lower Mainland which is shown
in colour-coded form in Figure 16-4. Table 16-1 gives a
legend for the interpretation. The description consists of seven
Geo-Systems, four of which are Islands, one is Sea, one is Lake
and the land area bordering the frame is interpreted as the
Mainland. Mapsee2 discovers two separate Road-Systems, one
of which is located on the Vancouver Mainland and contains
the Roads, Bridges, and Towns in that area. The second Road-
System is an isolated Town and Road on the Sechelt Peninsula
located in the upper left corner of the map. Finally, the
Mainland has two River-Systems, one representing the Fraser
River system, and the other the First Narrows connection

between the Sea and Burrard Inlet (which is interpreted as a Lake).

(2) *Schema models express scene relationships at an appropriate level of abstraction.*   A model constrains both the possible relationships of its components lower in the composition hierarchy and of the higher schemata of which it can be a part.   Thus, constraints need not be localized to small neighbourhoods of the image but may express global scene relationships in a natural way.

For example, in Figure 16-3, Road-Systems constrain their component parts to be connected Roads, Towns, and Bridges and simultaneously force the Geo-Systems, of which they are parts, to be Landmasses, as is shown in the interpretation in Figure 16-4 (See page 449).

(3) *Schemata support an intensional representation for object*

Colour	Interpretation	Colour	Interpretation
Red	Road	Blue	River Waterbody
Purple	Shore Bridge	Yellow	Town Mountain
Green	Landmass		

Table 16-1:   "Legend for Figure 16-4."

label sets. There is no explicit representation of all possible final interpretations for an object. Instead, a schema instance implicitly stands for all labellings that are consistent with its current description. The labels in this label set are not mutually exclusive but form a hierarchy called the *specialization hierarchy.* The top node of this hierarchy is a schema which represents a general class of objects. Each offspring node in the hierarchy represents a specialization of the class of its parent.

When a new instance is created, its label set includes every possible interpretation for any instance in the schema class. As components are added to its description, they provide additional constraints on the label set. Recognition of an instance is a process of refining its description, not deleting its labels. Consequently, recognition obeys the principle of reasoning from the general to the specific.

For example, the specialization hierarchy for Geo-Systems is given in Figure 16-5. A Geo-System is initially a set of undifferentiated Regions and embedded Chains in a sketch map. As additional constraints on a Geo-System are found during recognition, its interpretation can be refined first to either a Landmass or a Waterbody and finally to one of Island, Mainland, Lake, or Sea. Each of these specializations can be a distinct type of schema in the hierarchy.

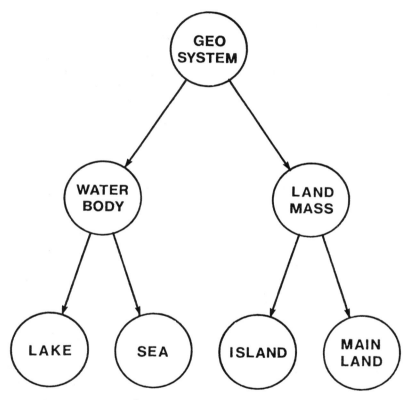

Figure 16-5:   "Geo-System Specialisation Hierarchy."

(4) *The size of the label set for each schema does not grow significantly with the complexity of the domain.* Each schema model has only a small number of possible interpretations. As a result, no compiler is required to exhaustively consider and represent explicitly all legitimate relations among objects in any scene. Conceptually, the function of the compiler has been distributed among the schema models and is invoked locally to

assign an interpretation to some instance of a model.

For example, in the Geo-System schema, the possible labels for any instance are only the nodes in its specialization hierarchy. As components are added to an instance, or the interpretation of any existing components modified, the possible interpretations for the Geo-System is re-examined and possibly refined. This computation is local to the schema and need not be computed beforehand for all possible scenes.

16.5. Achieving procedural adequacy

Controlling search in Artificial Intelligence systems is not well understood. Most of the theoretical work in knowledge representation has focussed on issues of descriptive adequacy. A prime motivation for the interest in schemata is their ability to represent both descriptive and procedural knowledge in a natural and effective manner.

(5) *Schemata can support a hierarchy of cues and models.* By representing complex objects as compositions of simpler components, search for these objects can exploit the structure of the composition and specialization hierarchies. Schema at the bottom of the composition hierarchy are invoked, as before, by context-free cues derived directly from the image features. In Mapsee2, the low-level cues are configurations of the chains present in the input sketch. Schemata higher in the composition hierarchy are invoked by abstract cues. When an instance has been fully instantiated (or nearly so), it can be used as a high-level cue to invoke schemata directly above it (bottom-up search) or schemata directly below it (top-down search) in the composition hierarchy. By using this *cue/model hierarchy*, the disparity between low-level cues and high-level models is avoided.

(6) *Procedural knowledge can be used to guide search efficiently.* Three distinct modes of search are possible: *top-down*, *bottom-up*, and a *hybrid* mode which combines desirable aspects of both. Top-down search in schema representations has been used frequently, (Minsky, 1975), (Schank, 1975). In this mode of search, a schema is proposed as a likely hypothesis by some schema higher in the

composition hierarchy. A new instance of the schema is created and invoked as a *subgoal* of the higher schema. Eventually, the subgoal must either succeed or fail, returning control to its caller.

Unfortunately, reliance on top-down search suffers from a number of known deficiencies, (Havens, 1983). Briefly, a schema must be hypothesized as a likely subgoal by some higher schema and control passed to the subgoal before any of its expertise becomes available to help guide the search process. Furthermore, the exploration of alternative subgoals is failure driven. One subgoal must be chosen as most likely and a commitment of resources made to it. Only if it eventually fails, will any alternatives be explored. Consequently, finding a correct combination of subgoals for a schema presupposes knowledge of which objects will be recognized in the scene. This is, of course, exactly the result the system is trying to compute. A reliance solely on top-down search can be very inefficient.

At the other extreme, bottom-up search can avoid some of the pitfalls of top-down search. An instance need only be recognized once. When complete, it is used as a component in every schema higher in the composition hierarchy of which it can be part. Each such higher schema becomes a *supergoal* of the completed instance and is invoked to look for its remaining components. The result is concurrently active hypotheses. However, no particular schema is in control to guide the recognition process. What is needed are mechanisms which allow top-down search to give overall guidance, yet permit bottom-up techniques to circumvent the inefficiencies of purely top-down schemes.

A third hybrid mode provides a mechanism which allows top-down search to give overall guidance, yet permits bottom-up techniques to circumvent the inefficiencies of purely top-down techniques. This technique makes extensive use of the procedural knowledge, called *methods*, attached to schemas, (Havens, 1983). In bottom-up search, when a schema has successfully incorporated a new component into its description, its method suspends awaiting the recognition of additional components. Instead, the method can retain control to direct the search for those components. For example, the method can focus the attention of the segmentation procedure to those areas of the image where its schema's components are likely to be found. If the method is successful, then another cue will be discovered in the scene which matches its schema. On the other hand, if the method fails or finds components which act as cues for other schemata, then the methods of those instances will be invoked instead. The advantage of this technique is that the schema can employ its methods to guide the search for its components without a commitment to top-down search. As long as it is successful, the schema retains control. However, as soon as components are found that can be part of a different schema, control is appropriately transferred to that schema.

(7) *High-level knowledge can guide segmentation processes.* (Glicksman, 1982) has shown that cooperative interpretation using schema-based systems can integrate information from separate *information sources*. His *Missee* system uses as input an aerial image and a sketch map drawn on top of the image outlining the major geographical objects which can be found. For example, Figure 16-6 is an image of part of Ashcroft, British Columbia with an overlayed map of a river (shown in yellow), a mountain-range, a bridge, and a road-system (all shown in green). Mapsee2 is first used to provide a structural description of the map. This interpretation is then used to guide the spectral segmentation process operating on the aerial image. Figure 16-7 shows the final segmentation for River-1 in the image (again shown in yellow). Corresponding image regions are also found for the other objects represented in the sketch map description.

16.6. Conclusion

We have argued that all levels of visual perception are domain-dependent and require specific knowledge of the objects of interest to the system. This knowledge necessarily includes both descriptive and procedural aspects. Furthermore, efficient visual processing requires a search of the knowledge base with a combination of data and goal-driven methods. We outlined previous research in high-level vision from the perspective of

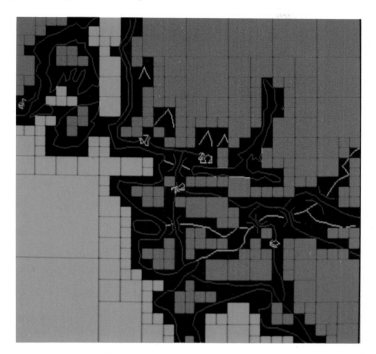

Figure 16-4:   "Interpretation of the Lower Mainland"

Figure 16-6:   "Sketch Map Superimposed on Image of
Ashcroft, British Columbia"

Figure 16-7:   "Missee River-1 Interpretation"

the knowledge representations used.   In particular, the network consistency representation, although successful, was shown to have a number of limitations.   We proposed a schema representation as a solution to these difficulties and outlined its advantages.

Acknowledgements

We are grateful to Jan Mulder, Rachel Gelbart, and Jay Glicksman for their contributions to Mapsee2.   This work was supported by NSERC under grants A9281, A5502, and SMI-51, the University of British Columbia, and NSF grant MCS-8004882.

17. On Representational Aspects of VLSI-CADT Systems

Hassan Reghbati and Nick Cercone

Laboratory for Computer and Communications Research
School of Computing Science
Simon Fraser University
Burnaby, British Columbia, CANADA V5A 1S6

Abstract

Designing anything as complicated as a state-of-the-art very large scale integrated (VLSI) circuit cannot be attempted without a full complement of computer-based design and test aids. This chapter focuses on information management and AI-related issues of computer-aided design and test (CADT) tools. These are the most important and least understood aspects of current and emerging VLSI-CADT systems.

After reviewing the VLSI design process, design knowledge and design representation issues are discussed. Then, application of AI techniques to the analysis, testing and diagnosis of VLSI circuits is also presented. Problems and recent advances in natural language interfaces are also discussed.

17.1. Introduction

Design of a system as complicated as a state-of-the-art very large scale integrated (VLSI) chip cannot even be attempted without the assistance of computer-based tools. Circuits have become smaller and manufacturing costs have dropped dramatically. Design and test are becoming the dominant cost. This is leading to a substantial interest in understanding design processes, design for testability, and built-in self-test (Reghbati, 1985).

Computer-aided design systems for VLSI testing consist of synthesis, analysis, testing and information management tools. *Synthesis tools* assist the design team in creating their circuit. Examples of tools in this category include circuit layout editors, silicon compilers for generating datapaths, and program logic array (PLA) generators for generating control. In the past few years, synthesis tools have been developed to act as expert assistants for stages in the VLSI design process, from architecture definition to layout (Kowalski et al., 1985), (Joobani and Siewiorek, 1985).

Analysis tools assist the designers in checking that the design is well-formed and behaves as expected (with the desired performance). Examples of these include *design rule checkers* for verifying that geometries are well-formed, *electrical rules checkers* for insuring that the circuit is electronically well-behaved, and various simulators that show that the circuit performs its function with the desired performance (Reghbati, 1985). Currently, software tools are being developed to provide the designer with expert advice on circuit behaviour (Williams, 1984). This requires a formalism that links the intuitions of the expert circuit analyst with the corresponding principles of formal theory, and that makes each underlying assumption explicit.

Testing tools aid the designer for the purposes of test generation and diagnosis (Reghbati, 1985). The traditional separation of design and test has given way to the design-for-testability approach (Horstmann, 1984), (Abadir and Breuer, 1985). Thus, the above classes of tools should not necessarily be considered as disjoint entities.

Information management tools organize the structure of the design data, and form the foundation upon which the other kinds of tools can be built (Katz, 1983). A related, and equally important issue, is the management of the design plan (Steinberg and Mitchell, 1985). This is especially important for redesign purposes.

The ubiquity of VLSI-CADT tools has forced the issue of *user interface* for CADT to prominence. One type of user interface which is under intensive investigation is the natural language interface. An example of such an interface is CLEOPATRA which currently deals with circuit-simulation post-processing, (Samad and Director, 1985).

In this chapter we will touch on some of the AI/VLSI issues. In section 17.2 the design process is examined. The VLSI design process can be characterized as a dialectic between goals and possibilities. This dialectic reflects the absence of a complete synthetic theory of design. Designers must begin without knowing exactly what they want or what is possible. Knowledge about design is the topic of section 17.3. Since VLSI design knowledge is changing rapidly and community practice is fragmented, such a problem domain is not ready for the development of an expert system. In section 17.4 representation of the circuit and the design plan are considered. Analysis and testing related issues form the topic of section 17.5. The CADT domain is substantially more complex than the domain for which previous natural language interfaces have been built. Problems and recent advances in this area are discussed in section 17.6. Some final remarks are made in the concluding section about the need for AI techniques to move out of the laboratory and into more widespread use in areas such as VLSI-CADT.

17.2. VLSI design process

The design process can be characterized as a dialectic between goals and possibilities. This dialectic reflects the absence of a complete synthetic theory of design. Designers must begin without knowing exactly what they want or what is possible. They explore parts of the design space as driven by their current goals and they sharpen their goals as they learn what is possible. They decide how far the overall design should be completed before designs for particular subsystems should be developed. When designers work bottom-up on particular subsystems, they gain information about what is possible in isolated parts of the design space. When designers work top-down, they decompose designs to reflect subgoals. Sometimes a reformulation of subgoals yields a simplification of interfaces between subsystems.

17.2.1. Use of multiple perspectives

Designs are specified with design perspectives. A *design perspective* provides a conceptual model for viewing the structure or the behaviour of a circuit that emphasizes certain features while suppressing others. For example, a sequential circuit can be viewed as a finite state machine or as a collection of clocked storage registers and combinatorial logic elements.

A *structural perspective* is defined by the types of components allowed when partitioning a circuit into constituent components with respect to that perspective. The definition of a perspective also includes composition rules that limit the ways in which components can be interconnected. These rules help ensure that circuits specified from a perspective are correct with respect to that perspective's concerns. The concerns of each perspective are characterized by specific classes of bugs that can be avoided when the composition rules are followed.

Collectively, the perspectives factor the concerns of the VLSI designer. A set of perspectives proposed by Stefik et al (Stefik et al., 1982) for the Mead-Conway design style consists of four levels (see Figure 17-1). The linked module abstraction (LMA) level is concerned with the sequencing of computational events. It describes the paths along which data can flow, the sequential and parallel activation of computations, and the distribution of registers. The LMA composition rules preclude bugs of starting computations before the data are ready, and deadlock bugs that arise from the use of shared modules. The clocked registers and logic (CRL) level is concerned with the composition of stages of combinatorial logic and registers. The CRL rules preclude various bugs related to clocking in a two-phase system. The clocked primitive switches (CPS) level distinguishes between different uses for logic (such as steering, clocking, and restoring) and is concerned with the digital behaviour of a system. The composition rules of this level prevent bugs of non-digital behaviour caused by charge sharing and invalid switching levels.

Description level	Concerns	Terms	Composition rules	Bugs avoided
Linked module abstraction LMA	Event sequencing	Modules Forks Joins Buffers	Token conservation Fork/join rules	Deadlock Data not ready
Clocked registers and logic CRL	Clocking 2 phase	Stages Register transfer Transfer functions	Connection of stages	Mixed clk bugs Unclocked feedback
Clocked primitive switches CPS	Digital behavior	Pull—ups Pull—downs Pass Transistors	Connection of switch networks Ratio rules	Charge sharing Switching levels
Layout	Physical dimensions	Colored rectangles	Lambda rules	Spacing errors

Figure 17-1: Structured Perspectives

Structured perspectives with the types of components (that is, terms) that they allow, and the composition rules that they enforce.)

At the layout level, the bugs to be avoided correspond to the function and performance problems caused by inadequate physical spacing. The composition rules provide a simple shallow model of composition that is based on a deep model of electrical properties and fabrication tolerances.

17.2.2. Almost hierarchical design

In a fully structured design process, design refinement proceeds uniformly through a sequence of structural perspectives, from the most abstract to the most concrete. Such a fully structured design process is rarely possible, and even when it is possible, it often results in a highly suboptimal design.

A fully structured design process has two major problems. First, it requires a complete partitioning of a component into the component types of one structural perspective before considering partitions at a less abstract perspective. Considering that design is an exploratory process, designers sometimes work on more detailed specifications for particular components, to discover what can be achieved in the overall design. Second, a ·fully structured hardware design process requires a conceptual view of the component hierarchy as tree-like. This does not allow for structure-sharing and structure-merging (Sussman and Steele, 1980).

Thus, one aspect of developing a more powerful theory of the VLSI design process than "structured design" is the development of descriptive mechanisms which capture the power of the decomposition strategy without the restrictions on what can actually be expressed imposed by a simple hierarchical development. The above problems with structured design theories are not in any way restricted to the world of digital VLSI circuits. Engineers in any discipline need to examine the systems they are designing from many points of view. Each of these viewpoints imposes its own decomposition of the system under examination, and each provides structure and information to processes working from other viewpoints.

17.2.3. Constraints and partial specifications

Designers often make significant changes late in the design cycle. They often must alter large portions of a design that are disturbed by a seemingly minor change. This is inconvenient with current design tools, which do not capture the dependencies among decisions. In such exploratory design situations it is often useful to represent explicit dependencies and constraints.

A *dependency* is a situation where one quantity depends on others. This is similar to the algebraic distinction between dependent and independent variables. Dependencies can be used in a design to represent situations where the system could automatically make changes in one part of a design to reflect changes made in another part. A *constraint* is a situation where several quantities are interrelated. Unlike dependencies, a constraint does not distinguish between dependent and independent quantities.

In AI programs, constraints are coupled with knowledge for propagating and satisfying sets of constraints. An example of such a program is SYN (Sussman and Steele, 1980), which was applied to the task of determining the parameters of the parts of a network (that is, circuit synthesis). SYN uses constraints for representing assertions about a circuit. Much of a constraint's power is that it allows a designer to specify only part of a circuit; for example, imposing a constraint that the bias current be 10% of the transistor current does not completely determine what the bias current is. From the point of view of bias stability, the exact value is irrelevant. Other constraints can be imposed to determine its value.

Constraints are an important vehicle for partial specifications. For example, constraints can describe requirements for parts of a structure whose implementation is yet to be worked out. Using constraints to characterize partial specifications can be particularly useful for representing interface contracts between parts of a design, especially when different people design the parts. A design system that includes the means for communication between designers could provide support for negotiating changes to interfaces. Such a system would help mediate the tension between defining interfaces early to divide the labour, versus revising interfaces later as a design is fleshed out. It would also make it easier for designers and managers to see when interface contracts are violated, and also to weigh the effect of proposed changes.

17.3. VLSI design knowledge

Over the past decade circuits have become more dense and manufacturing costs have dropped dramatically. This has led to a substantial interest in understanding VLSI design knowledge.

The tendency to specialize and the shifting of the technological base are forces for diversity in the integrated circuits design community. The picture is further complicated by the traditional stress on secrecy within the integrated circuits industry. All these factors have led to a state where design practices appear to be extremely complex and in a constant state of tumultuous change.

VLSI design knowledge is changing rapidly, and community practice is fragmented. If durable expert knowledge about how to design VLSI systems exists at all, it has not been widely recognized in the design community. It has been the conventional view of the knowledge engineering community that such a problem domain is not ready for the development of an expert system.

Recently, Mead and Conway (Mead and Conway, 1980) seized the opportunity inherent in the accumulated technology for a major restructuring and redesign of digital system design knowledge. When using the Mead-Conway approach, an individual designer can conceptualize a design and make all the decisions from architecture to chip layout. Thus, it becomes possible to explore the design space and optimize an overall design in ways precluded when the design is forced through the usual sequence of narrow specialties.

17.3.1. Knowledge about VLSI design

Domain-specific knowledge about VLSI design, can be classified into three categories: knowledge of implementation methods, control knowledge, and causal knowledge. These categories of knowledge are distinguished by the classes of questions that they are meant to answer during the design process.

Implementation-methods knowledge is for answering the

question "Given the specifications of a circuit module, what is one way to refine it a step closer to being implemented?". Knowledge of methods for implementing specifications is essential to hierarchical design. Implementation rules are interpreted as describing legal, correct implementations, but not necessarily optimal or even preferred implementations. In this sense, they define the "legal moves" in the search for possible circuit implementations, but not a strategy for choosing among alternatives.

Whereas knowledge of implementation methods defines the legal moves in the search for a circuit implementation, *control knowledge* provides the basis for guiding this search. At least two kinds of control knowledge can be identified: task selection knowledge and tradeoff knowledge. *Task selection knowledge* deals with questions of the form "Which of the design subproblems (circuit submodules) should be attempted next?". *Tradeoff knowledge* deals with questions such as "Given multiple implementation rules which suggest alternative refinements to a module, which implementation should be selected?".

In order to propagate information about circuit behaviour and design constraints from one part of the circuit to another, *causal knowledge* is needed. It is used to answer questions of the form "If the input signal to module M is X, then what will the output be?" and "If the output of module M must be Y, then what must the input be?".

Knowledge about design should be engineered to separate composition knowledge from optimization knowledge (Stefik et al., 1982).

17.4. VLSI design representation

The representational and structural details of a VLSI circuit design can be described in different ways (Adolph, Reghbati, and Sanmugasunderam, 1986). The representational aspects deal with the choice of how to represent design primitives, such as layout rectangles, transistors, or logic gates. The structural aspects deal with how to organize these primitives into aggregations of interrelated and hierarchically constructed design objects, across several design representations.

The planning aspects of the design are captured in the design plan.

17.4.1. Representation of designed artifact

The VLSI design domain is particularly interesting because of the rich set of representations needed to describe a design. A sampling of design representations are the following:

1. *Block diagram*:   Circuit subsystems are represented as named boxes, with input/output signals to denote control and data flow.   This representation is used primarily as a documentation and organizational aid.

2. *Behavioural representation*:   In the behavioural representation, the output signals of each block are defined as functions of the input signals.   This description is most frequently used to partition the design among subsystem designers..

3. *Physical representation*:   A physical representation describes how pieces (that is, tiles) of a design are physically placed.   If the tiles represent units of polysilicon, diffusion, metal, etc., then the description is called the layout representation.   If the tiles are similar to block diagrams, except that they have topologically accurate placements of the input/output connection points, then the representation is called the floorplan.   Design rule checkers check the validity of the layout.

4. *Electrical representation*:   An electrical representation describes a design in terms of a circuit schematic, that is, interconnected transistors with associated resistances and capacitances.   This representation is appropriate for detailed timing simulations (for example, using SPICE).

5. *Sticks*:   This representation combines the topological

properties of geometries with transistor switches. A sticks description is easy to stretch and compact, making it a higher level description from which the geometries of the physical layout can be synthesized. It is validated by switch level simulation.

Design objects are convenient aggregations of design information. They can be classified as representation objects or index objects. *Representation objects* describe a portion of the design in one of the above representations, and thus are of a particular type (for example, a sticks object). *Index objects* group these together for structural purposes.

Each representational object is constructed from the composition of its type's representation primitives. Representation objects provide the mechanism for describing the hierarchical decomposition of a design within a representation. On the other hand, index objects identify (i) equivalence (objects which are different representations of the same thing), (ii) versions (objects which are different evolutionary versions of the same generic object), (iii) alternatives (objects which are different implementations of the same generic object), and (iv) common attributes (objects which have something in common). Index objects provide a way to group objects together outside of the normal decompositions.

17.4.2. Design plan

Several types of questions arise in redesigning a circuit. To answer these questions, two separate models of reasoning are required: one, based on a causal model of a circuit, to analyze circuit operation; and one to reason about the purpose of circuit submodules (that is, their roles in implementing the global circuit specifications). These two modes of reasoning are combined to provide assistance at various redesign stages.

The design plan is a data structure that shows how circuit specifications are decomposed and implemented in the circuit, as well as the conflicts and subgoals that arise during design. It contains enough information to allow "replay" of the original design. In essence, the design plan is a recording of the reasoning that went into the design of the original circuit.

17.5. Analysis, testing, and diagnosis of VLSI circuits

Two types of computer-aided design and test (CADT) tools can be distinguished: those which help the synthesis process by which new designs are created, and those which help the analysis process by which new designs are validated. For example, the EL and SYN programs developed at MIT, help a designer analyze and synthesize analog circuits. Key to these two systems is the idea that the possible values for parameters describing circuits are represented and manipulated in terms of constraints (Sussman and Stallman, 1975).

17.5.1. Reasoning with constraints

A constraint is a situation where several quantities are interrelated. EL is an example of an AI system that represents and manipulates constraints (Sussman and Stallman, 1975). As an aid to designers analyzing analog circuits, EL computes electrical parameters of a circuit using circuit behaviour laws, such as Ohm's law and Kirchoff's current law. EL's knowledge about the values of voltages and currents at different parts of a circuit is represented as symbolic constraints.

Much of EL's power stems from the ability to reason with constraints by propagating them algebraically through a circuit description. For example, using Ohm's law constraints can be propagated in three ways. First, if the voltage across the resistor is known, and the resistance is known, the current through it can be assigned. Second, if the voltage across the resistor is known, and the current through it is known, the resistance can be assigned. And third, if the current through the resistor is known, and the resistance is known, the voltage across the resistor can be assigned.

Dependency and constraint records are valuable in systems that reason heuristically, then revise decisions. For example, in analyzing circuits, EL follows a heuristic approach from electronics engineering called the method of assumed states. This method uses a piecewise linear approximation for complicated devices. It also requires making an assumption specifying a linear region for device operation. Thus, EL has two possible states for diodes (on and off) and these states for transistors (active, cutoff, and saturated). Once a state is assumed, EL can use tractable linear expressions for the propagation analysis as before.

After making an assumption, EL must check whether the assumed states are consistent with the voltages and currents predicted for the devices. Incorrect assumptions are detected when a contradiction is detected. When this happens, some assumptions need to be changed. This is where the dependency records come in. EL uses these records to save justifications for each of its one-step deductions. These justifications enable EL to identify the assumptions behind a contradiction. Knowing what information in the analysis is dependent on contradictory assumptions enables EL to focus its attention in revising the analysis. First it decides which assumptions to withdraw, then it can gracefully withdraw those additional decisions that are dependent on the original bad assumptions. Contradictions are remembered so that combinations found to be inconsistent are not tried again.

17.5.2. Qualitative analysis

"When an engineer analyzes a circuit he rarely resorts to the heavy artillery of differential calculus. He usually attempts to provide a qualitative description of how the circuit works. This description could either be how the circuit equilibriates after receiving an input disturbance or how the circuit operates while in equilibrium". (Williams, 1984).

In qualitative analysis, descriptive terms such as "rises" and cliches such as "pulldown" and "pullup" are used to describe the circuit's operation. There is also a temporal ordering of events, i.e. a cause and effect relationship between events. Qualitative descriptions make a number of implicit assumptions and leave out parts of the explanation which are assumed to be obvious to the audience to whom the explanation is addressed. A system which analyzes circuits must be able to make these assumptions explicit.

It should be clear that qualitative analysis offers a powerful tool for determining how a circuit works. A system which can reason how a circuit works could potentially guide quantitative systems in the analysis of a newly designed circuit by knowing what features are important to examine and which features could, at least for the time being, be ignored.

The causal reasoning used for analyzing circuits is based on earlier work on qualitative physics. One of the ultimate goals of qualitative physics research is to develop a sufficiently complete account of reasoning about designed artifacts (such as electrical circuits) so that it can be automated. Johan De Kleer has been extremely prolific in his research on qualitative physics, and has developed a system called EQUAL which models an engineer's common sense reasoning about circuits (DeKleer, 1984). When given a circuit topology, EQUAL can construct a description of the mechanism by which the circuit operates.

Although qualitative physics describes the behaviour of physical artifacts, it says little about their function. Devices are designed by man to achieve some purpose. These purposes provide an alternative method for understanding the behaviour of physical systems. De Kleer (DeKleer, 1984) presents a theory for how the function of a device is related to its structure. The basic idea is that the qualitative physics relates structure to behaviour and teleology relates behaviour to function. Thus, it is possible to construct a complete account for how a particular device achieves its intended function.

17.5.3. Design for testability frames

A designer whose goal is to design an easily testable VLSI chip is faced with two serious problems. First, he may not be aware of all the design for testability (DFT) techniques that exist. Second, he may not know all the ramifications of these techniques when used in his particular circuit. Most DFT techniques are only applicable to a particular class of logic. A VLSI chip usually consists of various types of logic structures, each having different fault modes and detection mechanisms. Thus, different DFT techniques may be needed for different parts of the design, leading to questions of compatibility of various techniques and selection of a technique suited to the chip's architecture.   As an example of the richness of the DFT field, more than twenty techniques are available for PLAs alone, and so the task of simply designing a testable PLA may require expert assistance.

Clearly, the DFT problem can be characterized as a task requiring expertise.   Attempting to emulate the knowledge and behaviour of a testability expert is very challenging.   Abadir and Breuer (Abadir and Breuer, 1985) have developed an expert system called TDES (Testable Design Expert System) to aid in creating easily testable VLSI chips.   A prototype of TDES has been implemented in Lisp and runs on a Dec-20.   TDES is part of the USC Advanced Design AutoMation (ADAM) system.   A behavioural specification of the required circuit would first be compiled to a register-transfer level structural description. TDES then takes the RT level description of the circuit, along with its design goals and constraints, and using its knowledge of design for test methods, modifies the circuit such that it's design goals and constraints are met and at the same time it is easily testable.

17.5.4. Logic programming in VLSI design

Logic programming is one way to mimic the human reasoning process.   This method uses a type of automatic deduction to work towards a specified goal from a set of facts or assertions.   The work of Horstmann (Horstmann, 1984) has been oriented towards using logic programming to solve some basic VLSI design problems, in the areas of design for testability (DFT), functional simulation, fault diagnosis, and automatic test generation.   For a discussion of logic programming the reader is referred to Chapter 12 by Veronica Dahl.

17.5.5. Diagnostic reasoning

The traditional machinery for troubleshooting focuses primarily on test generation and its use in verification of device behaviour. The work by Davis (Davis, 1984) is better characterized as diagnosis in the presence of known symptoms, in devices complex enough that it is important to use the symptoms to help guide the troubleshooting.

Although Davis's work is mainly directed at the problem of troubleshooting printed circuit boards, many of his ideas are directly applicable to the diagnosis of VLSI circuits.

17.6. Natural language interfaces

We mentioned the importance of the *user interface*, in particular the natural language interface, as part of a complete set of VLSI-CADT tools. The CLEOPATRA natural language interface represents the first step toward a natural language interface for CAD, see (Samad and Director, 1985). This interface currently deals with circuit-simulation post-processing.

Samad and Director describe the following advantages of natural language interfaces for CADT:

1. Natural language interfaces are not tool specific and can therefore serve to insulate the user from idiosyncracies of the tool (such as memorizing particular formats or formal query language commands).

2. Natural language interfaces allow natural expressions.

3. Natural language interfaces are easy to learn.

CLEOPATRA's authors contend that the CAD domain is substantially more complex than the domains for which previous natural language interfaces have been built and therefore recommend a new approach to building such interfaces. They would include three main features in their approach to distinguish CLEOPATRA from previous approaches. including a greater degree of *flexibility* (avoiding any explicit notion of a grammar), *parallelism* (carrying around several "parse states" in parallel while the "correct" parse is calculated), and *redundancy* (which corrects for misspellings and reference disambiguation). Unfortunately Samad and Director have not consulted the literature widely. Otherwise they would have realized that much flexibility, parallelism, and redundancy (as per their definitions of these terms) have been incorporated into the more traditional approaches to constructing natural language systems. Nevertheless, the points they make are valid to a degree and merit further commentary.

One of the major areas of current research into natural language interfaces has been in connection with natural language interfaces to relational databases. A recent article espouses the need for knowledge of the domain, knowledge of the query, and knowledge of the user as crucial for constructing any successful natural language interface to a relational (or other) database, see (Cercone and McCalla, 1986). Since much of the design information of a VLSI-CADT system can be stored in such databases, the approaches they survey are relevant. (Cercone and McCalla, 1986) argue that six concerns represent particularly important issues which must be dealt with in natural language systems (and natural language interfaces more specifically). They write:

1. the full complexity of English is overwhelming which means that the kinds of language used when interfacing with a database are usually constrained; ways must be found of expanding the linguistic coverage of natural language systems;

2. the "stratified approach" of doing syntactic analysis, then semantic interpretation, then query evaluation is ineffective; techniques must be evolved to integrate syntax, semantics, and pragmatics so that whatever action is appropriate at a given time can be done;

3. the separation of the linguistic component from the

database component sets up an arbitrary barrier which may have become counterproductive; a means of re-integrating data and language must be found;

4. traditional (relational) database structures are not necessarily conducive to promoting the kinds of inferences which need to be made for the query to be comprehended or answered properly; more sophisticated structures must be devised;

5. the user's understanding of the capabilities of the linguistic and database components is an important aspect of the man-machine communication, which must be taken into account; the user cannot be ignored; and

6. even in a restricted linguistic domain such as natural language database interfacing, many discourse phenomena arise which must be accounted for if the natural language system is to behave cooperatively. [(Cercone and McCalla, 1986) p. 4.]

Research in natural language database access has addressed issues arising out of these six concerns. Indeed, as Samad and Director have observed, much of the early and intermediate term research into natural language understanding was directed at expanding the linguistic coverage, concern (1), and at devising parsing strategies that allowed the integration of the various levels of linguistic analysis, concern (2). How we deal with concerns (3) through (6) will determine how successful natural language interfaces to VLSI-CADT systems can be. Cercone and McCalla investigate these six concerns by drawing upon a wealth of examples from recent literature (see their reference list) on natural language database systems, literature primarily ignored by Samad and Director.

(Cercone and McCalla, 1986) summarize by stating that concerns (1) and (2) will not provide the main stumbling blocks to the construction of the ideal interface. Although much progress has been made regarding concerns (3) and (4) (for example, the use of frames, scripts, semantic networks, and/or other representational schemes is almost taken for granted in theory) little practical use of these devices for incorporating knowledge structures, either for interpretation or information access, has been made.[47]   Despite these developments, the ability to incorporate knowledge is still a major source of difficulty confronting the designer of a natural language interface. Finally, concerns (5) and (6) present the most challenging aspect to the construction of a good interface. In addition to the devices specified by Samad and Director, the computational framework of a discourse theory (such as speech act theory) needs to be specified and incorporated into the natural language interface. Progress in constructing natural language interfaces is incremental, and several impressive interfaces have been constructed at the prototype level.

17.7. Concluding remarks

In assessing the potential impact of expert systems on VLSI-CADT it is interesting to look for limiting factors. One critical factor is the small number of people with experience in building expert systems. Only a tiny fraction of this small number have a substantial interest in VLSI-CADT. To maximize its impact, it is essential for AI to simplify its methods and to export its ideas.

There are several encouraging signs, however. For instance, several large companies with an interest in VLSI-CADT, including Tektronix, Hewlett Packard, Schlumberger, and Texas Instruments, have organized AI laboratories. Also powerful personal workstations supporting appropriate AI languages (for example, Lisp), programming environments, and graphics are now available from many companies including LMI, Symbolics, and Xerox. Finally, knowledge representation

---

[47] A notable exception is the work of (Kao, 1986) in which she outlines relations which incorporate traditional generalization and aggregation knowledge structure hierarchies, among others, into a traditional relational database. She then uses these structures (relations) in order to provide quality responses in situations when the database response would normally be null (primarily due to user misconceptions).

languages tailored for expert systems are emerging: LOOPS (Xerox), MRS (Stanford University), and OPS5 (Carnegie-Mellon University) are among the most widely known of these languages.

Already there are many prototypical expert systems for assisting the VLSI-CADT community. However, the widespread use of expert systems in this area is several years away.

Acknowledgements

We wish to express our gratitude to Canada's Natural Science and Engineering Research Council for its financial support of our various research endeavours.

References

Abadir, M.S. and Breuer, M.A. A Knowledge-Based System for Designing Testable VLSI Chips. *IEEE Design and Test,* August 1985, *2(4),* 56-68.

Abelson, R. Concepts for Representing Mundane Reality in Plans. In Bobrow, D., and Collins, A. (Eds.), *Representation and Understanding,* New York: Academic Press. 1975.

Adolph, W.S., Reghbati, H.K. and Sanmugasunderam, A. *A Frame-Based System for Representing Knowledge About VLSI Design,* pages . ACM-IEEE, 1986.

Aho, A., Hopcroft, J., and Ullman, J. *Data Structures and Algorithms.* Reading, Massachusetts:Addison-Wesley, 1983.

Aiello, N. *A Comparative Study of Control Strategies for Expert Systems: AGE Implementation of Three Variations of PUFF.* AAAI, Washington, 1983.

Allen, J. *Maintaining Knowledge about Temporal Intervals.* Technical Report TR-86, Department of Computer Science, University of Rochester, 1981.

Allen, J. Recognizing Intentions from Natural Language Utterances. In M. Brady (Ed.), *Computational Models of Discourse.* Cambridge, Massachusetts: M.I.T. Press, 1982.

Allen, J. Maintaining Knowledge about Temporal Intervals. *Communications of the ACM,* 1983, *26(11),* 832-843.

Allen, J., and Kautz, H. A model for naive temporal reasoning. In Hobbs, J. and Moore, R. (Ed.), *Formal Theories of the Commonsense World,* Norwood, New Jersey: Ablex, 1985.

Almeida, Michael J. *Reasoning about the Temporal Structure of Narrative Texts.* Technical Report 86-00, SUNY Buffalo Department of Computer Science, 1986.

Almeida, Michael J., and Shapiro, Stuart C. *Reasoning about the Temporal Structure of Narrative Texts.* Cognitive Science Society, University of Rochester, 1983.

Appelt, D. *Planning Natural Language Utterances to Satisfy Multiple Goals.* Technical Report TR, SRI International, 1982.

Ari, M. Ben, Manna, Z., and Pneuli, A. *The Temporal Logic of Branching Time,* pages 222-235. Eight Annual ACM Symposium Principles of Programming Languages, , 1981.

Bailes, A. *Response Generation.* Technical Report M.Sc. thesis, Department of Computing Science, University of Alberta, 1986.

Baldwin, J.F. and Zhou, S.Q. *A Fuzzy Relational Inference Language.* Technical Report EM/FS132, University of Bristol, 1982.

Barr, A., and Feigenbaum, E. *The Handbook of Artificial Intelligence: Volume 1* Stanford, California:Harris Tech Press, 1981.

Barrow, H., and Tenenbaum, J. *Representation and the Use of Knowledge in Vision.* Technical Report TR 108, SRI International, 1975.

Barrow, H., and Tenenbaum, J. Recovering Intrinsic Scene Characteristics from Images. In A. Hanson and E. Riseman (Eds.), *Computer Vision Systems,* New York: Academic Press, 1978.

Bartlett, F. *Remembering: A Study in Experimental and Special Psychology.* Cambridge, England:Cambridge University Press, 1932.

Bellman, R.E. and Zadeh, L.A. Local and Fuzzy Logics. In Epstein, G. (Ed.), *Modern Uses of Multiple Valued Logic,* Dordrecht: Reidel, 1977.

Birren, F. (ed). *Ostwald. The Color Primer.* New York, New York:Van Nostrand Reinhold Co., 1969.

Birren, F. (ed). *Munsell A Grammar of Color.* New York, New York:Van Nostrand Reinhold Co., 1969.

Black, F. A Deductive Question Answering System. In Minsky, M. (Eds.), *Semantic Information Processing,* Cambridge, Mass.: MIT Press, 1968.

Blum, R. Discovery and Representation of Causal Relationships from a Large Time-Oriented Clinical Database. In *Lecture Notes in Medical Informatics 19,* Springer-Verlag, 1982.

Bobrow, D. Dimensions of Representation. In Bobrow, D., and Collins, A. (Eds.), *Representation and Understanding,* New York: Academic Press, 1975.

Bobrow, D. *Special Issue on Non-Monotonic Logic of Artificial Intelligence Journal.* Amsterdam:North Holland, 1980.

Bobrow, R., and Webber, B. *Knowledge Representation for Syntactic/Semantic Processing,* pages 316-323. Proceedings of the 1st AAAI, Stanford, California, 1980.

Bobrow, D., and Winograd, T. An Overview of KRL: a Knowledge Representation Language. *Cognitive Science,* 1977, *1(1),* 3-46.

Boland, J., and Lekkerkerker, C. Representation of a Finite Graph by a Set of Intervals on the Real Line. *Fundamentals Mathematics,* 1962, *11(1),* 45-64.

Booth, K., and Lueker, G. *Linear Algorithms to Recognize Interval Graphs and Test for the Consecutive Ones Property,* pages 252-265. Proceedings of the 7th ACM Symposium on the Theory of Computing, , 1975.

Brachman, Ronald J. What's in a Concept: Structural Foundations for Semantic Networks. *International Journal of Man-Machine Studies,* 1977, *9,* 127-52.

Brachman, Ronald J. On the Epistemological Status of Semantic Networks. In Findler, N.V. (Ed.), *Associative Networks: Representation and Use of Knowledge by Computers,* New York: Academic Press, 1979. reprinted in Brachman and

Levesque 1985: 191-215.

Brachman, R. *What IS-A is and Isn't.* CSCSI, Saskatoon, 1982.

Brachman, R. What IS-A Is and Isn't: An Analysis of Taxonomic Links in Semantic Networks. *IEEE Computer*, 1983, *16(10)*, 30-36.

Brachman, R., and Levesque, H. *Readings in Knowledge Representation.* Los Altos, Ca.:Morgan Kaufmann, 1985.

Brachman, R., and Schmolze, J. An Overview of the KL-One Knowledge Representation System. *Cognitive Science*, 1985, *9(4)*, 171-216.

Brachman, R., and Smith, B. *Special Issue on Knowledge Representation, SIGART Newsletter.* New York:ACM, 1980.

Brachman, R., Fikes, R., and Levesque, H. KRYPTON: A Functional Approach to Knowledge Representation. *IEEE Computer*, 1983, *16(10)*, 67-74.

Brachman, Ronald J.; Gilbert, Victoria P.; and Levesque, Hector J. *An Essential Hybrid Reasoning System: Knowledge and Symbol Level Accounts of KRYPTON*, pages 532-39. IJCAI, 1985.

Brower, R., Meester, G. *The Shape of the Human Left Ventricle: Quantification of Symmetry.* Computers in Cardiology, Florence, 1981.

Brown, J. S., and Burton, R. Diagnostic Models for Procedural Bugs in Basic Mathematical Skills. *Cognitive Science*, 1978, *2(2)*, 155-192.

Brown, J., Burton, R., and Bell, A. *SOPHIE: A Sophisticated Instructional Environment for Teaching Electronic Troubleshooting (An Example of AI in CAI).* Technical Report BBN Report No. 2790, Bolt Beranek and Newman, Inc., 1974.

Brown, J., Burton, R., and de Kleer, J. Pedagogical, Natural Language and Knowledge Engineering Techniques in

SOPHIE I, II, and III. In Sleeman, D., and Brown, J. (Eds.), *Intelligent Tutoring Systems*, New York: Academic Press, 1982.

Buchanan, B., Sutherland, G., and Feigenbaum, E. Heuristic DENDRAL: A Program for Generating Explanatory Hypothesis in Organic Chemistry. In B. Meltzer and D. Michie (Eds.), *Machine Intelligence 4*, Edinburgh: Edinburgh University Press, 1969.

Buchanan, B., and Shortliffe, E. Rule Based Expert Systems: The Mycin Experiments of the Stanford HPP. In Buchanan, B., and Shortliffe, E. (Eds.), *Rule Based Expert Systems: The Mycin Experiments of the Stanford HPP*, Reading, Massachusetts: Addison-Wesley, 1984.

Bundy, A., and Silver, B. Using meta-level inference for selective application of multiple rewrite rules in algebraic manipulation. *Artificial Intelligence*, 1981, *16(2)*, .

Bundy, A., Byrd, L., and Mellish, C. *Special purpose, but domain independent, inference mechanisms.*, pages 67-74. AISB, Orsay, France, 1982.

Carbonell, J. POLITICS. In R. Schank and C. Reisbeck (Eds.), *Inside Computer Understanding*, Hillsdale, New Jersey: Lawrence Erlbaum Associates, 1981.

Carbonell, J., Michalski, J., and Mitchell, T. An Overview of Machine Learning. In Michalski, J., Carbonell, J., and Mitchell, T. (Eds.), *Machine Learning: An Artificial Intelligence Approach*, Palo Alto, California: Tioga Press, 1983.

Carnap, Rudolf. *The Logical Structure of the World.* Berkeley:University of California Press, 1967. R.A. George, translator.

Castañ, Hector-Neri. Thinking and the Structure of the World. *Philosophia*, 1974, *4*, 3-40. reprinted in 1975 in Critica 6(1972)43-86.

Castañeda, Hector-Neri. Individuals and Non-Identity: A New

476

Look *American Philosophical Quarterly,* 1975, *12,* 131-40.

Castañeda, Hector-Neri. Identity and Sameness. *Philosophia,* 1975, *5,* 121-50.

Castañeda, Hector-Neri. Perception, Belief, and the Structure of Physical Objects and Consciousness. *Synthèse,* 1977, *35,* 285-351.

Castañeda, Hector-Neri. Fiction and Reality: Their Basic Connections. *Poetica,* 1979, *8,* 31-62.

Castañeda, Hector-Neri. *Thinking and Doing: The Philosophical Foundations of Institutions.* Dordrecht:Reidel, 1975.

Cercone, N., and McCalla, G. Artificial Intelligence: Underlying Assumptions and Basic Objectives. *American Journal for Information Science,* 1984, *5(35),* 280-290.

Cercone, N., and McCalla, G. Accessing Knowledge Through Natural Language. In M. Yovits (Ed.), *Advances in Computers,* New York: Academic Press, 1986.

Cercone, N. and Schubert, L. *Toward a State-Based Conceptual Representation,* pages 83-91. IJCAI75, Advance Papers of the 4th International Joint Conference on Artificial Intelligence, Tbilisi, USSR, 1975.

Cercone, N., McCalla, G., and McFetridge, P. The Many Dimensions of Logical Form. In Bolc, L. (Eds.), *Translating Natural Language into Logical Form.* New York: Springer-Verlag, 1986. forthcoming.

Chandrasekaran, B., Gomez, F., Mittal, S., Smith, J. *An Approach to Medical Diagnosis Based on Conceptual Structures.* IJCAI, Tokyo, 1979.

Chapman, David. *Planning for Conjunctive Goals.* Technical Report 802, MIT Artificial Intelligence Laboratory, November 1985.

Cheng, M. *The Design and Implementation of the Waterloo UNIX Prolog Environment.* Technical Report Report 26, CS-84-47, University of Waterloo, 1984.

Clancey, W. Tutoring Rules for Guiding a Case Method Dialogue. In Sleeman, D., and Brown, J. (Eds.), *Intelligent Tutoring Systems*, London, England: Academic Press, 1982.

Clark, K., and McCabe, F. The control facilities of IC-PROLOG. In Michie, D. (Eds.), *Expert systems in the micro-electronic age*, Edinburgh, Scotland: Edinburgh University Press, 1979.

Clocksin. W., and Mellish, C. *Programming in Prolog*. Berlin:Springer-Verlag, 1981.

Codd, E. A Relational Model for Large Shared Data Banks. *Communications of the ACM*, 1970, *13(6)*, 377-387.

Cohen, P. *Planning Speech Acts*. Technical Report TR 118, Department of Computer Science, University of Toronto, 1978.

Collins, A. Reasoning from Incomplete Knowledge In Bobrow, D., and Collins, A. (Eds.), *Representation and Understanding*, New York: Academic Press, 1975.

Collins, A., and Quillian, M. How to Make a Language User. In Tulving, E., and Donaldson, W. (Eds.), *Organisation of Memory*, New York: Academic Press, 1972.

Colmerauer, A., Kanoui, H., Pasero, R., and Roussel, Ph. *Un Systeme de Communication Homme-Machine en Francais*. Marseille, France:Aix-Marseille University Press, 1973.

Colmerauer, A. *Un Systeme de Communication Homme-Machine en Francais*. Technical Report , Aix-Marseille University, 1973.

Covington, A. and Schubert, L. *Organization of modally embedded propositions and of dependent concepts.*, pages 87-94. CSCSI/SCEIO, Victoria, British Columbia, 1980.

Craig, J., et al. DEACON: Direct English Access and Control. *FJCC, AFIPS Conf. Proc.*, 1966, *29(1)*, 365-380.

Cresswell, M.J. *Logic and Languages*. London:Methuen, 1973.

478

Cullingford, R. *Script Application: Computer Understanding of Newspaper Stories*. Technical Report Research Report 116, Department of Computer Science, Yale University, 1978.

Dahl, V. Translating Spanish into Logic Through Logic. *American Journal of Computational Linguistics*, 1981, *7(3)*, x-y.

Dahl, V. On Database Systems Development Through Logic. *ACM Transactions on Database Systems*, 1982, *7(1)*, 102-123.

Dahl, V., and McCord, M. *Treating Coordination in Logic Grammars*. Technical Report TR-83, Simon Fraser University and University of Kentucky, 1983.

Dahl, V., and Sambuc, R. *Un Systeme de Banque de Donnees en Logique du Premier Ordre, en Vue de sa Consultation en Langue Naturelle*. Technical Report , Aix-Marseille University, 1976.

Date, C.J. *An Introduction to Database Systems*. Reading:Addison-Wesley, 1977.

Date, C.J. *An Introduction to Database Systems*. Reading, Massachusetts:Addison-Wesley, 1981.

Davis, R. Diagnostic Reasoning Based on Structure and Behaviour. *Artificial Intelligence*, 1984, *24(4)*, 347-410.

Davis, R., Buchanan, B., and Shortliffe, E. Production Rules as a Representation for a Knowledge-Based Consultation Program. *Artificial Intelligence*, 1977, *8(1)*, 15-45.

de Groot, A. Perception and Memory Versus Thought: Some Old Ideas and Recent Findings. In Kleinmuntz, B. (Eds.), *Problem Solving*, New York: Wiley, 1967.

De Kleer, J., and Brown, J. A Qualitative Physics Based on Confluence. *Artificial Intelligence*, 1984, *24(2)*, 7-83.

Dean, Thomas. *Temporal Imagery: An Approach to Reasoning about Time for Planning and Problem Solving*. Technical Report YALEU/CSD/RR #433, Yale University,

Department of Computer Science, October 1985.

deHaan, J. *Inference in a topically organized semantic net*. Technical Report M.Sc. thesis, Department of Computing Science, University of Alberta, 1986.

deHaan, J., and Schubert, L. *Inference in a Topically Organized Semantic Net.*, pages (to appear). AAAI, Philadephia, Pennsylvania, 1986.

DeKleer, J. How Circuits Work. *Artificial Intelligence*, 1984, *24*, 205-280.

Delgrande, J. *Steps Towards a Theory of Exceptions*, pages 87-94. Proceedings of the 5th National Conference of the CSCSI/SCEIO, London, Ontario, 1984.

Dennett, D. Why the Law of Effect will not go away. In (Eds.), *Brainstorms*, Cambridge, Massachusetts: Bradford Books, MIT Press, 1978.

Doran, J., Traill, T., Brown, D., Gibson, D. Detection of Abnormal Left Ventricular Wall Movement During Isovolumic Contraction and Early Relaxation. *British Heart Journal*, 1978, *40*, .

Doyle, J. *Some Theories of Reasoned Assumptions: An Essay in Rational Psychology*. Technical Report TR, Carnegie Mellon University, 1982.

Doyle, J. *A Society of Mind: Multiple Perspectives, Reasoned Assumptions, and Virtual Copies*, pages . Eight International Joint Conference on Artificial Intelligence, Karlsrhue, West Germany, 1983.

Dresher, B., and Hornstein, N. On Some Supposed Contributions of Artificial Intelligence to the Scientific Study of Language. *Cognition*, 1976, *4(4)*, 321-398.

Dresher, B., and Hornstein, N. Reply to Winograd. *Cognition*, 1976, *5(4)*, 377-392.

Dresher, B., and Hornstein, N. Response to Schank and Wilensky. *Cognition*, 1977, *5(2)*, 147-150.

480

DuBois, D. and Prade, H. Fuzzy Cardinality and the Modelling of Imprecise Quantification. *Fuzzy Sets and Systems*, 1985, *16*, 199-230.

Duda, R., Gashning, J., Hart, P., Konolige, K., Reboh, R., Barrett, P., and Slocum, J. *Development of the PROSPECTOR Consultation System for Mineral Exploration, Final Report, SRI Projects 5821 and 6415*. Technical Report 5821 & 6415, SRI International, 1978.

Elcock, E. Problem solving compilers. In Findler, N. (Eds.), *Artificial Intelligence and Heuristic Programming*, Edinburgh, Scotland: Edinburgh University Press, 1971.

Elcock, E., McGregor, J., and Murray, A. Data directed control and operating systems. *British Computer Journal*, 1972, *15(2)*, 125-129.

Etherington, D., Mercer, R., and Reiter, R. On the Adequacy of Predicate Circumscription for Closed Reasoning. *Computational Intelligence*, 1985, *1(1)*, 11-15.

Fagan, L. M. *VM: Representing Time Dependence Relations in a Medical Setting*. Technical Report Ph.D. Thesis, AI Laboratory, 1980.

Fahlman, S. *A System for Representing and Using Real World Knowledge*. Technical Report AI Lab Memo 331, Project MAC, M.I.T., 1975.

Fahlman, S. *NETL: A System for Representing and Using Real World Knowledge*. Cambridge, Mass.:M.I.T. Press, 1979.

Fahlman, S. *Design Sketch for a Million Element NETL Machine*, pages 249-252. Proceedings of the 1st AAAI, Stanford, California, 1980.

Fahlman, S. *Three Flavors of Parallelism*, pages 230-235. CSCSI 82, Proceedings of the 4th National Conference of the Canadian Society for Computational Studies of Intelligence, Saskatoon, Sask., 1982.

Fikes, Richard E. and Nilsson, Nils J. STRIPS: A New

Approach to the Application of Theorem Proving to Problem Solving. *Artificial Intelligence*, 1971, (2)}, 198-208.

Fikes, R., and Nilsson, N. STRIPS: A New Approach to the Application of Theorem Proving to Problem Solving. *Artificial Intelligence*, 1971, *2(3)*, 184-208.

Findlay, J.N. *Meinong's Theory of Objects and Values*. Oxford:Clarendon Press, 1963.

Fine, Kit. *A Defence of Arbitrary Objects*, pages 55-77. Aristotelian Society, 1983. Supp. Vol. 58.

Firby, R. James, Dean, Thomas and Miller, David. *Efficient Robot Planning with Deadlines and Travel Time*. IASTED, Santa Barbara, Ca., May, 1985.

Fodor, J. Tom Swift and His Procedural Grandmother. *Cognition*, 1978, *6(4)*, 229-247.

Forbus, K. Qualitative Process Theory. *Artificial Intelligence*, 1984, *24(2)*, 85-168.

Forgy, C., and McDermott, J. *OPS, A Domain Independent Production System Language*, pages 933-939. IJCAI77, Proceedings of the 5th International Joint Conference on Artificial Intelligence, Cambridge, Mass., 1977.

Foster, J., and Elcock, E. Absys 1: an incremental compiler for assertions: an introduction. In Meltzer, B., and Michie, D. (Eds.), *Machine Intelligence 4*, Edinburgh, Scotland: Edinburgh University Press, 1969.

Fujii, J., Watanabe, H., Koyama, S., Kato, K. Echocardiographic Study on Diastolic Posterior Wall Movement Left Ventricular Filling by Disease Category. *American Heart Journal*, 1979, *98*, .

Fulkerson, D., and Gross, O. Incidence Matricies and Interval Graphs. *Pacific Journal of Mathematics*, 1965, *15(11)*, 835-855.

Funt, B. Problem Solving with Diagrammatic Representations.

482

Artificial Intelligence, 1980, *13(3)*, 201-230.

Funt, B. A Parallel Process Model of Mental Rotation. *Cognitive Science*, 1983, *4(1)*, 1-23.

Gerbrands, J., Booman, F., Reiber, J. Computer Analysis of Moving Radiopaque Markers from X-Ray Films. *Computer Graphics and Image Processing*, 1979, *11*, .

Gershon, R. Explanation Methods for Visual Motion Understanding Systems. Master's thesis, Department of Computer Science, University of Toronto, 1982.

Ghosh, S. File Organization: the Consecutive Retrieval Property. *Communications of the ACM*, 1972, *15(12)*, 802-808.

Ghosh, S., Kambayashi, Y., and Lipski, W. Data Base File Organization, Theory and Applications of the Consecutive Retrieval Property. In Ghosh, S., Kambayashi, Y., and Lipski, W. (Eds.), *Data Base Organization*, New York: Academic Press, 1983.

Gibson D., Prewitt, T., Brown, D. Analysis of Left Ventricular Wall Movement During Isovolumic Relaxation and its Relation to Coronary Artery Disease. *British Heart Journal*, 1976, *38*, .

Glicksman, J. *A Schemata-Based System for Utilizing Cooperating Knowledge*, pages 33-39. Proceedings of the 4th National Conference of the CSCSI/SCEIO, Saskatoon, 1982.

Goebel, R. *Interpreting Descriptions in a Prolog Based Knowledge Representation System*, pages 711-716. IJCAI 85, Proceedings of the 9th International Joint Conference on Artificial Intelligence, Los Angeles, California, 1985.

Goldstein, I., and Burton, R. The Genetic Graph: A Representation for the Evolution of Procedural Knowledge. In Sleeman, D., and Brown, J. (Eds.), *Intelligent Tutoring Systems*, New York: Academic Press, 1982.

Goodwin, James. *Taxonomic Programming with KL-One*.

483

Technical   Report LiTH-MAT-R-79-5.   Informatics
Laboratory, Linkoeping University, 1979.

Green, C. *A Summary of the PSI Program Synthesis System*,
pages 380-381.   IJCAI77.   Proceedings of the 4th
International Joint Conference on Artificial Intelligence,
Cambridge, Massachusetts, 1977.

Hadley, R.   SHADOW: A Natural Language Query Analyser.
Computers and Mathematics, 1985, *11(5)*, x-y.

Hagan, A., et al.   Evaluation of Computer Programs for
Clinical Electrocardiography.   In D. Cady, Jr. (Ed.),
Computer Techniques in Cardiology, New York: Marcel
Dekker, Inc., 1979.

Halmos, P. *Lectures on Boolean Algebra.*   New York:Van
Nostrand Press, 1963.

Hanson, A., and Riseman, E.   VISIONS: A Computer Systems
for Interpreting Scenes.   In A. Hanson and E. Riseman
(Eds.), *Computer Vision Systems*, New York: Academic
Press, 1978.

Havens, W. *A Procedural Model of Recognition*, pages 263-264.
Proceedings of the 5th IJCAI, MIT, Cambridge, MA, 1977.

Havens, W. *A Procedural Model of Recognition for Machine
Perception*, pages 254-262.   Proceedings of the 2nd
National Conference of the CSCSI/SCEIO, Toronto, 1978.

Havens, W.   Recognition Mechanisms for Hierarchical Schemata
Knowledge.   *Computers and Mathematics*, 1983, *9(1)*,
185-200.

Havens, W.   A Theory of Schema Labelling.   *Computational
Intelligence*, 1985, *1(3)*, 101-120.

Hawrylak, I.   M.Sc. Thesis .   Master's thesis, Department of
Computer Science, University of Kentucky, 1985.

Hayes, P. *In Defence of Logic*, pages 559-565.   IJCAI77.
Proceedings of the 5th International Joint Conference on
Artificial Intelligence, Cambridge, Mass., 1977.

484

Hayes. P. The Logic of Frames. In B. Webber and N. Nilsson (Eds.), *Readings in Artificial Intelligence*, Palo Alto, California: Tioga Press, 1979.

Hayes-Roth, F. Using Proofs and Refutations to Learn from Experience. In Michalski, R., Carbonell, J., and Mitchell, T. (Eds.), *Machine Learning: An Artificial Intelligence Approach*, Palo Alto, California: Tioga Press, 1983.

Hayes-Roth, F., Waterman, D. A., and Lenat, D. B., (Editors). *Building Expert Systems*. Reading, Mass.:Addison-Wesley, 1983.

Hendrix, G. *Expanding the Utility of Semantic Networks Through Partitioning*, pages 115-121. IJCAI75, Advance Papers of the 4th International Joint Conference on Artificial Intelligence, Tbilisi, USSR, 1975.

Hendrix, G. Encoding Knowledge in Partitioned Networks. In N. Findler (Ed.), *Associative Networks: The Representation and Use of Knowledge by Machine*, New York: Academic Press, 1979.

Hewitt, C. *Description and Theoretical Analysis of PLANNER*. Technical Report Ph.D. Thesis, AI Laboratory, M.I.T., 1972.

Hobbs, J.R. and Moore, R.C. *Formal Theories of the Commonsense World*. Norwood:Ablex, 1984.

Hobbs, J.R. and Moore, R.C. *Formal Theories of the Commonsense World*. Norwood, NJ:Ablex, 1985.

Hoehne, K., Boehm, M., Nicolae, G. The Processing of X-Ray Image Sequences. In Stucki (Ed.), *Advances in Digital Image Processing*, Plenum Press, 1980.

Horowitz, S. A Syntatic Algorithm for Peak Detection in Waveforms with Applications to Cardiography. *Communications of the ACM*, May 1975, *18(5)*, .

Horstmann, P.W. *A Knowledge-Based System Using Design for Testability Rules*, pages 278-284. Proceedings of FTCS-14,

1984.

Israel, David J. Interpreting Network Formalisms. In Cercone, Nick (Ed.), *Computational Linguistics*, Oxford: Pergamon Press, 1983.

Johnson-Laird, P. Procedural Semantics. *Cognition*, 1977, *5*, 189-214.

Johnson-Laird, P. Mental Models in Cognitive Science. *Cognitive Science*, 1980, *4(1)*, 71-115.

Jones, M., and Poole, D. *An Expert System for Educational Diagnosis based on Default Logic*, pages 573-583. Proceedings of the 5th International Workshop on Expert Systems and their Applications, Avignon, France, 1985.

Joobani, R. and Siewiorek, D.P. *Weaver: A Knowledge-Based Routing Expert*, pages 266-272. ACM-IEEE, 1985.

Judd, D., and Wyszecki, G. *Color in Business, Science and Industry (2nd edition).* New York, New York:John Wiley and Sons, 1963.

Kahn, K., and Gorry, G. Mechanizing Temporal Knowledge. *Artificial Intelligence*, 1977, *9(2)*, 87-108.

Kameda, T. On the Vector Representation of the Reachability in Planar Directed Graphs. *Information Processing Letters*, 1975, *3(4)*, 75-77.

Kao, M. Turning Null Responses into Quality Responses. Master's thesis, School of Computing Science, Simon Fraser University, 1986.

Kaplan, J. Cooperative Responses from a Portable Natural Language Query System. *Artificial Intelligence*, 1982, *19(2)*, 165-187.

Katz, R.H. Managing the Chip Design Database. *IEEE Computer*, December 1983, *16(12)*, 26-40.

Kaufmann, A. and Gupta, M. *Introduction to Fuzzy Arithmetic.* New York:VanNostrand, 1985.

Kay, P. *Color Perception and the Meanings of Color Words*, pages 61-64. Cog. Sci. Soc., Berkeley, California, 1981.

Kosslyn, S. *Image and Mind.* Cambridge, Massachusetts:Harvard University Press, 1980.

Kowalski, R. *Predicate Logic as a Programming Language*, pages 569-574. North Holland Publishing Company, Amsterdam, 1974.

Kowalski, R. *Logic for Problem Solving.* New York, New York:North Holland Elsevier, 1979.

Kowalski, T.J., et al. The VLSI Design Automation Assistant: From Algorithms to Silicon. *IEEE Design and Test*, August 1985, *2(4)*, 33-34.

Kuipers, B. Commonsense Reasoning about Causality: Deriving Behaviour from Structure. *Artificial Intelligence*, 1984, *24(2)*, 169-202.

Kunz, J.C. *Analysis of Physiological Behavior using a Causal Model based on First Principles.* American Association for Artificial Intelligence, August, 1983.

Kuratowski, K., and Mostowski, A. *Set Theory.* New York:North Holland, 1982.

Lambert, Karel. *Meinong and the Principle of Independence.* Cambridge, England:Cambridge University Press, 1983.

Langley, P., Bradshaw, G., and Simon, H. Rediscovering Chemistry with the Bacon System. In Michalski, R., Carbonell, J., and Mitchell, T. (Eds.), *Machine Learning: An Artificial Intelligence Approach*, Palo Alto, California: Tioga Press, 1983.

Lenat, D. The Role of Heuristics in Learning by Discovery: Three Case Studies. In Michalski, R., Carbonell, J., and Mitchell, T. (Eds.), *Machine Learning: An Artificial Intelligence Approach*, Palo Alto, California: Tioga Press, 1983.

Levesque, H. *A Procedural Approach to Semantic Networks.*

Technical Report TR-105. Department of Computer Science, University of Toronto, 1977.

Levesque, H. *A Formal Treatment of Incomplete Knowledge Bases.* Technical Report Ph.D. Thesis. Department of Computer Science, University of Toronto, 1981.

Levesque, Hector J., and Brachman, Ronald J. A Fundamental Tradeoff in Knowledge Representation and Reasoning. In *in Brachman and Levesque 1985.* Morgan Kaufmann, 1985. Revised Version.

Levesque, H., and Mylopoulos, J. A Procedural Semantics for Semantic Networks. In N. Findler (Ed.), *Associative Networks: The Representation and Use of Knowledge by Machine.* New York: Academic Press, 1979.

Lispki, W. Information Storage and Retrieval. *Theoretical Computing Science,* 1976, *3(3),* 183-211.

Lipski, W. *Logical Problems Related to Incomplete Information in Databases.* Technical Report Preprint #452, Universite de Paris-Sud, Orsay, 1977.

Long, W. *Reasoning about State from Causation and Time in a Medical Domain.* American Association for Artificial Intelligence, August, 1983.

Long, W., Russ, T., *A Control Structure for Tim-Dependent Reasoning.* IJCAI, Karlsruhe, Germany, 1983.

Loveland, D. *Automated Theorem Proving: A Logical Basis.* Amsterdam:North Holland, 1978.

Lukasiewicz, J. *Aristotle's Syllogistic.* Oxford:Clarendon Press, 1951.

Mackworth, A. Consistency in Networks of Relations. *Artificial Intelligence,* 1975, *8(1),* 99-118.

Mackworth, A. Model Driven Interpretation in Intelligent Vision Systems. *Perception,* 1976, *5( ),* 349-370.

Mackworth, A. How to See a Simple World. In E. Elcock

and D. Michie (Eds.), *Machine Intelligence 8*, New York: Halstead Press, 1977.

Mackworth, A. Vision Research Strategy: Black Magic, Metaphors, Mechanisms, Miniworlds, and Maps. In A. Hanson and E. Riseman (Eds.), *Computer Vision Systems*, New York: Academic Press, 1978.

Mackworth, A. *Constraints, Descriptions and Domain Mappings in Computational Vision*, pages . Royal Society Symposium on Physical and Biological Processing of Images, London, 1983.

Mackworth, A., and Freuder, E. *The Complexity of Some Polynomial Network Consistency Algorithms for Constraint Satisfaction Problems*. Technical Report TR 82-6, University of British Columbia, 1982.

Mackworth, A. and Havens, W. *Structuring Domain Knowledge for Visual Perception*, pages 625. IJCAI81, Proceedings of the 7th International Joint Conference on Artificial Intelligence, Vancouver, Canada, 1981.

Maida, Anthony S. and Shapiro, Stuart C. Intensional Concepts in Propositional Semantic Networks. *Cognitive Science*, 1982, *6*, 291-330. Reprinted in Brachman and Levesque 1985: 169-89.

Maier, D. *The Theory of Relational Databases*. New York:Computer Science Press, 1983.

Mamdani, E.H. and Gaines, B.R. *Fuzzy Reasoning and its Applications*. London:Academic Press, 1981.

Marr, D. *Vision*. San Francisco, Ca.:W.H. Freeman, 1982.

Martins, João and Shapiro, Stuart C. *Reasoning in Multiple Belief Spaces*, pages 370-73. IJCAI-8, 1983.

Martins, João. *Reasoning in Multiple Belief Spaces*. Technical Report 203, SUNY Buffalo Dept. of Computer Science, 1983.

Martins, João. Belief Revision. In Shapiro, S.C. (Ed.),

Encyclopedia of Artificial Intelligence, New York: John Wiley, 1987.

Martins, João and Shapiro, Stuart C. *A Model for Belief Revision*, pages 241-94. AAAI, 1984.

Martins, João and Shapiro, Stuart C. Theoretical Foundations for Belief Revision. In Halpern, J.Y. (Ed.), *Theoretical Aspects of Reasoning About Knowledge*, Los Altos, California: Morgan Kaufmann, 1986.

Martins, João and Shapiro, Stuart C. *Hypothetical Reasoning*, pages 1029-42. AAAI, Berlin, 1986.

Martins, João and Shapiro, Stuart C. *Belief Revision in SNePS*, pages 230-34. CSCSI, 1986.

Mathlab Group. *MACSYMA Reference Manual*. Cambridge, Massachusetts:Computer Science Laboratory, Massachusetts Institute of Technology, 1977.

Mays, E. *Correcting Misconceptions About Database Structure*, pages 123-128. Proceedings of the 3rd CSCSI National Conference, Victoria, British Columbia, 1980.

Mays, E. *Monitors as Responses to Questions: Determining Competence*, pages 421-423. Proceedings of the National Conference on Artificial Intelligence, Pittsburgh, Pennsylvania, 1982.

McCalla, G. *An Approach to the Organisation of Knowledge for the Modelling of Conversation*. Technical Report PhD Thesis, University of British Columbia, 1978.

McCalla, G., and Cercone, N. Techniques and Issues in the Design of Applied Artificial IntelligenceSystems. *Computers and Mathematics*, 1985, *11(5)*, 421-430.

McCarthy, J. First Order Theories of Individual Concepts and Propositions. In Hayes, J.E., D. Michie, and L. Mikulich (Ed.), *Machine Intelligence 9*, Chichester, England: Ellis Horwood, 1979. reprinted in Brachman and Levesque 1985: 523-533.

McCarthy, J. Circumscription: A Form of Non-Monotonic Reasoning. *Artificial Intelligence*, 1980, *13(1,2)*, 27-39.

McCarthy, J. *Applications of Circumscription to Formalizing Commonsense Knowledge*. Technical Report AI Technical Report, Stanford, November 1984.

McCarthy, J., and Hayes, P. Some Philosophical Problems from the Standpoint of Artificial Intelligence. In Meltzer, B., and Michie, D. (Eds.), *Machine Intelligence*, New York: American Elsevier, 1969.

McCarty, L. and Sridharan, N. *The Representation of an Evolving System of Legal Concepts II: Prototypes and Deformations*, pages 246-253. IJCAI81, Proceedings of the 7th International Joint Conference on Artificial Intelligence, Vancouver, Canada, 1981.

McCoy, K. *Augmenting a Database Knowledge Representation for Natural Language Generation*, pages 121-128. Proceedings of the 20th ACL, Toronto, Ontario, 1982.

McDermott, Drew. *The DUCK Manual*. Technical Report YALEU/CSD/RR #399, Yale University, Department of Computer Science, June 1985.

McKay, Donald P., and Martins, João. *SNePSLOG User's Manual*. Technical Report SNeRG Technical Note #4, SUNY Buffalo Department of Computer Science, 1981.

McKay, Donald P., and Shapiro, Stuart C. *MULTI - A LISP-Based Multiprocessing System*, pages 29-37. AAAI, Stanford University, 1980.

McKeown, K. *The TEXT System for Natural Language Generation: An Overview*, pages 113-120. Proceedings of the 20th ACL, Toronto, Ontario, 1982.

McSkimmin, J.R., and Minker, J. *The Use of a Semantic Network in a Deductive Question-Answering System*, pages 50-58. IJCAI77, Proceedings of the 5th International Joint Conference on Artificial Intelligence, Cambridge, Mass., 1977.

McSkimmin, J.R., and Minker, J.   A Predicate Calculus Based Semantic Network For Deductive Searching.   In N. Findler (Ed.), *Associative Networks: The Representation and Use of Knowledge by Machine*, New York: Academic Press, 1979.

Mead, C. and Conway, L.   *Introduction to VLSI Systems*. Reading, Massachusetts:Addison-Wesley, 1980.

Meinong, Alexius.   Über Gegenstandstheorie.   In Haller, R. (Ed.), *Alexius Meinong Gesamtausgabe, Vol. II*, Graz, Austria: Akademische Druck-u. Verlagsanstalt, 1904. English Translation *The Theory of Objects* by I. Levi et al., pp. 76-117 in R.M. Chisholm (ed.), *Realism and the Background of Phenomenology* (New York: Free Press, 1960).

Meinong, Alexius.   *On Assumptions*.   Berkeley:University of California Press, 1983.

Mercer, R., and Reiter, R.   *The Representation of Presuppositions Using Defaults*, pages 103-107.   Proceedings of the 4th National Conference of the CSCSI/SCEIO, Saskatoon, 1982.

Miller, David P.   *Planning by Search Through Simulations*. Technical Report YALEU/CSD/RR #423, Yale University, Department of Computer Science, October 1985.

Minsky, M.   A Framework for Representing Knowledge.   In P. Winston (Ed.), *Psychology of Computer Vision*, New York: McGraw Hill, 1975.

Minsky, M.   *Learning Meaning*.   Technical Report AI Lab Memo, Project MAC, M.I.T., 1980.

Minsky, M.   Why People Think Computers Can't.   *Artificial Intelligence Magazine*, 1982, *3(4)*, 3-15.

Moore, R.   *Reasoning About Knowledge and Actions*.   Technical Report Tech note 191, SRI International, 1980.

Moore, R.   *The Role of Logic in Knowledge Representation and Commonsense Reasoning*, pages 428-433.   Proceedings of the 2nd AAAI, Pittsburgh, Pennsylvania, 1982.

Mostow, D.J., Hayes-Roth, F. A Production System for Speech Understanding System. In Waterman and Hayes-Roth (Ed.), *Pattern Directed Inference Systems*, Academic Press, 1978.

Mylopoulos, J., Shibahara, T., and Tsotsos, J. Building Knowledge-Based Systems: The PSN Experience. *IEEE Computer special issue on Knowledge Representation*, 1983, *16(10)*, 83-89.

Neal, Jeanette G. *A Knowledge Based Approach to Natural Language Understanding*. Technical Report 85-06, SUNY Buffalo Department of Computer Science, 1985.

Newell, A. Production Systems: Models of Control Structure. In W. Chase (Eds.), *Visual Information Processing*, New York: Academic Press, 1973.

Newell, A. and Simon, H. *Human Problem Solving*. Englewood Cliffs, NJ:Prentice-Hall, 1972.

Nii, H., and Aiello, N. *AGE: A Knowledge-Based Program for Building Knowledge-Based Programs*, pages 645-655. IJCAI79, Proceedings of the 6th International Joint Conference on Artificial Intelligence, Tokyo, Japan, 1979.

Nilsson, N. *Problem Solving Methods in Artificial Intelligence*. New York, New York:McGraw Hill, 1971.

Nilsson, N. *Principles of Artificial Intelligence*. Palo ALto, California:Tioga Press, 1980.

Nilsson, N. Artificial Intelligence: Engineering, Science, or Slogan? *Artificial Intelligence Magazine*, 1982, *3(1)*, 2-8.

Noguchi, K., Umano, M., Mizumoto, M., and Tanaka, K. *Implementation of Fuzzy Artificial Intelligence Language FLOU*. Technical Report, Univ of Tokyo, 1976. Technical Report on Automation and Language of IECE.

Norman, D., and Rumelhart, D. *Explorations in Cognition*. San Francisco, Ca.:W.H. Freeman, 1975.

Papalaskaris, M. *Special Purpose Inference Methods*. Technical

Report M.Sc. thesis. Department of Computing Science. University of Alberta, 1982.

Papalaskaris, M.. and Schubert, L. *Parts Inference: Closed and Semi-closed Partitioning Graphs*, pages 304-309. IJCAI, Vancouver, British Columbia, 1981.

Papalaskaris, M., and Schubert, L. *Inference, Incompatible Predicates and Colours*, pages 97-102. CSCSI/SCEIO, Saskatoon, Saskatchewan, 1982.

Parsons, Terence. *Nonexistent Objects.* New Haven:Yale University Press, 1980.

Patil, R.S. *Causal Representation of Patient Illness for Electrolyte and Acid-Base Diagnosis.* Technical Report MIT/LCS/TR-267, Laboratory for Computer Science, Massachusetts Institute of Technology, 1981. PhD Thesis.

Patil, R., Szolovits, P., Schwartz, W. Modeling Knowledge of the Patient in Acid-Base and Electrolyte Disorders. In P. Szolovits (Ed.), *Artificial Intelligence in Medicine.* Westview Press, 1982.

Pereira, F., and Warren, D. Definite Clause Grammars for Language Analysis. *Artificial Intelligence*, 1980, *13(3)*, 231-278.

Poole, D. *A Logical System for Default Reasoning*, pages 373-384. Proceedings of the AAAI Workshop on Nonmonotonic Reasoning, New Paltz, New York, 1984.

Poole, D. *On the Comparison of Theories: Preferring the Most Specific Explaination*, pages 144-147. IJCAI 85, Proceedings of the 9th International Joint Conference on Artificial Intelligence, Los Angeles, California, 1985.

Poole, D., and Goebel, R. On Eliminating Loops in Prolog. *ACM SIGPLAN Notices*, 1985, *20(8)*, 38-41.

Pople, H. *The Formation of Composite Hypotheses in Diagnostic Problem Solving - An Exercise in Synthetic Reasoning*

494

[INTERNIST], pages 1030-1037. IJCAI77, Proceedings of the 5th International Joint Conference on Artificial Intelligence, Cambridge, Massachusetts, 1977.

Pople, H. Heuristic Methods for Imposing Structure on Ill-Structured Problems: The Structuring of Medical Diagnostics. In P. Szolovits (Ed.), *Artificial Intelligence in Medicine*, Westview Press, 1982.

Popper, K. *The Logic of Scientific Discovery.* New York, New York:Harper and Row, 1958.

Putnam, H. The Meaning of 'Meaning'. In Putnam, H. (Ed.), *Mind, Language, and Reality*, Cambridge, England: Cambridge University Press, 1975.

Pylyshyn, Z. What the Mind's Eye Tells the Mind's Brain: A Critique of Mental Imagery. *Psychological Bulletin*, 1973, *80(1)*, 1-24.

Pylyshyn Z. The Imagery Debate: Analog Media versus Tacit Knowledge. In Block, N. (Ed.), *Imagery*, Cambridge, Ma.: M.I.T. Press, 1981.

Quillian, M. Semantic Memory. In Minsky, M. (Ed.), *Semantic Information Processing*, Cambridge, Ma.: M.I.T. Press, 1968.

Quillian, M. The Teachable Language Comprehender. *Communications of the ACM*, 1969, *12(8)*, 459-476.

Quine, W. *Word and Object.* Cambridge, Ma.:M.I.T. Press, 1960.

Quine, W., and Ullian, J. *The Web of Belief.* New York, New York:Random House, 1978.

Rapaport, William J. *Intentionality and the Structure of Existence.* PhD thesis, Indiana University Department of Philosophy, 1976.

Rapaport, William J. Meinongian Theories and a Russellian Paradox. *Noûs*, 1978, *12*, 153-80. errata, Noûs 13(1979)125.

Rapaport, William J. How to Make the World Fit Our Language: An Essay in Meinongian Semantics. *Grazer Philosophische Studien,* 1981, *14,* 1-21.

Rapaport, William J. Meinong, Defective Objects, and (Psycho-)Logical Paradox. *Grazer Philosophische Studien,* 1982, *18,* 17-39.

Rapaport, William J. Critical Notice of Routley 1979. *Philosophy and Phenomenological Research,* 1984, *44,* 539-52.

Rapaport, William J. *Belief Representation and Quasi-Indicators.* Technical Report 215, SUNY Buffalo Department of Computer Science, 1984.

Rapaport, William J. *Meinongian Semantics for Propositional Semantic Networks,* pages 43-48. ACL, 1985.

Rapaport, William J. To Be and Not to Be. *Noûs,* 1985, *19,* 255-71.

Rapaport, William J. Review of Lambert 1983. *Journal of Symbolic Logic,* 1986, *51,* 248-52.

Rapaport, William J. Logical Foundations of Belief Representation. *Cognitive Science,* 1986, *10,* 00-00.

Rapaport, William J., and Shapiro, Stuart C. *Quasi-Indexical Reference in Propositional Semantic Networks,* pages 65-70. ACL, Stanford University, 1984.

Raphael, B. SIR: Semantic Information Retrieval. In Minsky, M. (Ed.), *Semantic Information Processing,* Cambridge, Mass.: MIT Press, 1968.

Reghbati, H.K. *VLSI Testing and Validation Techniques.* IEEE Computer Society Press, 1985.

Reiter, R. A Logic for Default Reasoning. *Aritificial Intelligence,* 1980, *13(1),* 81-132.

Reiter, R., and Crisculo, G. Some Representational Issues in Default Reasoning. In Cercone, N. (Ed.), *Computational*

Linguistics. London: Pergamon Press, 1983.

Rich, C. *A Formal Representation for Plans in the Programmer's Apprentice.* IJCAI, Vancouver, British Columbia, 1981.

Rich, C. *A layered architecture of a system for reasoning about programs,* pages 540-546. IJCAI, Los Angeles, California, 1985.

Rieger, C., Grinberg, M. *The Causal Representation and Simulation of Physical Mechanics.* Technical Report TR-495, University of Maryland, November 1976.

Roberts, L. Machine Perception of Three-Dimensional Objects. In J. Tippet (Eds.), *Optical and Electro-Optical Information Processing,* Cambridge, Massachusetts: MIT Press, 1965.

Roberts, R. and Goldstein, I. *The FRL Primer.* Technical Report AI Memo 408, MIT, November 1977.

Robinson, J. A Machine-Oriented Logic Based on the Resolution Principle. *Journal of the ACM,* 1965, *12,* 23-41.

Robinson, J. *Logic: Form and Function.* Edinburgh, Scotland:Edinburgh University Press, 1979.

Robson, D. Object-Oriented Software Systems. *Byte,* 1981, *6(8),* 74-86.

Rosenschein, S., and Shieber, M. *Translating English into Logical Form,* pages 1-8. Proceedings of the 20th ACL Conference, Toronto, Ontario, 1982.

Roussel, P. *PROLOG: Manuel de Reference et d'Utilization.* Technical Report , Aix-Marseille University, 1975.

Routley, Richard. *Exploring Meinong's Jungle and Beyond.* Technical Report, Australian National University, Research School of Social Sciences, Department of Philosophy, 1979.

Rumelhart, D., and Ortony, A. *The Representation of Knowledge in Memory.* Technical Report TR 55, Department of Psychology, University of California, San Diego, 1976.

Sacerdoti, E.D. *A structure for plans and behavior*. Technical Report 109, SRI Artificial Intelligence Center, 1975.

Samad, T. and Director, S.W. Natural Language Interface for CAD: A First Step. *IEEE Design and Test*, August 1985, *2(4)*, 78-86.

Sandewall, E. A Functional Approach to Non-Monotonic Logic. *Computational Intelligence*, 1985, *1(2)*, 69-81.

Schank, R. Conceptual Dependency: A Theory of Natural Language Understanding. *Cognitive Psychology*, 1972, *3*, 552-631.

Schank, R. The Role of Memory in Language Processing. In C. Cofer (Ed.), *The Structure of Human Memory*, San Francisco: Freeman, 1975.

Schank, R., and Abelson, R. *Scripts, Plans, and Knowledge*. pages 151-157. IJCAI75, Advance Papers of the 4th International Joint Conference on Artificial Intelligence, Tbilisi, USSR, 1975.

Schank, R., and Abelson, R. *Scripts, Plans, and Understanding*. Hillsdale, New Jersey:Lawrence Erlbaum Associates, 1977.

Schank, R., and Rieger, C. Inference and the Computer Understanding of Natural Language. *Artificial Intelligence*, 1974, *5(4)*, 373-412.

Schank, R., and Wilensky, R. Response to Dresher and Hornstein. *Cognition*, 1977, *5*, 133-146.

Schank, R., Goldman, N., Rieger, C., and Riesbeck, C. *Margie: Memory, Analysis, Response Generation and Inference on English*, pages 255-261. IJCAI73, Proceedings of the 3rd International Joint Conference on Artificial Intelligence, Stanford, Ca., 1973.

Schlipf, J. Private Communication. , 1986, ( ), .

Schubert, L. *Extending the Expressive Power of Semantic Networks*, pages 158-164. IJCAI75, Advance Papers of the 4th International Joint Conference on Artificial

498

Intelligence, Tbilisi, USSR, 1975.

Schubert, L.   Extending the Expressive Power of Semantic Networks. *Artificial Intelligence*, 1976, 7, 163-198.

Schubert, L.   *Problems with Parts*, pages 778-784.   IJCAI, Tokyo, Japan, 1979.

Schubert, L.   *An approach to the syntax and semantics of affixes in 'conventionalized' phrase structure grammar*, pages 189-195.   CSCSI/SCEIO, Saskatoon, Saskatchewan, 1982.

Schubert, L.   *On Parsing Preferences*, pages 247-250.   Coling, Stanford, California, 1984.

Schubert, L., and Pelletier, F.   From English to Logic: context-free computation of conventional logical translations. *Am. Journal of Computational Linguistics*, 1982, 8(1), 26-44.

Schubert, L., Goebel, R., and Cercone, N.   The Structure and Organisation of a Semantic Network for Comprehension and Inference.   In N. Findler (Ed.), *Associative Networks: The Representation and Use of Knowledge by Machine*, New York: Academic Press, 1979.

Scragg, G.   *Answering Questions About Processes, Ph.D. Thesis*. Technical Report, Department of Computing Science, University of California, San Diego, 1975.

Shapiro, S.   *A Net Structure for Semantic Information Storage, Deduction, and Retrieval*, pages 512-523.   IJCAI71, Proceedings of the 2nd International Joint Conference on Artificial Intelligence, London, England, 1971.

Shapiro, Stuart C.   *The MIND System: A Data Structure for Semantic Information Processing*.   Technical Report Report Number R-837-PR, The Rand Corporation, 1971.   also AD Number 733 560, Defense Documentation Center, Alexandria, VA.

Shapiro, Stuart C.   *A Net Structure for Semantic Information Storage, Deduction and Retrieval*, pages 512-23.   IJCAI, 1971.

Shapiro, Stuart C. *Representing and Locating Deduction Rules in a Semantic Network*, pages 14-18. IJCAI, 1977.

Shapiro, Stuart C. Path-Based and Node-Based Inference in Semantic Networks. In Waltz, D. (Ed.), *Tinlap-2: Theoretical Issues in Natural Language Processing*, New York: ACM, 1978.

Shapiro, S. The SNePS Semantic Network Processing System. In N. Findler (Ed.), *Associative Networks: The Representation and Use of Knowledge by Machine*, New York: Academic Press, 1979.

Shapiro, Stuart C. The SNePs Semantic Network Processing System. In Findler, N.V. (Ed.), *Associative Networks: The Representation and Use of Knowledge by Computers*, New York: Academic Press, 1979.

Shapiro, Stuart C. *Numerical Quantifiers and Their Use in Reasoning with Negative Information*, pages 791-96. IJCAI, 1979.

Shapiro, Stuart C. Generalized Augmented Transition Network Grammars for Generation from Semantic Networks. *American Journal of Computational Linguistics*, January-March, 1982, *8.1*, 12-25.

Shapiro, E. *A Subset of Concurrent Prolog and its Interpreter*. Technical Report CS83-06, Weizmann Institute of Science, 1983.

Shapiro, Stuart C.; and McKay, Donald P. *Inference with Recursive Rules*, pages 151-53. AAAI, 1980.

Shapiro, Stuart C., and Wand, Mitchell. *The Relevance of Relevance*. Technical Report 46, Indiana University Department of Computer Science, 1976.

Shapiro, Stuart C.. and Woodmansee, G. H. *A Net Structure Based Relational Questions Answerer: Description and Examples*, pages 325-46. IJCAI, 1969.

Shapiro, Stuart C.; Martins, João; and McKay, Donald P.

Bi-Directional Inference. pages 90-93. Cognitive Science Society, 1982.

Shapiro, Stuart C.; McKay, Donald P. Martins, João; and Morgado, Ernesto. *SNePSLOG: A 'Higher Order' Logic Programming Language.* Technical Report SNeRG Technical Note Number 8, SUNY Buffalo Department of Computer Science, 1981. Presented at the 1981 Workshop on Logic Programming for Intelligent Systems, Long Beach, California.

Shapiro, Stuart C.; Srihari, Sargur N.; Geller, James; and Taie, Ming-Ruey. A Fault Diagnosis System Based on an Integrated Knowledge Base. *IEEE Software,* March 1986, *3.2,* 48-49.

Shapiro, Stuart C.; Woodmansee, G. H.; and Kreuger, M. W. *A Semantic Associational Memory Net that Learns and Answers Questions (SAMENLAQ).* Technical Report 8, University of Wisconsin Computer Sciences Department, 1968.

Shepard, R. The Mental Image. *American Psychologist,* 1978, *33(6),* 125-137.

Shepard, R., and Cooper, L. *Mental Images and Their Transformations.* Cambridge, Mass.:MIT Press, 1982.

Shibahara, T. *On Using Causal Knowledge to Recognize Vital Signals: Knowledge-based Interpretation of Arrhythmias.* IJCAI, Los Angeles, California, 1985.

Shibahara, T., Tsotsos, J., Mylopoulos, J., Covvey, H. *CAA: A Knowledge-Based System Using Causal Knowledge to Diagnose Cardiac Rhythm Disorders.* IJCAI, Karlsruhe, W. Germany, August, 1983.

Shortliffe, E. *Computer - Based Medical Consultation: MYCIN.* New York:North-Holland, 1976.

Simon, H. Rational Choice and the Structure of the Environment. *Psychological Review,* 1956, *63( ),* 129.

Slager. C., et al. *Left Ventricular Contour Segmentation from Anatomical Landmark Trajectories and its Application to Wall Motion Analysis.* Computers in Cardiology, Geneva, 1979.

Sleeman, D., and Brown, J. (eds). *Intelligent Tutoring Systems.* New York, New York:Academic Press, 1982.

Sloman, A. *Afterthoughts on Analogical Reasoning,* pages 178-182. Proceedings Theoretical Issues on Natural Language Processing, Cambridge, Massachusetts, 1975.

Smith, B. *Refections and Perspectives in a Procedural Langauge.* Technical Report TR-272, M.I.T., 1982.

Sowa, M., Scott, A., and Shortliffe, E. Completeness and Consistency in Rule Based Systems. In Buchanan, B., and Shortliffe, E. (Eds.), *Rule Based Expert Systems*, Reading, Mass.: Addison-Wesley, 1985.

Srihari, Rohini K. *Combining Path-Based and Node-Based Inference in SNePS.* Technical Report 183, SUNY Buffalo Department of Computer Science, 1981.

Srihari, Sargur N.; Hull, Jonathan J.; Palumbo, Paul W.; Niyogi, Debashish; and Wang, Ching-Huei. *Address Recognition Techniques in Mail Sorting: Research Directions.* Technical Report 85-09, SUNY Buffalo Department of Computer Science, 1985.

Stefik, M. et al. *The Partitioning of Concerns in Digital System Design,* pages 43-52. IEEE, 1982.

Steinberg, L.I. and Mitchell, T.M. The Redesign System: A Knowledge-Based Approach to VLSI CAD. *IEEE Design and Test,* February 1985, *2(1),* 45-54.

Stickel, M. *Theory Resolution: Building in Nonequational Theories.,* pages 391-397. AAAI, Washington, D.C., 1983.

Stickel, M. *Automated Deduction by Theory Resolution,* pages 1181-1186. IJCAI, Los Angeles, California, 1985.

Suchin, Jennifer. *A Semantic Network Representation of the*

Peripheral Nervous System. Technical Report Project Report, SUNY Buffalo Department of Computer Science, 1985.

Sussman, Gerald J. *A Computer Model of Skill Acquisition*. American Elsevier Publishing Company, Inc., 1975.

Sussman, G.J. and Stallman, R. Heuristic Techniques in Computer-Aided Circuit Analysis. *IEEE Transactions on Circuits and Systems*, November 1975, *CAS-22(11)*, 205-280.

Sussman G.J. and Steele, G.L. CONSTRAINTS - A Language for Expressing Almost-Hierarchical Descriptions. *Artificial Intelligence*, August 1980, *14(1)*, 1-39.

Szolovits, P. and Pauker, S.G. Categorical and Probabilistic Reasoning in Medical Diagnosis. *Artificial Intelligence*, 1978, *11*, 115-144.

Tate, Austin. *Generating Project Networks*. IJCAI, AAAI, 1977.

Taugher, J. *A Representation for Time Information*. Technical Report M.Sc. thesis, Department of Computing Science, University of Alberta, 1983.

Taugher, J., and Schubert, L. Fast Temporal Inference. 1986, ( ), (to appear).

Tenenberg, J. *Taxonomic Reasoning*. pages 191-193. IJCAI, Los Angeles, California, 1985.

Tomberlin, James E. *Agent, Language, and the Structure of the World*. Indianapolis:Hackett, 1984. R.A. George, translator.

Tranchell, Lynn M. *A SNePS Implementation of KL-ONE*. Technical Report 198, SUNY Buffalo Department of Computer Science, 1982.

Tsotsos, J. *Representational Axes and Temporal Cooperative Processes*. Technical Report RBCV-TR-2, Department of Computer Science, University of Toronto, May 1984.

Tsotsos, J.K. Knowledge Organization and Its Role in Representation and Interpretation for Time-Varying Data: The ALVEN System. *Computational Intelligence*, 1985, *1(1)*, .

Tsotsos J.K., Mylopoulos, J., Covvey, H.D., Zucker, S.W. A Framework For Visual Motion Understanding. *IEEE Transactions on Pattern Analysis and Machine Intelligence*, November 1980, }, .

Ullman, J. *Principles of Database Systems*. New York:Computer Science Press, 1984.

Umrigar, Z., and Pitchumani, V. An Experiment in Programming with Full First Order Logic. *IEEE 1985 Symposium on Logic Programming*, 1985, *1(1)*, 40-47.

van Emden, M. Programming with Resolution Logic. In Elcock, E. and Michie, D. (Ed.), *Machine Intelligence 8*, Chichester, UK: Ellis Horwood, 1977.

van Emden, M., and Kowalski, R. The semantics of predicate logic as a programming language. *Journal of the ACM*, 1976, *23(4)*, 733-742.

van Melle, W. *A Domain Independent System that Aids in Constructing Consultation Programs (EMYCIN)*. Technical Report STAN-CS-80-820, Department of Computer Science, Stanford University, 1980.

Vere, Steven. Planning in Time: Windows and Durations for Activities and Goals. *IEEE Transactions on Pattern Analysis and Machine Intelligence*, 1983, (PAMI-5/3)}, 246-267.

Vilain, M. *The restricted language architecture of a hybrid representation system*, pages 547-551. IJCAI, Los Angeles, California, 1985.

Vilain, M., and Kautz, H. *Constraint Propagation Algorithms for Temporal Reasoning*, pages (to appear). AAAI, Philadephia, Pennsylvania, 1986.

504

Wallis, J., Shortliffe, E. *Explanatory Power for Medical Expert Systems: Studies in the Representation of Causal Relationships for Clinical Consultations.* Technical Report STAN-CS-82-923, Stanford University, 1982.

Walther, C. *A many-sorted calculus based on resolution and paramodulation,* pages 882-891. IJCAI, Karlsruhe, West Germany, 1983.

Waltz, D. Understanding Line Drawings of Scenes with Shadows. In P. Winston (Ed.), *Psychology of Computer Vision,* New York: McGraw Hill, 1975.

Warren, D., and Pereira, S. An Efficient Easily Adaptable System for Interpreting Natural Language Queries. *American Journal of Computational Linguistics,* 1982, *8(3-4),* 110-122.

Warren, D., Periera, L., and Periera, F. PROLOG - the language and its implementation compared to LISP. *Sigart Newsletter,* 1977, *8(64),* 109-115.

Weiss, S. M., and Kulikowski, C. A. *A Practical Guide to Designing Expert Systems.* Totowa, New Jersey:Rowman and Allanheld, 1984.

Weyhrauch, R. Prolegomena to a Theory of Mechanized Reasoning. *Artificial Intelligence,* 1980, *13(2),* 133-170.

Wilensky, R. *Understanding Goal-Based Stories.* Technical Report Research Report 140, Department of Computer Science, Yale University, 1978.

Williams, B.C. Qualitative Analysis of MOS Circuits. *Artificial Intelligence,* 1984, *24,* .

Wilson, K. *From Association to Structure.* Amsterdam:North Holland, 1980.

Winograd, T. *Understanding Natural Language.* New York:Academic Press, 1972.

Winograd, T. Breaking the Complexity Barrier Again. *SIGPLAN Notices,* 1974, *9(6),* x-y.

Winograd, T. Frames and the Procedural-Declarative Controversy. In Bobrow, D., and Collins, A. (Eds.), *Representation and Understanding*, New York: Academic Press, 1975.

Winograd, T. Towards a Procedural Understanding of Semantics. *Revue International de Philosphie*, 1976, *3-4(1)*, 260-303.

Winograd, T. On Some Contested Suppositions of Generative Linguistics about the Scientific Study of Language. *Cognition*, 1977, *5(3)*, 151-179.

Winston, P. *Learning Structural Descriptions from Examples*. Technical Report MAC-TR-76, PRoject MAC, M.I.T., 1970.

Woods, W. *Semantics for a Question-Answering System*. Technical Report Ph.D. Thesis, Division of Engineering, Harvard University, 1967.

Woods, W. What's in a Link. In Bobrow, D., and Collins, A. (Eds.), *Representation and Understanding*, New York: Academic Press, 1975.

Woods, W. Cascaded ATN Grammars. *American Journal of Computational Linguistics*, 1980, *6(1)*, 1-15.

Woods, W. What's Important about Knowledge Representation. In McCalla, G., and Cercone, N. (Eds.), *IEEE Computer special issue on Knowledge Representation*, New York: IEEE, 1983.

Woods, W. Problems in Procedural Semantics. In Pylyshyn, Z., and Demopoulos, W. (Eds.), *Meaning and Cognitive Structure*, New Jersey: Ablex Publishing Company, 1986.

Woods, W., Kaplan, R., and Nash-Webber, B. *The Lunar Science Natural Langauge Report*. Technical Report TR2378, Bolt Beranek and Newman, Inc., 1972.

Wright, M., and Fox, M. *SRL/1.5 User Manual*. Technical Report TR, Carnegie Mellon University, 1982.

Wygralak, M. Fuzzy Cardinals based on the Generalized

Equality of Fuzzy Subsets. *Fuzzy Sets and Systems 18*, 1986, }, 143-158.

Xiang, Zhigang, and Srihari, Sargur N. *Spatial Structure and Function Representation in Diagnostic Expert Systems*, pages 191-206. IEEE, 1985.

Xiang, Zhigang; Srihari, Sargur N.; Shapiro, Stuart C.; and Chutkow, Jerry G. *Analogical and Propositional Representations of Structure in Neurological Diagnosis*, pages 127-32. IEEE, Silver Spring, MD., 1984".

Zadeh, L.A. Similarity Relations and Fuzzy Orderings. *Inf. Sci.*, 1971, *3*, 177-200.

Zadeh, L.A. The Concept of a Linguistic Variable and its Application to Approximate Reasoning. *Information Science*, 1975, *8*, 199-249, 301-357.

Zadeh, L.A. *A Theory of Approximate Reasoning*. Technical Report Memorandum M77/58, Electronics Research Laboratory, 1977. also appears in Machine Intelligence 9, Hayes, J.E., Michie, D., and Kulich, L.I., (eds.) New York: Wiley, pp. 149-194, 1979.

Zadeh, L.A. *A Theory of Approximate Reasoning*. Technical Report Memorandum M77/58, Electronics Research Laboratory, 1977. also appears in Machine Intelligence 9, Hayes, J.E., Michie, D., and Kulich, L.I., (eds.) New York: Wiley, pp. 149-194, 1979.

Zadeh, L.A. PRUF - A Meaning Representation Language for Natural Languages. *Int. J. Man-Machine Studies*, 1978, *10*, 395-460.

Zadeh, L. A Theory of Approximate Reasoning. *Machine Intelligence*, 1979, *9*, 149-194.

Zadeh, L.A. *Possibility Theory and Soft Data Analysis*. Technical Report Memorandum M79/59, Electronics Research Laboratory, 1979. also appears in Mathematical Frontiers of the Social and Policy Sciences, Cobb. L. and Thrall, R.M. (eds.), Boulder: Westview Press, pp. 69-129,

1981.

Zadeh, L. A Computational Approach to Fuzzy Quantifiers in Natural Language. *Computers and Mathematics*, 1983, *9(1)*, 149-184.

Zadeh, L.A. Fuzzy Logic as a Basis for the Management of Uncertainty in Expert Systems. *Fuzzy Sets and Systems 11*, 1983, }, 199-227.

Zadeh, L.A. A Fuzzy-set-theoretic Approach to the Compositionality of Meaning: Propositions, Dispositions, and Canonical Forms. *Journal of Semantics*, 1983, *3*, 253-272.

Zadeh, L.A. Syllogistic Reasoning in Fuzzy Logic and its Application to Usuality and Reasoning with Dispositions. *IEEE Transactions on Systems, Man and Cybernetics*, 1985, }, 754-763.

Zalta, Edward. *Abstract Objects*. Dordrecht:D. Reidel, 1983.

Zucker, S. Production Systems with Feedback. In Waterman and Hayes-Roth (Ed.), *Pattern-Directed Inference Systems*, Academic Press, 1978.

Index